THE MISINTERPELLATED SUBJECT

JAMES R. MARTEL

THE MISINTERPELLATED SUBJECT

Duke University Press   Durham and London   2017

Printed in the United States of America on acid-free paper ∞
Text designed by Courtney Leigh Baker
Typeset in Quadraat Pro by Westchester Publishing Services

Library of Congress Cataloging-in-Publication Data
Names: Martel, James R., author.
Title: The misinterpellated subject / James R. Martel.
Description: Durham : Duke University Press, 2017. |
    Includes bibliographical references and index.
Identifiers: LCCN 2016035967 (print)
LCCN 2016037767 (ebook)
ISBN 9780822362845 (hardcover : alk. paper)
ISBN 9780822362968 (pbk. : alk. paper)
ISBN 9780822373438 (e-book)
Subjects: LCSH: Authority. | Anarchism—Social aspects. | Political
    sociology. | Political culture. | Identity (Philosophical concept)
    in literature.
Classification: LCC HM1251.M375 2017 (print) | LCC HM1251
    (ebook) | DDC 306.2—dc23
LC record available at https://lccn.loc.gov/2016035967

The introduction was originally published as "When the Call Is Not
Meant for You: Misinterpellation, Subjectivity and the Law" in
Philosophy and Rhetoric 48(4): 494–515, 2015. It is republished with
permission from Penn State University Press.

COVER ART: Photo by Trent Parke / Magnum Photos

For Nasser

CONTENTS

ACKNOWLEDGMENTS

While Mark Antaki should get first mention for having come up (spontane-ously, although I've heard the term since) with the term "misinterpella-tion" right before my eyes, the person with the biggest impact on this book is Bonnie Honig, with whom I have a running conversation throughout the book (as in life). She read several versions of many chapters and read the whole manuscript carefully in ways that often superseded and improved upon anything that I had to say. One of the greatest joys of writing this book was to have that conversation with her.

I also had a great deal of help, guidance, and close reading by Sarah Bur-gess and Keally McBride, both of whom read several chapters, sometimes a few times over. It has been a true pleasure to watch each other's writing projects develop and grow.

Several venues helped me refine and rewrite key chapters of this book.

In September 2014 I discussed parts of chapter 6 at a conference at the University of Alberta, Edmonton. Thanks to George Pavlich for inviting me and thanks to Richard Westerman for his very helpful commentary, Thanks also to my fellow panelists, Matthew Unger, Renisa Mawani, Keally Mc-Bride, Jennifer Culbert, and Mark Antaki.

I presented parts of chapter 5 at the Western Political Science Associa-tion in April 2015. I got great commentary from the audience—especially George Schulman—as well as my copanelists and dear friends, Jodi Dean and Jennifer Culbert.

In March of 2015 I presented parts of chapter 1 to a group at Williams College. My thanks to Mark Reinhardt for inviting me. Thanks also to those present for their deeply insightful commentary and criticism: Anita Sokol-sky, Laura Ephraim, Nimu Njoya, Christian Thorne, Seulghee Lee, and Walter Johnston.

In May of 2015 I had the very great pleasure of serving as a writer in residence at Birkbeck College in London. I had the wonderful opportunity there to present the work from this book to a gifted and brilliant group of students and faculty. I think of Birkbeck as my home away from home. Thanks to Nathan Moore for helping to set that up. Thanks also to Maria Aristodemou, Elena Loizidou, Costas Douzinas, Patrick Hanafin, Başak Ertür, Julia Chryssostalis, Marinos Diamantides, Stewart Motha, Piyel Haldar, Patricia Truitt, and Peter Fitzpatrick, who are some of the wonderful faculty at the law school and all good friends. Thanks also to the many fantastic students, including Tara Mulqueen (who is now a faculty member in her own right!), Kojo Koram, Leticia Da Costa Paes, Ozan Kamiloğlu, Sara Paiola, David Thomas, and so many others who took part in these workshops.

While in England, I also presented work at Goldsmiths College. Thanks to Saul Newman, Julia Ng, Alberto Toscano, and John Ackerman. I was also able to discuss this work at the University of Kent in Canterbury, United Kingdom, during the previous year. Thanks to Maria Drakapoulou and Connal Parsley for their invitation and support and friendship.

More recently, in December of 2015, I got to present my chapter on Nietzsche at the Australasian Society for Continental Philosophy in Sydney, Australia. Thanks to my fellow panelists, Dimitris Vardoulakis and Peg Birmingham, and many of the great thinkers and friends that live down under: Miguel Vatter, Charles Barbour, Vanessa Lemm, Jess Whyte, Daniel McLoughlin, Penny Crofts, Chris Peterson, Ben Golder, and (leaving Sydney and heading yet further south) Pete Burdon, Richard Joyce, Alison Young, and Peter Rush.

Most recently of all, in June 2016, I had the great pleasure of teaching a course about this book at the Kent Summer School in Critical Theory in Paris, France. My students were beyond wonderful and, as I was working on my last draft at the time of the class, many of my final thoughts and emendations came out of my conversations with them both in and out of the classroom. Therefore I want to thank Sanders Bernstein, Jonjo Brady, Kristina Cufar, Melanie M. Sherazi, Masumi Matsumoto, Maru Pabon, Jan-Jasper Persijn, Benjamin Ratskoff, Noga Rotem, Silindiwe Sibanda, Sid Simpson, Sara Sisun, Alberto Tondello, Michelle Velazquez-Potts, and Kangle Zhang for their participation in that seminar and for the way they contributed to thinking about the question of misinterpellation. Thanks also to Maria Drakapoulou and Connal Parsley (once again) for making this class possible, along with the presence of Sam Frost as a co-teacher and (I think) fellow co-conspirator about the question of agency and selves.

Diego Arrocha was a pleasure to get to know, and he suggested many thinkers for me to consider, ranging from Frank Wilderson III to Fred Moten to Sylvain Lazarus. Shalini Satkunanandan was not only helpful in thinking about some of the concepts that I was grappling with but also has a magical effect insofar as whenever we worked together at a café (always the same one), I always managed to think and write more clearly. Kate Gordy has also been a great friend and café workmate. She is a wonderful thinker and writer, and her book *Living Ideology* got me seriously thinking about ideology more generally.

Courtney Berger is everything that one could ask for in an editor. She got my project immediately, even during a meeting after she had gotten zero sleep because an arsonist had tried to set her hotel on fire (a true story). Thanks at Duke University Press also to Sandra Korn for her help with getting the manuscript ready for publication and Chris Dahlin for expert copyediting.

Melody Herr, formerly at University of Michigan Press, was also supportive and helpful as always. I feel very fortunate to know these wonderful editors.

My lovely family has, as always, been supportive and nurturing. I am so lucky to have them all in my life.

My dear friend Nasser Hussain was too beautiful and wonderful for this world and yet the world (my world, certainly) is bereft without him. I dedicate this book to his memory.

An earlier version of chapter 1 appeared as "When the Call Is Not Meant for You: Misinterpellation, Subjectivity and the Law" within a special issue on representation in *Philosophy and Rhetoric* 48, no. 4 (2015).

A much earlier version of chapter 4 appeared as "Nietzsche's Cruel Messiah," *Qui Parle* 20–22, no. 2 (Spring/Summer 2012).

Part of chapter 6 appears as "Guilty without Accusation: Legal Passions and the Misinterpellation of Subjects in Althusser and Kafka," in *Accusation, Criminality and the Legal Subject*, ed. George Pavlich, University of British Columbia Press, forthcoming.

An earlier version of chapter 7 appeared in *Breaking the Rules: Gender, Power, and Politics in the Films of Lars von Trier*, ed. Bonnie Honig and Lori J. Marso, *Theory and Event* 18, no. 2 (2015). This issue will be reprinted as a book, forthcoming from Oxford University Press.

Please note that in the citations that follow all emphasis is in the original. I haven't added any myself.

Unsummoned! When the Call Is Not Meant for You

Another Abraham

In his parable "Abraham," Franz Kafka offers us a narrative wherein the call that motivated Abraham to attempt to sacrifice his son Isaac was not perceived by the famous Abraham alone but had many other, unintended interlocutors—all of whom also happened to be named Abraham—as well.[1] Kafka tells us that besides the "real Abraham"—that is, the one that we all know about, someone who "already had everything, and yet was to be raised still higher"—there is "another Abraham ["einen anderen Abraham"]" or possibly even several other Abrahams.[2] One such other Abraham, Kafka tells us, "was prepared to satisfy the demand for a sacrifice immediately, with the promptness of a waiter, but was unable to bring it off because he could not get away, being indispensable; the household needed him, there was perpetually something or other to put in order."[3] For yet other Abrahams, "it is possible that they did not even have a son, yet already had to sacrifice him."[4] Whether the call to Abraham was ever intended for these other Abrahams or not, they do not ultimately respond; Kafka writes of them that "only the suspicion remains that it was by intention that these men did not ready their houses, and—to select a very great example—hid their faces in magic trilogies in order not to have to lift them and see the mountain standing in the distance."[5]

There is one last, final—and clearly lowliest—Abraham who, of all these figures, is the least likely to be intentionally called; this is a figure, it seems, who seems to neither deserve nor understand this call to sacrifice yet he answers the call nonetheless. Kafka describes him as follows:

> But take another Abraham. One who wanted to perform the sacrifice altogether in the right way and had a correct sense in general of the whole affair, but could not believe that he was the one meant, he, an ugly old man, and the dirty youngster that was his child. True faith is not lacking to him, he has this faith; he would make the sacrifice in the right spirit if only he could believe he was the one meant. He is afraid that after starting out as Abraham with his son he would change on the way into Don Quixote. The world would have been enraged at Abraham could it have beheld him at the time, but this one is afraid that the world would laugh itself to death at the sight of him. However, it is not the ridiculousness as such that he is afraid of—though he is, of course, afraid of that too and, above all, of his joining in the laughter—but in the main he is afraid that this ridiculousness will make him even older and uglier, his son even dirtier, even more unworthy of being really called. An Abraham who should come unsummoned! It is as if, at the end of the year, when the best student was solemnly about to receive a prize, the worst student rose in the expectant stillness and came forward from his dirty desk in the last row because he had made a mistake of hearing, and the whole class burst out laughing. And perhaps he had made no mistake at all, his name really was called, it having been the teacher's intention to make the rewarding of the best student at the same time a punishment for the worst one.[6]

This Abraham serves as a model for what I am calling the misinterpellated subject. This Abraham is, as already noted, seemingly unexpected ("unsummoned!"); he is not called (not interpellated), yet he responds nonetheless. He is the one who gets interpellation wrong; he turns a call by authority into farce, or perhaps—considering who is doing the calling—something far more subversive than farce. This Abraham's very presence is a challenge to and an interruption of the intended narrative. Even if his intentions are good—and we know that they are because "true faith is not lacking to him"—this Abraham seems incapable of doing what is asked of him. He is the wrong person at the wrong place and the wrong time.

Even in the unlikely event that God did intend to call this Abraham ("it having [perhaps] been the teacher's intention to make the rewarding of the best student at the same time a punishment for the worst one"), it seems that the point of such a calling has nothing to do with him. He is either totally unexpected or a pawn for the interplay between the powerful and the desired; he is a bystander at best, an unwanted intruder at worst.

My interest in this parable lies not so much in the intention of the caller, however—that is, in terms of whom God meant to call—and much more with what happens to this subject when she or he actually shows up. What does this subject do at this point (after what must be a highly awkward pause)? Does this other Abraham also attempt to sacrifice his son? Would God show him the same mercy that was shown to the "real" Abraham? Most critically, what happens when this Abraham realizes that the joke is on him? What happens when all the hope and faith this Abraham experiences when he hears the call conflict with his discovery that he was never the intended subject of the call in the first place?

It seems that this other Abraham, for all his fear of being ridiculed or "chang[ing] into Don Quixote," has the potential to cause an unprecedented kind of mayhem; all the schemes of the mighty and the powerful could—and also just as easily could not—be unmade or undone by this unexpected arrival (or, if expected, still not conforming to what that arrival was supposed to produce). His arrival at the scene of interpellation challenges the very notion that God (or whoever the caller may be) is in charge of the situation; here, the knowledge and the authority of the caller are put into question. This has consequences, not just for this Abraham, but for all the others, including the "right" Abraham. Insofar as the call for sacrifice occurs within the context of a script (God calls, God demands sacrifice, God prevents the sacrifice from happening), that script is ruined by the arrival of this unwanted other person; the very idea that the Abraham we all know would willingly sacrifice his beloved son rests on the notion that an all-knowing deity is in charge, is in control of the situation. Once this other, unsummoned Abraham shows up, that order is wrecked; almost anything, it seems, suddenly becomes possible.

As Kafka imagines it, this scene of misinterpellation could have a very anticlimactic ending: this other Abraham might show up, realize his mistake, and slink off into the distance. But, as I've already started to suggest, misinterpellation always has a radical potential. This book is about that potential, about how people respond to perceived calls (calls to freedom, calls to sacrifice, calls to justice, calls to participation, calls to identity) that are not meant for them, and how the fact that they show up anyway can cause politically radical forms of subversion. What does it mean when the uninvited subject, thinking that she has been called, shows up and refuses to go away? What if the subject turns her fury at being rejected and humiliated into a source of resistance to the power structures that have denied her? What forms of displacement of and challenges to subjectivity are produced by this phenomenon and with what result for the workings of "business as usual"? How does such a subject interact with the ongoing effects of state power and authority (and other related forms of power and authority as well)?

In *The Misinterpellated Subject* I examine this phenomenon in its historical, political, and literary forms in order to think about what misinterpellation can become, and what it has always potentially been: a radical, even revolutionary force among us. In particular, I will focus on the connection between misinterpellation and liberal capitalism insofar as, in our time, calls for subjectivity, poses of authority, and demands for obedience are generally—although not exclusively—issued from within this system.[7] Looking at the way that recognition normally subjectivizes (taken in both the Hegelian and Althusserian sense of that word) human beings, I will examine how the failure to be properly recognized under conditions of liberal capitalism is sometimes highlighted, made too visible to be ignored or papered over. Misinterpellation, which I will argue happens all the time, takes place in forms that are both more and less accidental; generally, it is never even noticed and yet sometimes it changes the world. The stronger version of this claim, which I will try to develop over the course of this book, is that misinterpellation is a principal way that radical change happens in a world dominated by global capitalism and liberal ideology. To the liberal stance of "There is no alternative [to liberalism]" (conveniently shorthanded to TINA), I argue that we don't necessarily need an alternative.[8] Liberalism itself, through its failure (its misfirings, its misreadings and miscallings), produces its own radical response and, through that response—the refusal to meekly slink away—the possibility of an alternative is produced after all. Or, perhaps more accurately, liberalism occasionally enables an already-existent alternative, one that is not itself part and parcel of liberal subjectivity and authority, to be noticed, to emerge into visibility through liberalism's own internal breakdowns.

Misinterpellation is therefore built into the very system that would oppose and obfuscate it. Whatever magic leaven that has allowed a force as unjust and illicit as liberalism to remain in control for some three hundred years (and counting) is to some extent the same force that produces this radical response. The subversive subjects that misinterpellation produces tend, as I will show both through historical and literary examples, either to be true believers in liberalism, or at least subjects who practice their resistance stealthily and in ways that permit some kind of modus vivendi with the reigning powers (more on that in a moment). The misinterpellated subjects of this book are definitively acting "within" the system that they contest. As I will discuss further, these subjects do not generally initially come with the intention to subvert and revolt; their radical response is the result of an increasingly legible mismatch between what they believe (what they think they have been called to do) and what those in power believe (who they have actually intended to call and why they have done so).[9]

Because misinterpellation comes from deep within the maw of established forms of power, the power of its threat to the status quo is seldom recognized. Accidents, misreadings, and the like seem the stuff of banality, like leaving your keys at home or having your shoelaces come untied. But such accidents, exactly because they are unexpected—generally not only by the dominant forces but at times even by the subjects of misinterpellation themselves—do maximum damage from inside the apparatus of liberal orthodoxy. Ever vigilant to threats from without (communists, terrorists, etc.), capitalism has no way of guarding against the threats that come out of its own phantasms. It is precisely because liberalism not only dabbles in but utterly depends upon untruths, namely phantasms of authority and nature, reason, and orderliness, that it is highly vulnerable to misinterpellation. Insofar as (as Foucault shows us) there is always a epistemological gap between the subject and the disciplinary regime she lives under, a less-than-perfect match even among the most ardent devotees, misinterpellation both constitutes and expands that gap; the mismatch between the claims of liberal agency, autonomy, and freedom, and the actual practices of the international global order produces endless misreadings, misunderstandings, and mistakes. These mistakes come and go all the time without taking root, without producing radical responses. But occasionally they produce effects that are so dramatic that nothing is ever the same again.

In thinking about misinterpellation as a set of accidents or built-in fail-ures of liberal subjectivity, I wish to push things further in the pages of this book. I will try to think about how to make misinterpellation something more than an accident, about how to expand upon and enhance this seem-ingly occasional phenomenon so that its more visible manifestations happen more often and with broader, deeper, and more sustained radical results. In order to do so, I will look at certain thinkers, particularly Nietzsche and Fanon, who I think have already shown how this is done. The political agenda I am advancing here, then, is to think about a phenomenon that is ongoing and to try to understand why it happens, how it could be multiplied and extended, and, finally, what the results of such subversion are in terms of the kinds of subjects that emerge from this process. I will argue that this subject is an anarchist one and that misinterpellation is itself an inherently anarchist phenomenon exactly because it decentralizes and opposes those highly regulated and singular selves that interpellation tells us that we are and have always been. More accurately, as I'll explain further, I see the sub-ject as having always been anarchist, decentralized, and multiple within herself, but I will argue that it takes a phenomenon like misinterpellation to make that evident to the subject herself. Normally the subject feels that she is what interpellation tells her that she is: unitary, internally harmoni-ous, and in keeping with the larger normative ordering of politics and soci-ety. This is one of the reasons that misinterpellation can have such radical results; it returns the subject, in a sense, to being the heteronymous—and hence both highly resistant and deeply interconnected—creature that she has always been, offering a state of noncompliance and complexity that is always hers to draw upon, if she wishes (or sometimes even if she doesn't).

Throughout this book there is a tension between the accidental and the deliberate qualities of misinterpellation; this tension is unresolvable in-sofar as the accidental subjects that come out of this process are the very "agents" who further its effects. There is no clear division between those who are "in the know" and those who stumble on radical outcomes. As I will show, there are vast overlaps between these states of being insofar as subjectivity itself—the source of both submission and rebellion—is what is in question.

In the service of furthering and deepening the radical potential of mis-interpellation, a key claim that I make in this book is that every moment of interpellation—that is, every time a political subject answers a call, acqui-esces to authority, and becomes a "proper" subject—is, simultaneously, a moment of misinterpellation. I will reject the idea that the law or the state—or whatever other authorizing body I may be discussing—ever "knows" who it is calling or that there is a direct and absolute connection between the intentions of the powerful (those who put out the call) and the subjects that are produced in response to that power. As I will argue further, there is always a built-in lack of certain knowledge of who is being called; the subject in question is more of an assumption than a fact (indeed, that act of assumption is the basis of interpellation). Thus, there is always an element of randomness and unknowingness at the heart of the interpellative process. Even when that randomness is not recognized 99.99 percent of the time (or nine times out of ten to use Althusser's more generous figure), that same radical potential lurks in every one of us and at every moment.

Understanding misinterpellation as a source of permanent vulnerability is critical for resisting a system that, for all its problems, seems fantastically good at adjusting to various challenges (leaving the left, among liberalism's other adversaries, often in a state of deepest despair). Thinking in terms of misinterpellation, we see that we have never been the subjects we thought we were. This is the case both in the sense of not being the individuals that interpellation tells us that we are and also in the secondary sense that we are not in fact utterly determined and controlled by those identities we receive. The drama of the moment of recognizing the misfirings of interpellation—as exemplified by Kafka's story of Abraham—attests to the dislocations of subjectivity that occur whenever we are called by authority (I will argue later, there are other forms of recognition or counterinterpellation as well, forms that do not have the same authority structure as the sort I am discussing here). In this way, I seek to think more closely and strategically about how and when liberalism misfires—or is read as misfiring—and how attending to such misfiring can help those of us on the left rethink or enhance our approach to politics, to authority, and even to revolution.

Layout of the Book

In order to explore this question, I divide this book into two parts. The first part of the book focuses on the theory and historical practice of misinterpellation within the context of an ongoing system of interpellated power and authority. This part addresses these questions: How does interpellation work? How has it been resisted in the past and with what results? The second part of the book focuses more on what happens beneath and beyond the umbrella of interpellation. This part takes a more philosophical and literary approach in order to answer a different but critically related set of political questions: What kind of subject emerges from the breakdown of interpellation? What strategies does this subject employ to maximize her disruption of interpellated identities? What kind of politics does this subject express and with what implication for thinking about questions of contemporary forms of resistance?

Each chapter of the book is organized around a central call. The first part of the book engages mainly with interpellating calls such as Louis Althusser's classic "hey, you there!" and Frantz Fanon's "tiens, un Nègre" ("look, a black person"), although I will consider Lauren Berlant's "wait up!" as an alternative kind of calling in chapter 1. The second part of the book features calls that further misinterpellation, calls that recognize the multiple anarchist subjects that we always have been but do not usually recognize as such.

Throughout the book, I will, as already noted, look at how to maximize the subversion of the kinds of subjects that we are usually asked to be, how, that is, to enhance the decentered and radicalized forms of subjectivity that emerge from the processes of misinterpellation. Turning from calls that interpellate us to calls that scatter and subvert that form of address is a key part of how I try to accomplish that.

In chapter 1, I look at the theory of misinterpellation by examining Althusser's theory of interpellation, as well as interventions to that theory by Judith Butler, Mladen Dolar—especially as Butler reads him—and Lauren Berlant, among other critics. In this chapter, I will attempt to protect the value of Althusser's observation from some of his detractors even as I am myself critical of the way Althusser seems to accept—or at least insufficiently challenge—the validity of interpellation as a process of political subjectivity. Even as he opposes the basis of the systems that interpellation supports, Althusser claims that "nine times out of ten" the person who is the subject of the interpellator's hail is "really" the one who was meant to be hailed. What happens, I ask, if we focus, by contrast, on the one time out of ten, the unintended, unsummoned subject of interpellation (i.e., the "wrong" Abraham)? If we adopt this viewpoint, we see better how interpellation is not a monolithic and fail-safe system; if it fails one in ten times, that imperils the notion that interpellation is "always right"—or even ever right—with implications for the cases when it supposedly "correctly" identifies the subject. Althusser knows this but his analysis of the workings of interpellation distracts attention from the productivity of its failures, something I try to correct for in this chapter.

In chapter 2, I look at three historical examples of misinterpellation: the Haitian revolution at the turn of the nineteenth century and its response to the French Declaration of the Rights of Man and Citizen; the so-called Wilsonian moment involving Woodrow Wilson's promotion of national self-determination at the end of World War I and its effect on those who would become leaders of the anticolonial movement; and the case of Mohamed Bouazizi's self-immolation and the origins of the Arab Spring in the winter of 2010–2011. In each case, there was a perceived call (very clearly in the first two instances; in a more diffused sense in the latter case) that was interpreted as having universal application but that revealed itself not to apply to the person or persons I am looking at (not for the slaves of Haiti, not for colonial subjects of European empires, not for the modern Tunisian underclass). Yet these people answered the call nonetheless, acting "as if" the call were for them after all.[10]

In looking at this question, I consider forms of resistance at both the elite and subaltern levels (especially in the first two cases; with the case of Bouazizi, resistance came much more definitively from the subaltern level). I argue that although at the elite level (such as with Toussaint Louverture or the leaders of anticolonial movements in the aftermath of World War I) there is a high degree of buy-in to liberal universalism, at the subaltern level, such influences are much weaker but still present.

In seeking an explanation for why these cases represented such a radical break with the status quo (when countless other moments of misunderstood calls, humiliations, and the like produced nothing at all), I turn, at the end of the chapter, to Machiavelli for an explanation as to why there are times that the operations of authority and ideology are maintained indefinitely and why sometimes they are exposed and ruined as with the three case studies in question. In his writings about the religion of the Roman republic, Machiavelli tells us how authority in a society can be produced and bolstered via projection onto externalities (like God, the law, or the state, the process of interpellation itself) and also, if we read him in a more conspiratorial fashion, how that same process can be subverted and resisted.

Chapter 3 is a reading of Fanon as a misinterpellated subject. Fanon, a black Martinican, was raised thinking he was both a French and universal subject, with all the rights and privileges that this identity brought with it. It was only when he went to France and was seen—and indirectly hailed—as a black man ("tiens, un nègre!") that he realized that he wasn't who he thought he was (or at least he wasn't thought of in the way he himself believed to be true). His knowledge and identity as an "insider"—that is, a Frenchman and universal subject—and his experience of rejection made for a potent and radical response. In this instance, Fanon's dual subject position allows him maximum access and damage to the ideology of race and colonialism that his experience of misinterpellation helped him to ultimately subvert and resist. In this chapter, I treat Fanon both as a prime example of a misinterpellated subject and, at the same time—and relatedly—as a uniquely situated critic of the kinds of identity that interpellation produces. Fanon is, accordingly, a keen observer of the possibilities for the misinterpellated subject to subvert and even topple illicit power structures and identities.

In chapter 4, which begins the second part of the book, I engage in a more literary and philosophical exploration of the misinterpellated subject by looking at the work of Friedrich Nietzsche (a figure who will dominate the rest of the book even if I'm not discussing him directly). As I see it, Nietzsche supplies us with a way to think about a subject who is not just responding to a mistake but who is fundamentally broken off from and deeply resistant to the system that produced her nominal identity. In this way, Nietzsche moves even beyond the misinterpellated subject that Kafka depicts. His subject not only refuses to go away but also allows for an entirely alternative form of subjectivity to emerge (or at least become visible) in the wake of that refusal. This is an anarchic and multiple self that defies the organizing principles of interpellating forms of subjectivity.

Nietzsche does this by supplying us with a series of messianic figures (his own authority in the text, the prophet Zarathustra, and the messianic figure of the overman) who pose as a succession of saviors who do not in fact save us. Instead, they disappoint and abandon us, leaving us very much on our own. Not only do these figures fail to save us but they effectively ruin—at least temporarily—the possibility for salvation. By taking on the pose of the savior and voiding that position with their own failure to act, Nietzsche prevents us from being saved by anyone else either. What emerges in the wake of that disappointment is not the shining, higher beings that we are promised to be but our mundane fleshy selves. As ourselves, we are never the person we want to be when we answer the calls of authority, but we are the ones who show up anyway. This self, the one who shows up to answer the call, is the one Nietzsche instructs us to love when he speaks of *amor fati*.

Chapter 5 looks at two works of literature, Herman Melville's "Bartleby, the Scrivener" and Virginia Woolf's *To the Lighthouse*, in order to exemplify what a Nietzschean (and therefore misinterpellated) subject might look like and, in particular in this chapter, how their seemingly marginal or invisible status disguises both a very complicated and very powerful form of subjectivity (more powerful, I will argue, than any other character in their respective texts). I read Bartleby not as a passive figure but as an active underminer of established hegemonies. And, whereas the erstwhile heroine of *To the Lighthouse* is the seductive and magnificent Mrs. Ramsay, I argue that Lily Briscoe, who normally exists entirely in Mrs. Ramsay's shadow, is the true—and misinterpellated—protagonist in that text.

In order to read these texts in this way, I suggest that we need to approach the texts themselves via a misinterpellated form of reading, that is, against the grain, in tension with established authorities and figures in the novel and even with the way the novel seems to insist on being read.[11] When read in such a manner, we experience the way these characters are disorganized, decentralized, and multiply subjected; we read, that is, the anarchy of the subject(s) in and through the text.

In chapter 6, I revisit Althusser's imagined scene of interpellation (wherein a police officer calls out "hey, you there!" to an individual who, responding, becomes a subject) via a turn to yet other literary, and one nonfiction, works: Kafka's *Amerika*, Ralph Ellison's *Invisible Man*, and Ta-Nehisi Coates's *Between the World and Me*. In this chapter, I focus on the strategies of failure and refusal in terms of weapons that are available to the misinterpellated subject to enhance and expand her resistance.

In all three texts, I argue that we see a complication and a subversion of Althusser's narrative by offering different readings of the encounter between a police officer and an individual. In the case of *Amerika*, Kafka offers us a subject—Karl Rossmann—who is so failed, so unavailable, that he cannot help but be misinterpellated. In his encounter with a police officer, he cannot play his part, cannot project authority, and so the moment of interpellation is foiled. In the case of Ellison's and Coates's narratives, there is no possibility for such a form of failure. In these cases, the fact that the subjects in question are black means that the police "know" whom they are dealing with—and kill them accordingly—regardless of what the subject does or says. Instead of failure, then, I argue that these latter two books describe and advocate a practice of refusal, a refusal to submit to the false identities that are placed on black subjects and other subjects of color on the one hand, as well as a refusal to partake in a language of redemption, teleology, and hope that underlies the liberal universal values that are for these subjects a trap rather than a promise. This refusal is not purely negative (just as Nietzsche's no saying is also always a yes saying); it has creative and productive aspects wherein these authors (like Fanon) take blackness not as a fate that they cannot escape, but as a subjectivity of their own devising, and in the face of the demand of liberalism that they be the kind of black subject (obedient, downtrodden, etc.) that it calls them to be.

In chapter 7, I look at a Lars von Trier film, *Breaking the Waves*, to consider ways to maximize the rupturing of the circuitry of interpellation. In this case, I focus on the strategy of turning interior complexity and plurality into being itself a form of resistance to interpellated identity (and, in particular, to its monolithic and unitary quality). The movie features a character, Bess McNeill, who talks to herself with the voice of God. Unlike the other characters in the movie, most of whom obey and fear a stern and universal, transcendent God, Bess engages with a God who is more of an accomplice and a co-conspirator than a punishing deity (although her God can be that too at times). Accordingly, Bess's God works to disrupt the original chain of command that Althusser models between God and the first political subject, Moses. This God comes in to save her from the interpellating deity (Althusser's "God the Subject"), which lies behind the forms of subjectivity that all subjects suffer from in one way or another. This too, I argue, is a form of Nietzschean salvation, and in the process, Bess, unlike any other character in the film, can love her fate and accept her misinterpellation (even as her actual fate in the film is quite horrific). By housing within herself another subject—and not just any subject but God—Bess shows a way to make herself (relatively) immune to being colonized or recolonized by interpellative forms of identity.

Finally, in the conclusion, I look at the forms of address that have been gathered in the preceding chapters, moving from the "hey, you there!" of Althusser to Bartleby's "I would prefer not to" to Orlando's "come, come!" (a character from a different writing of Virginia Woolf that is briefly considered at the end of chapter 5). These various forms of address, I argue, offer us many different modes of engagement, different political possibilities, and different ways to subvert the power of interpellation, what could be called a practice of counterinterpellation. Collectively, these form a network of callings, a set of choices that bring various degrees of resistance and challenge to norms of identity and ideology in terms both of personal and political subjectivity. I argue here once again that attention to these other forms of calling offer an anarchist politics, as well as an anarchist and misinterpellating form of reading to challenge the seeming inevitability and destiny of archism and interpellative authority.

Passivity and Subordination

Before getting into the chapters proper, a preliminary discussion of the question of political passivity as well as the larger question of how to undertake an anarchic reading of subjectivity is in order. In terms of passivity, I do not want to give the impression that prior to moments of misinterpellation, the general populace is either entirely bought into dominant ideology or simply marking time. I want to firmly reject any notion of false consciousness or quiescence as the historical record supports neither of these readings. Such readings, even when put forth by radical thinkers, tend, I think, to reinforce the trap of TINA. If resistance only happens during moments of revolution, and revolutions invariably seem to fail or get corrupted, then, the liberal can argue that there truly is no alternative (and so we might as well acquiesce to liberal political and economic power). Seeing that resistance is, in fact, constant and ubiquitous helps us to see that the power and authority of states and other institutions under liberalism are much weaker and more tenuous than they normally appear. Such an understanding also helps us better appreciate the context that misinterpellation comes out of, what comes "before" and "after" this phenomenon.

A key thinker to help challenge the idea of quiescence on the part of subordinated communities is James C. Scott. Two of his books, *Weapons of the Weak* and *Domination and the Arts of Resistance*, are particularly useful in this regard. In the latter work, Scott does a great deal of damage to the idea of false consciousness as it is expressed by thinkers ranging from Antonio Gramsci to Althusser himself. For Scott, the tendency to see subordinated communities such as peasants, serfs, and slaves as passive or quiescent constitutes an acceptance of what he calls the "public transcript," the formal and official discourse that occurs between the ruling and ruled classes.

Such a reading of power relations lies in distinction to the "hidden transcripts" that Scott focuses on, especially in the second half of *Domination and the Arts of Resistance* (*Hidden Transcripts* is the subtitle of that book). The hidden transcript takes note of the mocking songs, the jokes, the rituals, the gatherings, the foot dragging, the pilfering, the sabotage, and other acts of resistance that do not necessarily amount to open revolt but that collectively form a long and steady means of countering the hegemonic manifestations of authority at all levels of interaction.[12] This resistance very much includes the level of thought. As Scott puts it, "The obstacles to resistance, which are many, are simply not attributable to the inability of subordinate groups to *imagine* a counterfactual order."[13] As Scott shows, subordinate communities imagine an alternative frequently and well.

Indeed, for Scott, it is particularly at the level of ideology that resistance to dominant power is strongest. This goes in direct opposition to the work of Gramsci and Althusser (more the former than the latter) as they are usually read. Their prime argument is usually taken to be that it is precisely via ideology that groups are dominated; their objective class interests are given over to the interests of their overlords via superstructural operations at the level of culture, education, family, and even political consciousness. For Scott, such views amount to replacing an economic determinism (which is precisely what this turn to ideology was meant to correct for) with an ideological determinism.[14] As Scott sees it, "The concept of [ideological] hegemony ignores the extent to which most subordinate classes are able, on the basis of their daily material existence, to penetrate and demystify the prevailing ideology."[15]

In Scott's account, even the public transcripts, the official records that look like a compendium of subordinate devotion, are not simply accounts of obedience but are themselves the product of what he calls a "dialogue with power that may have a greater or lesser strategic dimension."[16] He details how both sides have a shared interest in portraying the negotiations that mark relations between dominant and subordinate groups as being fairly harmonious. The powerful wish to hide the extent to which their power is vulnerable, the degree to which they are in fact negotiating and jockeying with their own subordinates. The subordinates, in turn, can use the cover of subservience as a way to hide their true intentions, making themselves seem harmless or covering themselves with plausible deniability if any overt efforts should fail.

Clearly, there is a difference between open revolution and the kinds of hidden power struggle that Scott discusses in these books. In Scott's telling, the difference between open and covert resistance is less one of kind and more a matter of degree. There is, for him, a continuum of acts of resistance and counterideologies that the dominated have been practicing for years, decades, or centuries. He tells us that it is often the case that insurrection starts off as a call for reform within the system (something that is in keeping with the story of misinterpellation that I will be telling in later pages). Yet he argues that this does not indicate a true buy-in to the ideologies that are being resisted on the part of the subordinated community. To give just one—but a critical—example, Scott writes, "Revolutionary actions on behalf of reformist goals, such as an eight-hour day, an end to piecework, a minimum wage, politeness from management, cooking and toilet facilities, were the driving force behind the Bolshevik revolution."[17] For Scott, effectively all forms of resistance, even when they lead to no discernible change for the supplicant or supplicants in their lifetime, can be read as a kind of dress rehearsal for insurrection.[18]

For Scott, then, what looks like a history of perfect passivity, marked only by the occasional—and seemingly inexplicable—open revolts, is in fact the reflection of a long history of intense and often bitter contestation that goes underground and then comes to the surface (often only to go underground again). Power is never as confident as it seems, and resistance is never as hopeless or absent as it is portrayed. What is often portrayed as a "spontaneous" uprising has deep roots in practices of resistance that effectively never cease.

Such an insight is vital to understanding what forms of resistance are possible and where they come from. As Bonnie Honig writes in *Emergency Politics*, what is often depicted and understood as an individual act of resistance—for example, Rosa Parks's not moving from her seat—is actually the result of a mobilized and collective form of counterpower.[19] As Honig also notes, attempts by liberals to portray the individual in question as a sui generis heroic figure serve to neutralize and distract from the actual and collective politics being presented by their act, masking the true threat that such actions pose.

In this way, there is no consensus on the part of subordinated communities that a dominant power is "inevitable," or natural or desirable in any way. As Neil Roberts shows in his study of the Caribbean during the era of slavery, even under the direst conditions, there is always resistance, marronage, and other forms of flight and counterpower.[20] If this can occur even under conditions of slavery, it is clear that no state is ever so dominant as to be in a position to reduce its people to abject powerlessness. To put it in a nutshell, there is no TINA.

Resistance and Misinterpellation

How does this understanding of resistance then square with the story that I am going to tell about misinterpellation, which seems to suggest, on the contrary, that everyone is duped by systems of power until a misfiring of the linkages between the system and its reception produces a break in hegemony? In response to this question I have three points to make. First, as will become clearer in the next three chapters, to think in terms of notions like interpellation and misinterpellation does not commit one to a theory of false consciousness for all the times in between revolutions. I read many of the authors that Scott criticizes as having somewhat more nuanced readings of the situation than he implies, especially Althusser, about whom I do not share all of Scott's reservations. Nevertheless, I take Scott's main point about the porousness of ideology. As I'll attempt to show further in the following chapters, subordinate communities are never dupes. Their use of dominant ideology is, as Scott suggests, generally strategic, used as much to hide other agendas as it is to seek justice within a given system.

At the same time, there is a value to thinking about the role of ideology in allowing dominant systems to perpetuate themselves. If ideology is more of a two-way street than Gramsci or even Althusser might let on, akin to Hegel's master/slave dialectic, it effectively remains a basis for what is ultimately a kind of accommodation. I can imagine an unusually candid capitalist apologist reading Scott's books and thinking, "well, fine. As long as I keep getting my money who cares what is going on under the surface?"

We can see the operations of ideology most clearly by focusing on those moments when it is ripped asunder. If Scott's analysis allows us to see a continuum between the mildest forms of resistance and outright revolt, even he recognizes that there is a line between these forms of resistance.[21] The hidden transcript may suggest a dress rehearsal for the uprising, it may even give a form to that uprising, but the sudden openness of that resistance in moments of outright revolt is itself novel and critical. An actual uprising—assuming it is successful—scrambles and reconstitutes existing modes of understanding and actions. Critically, such a moment represents a definitive breaking of the fabric of ideology; whatever modus vivendi allowed the system of domination to perpetuate itself suddenly breaks down.

The effects of such a breakdown are dramatic and, I think, alter even the subversive practices that have been going on during the long periods of secrecy and domination that come between uprisings. If, as Scott tells us, the Bolshevik revolution came out of initially reformist demands for accountability and improved conditions, the workers' councils that emerged during the revolution created an entirely different relationship to authority and ideology (before having that authority eventually ceded to the Bolsheviks). In this way, strategic engagement with dominant ideology plays a crucial role in making revolutions possible but it doesn't preclude or overshadow the possibility of a move into other forms of politics that neither the subordinated or dominated communities could have envisioned in their ordinary subordinated conditions. Misinterpellation, in this regard, can be viewed as first the bending and then the breaking of the kinds of arrangements—the structures of address—that permit domination to remain intact for long periods of time. As the mismatch becomes more acute, the resulting radicalization of ideas, actions, and relationships may—but also may not—expand and develop accordingly.

The upshot of this point is that one doesn't have to be a dupe to work with and accommodate a repressive system. Ideology doesn't need to be "real" in the sense that it completely obfuscates and controls subordinate people. It simply needs to help organize and perpetuate a particular form of status quo, something that it does very well.

A second point to make involves making a distinction between the kinds of societies that Scott is addressing—generally peasant, serf, and slave societies—and contemporary conditions of liberal capitalism.[22] Here, the whole question of consciousness—however we define it—is strongly affected by the particularities of liberal capitalism. Contemporary capitalism has its own particular forms of ideology and the kinds of servitude that come with it are perhaps unique or at least different from the forms that Scott mainly studies. One key distinction under conditions of liberal capitalism is the ideology of individualism itself. This ideology is ingenious in that it essentially states that whatever class status a person has, it is her own fault. If she is poor, it's because she is lazy or stupid or just not working hard enough. If she is rich, she must similarly deserve her status (and if she doesn't, liberal ideology clearly states, she will lose her—or, since we are talking about liberalism, more likely his—birthright fairly swiftly; witness John Locke's notion of the "dissolute" landowner who squanders his fortune).[23] As Scott himself notes, if there is any chance of upward mobility, subordinate people are much more likely to buy in to the system. Liberalism produces this buy-in by virtue of its belief in individual merit and also via the belief it promotes in the fair and nonarbitrary power of the market to determine "winners" and "losers."

If the typical peasant doesn't need to read Barrington Moore to know that he or she is oppressed, and that class and status are based on arbitrary rules that work to their disfavor, the subject of liberal capitalism has a much harder time in being clear about this. Here again, I want to strenuously avoid the concept of "false consciousness" but want instead to note the prevalence under conditions of capitalism of various forms of political fetishism, phantasms of upward mobility, dessert, and the lures and promises of wealth that Walter Benjamin collectively labels "the phantasmagoria."[24] For Benjamin, reality—or at least what passes for reality—itself conspires to make us willing or at least semiwilling subjects of capitalism and the states that serve it. The effects of commodity fetishism produce in us a state of being wherein our desire to belong and to succeed is part of our bondage to the system.

It's not, of course, that the wage earner, the worker, or the member of the "working poor" toiling at McDonald's for minimum wage imagines that she is doing well. She may indeed recognize the degree to which she is suspended in an arbitrary power relation that she is not benefiting from in any way. Yet there are so many countering forces: the practices of commodity fetishism, the blandishments of liberal ideology that collectively serve to give the subject hope. Things like lotteries, media (in the United States, Bravo is a TV channel that, as I see it, is dedicated to the worship of wealth and glamour), Facebook, Twitter, Instagram, popular music, and a myriad of other factors don't so much make life bearable as they offer people a way to live a different and simultaneous life that is much more pleasant.[25] I wouldn't speak in this case of "false" consciousness but just of consciousness, full stop. Our life is flooded with conflicting signals, assuagement, despair, anger, and joy. So, for that matter, is the life of other communities who don't directly live under contemporary forms of capitalism (as Scott's attention to the hidden transcripts attests). Yet, under modern capitalism, domination has become very good at looking like a lot of different things so that it becomes much more difficult—but obviously not impossible—to refuse the status that is conferred by interpellation.

In the United States, it is easy for leftists and liberals alike to call members of the Tea Party "crazy" and "stupid," to argue (as Thomas Frank's *What's the Matter with Kansas?* does) that white working-class people in America have been duped by the Republican Party into trading their own class interests for feelings of superiority in being white (although that consensus is clearly breaking down with Donald Trump's ascendancy). Undoubtedly racism and other forms of hostility to "the other," however they are defined, are major tools of capitalist power and class oppression. Yet from a Benjaminian position, underneath all the devotion to capitalism, all the self-defeating support for a 1 percent that cares nothing for those who continuously vote for policies that they favor (and pay for) is a yearning on everyone's part for the promises of freedom, equality, wealth, and long (possibly eternal) life that capitalism promises via its mechanisms of interpellation. Benjamin clearly—and correctly—condemns the liberal and the fascist for their beliefs, but he also recognizes that behind and beneath this belief is a desire that is not itself evil; it comes rather from a set of "wishes images," as Benjamin puts it, for a better world.[26] This doesn't mean that we have to be "nice" or sympathetic to rich people and anyone else who oppresses others for their own benefit (the equivalent of that horrible retort to Black Lives Matter that "All Lives Matter"). It just means that their hold on power is far more tenuous then they—and often the rest of us—believe; their authority and power are not based on some truth that they have access to but rather quite the opposite. In this way everyone is similarly cut off from any firm or true forms of knowledge (whether about identity, power, or anything else). We don't therefore need to resort to a theory of false consciousness because to do so is to assume that there is a clear and authentic position from which we can regard the workings of capitalism whereas, in fact, such a position does not exist.

As Scott tells us too (working off of Foucault), both dominance and resistance to capitalism are internal to it. There is indeed no "outside" from which we can judge who is stupid, who is passive, who is false, and who is true. We are all, in the end, fetishists to one degree or other: hence my desire to stop using the term "false consciousness" and start just speaking of consciousness, the way that we experience our location in the midst of the miasma of liberal capitalist phantasm, fetishism, projections of authority, and corresponding forms of resistance.[27] If, under conditions of advanced liberal capitalism—or, in our own time, neoliberalism—the challenges to resistance are that much stronger, a theory of misinterpellation offers a set of strategies that gets at the nexus of consciousness and subjectivity that normally gives liberal capitalism an advantage over its adversaries. It suggests that even the most compromised among us need not be written off (as "falsely conscious") but are instead as vulnerable to the misfirings—and the radical potential—of interpellation as anyone else.[28]

The third, and related, point to make here—and this is where I bend a bit closer to Althusser than Scott does—is to argue, as I'll show in the next three chapters, that interpellation and the consciousness that it produces work like a circuit and are hence not a unidirectional or hydraulic system. As Katherine Gordy argues in her study of Cuba, ideology is not something that any one group owns or operates; it is a dynamic, a struggle, and a contest but it is also something that ties people together.[29] In this way, the division between "dupes" and those "in the know" becomes, once again, much blurrier, impossible to sustain. Nor in a sense are any of us wholly innocent of the power and lure of interpellation. There is a flow of interpellation, identity, information, and phantasm between the imagined origins of any power system and its peripheries. But this flow goes in two directions; as Scott clearly informs us, the modi vivendi that are created under conditions of capitalism are dynamic and in play, subject to renegotiation. Sometimes—as in our current period—the dominant groups can pretty much call the shots, although even in such cases there is continuous and endless resistance to their power. Other times the record is more mixed and then there are periodic revolutions when all bets are off. But at all times, there is a circularity of reception where the caller and callee are both caught up in the drama of interpellation. The caller imagines the power of the call, and the callee in turn imagines herself as the subject of that call, reproducing the authority of the caller, which otherwise seems entirely exterior to her.[30] This dynamic and charged call and response then is the circuitry of authority and power that constitutes what could broadly be considered as the pathways of interpellation. For this reason, both interpellation and misinterpellation are not merely single moments (Althusser's famous "hey, you there!") but are ongoing and fluid mechanisms, forms of representation and response—as well as the failures of those structures of address—that constitute the scenes of address.

The fact that interpellation itself depends on a kind of response makes it permanently vulnerable to the threat that misinterpellation poses. As I will show further, the dominant powers need us to respond to their calls far more than we need them to call us (actually, we don't need them to at all). For all the power and authority being generated from the capitalist classes and state overlords, there are counterveiling forces. As I will show further, there are countercircuits and subcircuits. All of this helps explain why the operations of interpellation never work as well as one would think (including for Althusser himself). Interpellation is less of a hydraulic force and more of a hot mess. More accurately, it is structured with regular and predictable forms of address—those apparatuses that gives form and structure to liberal capitalism—but those patterns and regularities disguise the way in which the circuitry itself is random, without origin, and far more vulnerable than it would appear to be.[31] A focus on misinterpellation allows us to question how to make that mess even messier, how to thwart and upset and overturn the operations of the status quo, how to align with subcurrents, and how to use circuit against circuit to maximum effect.

At the end of *Weapons of the Weak*, Scott evinces a lot of pessimism about revolutions. He notes that, almost inevitably, the oppressed groups who participate in revolutions end up experiencing new forms of oppression from new masters. His own energy therefore is directed at small acts of resistance and learning to live with states.

This is one place where I disagree very strongly with Scott (in part because his own analysis shows how states will seek out and attempt to destroy any competitors for political authority down to the most minor details). Rather than accepting the state or learning to "tam[e] the Leviathan," as Scott suggests, I believe that we can think more strategically about the nature of the breakdowns that lead to revolution.[32] If the production of authority is the critical factor in interpellation, the production of anti-authorities, the breakdown of the processes of ideology and interpellation, is vital for any consideration of ongoing resistance.

Accordingly, at the end of the day, this book is neither a defense nor a refutation of Althusser but a complication of his theory. One could read Althusser as arguing that at the level of ideology all subjects are brainwashed, filled with "false consciousness," and willfully obeying masters despite their own objective conditions to the contrary.[33] In such a reading ideology is determinant and that is that. If we stuck strictly to a theory of classical interpellation, we would not quite be able to understand how, if this is the case, resistance sometimes works nevertheless. It would seem that either we believe or we don't; either we get our subjectivity from this source or not. But if we interject the notion of misinterpellation, we get a much more vivid picture. Even as interpellation forms, misinterpellation unforms. Even as interpellation brings subjectivity, it is warped by its own failure, its own mismatch. Hence we get a subject who is continually being subverted at the same time she is receiving her identity from the state; this is a subject who has the potential to obey and disobey simultaneously. Indeed, following what Jacques Derrida says about J. L. Austin, we could say that the failure of interpellation, along with the intention of the caller, is a constitutive component of its "success" and furthermore—and relatedly—that interpellation needs the misinterpellation that could (and sometimes does) lead to its own undoing.[34]

For these reasons, I think it would be a grave mistake to continue to consider the role of ideology as something that dooms us to a certain political arrangement. When we shift our focus from ideology as a hydraulic force and think about it as a set of human interactions, we can see the myriad ways this ferment of resistance can be expanded, increased, and built upon. We see that there are forms of knowledge and action that can coexist even with the strongest and most oppressive (and obfuscating) forms of interpellation. Hence nothing is foreclosed and human actors are much more uppity and subversive than the official reading of history (the "public transcript") allows for.

The Banality of Resistance

In addition to concern about thinking about people as passive or as "dupes"— a way to overlook the real power that people exercise against dominant systems—a second critical, and related, preliminary issue to consider involves thinking about the relationship between extraordinary and ordinary moments of time, as well as the relationship between extraordinary actors and everyone else. In terms of the temporality of resistance, Jennifer Culbert alerts us to the dangers of thinking of major events as being exceptional and without precedent or connection to what comes before and after. In writing about Arendt's concept of the "banality of evil," Culbert suggests that Arendt herself misses the key import of such a concept. Banality for Culbert means that evil is not simply a matter of spectacular forms of violence, such as the Holocaust, but it also refers to the everyday (hence banal) questions of racism, police brutality, hierarchy, drudgery, microaggressions, and all the other aspects of life that make life "cruddy" (as she puts it, citing Elizabeth Povinelli).[35]

If we only look at events like the Holocaust or the transatlantic slave trade—although both had their own forms of quotidian, and evil, banality— we risk congratulating ourselves at how "good" things are now by contrast (another version of ignoring the "hidden transcript" that Scott discusses). Everyday indignities are not "evil" by this account and so are not really worth worrying or thinking about (it may be that Arendt's problematic reading of events like desegregation in Little Rock, Arkansas, may reflect a bit of this bias toward the spectacular manifestations of evil).

My interest in misinterpellation follows Culbert's logic. I share her concerns that by lionizing one moment in time, one renders all the "in between" times useless or, once again, passive. Since we tend to live in "in between" time ourselves, such a view would strip us of any sense of an ongoing possibility of revolt, much as the idea of the power of ideology reinforces a sense of the impossibility of resistance. This question has great resonance for how this book's argument is actually undertaken: although in the chapters that follow I will be looking at the more spectacular events—the Haitian revolution, the Arab Spring, and so on—I do so in order to reveal an architecture that is no different than what happens every day under the aegis of interpellation. I look at the "one time out of ten"—the exceptions that cannot be ignored when misinterpellation is undeniable, when it is highly visible and easy to spot—in order to think about the nine times out of ten, all the other times when it is deniable (or misrecognizable, to use Althusser's own term).[36]

There is a risk to this strategy.[37] The risk is the flip side of what Culbert examines with Arendt; it is that in looking at spectacular moments, I treat them as fundamentally different than other moments, ignoring their connection to more quotidian—or banal—moments in the process (and not just textually in terms of the amount of time spent on them, but conceptually as well). One of the key underlying ambitions of this book is to anarchize the way we think about time and agency, that is, to get us away from thinking about the big moments (the events) and big players (the revolutionary leaders) and think instead about the steady stream of resistance and subversion that constitutes politics, what might be called the misinterpellation of everyday life or, perhaps too, the banality of resistance.

In terms of thinking about time and its relationship to politics, like many US-based leftist political theorists, I am a product of an Arendtian-Wolinite school of thinking whereby we are taught to think of politics as only really occurring during wonderful glorious moments like the Paris Commune and the late 1960s. During the rest of the time, by implication, nothing really happens, at least politically speaking. While I would never abandon the vision I get from this tradition about what politics could (or should) look like, I think it's time for leftists—at least the ones who come from this tradition—to begin to think more broadly about what politics is, that is, to retrieve, as Culbert and Scott do, from the ordinary course of time, a politics of resistance that is always happening. To anarchize time means that every moment is the same as every other moment. No moment is special, not even moments like the Paris Commune. That moment (what Alain Badiou calls "18 March 1871") is unique in terms of what happened during that period of time but there is nothing about the temporality of that occasion— the materiality of the moment—that made the Commune any different than any other point in time; its eventfulness is not teleologically given by its particular temporality and any moment could be equally disruptive, even moments that have already happened and are now past.[38] In looking at spectacular examples—as I will—I seek to render the ordinary spectacular or the spectacular ordinary, to blur the line between these states and not give everything over to the exceptional. In this way temporality in general, and not just "special moments," is available for radical politics, everywhere and every time.

Similarly, there is a risk, in thinking about agency, to lionize the hero or even the antihero.[39] Rather than thinking about vanguardism or exceptional actors, I want to think about everyday acts of resistance, banal—because quotidian—and unnoticed (sometimes even by the resister herself). This is the essence of the misinterpellated subject: she is the one that no one wanted but she showed up anyway. Yet here too the examples that I look to—the life and work of Fanon; literary antiheroes like Bartleby, Lily Briscoe, and Karl Rossmann; and Ellison's narrator—risk making it seem like these are the only possible subjects who can successfully overcome their interpellation (so that it could never have happened to other characters in those texts, even as they are clearly affected and even radicalized by their encounter with the subjects that I focus on). There is a romance to the antihero no less than to the more standard and conventional form of heroism.

The point of this book is to argue that we are all misinterpellated and so what I say for Bartleby is equally true for you and me and everyone else. Rather than saying that everyone is special, I wish to argue that no one is. We are all failed as subjects, all deluded, all broken by interpellation (although our respective failures take on unique and different aspects for each of us and also, as I'll argue further, take on different valences for different groups). The purpose of the figures that I am looking at is not to make us admire them but to see that what is the case for them can be the case for everyone else as well, or may actually be the case already (at least potentially).

In selecting my examples, I tried to emphasize therefore the disappointment and wretchedness that afflict the actors in question (especially with the literary examples). I ultimately seek to deglamorize and deromanticize the stories that I am telling. The misinterpellated subject is someone whom no one wants to be: an uninvited, undesired, broken, and failed subject. The bad news is that we are all that person. The good news is that being that person can be the basis for a radical and anarchist politics that the subject is already fighting for even if she doesn't always (or even ever) know it. As already noted, in thinking not just about the one time out of ten but the nine times out of ten as well (the numbers are completely arbitrary) I wish to locate and enhance the failure for all subjects, the failure, that is, that we already have accomplished.[40]

In thinking about anarchizing the way we engage with time and agency, I will confess to feeling all the romance and the heroizing tendencies that these stories evoke and even to deploying these genres to tell these tales. I am as fetishistic as the next person (you are a fetishist too, I'm afraid). A braver author might try to evoke banality itself in the text, sticking to the purely quotidian and the mediocre (in her reading of Arendt, Culbert includes a reading of a story by Octavia Butler—one of my favorite authors— which is as Culbert puts it "one of her least interesting stories"; here, the banality of the story itself enhances and captures the banality of evil that she is looking for in the everyday).[41] If the stories I tell evoke a romantic or heroic affect, my hope is that they will work like a Trojan horse (but here I am giving away the big secret); we may read them and find them exciting and possibly tragic, but taking them in, considering them, we allow their antiheroic and banal premises to undermine those very same glamorizing effects. My wager is that the power of the stories I tell does not get us to simply respond archically and fetishistically, but rather—and also—to see ourselves in these figures, not as heroes, but as failures. In thinking about Kafka's adage about a hope that is "not for us," I seek to have the reader experience—in a way that is legible to her—her own failure.[42]

A Yet More Minor Literature

If Gilles Deleuze and Félix Guattari call for a "minor" literature, perhaps it could be said that this book asks for a "yet more minor" literature, a mode of reading that seeks not the end of the subject or even signification per se, but just the failure of those things (that is, the recognition of a failure that has already been accomplished).[43] In looking at the literary and filmic examples that are examined in part II in particular, I seek out examples of that failure in the margins of texts and novels and films (and sometimes too peripheral characters who exist at the dead center of texts, depending on the work in question). This is a style of reading that could be applied to any text. The method is simple: look for the losers and the outcasts, the one whom nobody wants to know or be. It is not a matter of seeing those losers as being secretly great and superior but rather of having their exclusion bring into question the very categories by which they are being excluded. When the differences among heroines, antiheroines, and everyone else become impossible to maintain or understand, then we are thinking (and reading) along the lines of misinterpellation; we are seeking—and finding—the disruption to dominant narratives that coexists in every story that we tell.

Just as critically, to read in the mode of misinterpellation means to avoid the stealth teleologies and patterns of understanding that usually accompany more "archist" modes of reading. The ideas of sacrifice and, in particular, of tragic loss and suffering are all forms of literary genres that reinforce the sense of destiny and inevitability that come with interpellated forms of subjectivity. In the same way that Kafka's parable about Abraham renders the moment of sacrifice into something completely different and unexpected, so in general does a misinterpellated reading reject standard conventions of loss and sacrifice for some perfect, golden—or at least glamorous—future. As we will see in chapter 6, Ellison and Coates both decisively oppose any notion of tragic loss or heroization for the subjects that they consider. The concept of tragedy assumes a kind of inevitability, a built-in destiny that cannot be resisted. The subjects of such a destiny are always fated, always called in ways that they cannot avoid. They exist under the spell of a "big plan." Things happen to them "for a reason." In reading about these characters and their fates we duplicate this way of thinking, tying their story into larger beliefs in progress and teleology, into archist forms of time and subjectivity. But a misinterpellated form of reading will always oppose such a view; it will seek to undermine the certainties of fate and destiny that come along with such a sense of subjectivity and to render the tragic into something far more complex, contingent, and anarchic.[44]

As already noted, in thinking about reading in this mode, over the course of this book I will be trying to build up a vocabulary of the kinds of calls that are put out by misinterpellated subjects. To Althusser's emblematic "hey, you there!" (the call of the interpellator), I will look to Berlant's "wait up!," Woolf's "come, come!," Bartleby's "I would prefer not to," along with several other forms of calls to those who find themselves on the wrong end of interpellation. These other forms of calling do not demand that we be a particular form of subject. Instead, they welcome multiplicity, complexity, anarchism, and resistance. As may be appropriate for a book that seeks to think about anarchizing subjectivity, there is no one "correct" alternative form of calling to oppose the call of the interpellator. Rather, there is a myriad of choices, all of which come with their own baggage, their own pluses and minuses (and zeros).

I will be speaking a lot about failure in this book but it is critical to note that by failure, I am referring to the failure of subjectivity, not of politics.[45] In fact, I think we will continue to fail politically—that is, to remain captive to capitalism and neoliberalism—so long as we do not realize that we are failed as subjects. The failure of the latter must precede a more "successful" form of politics. A failed subject is not a pile of useless mush; she is an incredibly dynamic complex and heterogeneous being. This being is the not-hero of my book; she serves as the unmaker of the heroes we all wish to be (all that we are interpellated to be). She is an anti-egoic force. Like the messiahs that Nietzsche offers us—one who serves to save us from messiahs—this not-hero just might serve to save us from heroism, from thinking that some time and some person and some place is unique and better than all the other times and persons and places, thereby depoliticizing the moments we live in and the people that we are. When we stop thinking exclusively in terms of heroes and tragedy, romance and loss—that is, once again, when we read these texts through a misinterpellating lens—an enhancement of the politics we all practice in a daily and banal way potentially becomes more potent, more evident, more subversive, and more powerful.

Misinterpellation and Anarchism

There are other explanations besides misinterpellation for how resistance breaks out after periods of apparent quiescence. Alain Badiou, for one, has his theory of the "event," which bursts out of the realm of impossibility into possibility by the sheer force of its coming into being. Before an event (the French revolution, the Paris Commune, the Chinese Cultural Revolution and even the Resurrection of Christ are key events in his view), Badiou tells us that whatever it comes to inaugurate simply doesn't—and can never—exist. Then, suddenly, the changes an event brings can and do exist in a way that can never be undone. I'm not sure this theory of misinterpellation is completely at odds with a theory of the event but it's certainly the case that misinterpellation does not look for the break that comes ex nihilo.[46] Nor, as already noted, does misinterpellation represent a unique and isolated moment in time. Misinterpellation always comes out of interpellation; new practices come out of the "dress rehearsals" of resistance and subversion that precede them. Even if the moment of the event is radically unlike that which it precedes, to think of the moment of rupture as special and unique—that is, to think of the moment of time itself as bearing some special quality that makes it different from every other moment in time—is akin, once again, to thinking of Rosa Parks or other political resisters as sui generis; it masks once again the ongoing collective threat—and hence the real power—posed by such moments.

There is also the Leninist model of slow and steady planning by a vanguard party that then inspires and causes revolution among others. I know and respect many people who hold to this view and I think that there has been some new and exciting work in Leninist thought—work by thinkers like Jodi Dean and Sylvain Lazarus—that challenges the old vision of elite-level domination.[47] Yet I remain skeptical about a party-based model of left politics. As Arendt's classic work *On Revolution* suggests, when revolutions happen—for reasons that I will set aside for the moment—they are massive, unscripted, and unpredictable. More accurately, they do follow patterns but it is not those set down by parties but rather by decades and centuries of resistance as Scott shows us. It is only later that a party shows up and announces that it has been "leading all along." Surely there are parties that are always ready to make claims for speaking for "the people" and in that sense they may precede the revolutions that they become associated with (temporally speaking), but their success has, I think, less to do with the way that they prefigured that revolution than with the way they manage to make themselves the spokesperson and representatives for a movement that is much broader, more diffuse, and more anarchic than anything that could have been "led." Furthermore, I would say that parties are themselves often agents of interpellation; they seek to put out calls and, for this reason, they are not part of the politics of misinterpellation I describe here (although their actions, of course, can produce misinterpellating responses of their own).

There are, as already noted, some exceptions to this understanding of Leninism. Jodi Dean, in a recent work, argues that the party is explicitly not in possession of some special knowledge, that it holds the place of the "Big Other," to use her Lacanian parlance, in order to prevent other aspirants from taking on that role (hence not unlike the role I ascribe to Nietzschean messiahs, who save us from salvation by occupying and ruining the position from which authority is thought to derive).[48] I definitely see the possibility of some kind of alignment between her theories (and those of a few others) and my own.

Yet, more generally, rather than aligning with Badiou or Leninism—at least with the more orthodox or standard versions of these theories—as already noted several times, a theory of misinterpellation is, in my view, largely and mainly consistent with anarchist theory and practice. The very model of call and response that sets up a theory of interpellation is inherently "archic," that is, tied up with ruling and statecraft, with authority asserted from above and beyond. Misinterpellation comes from an anarchist perspective; it comes out of collective patterns of behavior, a form of steady and ongoing resistance to interpellative authority. It pays attention to alternative calls, calls that come from within and beneath and among the communities and individuals in question. These calls form other sources and models of authority that may rival or displace archist forms of interpellation.[49] In this regard, I see misinterpellation as a key aspect of anarchist power, a product of endless ferment and resistance to a system that might seem utterly dominant but that is characterized by numerous and endless forms of vulnerability and dysfunction. Human actors do not need to wait for parties or events to take up the charge of revolt; misinterpellation makes that ability available to all of us at all times. In this way, misinterpellation can be seen as stemming from—and being connected to—what could be called the anarchism of everyday life, to the banal and ordinary forms of resistance that are usually overlooked but that collectively form a potent challenge to various forms of dominant orthodoxy.

Who Are "We"?

A final word about nomenclature: I've been talking about "us" and "we" a lot but, of course, as innumerable other scholars have noted, this we is a problem. As I'll be discussing, "we" are divided by many things, perhaps especially race, class, ability, sex, sexuality, and gender (in all of their variations). As

I'll discuss further in chapter 6, anarchism has had a lot of problems with negotiating this "we." This pronoun is often used to overwrite many critical and unbridgeable differences within this and other movements. There are too many assumptions about the audience, about their identity, about their equivalence to other subjects, and even about the way they can be thought of as separate entities. In my reading of things, all of these ways of thinking are antithetical to anarchism since assumption and projection, as I'll argue further in this book, is a hallmark of archism. But this doesn't mean that anarchists of today don't make these assumptions anyway. I take Foucault's claim that "we need to cut off the king's head" quite seriously, and I think this adage applies even—perhaps especially or at least most poignantly—to anarchism in many ways.[50]

How then can we even start to talk about "us" or "we" when such terms are so redolent of overwriting, of assumption, of archism itself? The "we" I have in mind is an assortment of failed subjects who hold on to all of the differences and cleavages that they've had all along (including all of the histories and divisions that come with those cleavages). The we I am thinking about is not an alliance but a conspiracy, a form of resistance based on a common rejection of the practices of law, politics, and economics—with an accompanying form of subjectivity—that are visited upon all of us but that some of "us" suffer from far more than others. Some of "us" in fact don't suffer at all and that is part of the problem of "we." As noted, the one thing that "we" all have in common is that we are all failed subjects, we are all misinterpellated. If that failure can become more visible, then "we" can start to act less like a family, with clear roles and hierarchies and much hidden misery and conflict and more like a conspiracy, a shifting and ongoing network of resistance that fights for some things in common and also some things that are different (including from each other).

The anarchism I am suggesting here, however, is not simply limited to the usual collective and social setting where we think politics tends to happen. There is a deeper "we" afoot, a "we" that resides in each person, that reflects overlapping and heterogeneous sources of identity. Just as Plato tells us that to understand the city we must first look at the soul, in this book I try to look at the anarchism of the soul or subject as a necessary complement to the anarchism of the city or community.[51] This more intimate and personal "we" is no more harmonious or coherent than the we that forms the city. It too has its discords and disagreements, antagonisms and cross-purposes, as I'll show further.

Thinking of these two forms of "we" in tandem offers a way, as I say in the conclusion, to think of human beings as being anarchist "all the way down" from the interpersonal to the intrapersonal level. To think from such a position, offers no, or at least less, refuge to the often occult archisms that construct—and dominate—us at so many levels (on the level of the personal, the collective, even the temporal and spatial). It gives us over to the many ways that misinterpellation is continually unforming us as subjects, offering the widest and most contingent possible understanding of "who we are." Such a viewpoint can be immensely powerful, as I will show, but it does not guarantee a happy ending. Some of the stories and texts that I will be looking at have distinctly awful endings. Actually a focus on misinterpellation doesn't guarantee anything. Guarantees are part of the patter of liberalism, a way of assuaging present injustices in the name of universalism and reason. All you get from paying attention to misinterpellation is a chance not to be predetermined by the teleologies, phantasms, and projections of liberalism. But that is quite a bit and this book is an attempt to think more pointedly about that possibility.

PART I. SUBJECTS OF THE CALL

CHAPTER ONE

FROM "HEY, YOU THERE!" TO "WAIT UP!"

The Workings (and Unworkings) of Interpellation

In this chapter, I look more closely at the notion of misinterpellation, asking how it might—or actually does—work, how an unintentional and uncontrolled kind of calling, one that works at cross-purposes with how calling is usually intended to work, can lead to radical outcomes. As already noted in the introduction, because their response to the call is unexpected, even unwanted, the arrival of the misinterpellated subject challenges the scene in which she arrives. Insofar as the act of interpellation establishes and cements authority and social norms—establishing even the sense of individual identity—misinterpellation works as a specifically and dangerously political force. As noted in the introduction too, the power of misinterpellation comes from the fact that it often initially presents itself as harmless, as a small mistake of understanding or identity whereby it is able to effect its subversion from deep within the heart of normativity and subjectivization. Yet, as I will attempt to establish further in this chapter, such moments are just indications of a much deeper flaw in the armature of interpellative authority, the veritable tip of the iceberg.

The political upshot of this discussion is that, as I see it, misinterpellation constitutes a potential antidote (there are others as well) to the otherwise seemingly overwhelming and irresistible power of global capitalism and liberalism, as well as to the phantasms that such systems produce. The hallmarks of misinterpellation, the refusal (or failure, which is not always the same thing, as I will explain further) to hear the siren calls of global powers in the way they are intended, the fact of showing up when unwelcome, of seeing oneself as being called when nothing of the sort is true, lead to resistance, radicality, and subversion, sometimes on a massive scale.

In order to demonstrate the way in which misinterpellation operates—and also how it might be enhanced and practiced more broadly—I will turn to the work of the key author of interpellation theory, Louis Althusser, as well as a few of his critics.

Althusser and Interpellation

Louis Althusser's notion of interpellation is the basis for much of what has passed for subjectivity theory in contemporary thought (at least in its leftist, radical variants, although, as I will show, plenty of leftists resist his influence). In "Ideology and the State," his well-known essay on the subject, Althusser tells us that ideology is "nothing but its functioning in the material forms of existence of that functioning."[1] In other words, ideology only exists insofar as it takes a material form, a style of categorization of the subject as a legal person, an entity recognized by the state and its power apparatus. For Althusser, this subjectivization is so deep, so intimate, that it is effectively naturalized (he tells us, riffing on Aristotle, that "man is an ideological animal by nature").[2]

Very famously, Althusser tells us that ideology

> "transforms" the individuals into subjects (it transforms them all) by that very precise operation which I have called *interpellation* or hailing, and which can be imagined along the lines of the most commonplace everyday police (or other) hailing: "Hey, you there!" [In French: "Hé, vous, là-bas!"] Assuming that the theoretical scene I have imagined takes place in the street, the hailed individual will turn around. By this mere one-hundred-and-eighty-degree physical conversion, he becomes a *subject*.[3]

This subject is thus produced, as we see, by this act of interpellation, although chronologically speaking, Althusser tells us that "you and I are *always already* subjects."[4] This act of interpellation reaches, as it were, both back and forward in time, producing a subject where there was merely an individual before. For Althusser, this is a tangible and material operation of ideology.

In describing this process, Althusser suggests, however obliquely, a way for the process to not quite go the way it usually is supposed to. Immediately following the passage just cited, Althusser asks,

> Why [does the interpellated individual become a subject]? Because he has recognized that the hail was "really" addressed to him, and that "it was *really him* who was hailed"; (and not someone else). Experience shows that the practical telecommunications of hailings is such that they hardly ever miss their man: verbal call or whistle, the one hailed always recognizes that it is really him who is being hailed.[5]

Note that in the way that Althusser describes this event, the focus is less on the intention of the police officer but rather on the way the supposed recipient of the call understands what has taken place. The knowledge of the police (and the rest of what Althusser calls the RSA, or repressive state apparatus) is assumed.[6] Or at least it appears to be. Even in the face of the projection of absolute authority that ideology (or the ISA, the ideological state apparatus) produces, there is some room for doubt. The critical phrase here for my purposes is "they hardly ever miss their man [or, presumably, woman]." If the act of interpellation, of hailing, "hardly ever miss[es]" their intended individual, that means that sometimes they do miss. Once in a while, it is possible that the hail is not "really" addressed to the right person and that it is not "really [he or she] who was hailed." In this way, the all-knowingness of the law, at least from the perspective of the legal subject, possesses a flaw, a crack in its façade of unimpeachable omniscience and authority.

Althusser also evokes the possibility of such a flaw in the next paragraph when he writes: "Somewhere (usually behind them) the hail rings out: "Hey, you there!" One individual (nine times out of ten it is the right one) turns around, believing/suspecting/knowing that it is for him."[7] If nine out of ten subjects are correctly hailed, then at least one in ten are not. What do we make of this mistakenly hailed subject? If the correctly hailed subject is interpellated, it makes sense to call the subject who was not intended, but who was hailed anyway, as "misinterpellated." Even if it happens in a minority of cases, at least in a tangible and unmistakable way, the fact that misinterpellation happens at all further suggests a flaw in the formula, a problem with the method by which authority is internalized and mapped onto human subjects.

God as Subject: The Circuitry of Interpellation

The importance of interpellation as well as its possible misfiring becomes clearer when we note the one chief example that Althusser furnishes and embellishes in his text, namely, the role of God as Subject—with a decidedly capital S—the original interpellator. Althusser tells us that the way Christians understand being called by God is a model for the way subjectivity works more generally. When God interpellates a subject, the subject responds by acknowledging that the identity that they are taking on is one that they have in fact always had. The subject replies, *"Yes; it really is me!"*[8] In this way the subject "obtains . . . the *recognition* that they really do occupy the place . . . designate[d] for them . . . a fixed residence."[9] Behind this operation, Althusser tells us, is the Subjecthood of God. In this case, rather than discussing God's calling to Abraham (the subject of Kafka's parable), Althusser talks about God's calling to Moses. Althusser writes that when God tells Moses "I am that I am," God is announcing that he is the "Subject *par excellence*."[10] Thus when God interpellates Moses (by crying out to him "Moses!"), Moses "recognizes that he is a subject, a subject of God, a subject subjected to God, *a subject through the Subject and subjected to the Subject.* The proof: he obeys him, and makes his people obey God's Commandments."[11]

Here, there is no hedging, no "nine times out of ten" for Althusser. God's interpellation is always correct. This primary subjectivity serves as the basis, the bedrock of all other subjects. And note that by having God serve as the model for interpellation, the assumption of omniscience of knowing who the subject "really is" is dramatically bolstered.

Yet, for all of this divine authority coming from God the Subject, Althusser tells us, "God needs men."[12] The Subject's own subjectivity requires other subjects to reflect on this one, original source of identity. Indeed, Althusser tells us further, that in the story of Christ, we see that "the Subject needs to become a subject, as if to show empirically, visibly to the eye, tangibly to the hands . . . that, if they are subjects, subjected to the Subject . . . they will reenter the Lord's Bosom, like Christ, i.e. re-enter the Subject."[13]

There is thus in interpellation, once again, a kind of circulation of subjectivity, a leaving from and entering into the original—and divine—basis of subjectivity. This mutuality is what Althusser calls a "mirror-structure" in which "God will *recognize* his own . . . i.e those who have recognized God, and have recognized themselves in Him."[14]

In terms of the circuitry that is produced by such a view of interpellation, we see that, in effect, human subjects have called to a God in order to have that God call out to them in turn. That is, interpellation is largely a movement of projection and then counterprojection, a basing of authority on some seemingly unimpeachable original Subject who can "really" know or call the subjects (with a very small s) into being who they (always) are. The device of having an original Subject, which is itself the product of the subject's phantasms of authority, means that the very ground for authority becomes more like quicksand. This is a circuit that disguises itself as being more unidirectional (more on that in a moment). It constitutes an endless set of imaginings and projections that are for the most part meekly followed as if they were always and forever true, as if there was no way to ever break this circuitry (an idea I will return to very explicitly in chapters 4 and 7).[15]

(Mis)interpellation and the State

For all this talk of God and Christ, Althusser is far from being a theologically inflected thinker (although, as we will see, Judith Butler, among others, suggests that he is, to some extent, captured by his use of this analogy, that it is not merely illustrative but determinant of his theoretical model). Althusser's analogy to God sets up a model for the state—and ultimately not just the state but the ruling class that uses the state as its instrument—wherein, once again, we see a form of subjectivity that circulates between the "original" and the "derivative" subject.[16] As with the religious analogy, it is only by the recognition of the state that we come into our own as citizens, that we can become who we are and have, therefore, always been (at least retroactively).[17]

Playing with the double meaning of the word "subject" (in both French and English) as both autonomous individual and submitted to another's rule, Althusser tells us that in this system: "The individual is *interpellated as a (free) subject in order that he shall submit freely to the commandments of the Subject, i.e. in order that he shall (freely) accept his subjection. . . . There are no subjects except by and for their subjection.*"[18] Thus the "freedom" that is produced by the act of subjectivization is only meant for the purposes of submitting ourselves to the rule of another (as Moses does with God).

Perhaps then it is already becoming clear how dangerous misinterpellation can be for this process. For the misinterpellated subject, the mirror-structure that is set up with the state is disrupted. The state does not recognize itself, does not get recognized, in a misinterpellated subject because that subject is not "really [he or she] who was hailed." Even the most "successful" cases of hailing are called into question (that is, even God's hailing of the "correct" Abraham) but this misfiring is especially apparent with the lesser, unwanted, and unexpected subjects of the call. Here the processes of circuitry and projection become much more legible exactly because they represent a situation that is out of the control (at least for that moment) of the authority in question. Such a state of affairs not only threatens the individual in question (since their subjectivity is bound to come out wrong) but far more radically, also threatens the great Subject of God or the state, the point of origin that "needs" subjectivization to work for its own sake far more than for the sake of those who submit to it. Even though Althusser's focus is resolutely on the recipient of the call—the "subject of subjectivity," one might say—the possibility of misinterpellation affects the state and its operatives as well. Insofar as it is the legal subject's imagined relationship to the state and its repressive mechanisms that is operative, to call the state's omniscience into question is to radically alter the way that power works for Althusser (the way that the ISA supports or even grounds the RSA, to use his terminology).

It seems clear that the misinterpellated subject—if her situation becomes evident to her—may not, probably will not, use her newly found freedom from interpellation, even if it is only temporary, to simply reassert her subjection to the state. In her case, the assertion of subjectivity leads not to harmony and acceptance, but to disruption, the introduction of unexpected and unknowable elements in a way that spreads back to the original subjectivity of the state.

Crucially, misinterpellation is not the same thing as the operation of misrecognition (méconnaissance) that Althusser describes in his essay.[19] For Althusser misrecognition is a vital cog in the workings of ideology. In his understanding, every act of recognition is at the same time an act of misrecognition. This is necessarily so. Speaking of the entire process of interpellation, Althusser tells us that what thus seems to take place outside ideology (to be precise, in the street), in reality takes place in ideology. What really takes place in ideology seems therefore to take place outside it. That is why those who are in ideology believe themselves by definition outside ideology: one of the effects of ideology is the practical *denegation* of the ideological character of ideology by ideology: ideology never says, "I am ideological."[20]

This refusal to acknowledge the basic function of recognition is what Althusser calls misrecognition, writing, "At work in this reaction is the ideological *recognition* function which is one of the two functions of ideology as such (its inverse being the function of *misrecognition—méconnaissance*")."[21]

Althusser ends "Ideology and the State" by writing, "The reality in question in this mechanism, the reality which is necessarily *ignored (méconnue)* in the very forms of recognition (ideology = misrecognition/ignorance) is indeed, in the last resort, the reproduction of the relations of production and of the relations deriving from them."[22] Here, we see how misrecognition is critical for the process of recognition and, thus, interpellation. If we remained aware of the process and function of interpellation, we would not be subjects in the double sense of that word; we would resist or disobey the law that supposedly gave us to ourselves. We need to see ourselves as being natural and given as we are rather than as a product of ideology. We must erase the act that produced our subjectivity (even though it does not necessarily have a prior temporal existence) in order to confirm that the being that was produced by such a moment of interpellation "really" is us. It is the status of this "really" that is therefore in question, the basis of the vulnerability of interpellation as a foundation for political authority. Without misrecognition then, the circuitry of interpellation could not function; we would too easily see the nature of our projections, the fact that we are obeying a seemingly inevitable power that has no actual or true origin.[23]

Misinterpellation is thus very different from misrecognition; it is in fact its opposite. It may derive from within the system but it is not part of the homeostatic processes by which individuals are produced and sustained. It is when misrecognition breaks down that we get misinterpellation instead (put differently, misinterpellation is what misrecognition shields from our view). Misinterpellation, the one in ten, the accident, the undesired and unexpected, is a challenge to, rather than a pillar of, the ISA.[24] Especially when we recall that for Althusser the state is itself an agent of capitalism and the interests of the ruling class, we can see that the misinterpellated subject's upending of the processes of ideology and subject formation is ultimately a challenge above all to capitalism itself, as well as the ideology of individualism that sustains it.

Althusser's Critics

Over the years, Althusser's theory of interpellation has been subjected to a great deal of criticism. Some thinkers, like Jacques Rancière, accuse Althusser of failing to link his theory of interpellation to class struggle.[25] In this viewpoint, Althusser effectively depoliticizes political subjectivity, rendering ideology less a tool of a dominant class (via the state) and more an instrument that affects everyone rich and poor alike (so that, presumably, even Donald Trump or Rupert Murdoch could conceivably be considered to be the subject of the hailing of a police officer and have their own political subjectivity formed in that moment).

From a more psychoanalytically oriented position, Mladen Dolar criticizes Althusser for the excessively neat way that he considers the formation of subjectivity (and in ways that completely bypass any psychological elements). Thus, Dolar writes that, with interpellation,

> there is a sudden and abrupt transition from individual—a preideological entity, a sort of *materia prima*—into ideological subject, the only kind of subject there is for Althusser. One becomes a subject by suddenly recognizing that one has always already been a subject: becoming a subject always takes effect retroactively—it is based on a necessary illusion, an extrapolation, an illegitimate extension of a later state into the former stage. A leap—a moment of sudden emergence—occurs.[26]

This "clean cut" seemingly comes out of nowhere even as it is, by Althusser's own admission, part of a much more complicated apparatus that predates the subject.[27]

Relatedly, for Dolar, such a view of the formation of subjectivity seems to disallow any kind of interaction between the internal and external states of the would-be subject. Dolar writes, "One could say that [with Althusser] materiality and subjectivity rule each other out: if I am (already) a subject, I am necessarily blinded in regard to materiality. The external conditions of ideology cannot be comprehended from within ideology; the institution of interiority necessarily brings about a denial, or better, a disavowal of its external origin."[28] In this way, Dolar is suggesting, there is no real creation of our interior reality via the material effects of ideology. If indeed we have "always already" been a subject, then the material interaction of the scene of interpellation does not actually change us; we are not, in fact, materially affected.

Finally, for Dolar, this sudden production of a subject who was not a subject before is not "clean" after all; part of the individual cannot fully pass into the subject. The subject is never "really" who she is, at least not entirely.[29] As Dolar puts it, "In short, the subject is precisely the failure to become the subject—the psychoanalytic subject is the failure to become the Althusserian one."[30]

For her own part, Jodi Dean argues that the subject that is produced via interpellation is never individual but rather collective. She writes, "My wager is that Althusser got it backwards. Ideological interpellation makes more sense as a theory of individuation than as a theory of subjection."[31] Dean points out, via Warren Montag, that the backdrop for Althusser's theory of interpellation was the protest movements of the 1960s. A crowd would be demonstrating and the police would single out one person as a form of individuation (setting up a model for Althusser's account of the "hey, you there!"). For Dean, this person is not acting as themselves but as part of a crowd and so the subjectivity of the person is a shared one. For Dean, then, interpellation is the process by which we are picked off from our collective subjectivity and isolated, subject only in the secondary sense of being reduced and dominated by that move.

There is a great deal of validity in each of these criticisms—some of them, I even agree with—but I would yet argue that Althusser's theory of interpellation remains worth taking seriously for a few reasons. First of all, I think his focus on materiality is valuable insofar as it takes us away from a strict focus on inner states and the previously discussed problematic of "false consciousness" that so many on the left still subscribe to (at least indirectly). Althusser's focus on interpellation as a material process takes us out of this interior space and into the realm of interpersonal subject formation, the power of the state, the circulation of authority, and other related matters. As I read him, Althusser gives us an account—and a plausible one at that—for how consciousness and the political subjectivity that comes along with it are formed, how these states are experienced via and through material processes. As Althusser describes it, consciousness is itself a material product. Our consciousness is not "ours," not private and alone in some realm of ideas, but shaped by countless external forces such as family, society, state, and so forth. Hence there is nothing "false" about consciousness; it merely reflects its context and inputs (put another way, all consciousness is equally false).

In this way, Althusser's focus is not so much on our internal psyche (as Dolar would have him do) nor on the nature of subjectivity per se (as Dean describes it; I think she is actually right about subjectivity being collective, although I would add it is collective *and* anarchic) but rather on the subjective and material experience of personhood under conditions of liberal capitalism. We do not necessarily need to get into a discussion of the nature of our actual subjectivity with Althusser (although I will engage in such a discussion myself later in the book).[32] We mainly need to observe the effects of living under the authority regime that we are submitted to. Even if the persons being created are patently false, a notion of interpellation still speaks to the questions of who answers when the law comes calling, who we think we are, and who we are thought to be.

Furthermore, because this form of subjectivity is so vulnerable, I see it as being far more amenable than Rancière does to questions of class struggle and other forms of resistance to domination. I think the same of Dolar's criticism as well. It is precisely because it is not clean and it does not "know" who we really are, that the process of interpellation helps to explain how radical outcomes come out of a system that is devoted to anything but radicalism. In other words, interpellation might seek to level us all out, to pick us off and isolate us, but, in practice, it creates very wobbly, poorly isolated, and potentially rebellious sorts of subjects. Dolar tells us that the subject of interpellation is meant to be "autonomous" and "self-transparent" even though it certainly is nothing of the kind.[33] The subject's autonomy, far from being given by this event, seems on the contrary to be rendered moot by this act of receiving identity from an external source (and furthermore a source as remote and formidable as the state or its operatives). And because this autonomy is meant to be asserted nonetheless, such a subject can hardly be "self-transparent." Indeed, Althusser tells us, via his theory of misrecognition, that the subject is built on an entire apparatus of deceit and vulnerability. The notion of interpellation is therefore valuable because it theatricalizes this kind of vulnerability. The very moment of "hey, you there!" is a testament not to the power of interpellation but to its weakness, its failure to produce the subject who is really meant to be called. And for this reason, we can begin to see already that interpellation and misinterpellation are not as far apart as they might initially seem to be. Far from being the occasional accident (one in ten) that Althusser himself depicts, his theory suggests strongly that the only difference between interpellation and misinterpellation is the illusion of success (i.e., misrecognition). When that veneer is stripped off—and I think Althusser's story is sufficiently self-subverting to do that stripping at least partially on its own—the shaky formula for autonomy and transparency collapses, leaving not proper and obedient subjects but the opposite.

In the end, interpellation must fail. First, because anyone can answer the call; the call itself is rather indiscriminant ("hey, you there!" "who, me?" "yes, you!"). Second, because even if the "right" person answers, there is no actual equivalence between state intention and individual subjectivity; the "you" in question is always an assertion, not a true identification.[34] The question is not whether interpellation "works" or "doesn't work," but rather whether and how we come to see its failure.

Butler's Critique of Althusser

In addition to those who largely reject Althusser out of hand, there are some critics of Althusser who, as I see it, try to remain working within his framework, at least to some extent. These thinkers, in my opinion, help us to further see the radical potential in Althusser's own formulations and in that way help us to think more about misinterpellation as well. In her own response to Althusser, Judith Butler complicates Althusser's model in ways that I think are highly conducive to thinking more about misinterpellation. Although Butler herself does not use the term "misinterpellation," her writing on the issue—and specifically her chapter entitled " 'Conscience Doth Make Subjects of Us All': Althusser's Subjection" in her book The Psychic Life of Power—helps to expand the space for the misfirings of interpellation that Althusser only hints at. Butler helps us see more clearly that, in fact, it is not just "one in ten" that are misinterpellated but all of us.

Butler begins her chapter by noting that the famous event that Althusser evokes of a policeman hailing someone by calling out "hey, you there!" (and with the newly enshrined subject thus turning around in response) does not have to take place in real life to remain meaningful. She reads this story as an allegory, specifically as an allegory in the Benjaminian sense wherein the "allegory is precisely what resists narration, what exceeds the narrativizability of events."[35]

What this process describes then is not so much an actual event as a way to understand the subject and, in particular, her temporality. Butler tells us that "although there would be no turning around without first having been hailed, neither would there be a turning around without some readiness to turn."[36] In other words, the interpellated subject is already bought in to her subjectivity. She comes into the world ready to receive her call (and for this reason, her hailing is itself extraneous, a formality that can be rendered allegorical). This is not to say that the moment of hailing is meaningless, as Dolar suggests. On the contrary, by evoking Benjamin's notion of allegory, Butler is implicitly pointing to how, for Benjamin, allegory serves to unmake the functions of persuasion. Rather than deliver a clear and true message, for Benjamin allegory exposes false messages, often quite inadvertently. Thus the imagined scene of a police officer saying "hey, you there!" is not the pinnacle of subjectivization but instead the moment where the flaw in the operation of the ISA becomes potentially evident. Even if only imagined, Althusser's depiction of the scene of interpellation suggests that when rendered visible—when it is theatricalized—the process of producing authority is exposed as fundamentally empty and failed.

For Butler, the problem with Althusser's account is that it seems to encircle itself within the very ideological apparatus that it critiques. It limits the means and ways of not being such a subject and therefore constitutes a kind of submission (subjection), despite Althusser's powerful wish that things be otherwise. As Butler puts it, "How does Althusser's sanctification of the scene of interpellation make the possibility of becoming a 'bad' subject more remote and less incendiary than it might well be?"[37]

This question, in my view, opens up the space for a kind of resistance that is, once again, hinted at in Althusser's account but not directly considered: the possibility of misinterpellation (and hence a maximization of the ways that allegory—taken in its Benjaminian sense once again—resists narrative). Here, the question becomes—to reverse Butler's phrasing—how do we "make the possibility of becoming a 'bad' subject [less] remote and [more] incendiary than it might well be?"[38]

In her own response to such questions, Butler notes the way that Althusser is perhaps less in control of his own essay than he would himself believe (thus performing the duality of being both recognized and misrecognized that he himself describes). As previously noted, she argues that although Althusser claims to turn to the example of God as original Subject only as an illustration of interpellation, his ideas can only be conceptualized in theological terms. The "concrete" example of the police officer interpellating a pedestrian by yelling "hey, you there!" is actually the abstraction of the real grounding of the functioning of ideology—at least as Althusser describes it—in theological terms. Butler writes, "The force of interpellation in Althusser is derived from the examples by which it is ostensibly illustrated, most notably, God's voice in the naming of . . . Moses."[39] Here, the example is in fact the paradigm and, once again, God is revealed to be not a subject but *the* Subject, above and beyond state or party or class (and hence unimpeachable, ideal for the purpose of fomenting misrecognition).

Althusser, it seems, does such a good job of envisioning a totalizing system of interpellation that he himself cannot escape it. Butler speaks of how Althusser "implicate[s] the text" through his use of a theological language that is meant to be "merely" figurative. The true authority of the text, she argues, comes from and through the figure (not in a way that is "true" but in a way that commandeers the text from its author's purported intent).[40]

The theological can be shown to overpower the process it is meant to illustrate in another sense as well, namely, in terms of the concept of original sin.[41] For Butler, insofar as guilt is presupposed in our turn toward the law, we are continually engaged in a process of "acquitting oneself of the accusation of guilt."[42] Because the law—for the criminal and obedient subject alike—is the source of our most basic identity, we must constantly return to it in order to confirm our own continued right to exist. This creates a feedback loop that once again binds Althusser: Butler notes that "the reason there are so few references to 'bad subjects' in Althusser is that the term tends toward the oxymoronic. To be 'bad' is not yet to be a subject, not yet to have acquitted oneself of the allegation of guilt."[43] Here again, we see that being "bad" is not all that radical an option for Althusser (despite his own desire that we be very bad indeed). We seem to be in a kind of trap whereby there is no way out, no way to not be a subject.

Perhaps more to the point, if we are all bad, all guilty, then there is really no true distinction between various subjects of the law. Determinations of who is "bad" and who is "good" are more a matter of the law's ability to make such distinctions to promote its own power of judgment, than any basis in "reality," in our ontological status as persons (I'll return to these questions in chapter 6). For this reason, we can start to think more seriously about how thin the line between interpellation and misinterpellation really is. If there are moments when the disjuncture between the law's intention to call ("hey, you there!") and the specific identity of the subject of that call is too great to ignore—moments when we cannot be convinced that we "really" are the intended subject of that call—every call, even a "successful" one, is nonetheless also, in some way, a missed call. Every call is not really about innocence or guilt at all but simply an exercise of power that we submit to (or don't).

Interpellation and Immaterialism

Is there a way to avoid the circumspection we see in Althusser (whether of the theological or rhetorical variety), a way to break beyond the limits of subjectivity we see in his political philosophy? One notion that seems promising on its face is to look beyond interpellation, to see other ways that the individual can be and act that aren't as compromised. Butler herself could be seen as arguing for something of this sort insofar as she speaks of interpellation as a form of a "turn . . . against the self."[44] Perhaps there is something about the self that might serve as an alternative basis for subjectivity.

Yet Butler makes it very clear that she rejects any kind of argument that looks "outside" or beyond interpellation when she argues against Dolar's own, previously noted response to Althusser's interpellation theory. She cites Dolar as writing "to put it in the simplest way, there is a part of the individual that cannot successfully pass into the subject, an element of 'pre-ideological' and 'presubjective' *materia prima* that comes to haunt subjectivity once it is constituted as such."[45] In making this claim, Dolar, as we have already seen, seeks to reimpose a kind of temporal ordering onto the subject as well as a separation between the material, tangible aspects of subjectivity and what he calls the "immaterial." For Dolar, the immaterial offers a promising means beyond the limits of interpellation; it gives us a basis for the subject that is beyond the control of the state (or any other authority figure).

Yet it is precisely a sense of materialism that Butler seeks to retain in Althusser. For Butler, one of the great advantages of Althusser's essay is that it collapses the old Marxist distinction between material production and the so-called superstructure by showing that even the most seemingly non-material aspect of the superstructure—ideology—is itself simply a set of material rituals, institutions, and practices (interpellation itself very much included).

For Butler, to think that one has resources "outside" of this materialism, that there is some kind of built-in resistance in the individual—even a resistance as complex as that which we find in various psychological concepts—risks resubjectivizing oneself to the very system one resists in the guise of escaping it for some nonmaterial or immaterial outside. Paradoxically, for Butler, Dolar can be read as being as circumscribed as Althusser himself (thus he is not as "outside" as he thinks he is). For one thing, she argues that Dolar too is captured by a kind of theological determinism that Butler connects to Descartes—she argues that Dolar's formulation has "strong Cartesian resonance"—and even Lacan.[46] Butler writes, "Theological resistance to materialism is exemplified in Dolar's explicit defense of Lacan's Cartesian inheritance, his insistence upon the pure ideality of the soul, yet the theological impulse also structures Althusser's work in the figure of the punitive law."[47] Tellingly, for Butler, Dolar turns to love, that most Christian concept, to argue that there is something "beyond interpellation" and hence beyond materialism as well.[48] For Dolar an immaterial other emerges out of the experience of love. Citing Dolar directly, Butler shows that in his view "Althusser covers up this non-materiality by talking about the materiality of institutions and practices."[49] Butler adds herself, still speaking somewhat in Dolar's voice (and not in a wholly critical way), that "the Other who is lost, introjected [i.e., interrupted by some outside, some nonmaterial, preideological aspect] who is said to become the immaterial condition of the subject, inaugurates the repetition specific to the symbolic, the punctuated fantasy of a return that never is or could be completed."[50]

Such a "lost Other," a "punctuated fantasy," may have its appeal but Butler is interested in looking elsewhere in order to radicalize the potential that she sees in Althusser. Butler asks,

> Are there other forms of "losing" the Other that are not introjection, and are there various ways of introjecting that Other? Are these terms not culturally elaborated, indeed, ritualized [and hence reinscribed into an Althusserian notion of materialism after all] to such a degree that no meta-scheme of symbolic logic escapes the hermeneutics of social description?[51]

In speaking of "various ways of introjecting the Other," Butler is offering a multitude of possible calls and forms of address (something that I will pay a great deal of attention to as this book progresses). At the same time, she calls into question some of the ways in which we think we can escape the doom of interpellation. Even love, Butler suggests, is not immune to ritual, to repetitive practices that produce its own "truth."[52] It too has a material form, is not "outside" after all. Indeed, Butler finds some use in Dolar's turn to love after all insofar as it helps us to think further about the strange passions that occur *within* the order of interpellation: "that the subject turns round or rushes toward the law suggests that the subject lives in passionate expectation of the law. Such love is not beyond interpellation; rather, it forms the passionate circle in which the subject becomes ensnared by its own state."[53]

Here, instead of looking beyond interpellation, Butler looks once again to the failure of interpellation, and this is where I see her argument as aligning most closely with my own. Although Dolar too ostensibly seeks the failure of the subject, in Butler's reading, his failure is not utter enough. His view of the subject's failure is that something remains that is not accounted for in the subject (however immaterial it may be) whereas the kind of failure that Butler describes has no residue or excess that is truer or more real than whatever interpellation itself produces. Rather than seeking to do an end run around ideology and interpellation, Butler seeks to explore and exploit the ways in which interpellation already doesn't work on its own terms. She seeks failure that is internal rather than external to interpellation. In my view, this amounts, once again, to a way of understanding how every act of interpellation is also an act of misinterpellation, how, even as we think we are called, we never really are, nor can we ever really be. The very notion of the successful call is a fantasy produced from within the bounds of liberal capitalism ("it's really me!"). It is part of the circuitry of authority that has wholly phantasmic origins (and, like other phantasms, it indicates the weakness as much as the effectiveness of what it projects).

Butler's turn to this deeper and more utter failure, to the way obstacles occur within the material structures, rituals, and practices of ideology, allows us access to the misperformances and misunderstandings that underscore ideology as a whole. Butler tells us that

> interpellation is "barred" from success not by a structurally permanent form of prohibition (or foreclosure), but by its inability to determine the constitutive field of the human. . . . According to the logic of conscience, which fully constrains Althusser, the subject's experi-

ence cannot be linguistically guaranteed without passionate attachment to the law. This complicity at once conditions and limits the viability of a critical interrogation of the law. One cannot criticize too far the terms by which one's existence is secured.[54]

Without denying or overcoming our passionate attachments to law and other forms of authority, we can see that the kinds of unexpected and unwanted meetings and revelations that are produced by misinterpellation exacerbate and subvert the workings of those passions. As already noted, when we think of the story of the police officer hailing a pedestrian through the lens of Benjaminian allegory, we have a way to resist the narrative without trying to somehow get free of the question of interpellation altogether, without thinking that somehow the passions that animate those narratives can be sidestepped or avoided.

In his own work, Benjamin always avoids the notion that one could somehow sidestep the network of phantasm that he collectively called "the phantasmagoria." He recognized that we are all deeply complicit with these phantasms and that resistance cannot therefore come from outside since there "is no outside," at least not for us.[55] Indeed, for Benjamin the more "inside" we are, the greater our potential for subversion to established networks of phantasm. As we see with Butler too, for Benjamin, rather than saying "no" to great systems that otherwise overwhelm us, we must become attuned to the way that they are not working, or do not work in the way that we expect, that is, we must become attuned to the radical potential of failure.

An interest in failure helps to explain Benjamin's great reverence for Kafka (returning us back to the parable about Abraham with which this book starts). For Benjamin, Kafka's greatest achievement was to fail in radical and unprecedented ways:

> To do justice to the figure of Kafka in its purity, and in its peculiar beauty, one should never lose sight of one thing: it is the figure of a failure. The circumstances of this failure are manifold. Perhaps one might say that once he was sure of ultimate failure, then everything on the way to it succeeded for him as if in a dream. Nothing is more remarkable than the fervor with which Kafka insists on his failure.[56]

It is due to his own regard for failure that Kafka is able, perhaps better than anyone else, to give us the story of "another Abraham," a failed version of "the real thing" and a deep subversion of the system of interpellation in a retelling of one of its paramount and exemplary illustrations (besides God's call to Moses, the call to Abraham is the other great interpellative moment in the Judeo Christian tradition; Paul's call and conversion on the road to Damascus is a third).

Thinking along the lines of such failure, if we read misinterpellation as a recognition—as opposed to misrecognition—of a more widespread failure, it helps us to see how it can be employed, not just on an accidental basis (for which we must wait) but also as a more widely disseminated, more "deliberate" form of action. If we take Benjamin's understanding as a basis of our reading of misinterpellation, we can argue that every attempt at communication, every "call" that is spoken or heard, is a failed attempt to represent, to definitively connect. The more we turn toward material practices—even if they are only imagined and allegorical—the more evident this failure becomes via the process of theatricalization that is inherent in material performances of interpellation. This is what Althusser helps us to realize (perhaps despite himself).

Even in the nine out of ten cases where, for Althusser, interpellation is "successful" ("it was *really him* [*or her*] who was hailed") our assumption is superimposed on a radical aporia in language and speech. Ideology itself can be said to consist of the attempt by human actors to promote or project consistency, commonality, and mutuality onto language acts (among other acts) that aren't necessarily connected. Perhaps, one might argue, we must act as though our speech acts are mutually clear in order to avoid total chaos—Hobbes says something like this—but even so, when we think of language in terms of interpellation, we can see that understanding political identity as being generated in this way creates an ideology of power and authority that superimposes itself over a much more contingent and uncertain scene of speech and human interaction (hence Althusser's requirement for misrecognition).

Nine times out of ten—the figures are arbitrary but illustrative—we don't notice the failures either of interpellation or of speech. Our own conceptions coincide with the act of calling and being called, which is only to say that ideology successfully naturalizes and disguises itself, including over the very fundamental question of what speech actually communicates. But one in ten times—actually far more rarely, unfortunately—an act of interpellation becomes impossible to sustain, impossible to "misrecognize" as part of the operation of ideology. The contradiction between our own ideological assurances and the experience of the act itself disrupts the fabric of ideology momentarily (I'll have more to say about that in the following chapter). This is, once again, not to say that "truth" appears in this space, but rather that we experience a disruption of the illusion of mutuality and commonality. This is a disruption that throws us not into chaos but into a more radically contingent, agonal, and undetermined state.[57]

The upshot of such a way of thinking is that we don't actually have to wait for the occasional breakdown of interpellation in order to resist. Once we are freed from the expectation based on the caller's intent (Did he or she mean to call me? Was I in fact the one who was called?), the caller's authority is disrupted and the subject is put in a much more fluid and contingent situation. More accurately, she recognizes the fluidity and contingency that has always been present even if she was not yet aware of this. If we realize that interpellation is never accurate, that we are never actually called, it changes the nature of our "waiting" to be hailed or the way that temporality is structured around the reception—or nonreception—of the call we are to receive. Furthermore, the trap that seems to bind Althusser—wherein whether good or bad we are still under the thumb of the state via the process of subjectivization—can be disrupted if we rethink what being a disobedient subject actually consists of (hence Butler's question to that effect). If being "bad" is no better than being "good" (a dilemma I will discuss in chapter 7), we can pursue our failure in both categories. Neither bad nor good subjects, we can seek the disruption of such fixed categories, leading to states of being that may be far messier and unstructured.

"Wait Up!"

In light of this, I now turn, very briefly, to an intriguing idea put forth by Lauren Berlant in her book *Cruel Optimism*. There, Berlant evokes Althusser as part of her textual analysis in ways that suggest how to more broadly subvert the operations of interpellation. Speaking of Dorothy and Justine, two characters in a novel by Mary Gaitskill entitled *Two Girls, Fat and Thin*, who engage in repetitive and seemingly compulsive forms of sexuality, eating, and thinking, Berlant writes,

> These repetitions can be read as establishing a regime of self-continuity that amounts to the constellation called "who I am." At the same time, the girls' capacity not to inhabit the case study version of their story

("Hey you!") that makes everything as a continuous symptom of the cultivated self suggests something else: an impulse to interfere with reproducing one's "personality." Their negativity can be read as a *departure from* rather than an *assumption of* a way of being "who they are." . . . Responding to trauma's haunting plenitude not with ascesis but with a formalist abundance, the girls' tactic of counterabsorption marks their will to live otherwise ("Wait up!").[58]

For Berlant, Dorothy and Justine both submit to and defy their interpellation ("Hey you!," the "case study" that is meant to explain and control them) through an engagement with failure. On the surface, the girls strive "not, for a minute, to be that failed person with that history." They try to conform, to accept their degradation, the abuse they suffer by peers and family. But, at the same time, they do fail and that failure gives them, in Berlant's eyes, a felicitous distance from the person they are striving to be (or are interpellated as being).

At one point, Justine, after a disastrous sexual encounter meant to promote her image—one that, badly backfiring, leads to her utter humiliation—walks "with her arms around her middle feeling loneliness and humiliation coupled with the sensation that she was, at this moment, absolutely herself."[59] Berlant writes of this that "at the moment of that holding thought she is having, perhaps, the best sex of her life."[60]

In the shift from "hey, you!" to "wait up!," Berlant is suggesting a more open-ended understanding of subjectivity, one that is more receptive to failure and loss (therefore less "optimistic," less caught up in the frenzy of subjection and subjectivization that normally marks us). Berlant doesn't suggest that "wait up!" is entirely freed from the processes of interpellation. She writes, "In the end, of course, it's a dialectic between the Althusserian 'Hey you!' and 'Wait up!' but these locutions are not antitheses either, because they each mark the subject's lag . . . with respect to the meanings and desires that organize her."[61] Yet, it seems, "wait up!" offers another way to think about the subject, a way that trades authority for openness and contingency.

In thinking about this kind of alternative form of subjectivity, I feel a bit of caution is needed. Berlant's description is intriguing but it risks a return to liberal subjectivity if it is not carefully thought through.[62] The notion of being "absolutely oneself" potentially allows a return to being a "true" subject and thus the opposite of a failed subject. I am not suggesting that this is Berlant's argument (I don't think it is) but there is a risk in this reading that we conclude that the resistance to interpellation is simply a matter of asserting one's true identity over and above what one is called to be. Instead, I read the moment of Justine's encircling her body with her hands as a moment not of self-realization, but simply as a description, and delineation, of the terrain in which her various and even competing forms of identity are enclosed. The site delineated by her hands is "her"; we can gather nothing further—certainly no central claims about identity—from that gesture. The complicated and rich mix of emotions that Justine is feeling at that moment (shame and humiliation and also a feeling that this is "the best sex" she's ever had) indicates an unresolved situation, not a triumphant discovery of self. Even a sensation of being "oneself" does not (as the discussion of misinterpellation more generally suggests) prove that one is what those feelings describe; it is just another emotion and sensation to be added to the myriad other emotions and sensations that collectively constitute "what we are."

As I will argue in the second half of this book, the experience of the failure of one's own subjectivity is a complex and ongoing movement, not a singular event that inaugurates a once-and-for-all resolution. This is why authors like Nietzsche and Woolf and Ellison repeatedly raise and then dash the reader's expectations for resolution; they do so in order to shake their readers from such false and easy fixes as the notion of "being oneself." In the case of Justine, we could say that this moment is not the end but the beginning of her failure as a subject and that this failure can be extended, multiplied, and shared with others on an ongoing basis. In the moment Berlant describes, Justine has located the site of her struggle but not the trajectory.

Read in this light, when Justine has the sensation that she is "at that moment, absolutely herself," the self in question is not the interpellated agent, the sure, ideologically corrected person that is "*really* [her]." Instead, it is a smaller, more failed, denuded self that emerges after it has been excised from its connections to phantasmic projections of self, when it becomes what Benjamin refers to as "pure means."[63] The self that emerges after the rejection and humiliation that comes along with misinterpellation is a sadder (less optimistic) self, to be sure. She is not "free," but at least she knows that she is on her own, however awful that realization may be for her.

In the end, I don't think it's as easy as going from "hey, you there!" to "wait up!" and I don't think that Berlant thinks that either. As she points out, this is not an escape from interpellation so much as a resistance to it from within. "Wait up!" may simply indicate, as Butler suggests, another "various way of introjecting that Other." "Wait up!" seems not to be a call between an authority figure and a subject (like "hey, you there!") but rather between equals (its very familiar informality suggests as much).[64] Instead of offering a "voice of authority," such a call just adds another voice. In this way, "wait up!" expands the vocabulary of misinterpellation; it welcomes the various and cacophonous voices that are stilled or overwhelmed when "hey, you there!" is the only sound that we hear and respond to.

Different Ways to Be Hailed

In thinking more about the various possibilities of address and interpellation in terms of Althusserian theory, Terry Eagleton writes,

> The fact that Louis Althusser's friends apparently never mistook his cheery shout of greeting in the street is offered here as irrefutable evidence that the business of ideological interpellation is invariably successful. But is it? What if we fail to recognize and respond to the call of the Subject? What if we return the reply: "Sorry, you've got the wrong person"? That we have to be interpellated as *some* kind of subject is clear: the alternative, for Lacan, would be to fall outside the symbolic order altogether into psychosis. But there is no reason why we should always accept society's identification of us as this particular sort of subject. Althusser simply runs together the necessity of some "general" identification with our submission to specific social roles. There are, after all, many different ways in which we can be "hailed."[65]

If there are "different ways . . . we can be hailed," then we see that "hey, you there!" does not have a monopoly on calling. Multiplying the kinds of calls (or our awareness of their plurality) helps to further disrupt the circularity of interpellation as a normativizing and subjectifying practice.

The term I would use for this kind of disruption and multiplication—the seeking out of failure rather than success and resolution—is anarchism. I don't mean anarchism in the sense that it is often used in liberal theory as chaos and destruction for destruction's sake. It is interpellation itself, I would argue, that is chaotic; its chaos comes from imposing a false sense of organization on a multiple and multiply influenced subject. The demand to *be* that subject is the source of chaos for us both as individuals and as members of a collectivity. Anarchism is both the resistance to that chaos and an attempt to see what develops as a result of the breakdown of such false orderings.[66] In this sense, we could repurpose Berlant's "wait up!" to be more of an anarchist call, a way to see, alone and together, what kinds of politics—and what kinds of subjects—emerge from the failures that interpellation produces.

CHAPTER TWO

"MEN ARE BORN FREE AND EQUAL IN RIGHTS"

Historical Examples of Interpellation and Misinterpellation

Having laid out some of the theoretical basis for misinterpellation, let me provide a few historical and contemporary examples to illuminate not only the power of misinterpellation but also the way it actually operates. Although, once again, such cases are just the "tip of the iceberg," the most obvious and glaring cases that cannot be papered over by misrecognition, they give us some insights into the phenomenon of misinterpellation more generally. As I have been discussing in the previous chapters, interpellation is like a circuit wherein agency and identity move from state to subject and back again. This circuitry is endlessly resisted and endlessly failing (the process of misinterpellation) but so long as the circuit continues, the operations of state, along with its accompanying hierarchies, go on as well. The examples that I am looking at constitute moments when the circuitry broke down, when the mismatch between intended subjects of authority and the formal agent bestowing that authority became visible. To return to Plato's metaphor of reading the soul by looking at the city, I'd say that by looking at these "extreme" cases of misinterpellation, we can more readily see what misinterpellation always is. Writ large, in ways that cannot be missed (as is the case with the city for Plato), misrecognition becomes that much harder to sustain.

The three examples I have chosen—the Haitian revolution at the turn of the nineteenth century, the so-called Wilsonian moment at the end of World War I, and the origins of the Arab Spring in Tunisia—show how this circuit can break down and how the complex and ongoing relationship between interpellation and misinterpellation can decisively shift in favor of the latter. I want to look at these phenomena both at the elite level—that is, at the level of the key subjects who stood at the intersection between state and resistance, such as Toussaint Louverture and the leaders of the anticolonialism movement in the late 1910s—and also at the ground, or "grassroots," level, at the way the breaking of the circuitry was understood and processed by ordinary people in their daily lives and daily forms of resistance. It is always more difficult to get this second perspective; subaltern studies is premised on the ways that such communities do not have a voice, are not recorded, and are not asked for their opinion.[1] Yet any concept of misinterpellation cannot leave out this perspective insofar as neither interpellation nor misinterpellation are exclusively elite-level phenomena. As my cases will suggest, the way that misinterpellation is understood and received changes as one moves down the levels of social hierarchy. Toussaint Louverture had a very different perspective and experience than the larger population of Haitian ex-slaves. Similarly, peoples across the colonialized world understood and responded to the breakdown of authority that stemmed from the "Wilsonian moment" in very different ways than their anticolonial leaders.

As I will try to show further, the trappings of authority—and the nature of resistance to that authority at the level of ideology—get diluted and abstracted from as one moves down the chain of hierarchy among resistant communities. What Toussaint understood was far more in keeping, in a sense, with the dominant ideology he was meant to accept. Although not himself directly called by the Declaration of the Rights of Man and Citizen, Toussaint could be said to have been "more called" than the vast community of Haitian slaves whom he led in rebellion against France. Even as he resisted and subverted that authority, he remained much more attuned to the siren call of the liberal universal, much more of a "true believer" in the kind of liberal rights and privileges that he saw himself and the Haitians in general being excluded from. At the very least Toussaint paid lip service to—and actually implemented the policies of—liberal ideology in a way that sets him apart from those who struggled beneath him.

On the grassroots level, there was much less buy-in—even at the level of lip service—to the kinds of ideologies that are used to constitute and preserve a dominant order. The Haitian ex-slaves in general were far less interested in "universal" French values than was Toussaint. But even on their level, as I will try to show further, there is yet a kind of coexistence with liberal ideology. It is certainly not the case that subaltern people accept dominant ideology. (Scott once again gives an enormous amount of evidence against such a view). Rather, they live with and amid such ideology, rejecting some of it out of hand, playing along with some other parts, adapting some of it for their own purposes, mixing some with of it their own traditions and values, and so forth.

Accordingly, the breakdown of dominant, interpellated ideology presents the nonelite members of resistant communities with a different set of challenges than it poses to their own leadership. In their case we find not so much the mixture of cognitive dissonance and strategy that we find with a figure like Toussaint, but rather a question of engaging both with a collapsing or exposed series of dominant ideologies as well as the complicated relationship that such a dance produces in their own leadership.

The case of the Arab Spring is quite different from the two earlier examples that I look at. In this case, the break in circuitry came not from the top but from closer to the bottom; Mohamed Bouazizi was a poor fruit vendor in a provincial city in inland Tunisia. His defiance of authority did not occur at the level of world powers but played before a very different, poor, and disenfranchised audience. Coming from below as it did, the revolution that Bouazizi initiated caught the would-be leaders of the resistance in Tunisia quite by surprise. The story of the origins of the Arab Spring is a useful one because it comes closer to revealing the anarchist sources of misinterpellation than the earlier cases do. In the earlier cases, we have to dig a bit to find the local and anarchist response (even as they are critical for the fuller implications of these cases). In the case of Bouazizi, it is much plainer to see. Minus the complex positioning of an elite (although all that was to come in Tunisia and elsewhere as the Arab Spring spread), the early moments of that revolt show how misinterpellation in general is not something that has to happen or occur to community leaders only. Instead, it is revealed to be a widespread and decentralized—indeed, anarchist—process where the long practices of resistance that these communities develop over decades and centuries can be brought out into the open. In this way, none of these uprisings can be said to be "spontaneous";

they come out of a history and a culture and a long set of established practices (for this reason, the tendency to equate anarchism and spontaneity disguises a much more complicated—and more interesting—history). As previously noted, rather than privilege these moments as the moment of breakage, I would rather read them in terms of their relationship to all of the moments that are similarly marked by failure and breakdown, all the moments of resistance—that is to say every moment that precedes (and follows) the examples in question—before (and after) misinterpellation broke out into the open.

The story of misinterpellation as an actual practice helps illustrate the point made in the previous chapter that, along with the circuitry of interpellation, which maintains existing schemes of domination, other circuitry (other hailings and mishailings) is simultaneously happening. Other forms of authority are present that are not beholden to existing power structures and that can be said to be marked by much more collective processes of authority. These other forms of authority (or counterauthority) emerge out of the practices and engagements of communities within dominant hierarchies. These other forms are no more "authentic" or true than the standard form of interpellation insofar as they too partake in no "truth," no absolute and eternal value as such. Nor are they any more immune to misinterpellation than standard interpellation is.[2] Their radical potential comes not from anything inherent to themselves but simply from the fact that they enable the distortion and failure of dominant forms of hailing to become more legible by virtue of their interference and competition with dominant narratives. In this sense, what unites these case studies is the way that misinterpellation is always aided—and extends—from below, from the "hidden transcript" of resistance and subversion that Scott details in his work.

If none of the stories I will look at in this chapter have a "happy ending," that is, if in each case domination, sovereignty, and the phantasms of rule and hierarchy are ultimately restored—even if in different guises, even if there is an exchange of commanders—the chance to see these alternative authority networks as they emerge from hiding allows us to better understand the truly subversive power that comes when the circuit of interpellation breaks down and malfunctions. It shows us how, when that breakdown occurs, other forms of address and alternative modes of politics and subjectivity can emerge from the great and obscuring shadow cast by liberal forms of subjectivity and interpellation.

At the end of this chapter, after examining the three cases in question, I turn to the work of Niccolò Machiavelli (whom Althusser himself was very interested in) for further illumination about the workings of interpellation and how it can be resisted. In Machiavelli's own explanations of the circulation of political authority, his understanding of how interpellation succeeds (and fails), we see both an explanatory model for the cases in question as well as a set of further strategies for resistance. Particularly when we read Machiavelli through a conspiratorial—or indeed, misinterpellated—lens, a more radical set of practices and subversion emerges. This in turn helps us to better understand the examples discussed in this chapter as well as the phenomenon of misinterpellation more generally.

Three Case Studies in Misinterpellation

Misinterpellation and Revolution in Haiti

In order to give a sense of the relevance and nature of misinterpellation, I begin with what I consider to be a paradigmatic example of this phenomenon: Haiti at the time of its revolution at the turn of the nineteenth century. I have written at some length elsewhere about the Haitian revolution as an exemplary moment of misinterpellation.[3] There, I argue that the Haitian revolution, as a response to the French 1789 Declaration of the Rights of Man and Citizen, was a moment when the breakdown of interpellative circuitry—the gap between the universal pretensions of the call and the fact that its articulation in fact produces hierarchies and exclusions—was exceptionally clear. This can be seen in the very language of the Declaration. The first sentence of the first enunciated right in the Declaration states, "Men are born free and remain free and equal in rights" ("Les hommes naissent et demeurent libres et égaux en droits") only to be swiftly qualified by the second sentence: "Social distinctions can be based only on public utility" ("Les distinctions sociales ne peuvent être fondées que sur l'utilité commune"). Besides being limited to men—something that was subsequently challenged when Olympe de Gouges wrote her own version of the Declaration—the whole clause shows itself to be first giving and then taking back supposedly universal and inalienable rights, subjecting them to social forms of control (that is, to whoever got to speak on behalf of "the public").[4] We can therefore consider the statement "Men are born free and remain equal in rights" to be a paradigmatic form of interpellation (akin to saying "Hey, you there! You have universal rights!" but then immediately following that up with "No, not you. YOU!" It's what one could imagine Abraham's God saying in response to all the other Abrahams who showed up in Kafka's parable).

Insofar as the Declaration goes on to assert classical liberal rights including the right to maintain property, the rights and freedoms promised by that Declaration were never intended for the French white working class, much less for the slaves of Haiti. Yet, for all of this, the Haitians responded to this call nonetheless. In his own writing on the subject, Illan rua Wall writes,

> [The Haitian slaves] (mis)understood the meaning of the idealistic phrases [such as the Declaration of the Rights of Man and Citizen]. It was a misunderstanding, of course, because the ideals of the revolution were hardly meant to apply to women and Jews, let alone slaves! However, the slaves knew that they were to be excluded from these declarations; theirs was not a mistake of ignorance. Thus, when they took up the words, they did so out of a purposive misunderstanding of the implicit logic and therefore they do not represent some sort of tabula rasa on which the enlightenment norms were projected, but rather active, thinking subjects who resisted "enlightenment" with its own norms.[5]

This idea of "resist[ing] 'enlightenment' with its own norms" is critical for my own argument, as is the concept of purposive misunderstanding. The concept captures the complicated dance between those who penned the document and its recipients in Haiti. The Haitian slaves (taken as a whole), while not the intended audience of the liberal bourgeois authors of this document, were not entirely outside of the system of liberal enlightenment thought and they were certainly not outside of its power. The elites of this community were, to some extent, schooled in the false universals that the French revolution produced (C. L. R. James tells us that Toussaint "had read Caesar's Commentaries" and many histories of colonialism), while the general population mainly knew France by the cruelties they suffered by its agents (whippings, torture, rapes, murder) and by the alienation of their (unpaid) labor to the white colonial settlers in Haiti and to the metropole itself.[6] Whatever their status, the Haitian slaves knew—at least to some extent—that the words of the Declaration were not addressed to them, that, in a sense, their exclusion is part of the intention of the law (in the complicated way that interpellation and misinterpellation are mutually constituted). Accordingly, their position of being (albeit to various degrees) within the orbit of French universalism gave them a kind of inside stand-point, a way to do maximal damage to the very structures that otherwise dominated them. Since it was surely "obvious" to the framers that slaves were not referenced by the Declaration, the slaves' own response, being so utterly unexpected, is that much more powerful.

If we consider the Haitian slaves to have been misinterpellated subjects—as I would strongly argue we should—we begin to see the power and logic of this operation vis-à-vis the larger and more obvious and naturalized workings of interpellation. These slaves laid claim to the banquet of rights that were being asserted in the Declaration of the Rights of Man and Citizen—among other proclamations coming out of France at the time—and, in doing so, they radically altered and subverted the liberal notions that were presented in that document and the revolution that was perpetrated in its name. In my read-ing, the story of the Haitian revolution does not prove that such rights are "real" and that the failure of liberalism is merely one of not distributing those rights more broadly (i.e., more "universally"). Instead, it suggests that even with as bogus and misleading a discourse as that of universal rights, once it is inserted into the world it can have radical and entirely unintended results precisely due to the nonexistence and phantasmic nature of those rights.[7]

As James asserts, the Haitian revolution, once it began, stirred the French white working class to their own forms of radical response.[8] They too were, as already noted, not directly called by the Declaration, but the Haitian slaves offered a highly tangible and exportable model for how liberal rights could be transformed into something altogether different. Of the white French workers' views on Haiti, James writes,

What has all this [i.e., the French revolution] to do with the slaves? Everything. The workers and peasants of France could not have been expected to take any interest in the colonial question in normal times, any more than one can expect similar interests from British or French workers to-day. But now they were roused. They were striking at roy-alty, tyranny, reaction and oppression of all types, and with these they included slavery. The prejudice of race is superficially the most irrational of all prejudices, and by a perfectly comprehensible reac-tion the Paris workers, from indifference in 1789, had come by this time [1792] to detest no section of the aristocracy so much as those whom they called "the aristocrats of the skin." On August 11th, the day after the Tuileries fell, Page, a notorious agent of the colonists in France, wrote home almost in despair "One spirit alone reigns here, it is horror of slavery and enthusiasm for liberty." Henceforth the Paris masses were for abolition, and their black brothers in San Domingo [i.e., the nation that would be renamed Haiti], for the first time, had passionate allies in France.[9]

For James, beyond establishing sympathy for the slaves' cause among the white workers of Paris, the example of the Haitian slaves helped to inspire the workers in their own struggles against capitalism. In *The Black Jacobins*, James has two chapters in a row describing this transformation. The first is entitled "The San Domingo Masses Begin" and the second is called "And the Paris Masses Complete." In this sequence, the fact of misinterpellation first becomes evident to the slaves of Haiti and then, by extension, became clear to the workers in Paris as well.

In this way, the Haitian revolution can be read as the spark that animated the revolution that has subsequently become *the* model for revolution worldwide. James is very clear that the Haitian radicalization came first and then spread back from the colony to the metropole. Insofar as the now radicalized French revolution went on to become *the* revolution, inspiring a series of later radical revolutions in turn, we can see the Haitians' "purposive misunderstanding" of the Declaration (which implicitly recognized the Declaration's misinterpellation of them) as the origin of a great portion of radical change in the world ever since.

TOUSSAINT LOUVERTURE. At the elite level of resistance to France, the leaders of the uprising—and in particular Toussaint Louverture—espoused liberal and enlightenment ideology even as they had no illusions about the degree to which the French were willing to exploit the natural and human capital in Haiti for their own nefarious purposes. If many of the advocates and bearers of French liberal ideology were suspect for them/him, the ideology itself was not (at least not overtly). As James describes him—but also as he describes himself—Toussaint epitomizes the kind of "purposive misunderstanding" Wall is referring to.

For example, James cites Toussaint as writing: "I took up arms for the freedom of my colour, which France alone proclaimed, but which she has no right to nullify. Our liberty is no longer in her hands: it is in our own.

We will defend it or perish."[10] Here, we see the complex mixture of belief and calculation that animated Toussaint's rebellion against France. "France alone" proclaimed the universal rights that he ardently believed in and, by the exact same token, France had no right to take those rights away once they were proclaimed. For James, what he calls Toussaint's "strange duality" was emblematic of a great mind. Toussaint was capable of being animated by enlightenment thinking and, at the same moment, he was a canny operator who resisted French hegemony.[11]

In his own *Mémoires*, written while he was in prison in France, Toussaint clung, at least textually, to the belief that both France and Napoleon were decent and living according to their own universalist principles. He felt that certain agents—and, in particular, Napoleon's local commander, General Leclerc, who was busily trying to subjugate Haiti and reimpose slavery—were acting on their own behalf without authorization from the French emperor. Thus he wrote,

> I observed that the intentions of the [French] government were peaceful and good towards myself and those who had contributed to the goodness that the colony enjoyed. General Leclerc surely had neither followed nor executed the orders that he had received since he came to the island like an enemy and engaging in evil solely for the pleasure of doing so.[12]

If we read these words from the perspective of Scott's *Domination and the Arts of Resistance* or *Weapons of the Weak*, we need not read this as a case of Toussaint being completely deluded. As Scott implies, there is an advantage to the subordinated person (and at this point Toussaint was nothing if not subordinated) to act as if they believed in the dominant ideology. This served to cover their own resistance and also to hedge their bets. Scott, for example, talks about the doctrine popular among the Russian peasantry of the "czar-deliverer," the idea that the czar was on the side of the people, allowing serfs to resist the czar's agents in the name of the czar himself (and in ways that might inoculate them from too much reprisal if they didn't succeed).[13] This is a form of using the tools of the state to bash at and resist the state, a long-held practice among groups and individuals who did not have access—at that moment, at least—to open confrontation. Toussaint's situation was desperate and it may be that he felt that this was the only way that he could safely articulate his critique of French policy toward Haiti.

At the same time, it seems that for most of his career as a resistance leader, Toussaint really did believe in the ideology of French liberalism and universalism, even as he saw France as failing utterly to practice what it preached. Ideas of universal subjectivity, individuality, and self-determination were foundational to the way Toussaint thought. His anger at France was fueled in part by the chasm between what he saw as such noble thoughts and the imperialist and self-interested actions of both the French capitalist class and the French state.

It may reflect this strange mixture of belief and canniness that Toussaint himself replicated some of the practices of the French that he himself was otherwise so critical of. As both C. L. R. James and the historian Carolyn Fick point out, Toussaint got rid of slavery but not capitalism; his goal was to keep Haiti functioning as a major producer of sugar and, ideally, within the French capitalist order, still competing with Britain, still producing a high level of surplus, only without the institution of slavery.[14]

As James writes of this,

> [Toussaint's] regulations were harsh. The laborers were sent to work 24 hours after he assumed command of any district, and he authorised the military commandments of the parishes to take measures necessary for keeping them on the plantations. The Republic, he wrote, had no use for dull or incapable men. It was forced labour and restraint of movement.[15]

Toussaint also allowed the white French planters' class to remain in control of the economy, very much against the wishes of the vast majority of Haitian former slaves. It is perhaps in this way especially that we can see that Toussaint's devotion to the French universal was not purely instrumental or lip service. When it came down to it, he remained, at least to some extent, bound within the ideological system that he was rebelling against in a way that those who followed him did not.

THE EX-SLAVES OF HAITI. Toussaint may have been a brilliant navigator of the cognitive dissonance between French enlightenment thought and the realities of French imperialism in Haiti, yet the revolution that he led did not exclusively result from this admixture. Below Toussaint and his generals was an entire network, a community of slaves (and then ex-slaves) who came at these political and economic questions from a very different perspective.

On one level, Toussaint is not as unconnected from the general population of Haitian slaves as might be expected. For one thing, Toussaint himself started his life as a slave, and his leadership is not unrelated to the context from which he comes. Scott says that we should not see a revolutionary leader of an oppressed community (including Toussaint, although Scott doesn't mention him) as being some kind of breakthrough figure, one whose "charisma" and personal leadership enable him or her to accomplish what no one else could and whose innovations have nothing to do (therefore) with the community he or she leads; this is another version of the "Rosa Parks" phenomenon, of seeing heroic figures as working on their own behalf rather than by and through a form of collective struggle.[16]

In other words, charisma and leadership are only relational, collective traits, the tip of a great social iceberg. Here we see some more evidence for a countercircuitry, a giving and receiving of authority that is not sanctioned by the state or market and that potentially works at cross-purposes to those entities. The forms of language used, the kinds of thinking employed, the cultural expressions, political responses, and the "leadership" that is exercised are all articulations of this much larger circuitry. The value of a leader is only a reflection of a set of practices that is itself entirely leaderless (i.e., anarchist).[17]

For all of this, it remains true that a leader's unique experience and perspective distinguishes him or her from those who are led and represented, at least in the way they respond to and think about their situation. The great number of Haitian ex-slaves experienced things quite differently than Toussaint. Without the complication of a Western ideology that is both attractive and repulsive, the general population's experience of resistance tended to be more pragmatic and far more local in character.

Even the initial response to events in France took on a very different form at the subaltern level.[18] While Toussaint and others were aware of the debates and the issues, at least to some extent, for the majority of Haitian slaves, events came to them only in the vaguest and most distorted form. In response to the Declaration and the events in Paris, a rumor swept the French Caribbean that the king of France had ended slavery and that the plantation owners in Haiti had colluded to hide this from the slaves, leading to an uprising.[19] In James's own narrative, the slaves caught the main idea, if not the specifics, of the revolution: The slaves "had heard of the revolution and had constructed it in their own image: the white slaves in France had risen, and killed their masters, and were now enjoying the fruits of the earth.

It was gravely inaccurate in fact, but they had caught the spirit of the thing. Liberty, Equality, Fraternity."[20] In terms of the role of the Declaration itself (or similar such documents) in relation to the subaltern community as a whole, a story widely repeated by scholars of the Haitian revolution has it that one rebel was killed:

> When they searched his body, they found in one of his pockets pamphlets printed in France, filled with common-places about the Rights of Man and the Sacred Revolution; in his vest pocket was a large packet of tinder and phosphate and lime. On his chest he had a little sack full of hair, herbs and bits of bone, which they call a "fetish." The law of liberty, ingredients for firing a gun, and a powerful amulet to call on the help of the gods: clearly a potent combination.[21]

Who knows why this rebel had this particular combination of things in his pocket? That revolutionary pamphlets were included along with certain sacred objects suggests that the ideas from France were not solely being recognized at the level of Toussaint but had an effect, at least possibly, among the general population that received them in ways that were connected to their own belief systems.

If the degree to which most ex-slaves were familiar with the specifics of French universalism is not clear, what is clear is that these former slaves were in no way in agreement with Toussaint's decision to keep a capitalist and exploitative form of economics. Toussaint's idea was to run the plantations and pay wages to the slaves by way of profit sharing (he also forbade whipping of newly enfranchised workers, although in practice whippings still occurred).

The ex-slaves had their own ideas about how they wanted to live their lives and what they wanted to do with their newfound freedom. Against the continued latifundia system Toussaint supported, the ex-slaves sought small landholdings and a release from the international market altogether. As Fick writes, for the former slaves, owning their own land and tilling it as they saw fit was their own definition of freedom:

> Freedom for the ex-slaves would mean the freedom to possess and till their own soil, to labor for themselves and their families, with no constraints other than their own self-defined needs, and to sell or dispose of the products of their labor in their own interest. Or, to put it another way, freedom would consist largely in subsistence farming,

based upon individual, small proprietorship of land, in direct contradiction, at that, with the demands of a colonial economy utterly dependent upon large-scale production for external markets.[22]

We see here how the different responses to misinterpellation have very different political effects. As we move from those who are more integrated with the metropole (such as Toussaint) to those who are far more excluded (the general population of former slaves), we see that the connection to the main ideological positions of French thought becomes more attenuated; the lures of capitalist forms of production, along with the liberal universal that supports it, become weaker. Similarly, the requirement Toussaint felt to allow the white planters to remain in their positions, as well as his (related) attempt to maintain Haiti as part of the international system of nations—and a capitalist one at that—yields, at the subaltern level, to a far more anarchist and local response.

Yet, even among the larger community there is yet an echo of the kinds of responses that we see at the elite level; here too an idea like freedom or rights gets requisitioned, adapted for different purposes than was originally intended. If the break in the circuitry of interpellation, however much or little it is believed in, occurs first at an ideological level—in Althusser's sense of the word—in relation to the French metropole, it quickly takes on other forms; it transforms into localized reappropriations and subversions of liberal doctrine, a set of counterideologies, all made possible by the highly visible breakdown in interpellative authority that the Haitian revolution produced.

I would like to argue here that the Haitian revolution offers a particularly "visible" instance of misinterpellation but in fact the opposite is true, historically speaking. The Haitian revolution was effectively silenced and forgotten for the next 150 years, give or take. Although it was recognized and remembered among slave societies in the Caribbean and the United States, among other places, there was a general attempt by the great European powers to hide and forget this singularly potent challenge to their authority.[23] This silencing, however, far from rendering the Haitian revolution less important as an example of misinterpellation, only shows how very powerful—how very legible—it is, how the answer to such an exposure of the vulnerabilities of Western interpellation is a heavy dose of misrecognition. If a group of slaves could manage to cast out the onslaught of European military and political power, nothing, it seems, is impossible or unthinkable.

A somewhat more recent moment of critical and widespread misinterpellation can be considered in what the author Erez Manela calls "the Wilsonian
moment."[24] Manela's book of the same name describes a time approach-
ing the end of World War I when US president Woodrow Wilson gave his
famous "Fourteen Points" speech in January 1918, calling for national self-
determination. As Manela notes, this call created a huge outpouring of
enthusiasm among many non-European and colonized communities. Activists and leaders ranging from Ho Chi Minh (then known as Nguyen Tat
Thanh) in Vietnam to Wellington Koo (Gu Weijun) in China enthusiastically praised Wilson and wrote directly to him, begging for his assistance
in sponsoring new and self-determining nations in the colonized world.
Manela notes that at this point in time, even the far more radically anticolonial Soviet declarations, coming as they did from Lenin and Trotsky, did not
have the same currency among aspiring independence leaders that Wilson
himself enjoyed.[25] It was felt that Wilson alone had both the power and the
desire to end colonialism once and for all. Despite the president's clear allegiance to the very order that had led to imperialism and colonialism in the
first place, Wilson was the hero of the hour.

As Manela notes, this moment was ripe with hope for change, a hope
that had very little to do with Wilson and his own interests:

> The major leaders who convened for the peace conference in Paris
> in January 1919 were concerned mainly with fashioning a settle-
> ment in Europe. But Europeans were not the only ones who had high
> hopes for the conference. For colonized, marginalized, and stateless
> peoples from all over the world—Chinese and Koreans, Arabs and
> Jews, Armenians and Kurds, and many others—the conference ap-
> peared to present unprecedented opportunities to pursue the goal of
> self-determination. They could now take the struggle against impe-
> rialism to the international arena, and their representatives set out
> for Paris, invited or otherwise, to stake their claims in the new world
> order. A largely unintended but eager audience for Wilson's wartime
> rhetoric, they often imagined the president as both an icon of their
> aspirations and a potential champion of their cause, a dominant fig-
> ure in the world arena committed, he had himself declared, to the
> principle of self-determination for all peoples.[26]

Manela's language here is telling: he speaks of would-be attendees "invited or not" and also speaks of "a largely unintended but eager audience." Yet their hopes could not be farther from what Wilson himself actually intended by his speech. Manela makes it very clear that, in fact, when Wilson spoke of self-determination (not unlike the drafters of the French Declaration of the Rights of Man and Citizen some 140 years earlier), he had in mind only people very much like himself; his intentions were focused on European peoples and his call was specifically for the cessation of the power of old empires that had long dominated Europe (the Hohenzollerns, the Habsburgs, and so on).[27]

In their own reading of Manela's work, Margaret Kohn and Keally McBride write,

> Unfortunately, Wilson presumably was thinking of European Countries when he made the statement [about self-determination]. His well-known racism (the Virginia-born president resegregated the federal workforce while he was president and was an enthusiastic audience for D.W. Griffith's film *The Birth of a Nation*) may have simply caused a blind spot. It was inconceivable to him that other races would assume that such universal principles applied to them. Whether this was the case or whether it was a more calculated ploy to disrupt the international system ultimately does not matter for the purposes of this argument. What is crucial is that nationalist leaders and movements did respond to Wilson's rhetoric, and made a play for the transfer of power to commerce.[28]

As Kohn and McBride note, the empires Wilson were referring to were not the only European empires in the world; Britain, France, and the United States had vast imperial (and also neoimperial) holdings over much of Africa, Asia, and the Pacific as well as Central America and the Caribbean. The subjects of these empires saw themselves as being similarly addressed by Wilson's call and this—not the intention of Wilson—was the critical point.

As Manela tells us, this international response was not well received by Wilson and his fellow planners of the Paris conference:

> Hundreds of [documents calling for Wilson's aid in fomenting non-European self-determination], many addressed to President Wilson himself, made their way to the Paris headquarters of the American Commission to Negotiate Peace at the Hôtel Crillon, but most got

no further than the president's private secretary, Gilbert Close. The president read only a small fraction of them, and he acted on fewer still. The complex and contentious issues of the European settlement were foremost on [Wilson's] mind during his months in Paris, and relations with the major imperial powers—Britain, France, Japan—loomed larger in the scheme of U.S. interests as Wilson saw them than did the aspirations of colonized groups or weak states. . . . The leading peacemakers had no intention of entertaining the claims for self-determination of dependent peoples elsewhere, least of all those that ran against their own interests.[29]

Yet, despite this indifference on the part of the powerful leaders of the major capitalist and imperialist powers, the "Wilsonian moment" was not something to be determined by Wilson and his allies alone. As with the events of the Haitian revolution, the contrast between what the supplicants read in Wilson's call—or at least wanted to read in it (as Wall shows, this can be a very complicated question)—and what was intended by Wilson himself became increasingly evident. As the fact of misinterpellation became clearer to all involved—the caller by seeing who shows up, the callee by seeing the response of the caller to their arrival—the mismatch of interpretations became dramatized, highly legible, in a way that was maximally inflammatory for a politics of resistance.

As Manela tells us in this instance,

As the outlines of the peace treaty began to emerge in the spring of 1919, it became clear that [expectations for "a more immediate and radical transformation" of the status of many in the colonial world] would be disappointed and that outside Europe the old imperial logic of international relations, which abridged or entirely obliterated the sovereignty of most non European peoples, would remain largely in place. The disillusionment that followed the collapse of this "Wilsonian moment" fueled a series of popular protest movements across the Middle East and Asia, heralding the emergence of anticolonial nationalism as a major force in world affairs.[30]

Eventually, as Manela shows, many of these supplicants turned in disgust from Wilson and moved instead toward the orbit of the Soviet Union, which issued a different sort of call. This is certainly the path that Ho Chi Minh was to take. But even the communist alternative was itself made possible by an earlier moment of misinterpellation; as already noted, the Haitian revolution radicalized the French revolution, which itself became the inspiration and model for a series of great revolutions (the Russian revolution very much included) that periodically wrenched the world.

The Anticolonial Leadership: Savvy or Stooges?

In looking at the reception of Wilson's call by various anticolonial subjects, we can ask the same questions as we did in the case of Haiti. In looking, first of all, at the elite level, the delegates who were actually present at the Treaty of Versailles—even if not necessarily invited—it is helpful to think about the degree to which they were bought into Western doctrine versus reading them as savvy manipulators of Western delusion. As with Haiti, there is no clear answer to this question; rather, we see once again a combination of clarity about the perfidy of the European powers—and the United States as well—and a real belief in the very values that the West promoted, values that had in no way been extended to the subjects of colonization. Here again, then, we can speak of "purposive misunderstanding" on the part of the leaders of these communities.

Manela's work, although not itself a radical critique of subjectivity, bears out this complicated subject position. Manela is very clear that the subjects of his book are far from stooges or starry-eyed lovers of all things Western and American, just as they were not master manipulators either. As he puts it,

> [These people] were neither naive victims of Wilson's hypocrisy nor, outside a few exceptions, radicals intent on revolutionary transformation, but rather savvy political actors, who, keenly aware of their weakness vis-à-vis the British and Japanese imperial projects [Manela's four case studies are Egypt, India, China, and Korea], sought to harness Wilson's power and rhetoric to the struggle to achieve international recognition and equality for their nations. They moved with dispatch to seize the opportunities that the Wilsonian moment seemed to offer to reformulate, escalate, and broaden their campaigns against empire, and worked to mobilize publics both at home and abroad behind their movements.[31]

In his case studies of various historical figures, we see a complex mixture of genuine misperception, calculation, belief, and deceit.

Manela describes, for example, the case of Lala Lajpat Rai, the Indian crusader for independence from Britain. Despite the man's great enthusiasm for the United States (he toured and wrote about the United States as a model for India's own "progress"), Manela writes that in response to Wilson's speeches

> Lajpat Rai was not naive, and he knew well that India was not foremost on Wilson's mind when the president spoke of self-determination. But he argued that it mattered little, since the president's forceful statements of his vision for the postwar order would serve as a powerful tool for the advancement of Indian self-rule regardless of his intentions.[32]

In Lajpat Rai's case, then, we see that it is possible to be both a pro-American idealist and an opportunist who knows how best to work his subject position. If anything, it is exactly because he is, to some extent, "bought in" to the liberal worldview that Lajpat Rai succeeds in helping to upend it. His inclusion in that worldview allows him to assume that Wilson's addresses are at least to some extent addressed to him and, in that calculation, there is room for recalibration and response. In this view, misinterpellation is perhaps not so much a game to be played and won (or lost) but rather a complex set of shared and overlapping readings of reality. As new possibilities emerged, the subject changes along with them, with their belief systems, as it were, bringing up the rear.[33]

Misinterpellation and the Subaltern

At the more grassroots level of the subaltern community itself, it is once again more difficult to have access to their perspective. The first thing to say is that the popular resistance to colonial rule long predates the Wilsonian moment (this is true, of course, at the elite level as well). Thus, in India, for example, Ranajit Guha describes how the entire nineteenth century was convulsed by rebellion and insurgency across the British Raj.[34] Histories and recordkeeping of the period (generally undertaken by the British themselves) tended to flatten out these insurgencies and deprive them of any truly revolutionary character; Guha tells us that the British treated these uprisings as purely security concerns and that "by making the security of the state into the central problematic of peasant insurgency, it assimilated the latter as merely an element in the career of colonialism. In other words, the peasant was denied recognition as a subject of history in his own right even for a project that was all his own."[35]

In thinking about the agency of these subjects, Guha, like Scott, rejects "mak[ing] the mobilization of the peasantry altogether contingent on the intervention of charismatic leaders, advanced political organizations or the upper classes."[36] He also attacks the way that

> Bourgeois-nationalist historiography has to wait until the rise of Mahatma Gandhi and the Congress Party to explain the peasant movements of the colonial period so that all major events of this genre up to the end of the First World War [and hence the period being specifically discussed here] may then be treated as the pre-history of the "Freedom Movement."[37]

Thus, for Guha, it is critical to discover the kinds of motivations and actions of the larger population to some extent independently of the leadership, which often gets retroactively mapped as anticipating or resulting from elite-level interventions. If the concerns of the elites were at the national level, with European power and doctrine, the kind of subaltern consciousness that functions beneath it is concerned largely with issues of peasant and landlord relations (the insurgency of the former and the authority of the latter). While this relationship both predates and postdates the British Raj, the incorporation of capitalist forms of production during this period gave the landlords new forms of power and new means to oppress and exploit their tenants. It was this form of power that was most keenly resented and resisted by the collectivity of Indian peasantry.

The fact that landlordism itself survived the end of British colonialism suggests how far the path of divergence between the anticolonial elite and the larger population (just as in Haiti) varied; while the leaders got what they wanted—independence from Britain—the extent to which other desires and concepts of freedom were delivered is far murkier.

Reynaldo Clemeña Ileto's discussion of popular resistance to colonialism in the Philippines suggests a similar track. In discussing this case, we leave behind Manela for the moment. This story culminates well before World War I and does not involve one of Manela's case studies. Yet the story Ileto tells correlates very well with the larger experience of subaltern communities and, in particular, illuminates the way that Western ideologies can often turn on their wielders, leading to radical, rather than reactionary outcomes. As Ileto tells us, in the Philippines, a growing anticolonial movement arose along with the capitalist development and exploitation of the territory. This development also produced internal changes in Filipino social structures.

A whole class of elite Filipinos called *ilustrados* (meaning something akin to "the enlightened ones") came into being; they had indigenous roots but prospered in the capitalist economy. The *ilustrados* were so named because they were influenced by Western liberal ideas and sought to bring European ideas about the enlightenment to the Philippines.

In his well-known account *Pasyon and Revolution*, Ileto looks at the Katipunan movement, a revolutionary uprising largely led by nonelite Filipinos, which the *ilustrados* became involved with as well. In speaking of what he perceives to be a split between these groups and their respective goals, Ileto writes,

> Agoncillo [a previous scholar of that movement] assumes that to all those who engaged in revolution, the meaning of independence was the same: separation from Spain and the building of a sovereign Filipino nation. We can rest assured that this was the revolutionary elite's meaning, which could very well be identical with that of revolutionary elites in Latin America and elsewhere. But the meaning of the revolution to the masses—the largely rural and uneducated Filipinos who constituted the revolution's mass base—remains problematic for us. We cannot assume that their views were formless, inchoate, and meaningless, apart from their articulation in ilustrado thought.[38]

For Ileto, the prime motivator for the majority of Filipinos was not sovereignty or independence but a sense of justice that comes in part from participation in Catholic religious ritual and in particular the Passion play (*pasyon*), which re-creates the last week of Christ's life in highly elaborate and often traveling ritual reproductions. Frequently the heroes of the Katipunan and other movements were associated with the life (and death) of Christ.[39]

For Ileto, these religious rituals and responses, far from being irrational and eventually giving way to the "real" revolutionary fervor, which is secular (read Western, read *ilustrado*), were in fact central to the revolution that they spawned. In effect, the passion plays served as the source of the main body of revolutionary authority in the Philippines. Of course, the doctrines and rituals of Catholicism that were being expressed in the passion plays were themselves a Western import. But non-elite Filipinos hijacked—in ways both deliberate and inadvertent—this institution in order to assert their own counternarratives.

Ileto writes that Catholicism was introduced among the *Indios*, or indigenous Filipinos, to "inculcate . . . loyalty to Spain and Church; moreover they encouraged resignation to things as they were and instilled preoccupation with morality and the afterlife rather than with conditions in this world."[40] Thus, in its origin, Catholicism in the Philippines serves as part of a very elaborate network of interpellation, a means of control and domination. Yet, as Ileto notes, there was a secondary effect of the spread of Catholicism, "which probably was not intended by the missionaries."[41] It also served "to provide lowland Philippine society with a language for articulating their own values, ideals, and even hopes of liberation."[42] Prime among the rituals of Catholicism that served this second purpose was the Passion play.

In the story of the Passion play, we can see another example of how interpellation can fail, can reveal itself to be—or perhaps be hijacked to become—misinterpellation after all (here again the question of what is deliberate and what isn't becomes deeply entangled). Here we also see the presence of countercalls and counterforms of interpellation; the call of the Passion play countered the call of imperial domination, thwarting the intentions of the ruling elites in ways that could not have been anticipated. This shows how institutions and practices intended for dominant ideological production can turn in on themselves, can be reappropriated and reused for radical purposes. The Filipinos' reappropriation of Catholic doctrine and pageantry for their own political purposes is another example of mass-level resistance via the mechanisms of misinterpellation.

For his own part, Manela himself doesn't write much about the subaltern perspective. His is a largely elite-level reading. But even in his account, you can see some evidence for the complex way that Western ideology is both resisted and reinterpreted or reappropriated in complex ways at the mass level. Thus, for example, in his case study of Egypt and its 1919 revolution (one that was highly impacted by the events he describes as the "Wilsonian moment" but that also, obviously, had a lot of antecedent causes in Egypt itself), Manela describes how "as the revolution unfolded in the streets, Egyptian protesters strove to obtain the support of the United States for their cause. One group of demonstrators attempted to march to the U.S. legation in Cairo with an American flag at its head, but British troops dispersed the crowd and confiscated the flag."[43] For Manela, this demonstrated a belief on quite a broad level among the populace that the United States was a benefactor and that Wilson's principles were universal and good. He said the movements that composed the 1919 revolution included elites but also Egyptians of all classes, religious minorities, and women (obviously these categories overlap a great deal). Manela also writes, "[The demonstrators] declared their faith in President Wilson and his Fourteen Points and called on the United States to come to their aid."[44] While this might again reflect the particular view of those anticolonial elites (he tells us, for example, that "fifteen notables from Alexandria" had written "Long live America, liberator of the world"),[45] it suggests that at least to some extent, many nonelite Egyptians too were responding to the perception that Western values might lift them out of their present situation and offer them the benefits of universal subjectivity.[46] These same people were to experience tremendous anger when it was discovered that the United States had no more interest in freeing them than did the United Kingdom or France. Here too the mismatch between ideology and practice was swiftly to become too pronounced to sustain misrecognition of the circuitry of interpellated political authority, with radical—and world-changing—results.[47]

As with the case of Haiti, the anticolonial movement that Wilson inadvertently helped to produce did far more than fit itself into liberal categories of rights and self-determination; in challenging its own exclusion from these rights, this movement radically altered and unmade the "liberal universal" that it was demanding admittance to.

Mohamed Bouazizi and the Arab Spring

A final and much more recent example of misinterpellation does not involve the ideologies that lie at the heart of liberal capitalism so much as the effects of liberal capitalist dogmas on a globalized and postcolonial world. In the case of the Arab Spring, we are dealing with a much more diffuse form of liberal identity formation and universalism. The brutal dictatorships that dominated the Arab world until very recently (and in Egypt at least has reemerged in a new and no less brutal form) were hardly democracies but they were supported by and used the language of liberal democracy nonetheless.

We live in a time where every almost country calls itself a democracy and where capitalism is nearly ubiquitous. Similarly, a global discourse of rights and freedoms exists as a kind of "universal" set of beliefs, regardless of the particular practices of individual nations. In Tunisia, where the Arab Spring began, the connection to France, the former colonial power, remains strong. Accordingly, the same discourse of universal subjectivity applies there as in France or elsewhere (the same universal that the Haitian slaves therefore encountered some two hundred years ago).

At the time of the beginning of the Arab Spring, Tunisia, under the rule of Zine El Abidine Ben Ali, was awash in a phantasm of French-inspired postcolonial discourse. While in practice Tunisians had no rights (except for the elite, who, it could be said, didn't need rights) and lived a life of harsh and brutal subordination, their lives as political subjects remained filled with the discourse of the French revolution. From Scott, we can surmise that their subordination was not born meekly or passively. Indeed, modern Tunisian history has several instances of outright rebellion, including a 1978 general strike against the former dictator Habib Bourguiba, which was brutally repressed with mass killings and arrests. In Tunisia, as elsewhere, we find a kind of double life where ghostly rights and privileges coexisted with the daily humiliations and domination of a hierarchical authoritarian regime.

All that changed with the singular act of Mohamed Bouazizi when he set himself on fire in December 2010. Bouazizi lived in Sidi Bouzid, a city in the interior of Tunisia. He came from a poor family and he had many siblings to support. Bouazizi sold fruits and vegetables from a stand and, like many others struggling to make a living, was constantly harassed by authorities for violating various laws that were oppressive and odious by design. In his telling of Bouazizi's story, Mohamed Bouamoud writes that Bouazizi was particularly targeted. In part this was because he was more openly resistant to the arbitrary rules that forbade selling fruit or other products on the street even while the local government profited from the fines and power that such a law produced amid a population for which such work was one of the few options for employment.[48] At one point after the umpteenth fine he had been forced to pay, Bouazizi is said to have cried out, "I swear I will end up turning this country upside down from top to bottom!" If he did indeed say this, these were highly prophetic words.[49]

On Friday, December 17, 2010, Bouazizi was approached by a female inspector who, as happened on a nearly daily basis, told him that he was not allowed to sell fruits on the street. He told her that he needed to do so for his livelihood and that he had no other choice. Angered by his resistance, the inspector took away his scales and then—at least in one version of the story—slapped him twice across the face in full public view.[50]

Incensed, Bouazizi went to the Gouvernorat, the administrative center of Sidi Bouzid, to complain about the inspector's actions. If he expected someone to listen to him or to afford him his rights as a citizen, he was quickly disillusioned. As Bouamoud puts it, "Poor Mohamed, he really thought he was in a state of rights and institutions. There, rather than listening to him, he was treated like a dog."[51]

Thoroughly humiliated, especially by being slapped in public—and by a woman at that, which was considered a great insult for a man in his community—Bouazizi bought gasoline at local store and sat in front of the administrative center. He poured the gasoline over himself, lit a match, and set himself on fire, yelling out a profession of Muslim faith as he did ("I testify that there is no God but Allah").[52] Witnesses said that the local officials just laughed at this spectacle and finally a passerby put her coat over him to put out the flames. His uncle was in the vicinity and it was he who called an ambulance to take Bouazizi (who was still alive at that point) to the hospital.[53]

Word of this event spread quickly, leading to protest demonstrations. That very night there were marches throughout the region in six locations, including in Sidi Bouzid itself. The next day, on December 18, there were even bigger demonstrations in Sidi Bouzid. Via social media, word spread to Tunis, the capital, creating agitation there, which was then censured and shut down by the authorities.[54]

For a couple of weeks, the country remained relatively stable, but there was a lot of tension and there were still demonstrations. In order to address the situation, President Ben Ali took to the airwaves. Rather than making any conciliatory claims, Ben Ali made a speech threatening to mercilessly crack down on all forms of civil disobedience. Reaction to this speech made the situation much more serious; the gap between the leaders' words and a discourse of rights became ever more visible. Thinking twice about his hard line, Ben Ali, on December 30, invited the Bouazizi family to his palace while he himself went to visit Bouazizi in the hospital. This trip backfired dramatically. The image of the president standing over Bouazizi, who lay wrapped in bandages, went viral, leading to a further escalation of protest and outrage.

Bouazizi died on January 4, 2011, from his burns. His death led to the biggest demonstrations yet. On January 5, almost five thousand people marched to the cemetery where he was to be buried. At this point, he had become a martyr. For his part, Ben Ali returned to type, speaking of resisting terrorism and the like, but to no avail. More and more cities were rising up, including Tunis. On January 13, a visibly humbled president took the air one more time. He said, "I have understood you" (*je vous ai compris*) but it was clearly too little, too late.[55] The very next day the uprising became a full-on revolution, calling for Ben Ali to be deposed. Ben Ali fled the country and the Arab Spring had begun in earnest.

In thinking about this story in terms of misinterpellation, there are, as previously noted, some key differences from the earlier stories that I told about Haiti and the anticolonial movement. Here, as already stated, we are not at the phantasmic heart of liberal capitalism but somewhere at its periphery. The main agitator in this case was much farther removed from liberal universalism than in the case of Toussaint Louverture or Lajpat Rai. Bouazizi was not well versed in liberal capitalist discourse; it's unclear from hagiographies like Bouamoud's what Bouazizi himself thought about rights and so forth. He never managed to complete high school (although he did several years of study) and was poor and isolated from larger liberal conventions. Nonetheless, it would appear that Bouazizi did expect something from the state. The fact that he went to complain about his treatment by the inspector suggests that he had at least a modicum of hope that he might receive some kind of justice. Or perhaps he knew he wouldn't but he wanted to go anyway, just to vent his rage and humiliation. At any rate, the experience with the inspector and his subsequent refusal by the Gouvernorat made something that he had been able to live with—however angry he was, however much he raged against the injustice he was subjected to on a daily basis—suddenly unbearable. The fabric of his sense of dignity and possibility had been rendered in a way that was now too visible or tangible to ignore. After years of accepting—more or less—his lack of rights despite being a "universal subject," something changed. Arriving at this particular scene of interpellation, Bouazizi was no longer able or willing to slink away.

In his encounter with the fruit inspector, we see a terrible revisitation of Althusser's scene of interpellation, one in which dysfunction instead of function prevails. Instead of a casual "hey, you there!," we see the full panoply of the assertion of power, humiliation, and the hubris of the state that comes along with interpellation. This moment marks the point where interpellation, the stuff of everyday life, shades into misinterpellation, a position where the bases of the call—its assertion of authority, the suggestion that it "really" is oriented toward the intended subject—become, to cite Judith Butler once again, "radically incredible."[56] The story of the fruit inspector and her encounter with Bouazizi, exactly because it parallels (and almost parodies) the original scene of interpellation as Althusser imagines it, exposes the earlier version as being entirely false, arbitrary, and without foundation. Similarly, Bouazizi's own attempt to assert his subject position nonetheless—his going to the Gouvernorat to get "justice"—signifies his final attempt to be the subject he believed he was meant to be (hence getting ushered into a real-life Kafkaesque situation). With that final refusal, he took the only path he felt that he could; denied any chance to be the subject he believed himself to be, he took that subjectivity into his own hands, ending his life (and in a very public way) in order to assert his own form of counter-agency or, at the very least, to allow his failure as a subject to be complete and undeniable.

What was true for Bouazizi in his personal experience became true for nearly everyone else in Tunisia as well. Somehow the story of his humiliation and his subsequent self-immolation exemplified or dramatized a form of injustice that was already present and already known but held back from, at least to some extent, because a patina of respectability remained. Once that patina was removed, what had been borne (with however much ill will and however many acts of daily defiance in relative isolation) was no longer possible and the decades-long authoritarian regime in Tunisia (first with Bourguiba and then his prime minister, Ben Ali) quickly fell apart.

In terms of this third example, we do not need to make as much of a distinction between elite and local-level responses as in the previous two cases because in this instance, the crisis was completely attributable to the acts of a nonelite person. Indeed, the swell of uprising that followed Bouazizi's act of self-immolation took the ordinary resistant elites by surprise and they had to scramble to stay ahead of their own revolution (something they ultimately managed to do, more or less).

The movements of the Arab Spring, certainly in Tunisia but also in Egypt and elsewhere, have strong anarchist tendencies and are very much leaderless in the sense that organization and action are not being planned by any one particular group. As Alcinda Honwana puts it, describing that moment in time, "In Tunisia, young people no longer appear to be bound by hegemonic political discourses and party ideologies, and are creating their own spaces of intervention to engage the state and society. . . . The Tunisian revolution, led mainly by disenfranchised youths, was a powerful example of 'citizenship from below' that has emerged outside traditional power structures and has opened up a space for major transformations."[57] Amira Aleya-Sghaier says something similar:

> The Tunisian revolution . . . is not a classical revolution like the French revolution with a transition from a feudal to a *bourgeois* revolution. It was not a communist class-driven revolution like the 1917 Bolshevik Revolution in Russia. Nor was it a national liberation like those of Vietnam and Algeria, or a revolution for human rights like the Eastern European revolution of the 1990s. The Tunisian revolution was unique. . . . It was special because it was spontaneous, lacking a centralized leadership, a clear ideology, or any pre-established political program.[58]

While this example may not be complicated, as the previous cases were, by the presence of a mix of "universal" and local ideologies (although both are clearly present in different quantities), it too shows the power of misinterpellation to unmake the workings of decades, if not centuries, of interpellative power.[59] That power, as I have been arguing, never had the force of authority it imagined itself to, yet its vanishing—even if only temporary—is singularly impressive.[60] The power projected by an interpellating authority is not so much one of convincing or persuasion—although it has that aspect too, at least with the elites who engage in resistance movements—but lies in some much more complicated mixture of strategy, threat, appropriation, and ideology more generally. Such a combination of forces obviously does not perfectly prevent uprisings but it has a deadening effect that, unless it is ripped asunder by a process like misinterpellation, seems to be able to hang on indefinitely. If it is exposed, the authority rendered by interpellation returns to being the nothing it has always actually been, disappearing seemingly in an instant.

In looking at the three examples in question, as already noted, there are clearly differences between them. The example of Haiti is the clearest case of a universal subjectivity being announced even as it was swiftly taken back. The mismatch in this case between announced authorial intention and the fact of exclusion is the most glaring and, perhaps for this reason, produced the most spectacular reaction. Wilson's Fourteen Points were not explicitly based on universal principles (although they referenced them) but had a more prosaic basis. Even so, the mismatch between the way the rights enumerated in that speech were intended versus the way that they were received led to radical and unpredictable results; this was the moment that the anticolonialism movement really broke out into the open. Finally, Mohamed Bouazizi—in addition to the way he himself was called by the fruit inspector—lived in the aftermath of those earlier liberal calls to citizenship and self-determination; he existed in the shadow of the expectations and hopes that the language of rights brings. In his case, the dramatization of the gap between promises and realities came through his own actions; he was the agent of dramatization and his act of self-immolation was itself a kind of call or countercall of its own for a huge number of unhappy subjects in Tunisia and elsewhere.

What unites these stories is the fact that each of them exposes the emptiness of the concept of universality (in all of its various guises). Unlike a thinker like Jürgen Habermas, who argues that there is a virtuous circle wherein even falsely determined rights can and will become true as part of an expanding notion of universality, these examples indicate that the universal is always built on exclusion, always false, and therefore always vulnerable to misinterpellation and radical and unscripted responses.[61] In my view, the usefulness of the concept of the universal is not that it is capacious enough to eventually include everyone after all but rather that the concept of the universal serves as a site upon which we can clearly observe the failure of the universal to appear.

Bad Signs: Machiavelli and the Power of Stories

We often resort to metaphors to explain what happens in particular political situations. We say, for example, that Tunisia was a "powder keg" that merely needed a match to set it off (in this case, quite literally; the gruesomely poetic title of Bouamoud's book, *Bouâzizi ou L'énticelle qui a destitué Ben Ali* [Bouazizi or the spark that deposed Ben Ali], suggests as much). Although useful as a metaphor for sudden political change, this image doesn't really help to explain how Tunisia's oppressive regime sustained its gunpowdery life for decade after decade, not to mention the endless series of sparks that could have set it off at any number of points (such as the aforementioned general strike). We must ask ourselves how one act of self-immolation brought down—seemingly overnight but actually through a much more complex and sustained process—an entire political apparatus in a way that spread rapidly to consume a large part of the Arab world and then inspired other movements, like Occupy Wall Street in the United States and the protest movements in Europe that same year. After all, there are countless stories of brave resistance, martyrdom, and self-sacrifice throughout the world at any given time. Witness, for example, the Tibetan monks and nuns who have self-immolated in recent years to protest their community's treatment by the Chinese government. This dramatic act happens on a fairly regular basis without (at least so far) triggering a world-changing event like the Arab Spring.

One thinker that may help us to understand what happened in Tunisia, as well as shedding more light on the process of misinterpellation itself, is Machiavelli. Although far removed from our current modern era, he was an astute observer of both his own time, as well as the classical era (and, in particular, the example of the Roman republic, to which he was quite devoted). Machiavelli is an avid and enthusiastic teller of great political stories. In Machiavelli's hands, these stories go well beyond entertainment, however wonderful or awful they may be. They also serve as instructions for how to engage with the substructures of political agency and how, it could be said, to both understand and subvert the ways that power is sustained and produced through the production of authority, depending on how we read those situations (or, more accurately, how we read Machiavelli's reading of them). Understanding his treatment of stories helps us to better see the operations of misinterpellation in the three stories I just told; it helps to explain how and why existing authority relations are suddenly no longer tenable and how to maximize that untenability. How, that is, can we reverse Judith Butler's question in the previous chapter once again to "make the possibility of becoming a 'bad' subject [less] remote and [more] incendiary than it might well be?"[62] Reading these stories via Machiavelli allows us to better see how to maximize the potential for misinterpellation, to more explicitly and ably politicize such moments (and, for that matter, every other moment as well).

In his Discourses on the First Ten Books of Livy, Machiavelli demonstrates a keen appreciation for the Romans' ability to read the world around them as a set of signs or a text in which they could interpret their fortunes, so as to maximize their own power and agency. After stating that "no great events ever occur in any city or country that have not been predicted by soothsayers, revelations, or by portents and other celestial signs," Machiavelli goes on to list some examples of such soothsaying as it relates to politics (including Savonarola's visions of the coming of Charles VIII of France).[63] He then states "it may be . . . that the air is peopled with spirits, who by their superior intelligence foresee future events, and out of pity for mankind warn them by such signs, so that they may prepare against the coming evils."[64]

Yet much of what Machiavelli writes about in the *Discourses* militates against this conclusion. Rather than being passive subjects who simply obey whatever fortune (or Fortuna, as he hypostatizes it) wills, Machiavelli sees the possibility of directly and materially engaging with signs as a way to maximize the possibilities of human agency.

For Machiavelli, what might be called the art of politics consists in "reading" the auguries and signs of the world in a way that accords with a person or community's own agenda or wishes. In this way, one becomes "authorized" to engage in said behavior by dint of an engagement with external (and presumably omniscient) sources. He traces this tendency back to Numa, the second king of Rome (and a favorite of Machiavelli's). As Machiavelli tells us, Numa saw that the Roman people were uncivilized and in need of law. But he also knew that they would not obey a law that he just invented out of whole cloth. Thus, Machiavelli tells us that Numa "feigned that he held converse with a nymph, who dictated to him all that he wished to persuade the people to."[65] He pretended that this nymph (in Titus Livy's telling, it is the goddess Egeria) gave him the laws and, suitably awed, the Romans responded by taking these laws to heart and obeying them.[66] And, Machiavelli goes on to tell us, all other great lawgivers acted similarly, cloaking their laws in divine or mystical origins. ("Thus did Lycurgus and Solon, and many others who aimed at the same thing.")[67] What for Numa was a lie becomes for the Romans a practice, a way of reading the world to give themselves agency and a call to political subjectivity; one could call this an origin story of interpellation.

We see here the origins too of the circuitry of authorization, the way that authority is sought out and projected and then returns in an alienated (and seemingly irrefutable) form. Numa's actions are a model for all future forms of authorization for the Romans (and maybe for the rest of us as well). Thus in his chapters on the Roman religion, Machiavelli gives several examples of such actions. He writes for example that

> when the Roman soldiers sacked the city of Veii . . . some of them entered the temple of Juno, and placing themselves in front of her statue, said to her, "Will you come to Rome?" Some imagined that they observed the statue make a sign of assent, and others pretended to have heard her reply, "Yes." Now these men, being very religious, as reported by Titus Livius [i.e., Livy] and having entered the temple

quietly, they were filled with devotion and reverence, and might really have believed that they had heard a reply to their question, such as perhaps they could have presupposed.[68]

For Machiavelli, these soldiers are not so much lying as interpreting the world around them in a way that offers them an externalized source for their own right and power to act; one could say that here they are actively self-interpellating, giving themselves a goddess to watch over their city and ensure their victory (and thus setting the interpellative circuitry into motion). But, as with Althusser's notion of misrecognition, they are not actively aware of this; to do so would be to ruin the agency that comes from such an act. The gift of the Romans was to truly believe that the statue they had spoken to (called for) had answered them. Juno becomes the externalization of the Romans' will, allowing them an authority that they would not otherwise have. In this way, the power of Numa's lie lived on as an institution of Roman (misrecognized) self-authorization.

Machiavelli also approvingly tells the tale of Junius Brutus, the founder of the Roman Republic and the way he interpreted a prophecy from the oracle at Delphi. Brutus, along with two relatives of the Tarquins—the foreign rulers of Rome at the time—went to the oracle. Rather presumptuously, they asked her, of the three of them, who would be the next ruler of Rome. The oracle's answer—as told by Livy—was "the one of you who first kisses your mother will be the authority over Rome."[69] The three of them drew straws to see which of them would first kiss their mother upon return to Rome but Brutus, who acted stupidly in order to avoid the envy and the attention of the Tarquins, had another plan. He pretended to fall to the ground and kissed the earth, "the mother of us all." Machiavelli tells us that in doing so, Brutus was "hoping thereby to propitiate the gods to his projects," that is, like the Roman soldiers at Veii, he sought to bend Fortuna to his will and thereby gain the authority (even if by this act of deceit) to overcome the tyranny of the Tarquins.[70] Admonishing Livy himself, who Machiavelli claims saw Brutus's deceptions as merely serving his own self-interest, Machiavelli writes that Brutus sought to gain favor with the Tarquins so as to better plot against them (perhaps also explaining his own behavior in ostensibly writing The Prince for the Medicis in the process). Machiavelli writes that "such intimacy will insure you tranquility without any danger, and enable you to share the enjoyment of the prince's good fortune with him, and at the same time afford you every convenience for satisfying your resentment."[71] Here too this is not mere lying on Brutus's behalf but rather serves as a complicated maneuver by which to gain an "external" source of authority for one's own actions. If he was just a plain liar, Brutus wouldn't have been concerned with the prophecy one way or the other; the ruse would have done nothing for him. Brutus needed to believe that the oracle was speaking of him—it had to become an external source of authority—in order to propel himself into power and so he acted to make that the case.

Misinterpellating Better

A final—and perhaps most critical—example of this type of self-interpellating behavior comes in Machiavelli's discussion of the way the Romans took auspices before every battle. On the eve of battle, the Romans had sacred poultry men, or Pollari, who would feed grain to sacred chickens. If the chickens pecked at the grain, all was well and they could move forward with battle. If they didn't, it was a bad sign and battle was averted.

Yet, here again, the Romans were not the passive sort who simply accepted a sign (just as Machiavelli himself seemingly refutes his own suggestion that the world is full of intelligent spirits who know better than we do when they give signs). Machiavelli supplies us with two contrasting stories about Roman generals dealing with the Pollari and their chickens. Together they suggest a more complicated lesson from Machiavelli than simply urging us to lie and interpellate (that is, to lie and then to believe those lies).

In the first story, Machiavelli speaks of Consul Papirius, who was faced with nonpecking chickens on the eve of a battle with the Samnites that he was sure he would win. Machiavelli writes,

> The chief of the Pollari, seeing the great desire of the army to fight, and the confidence in victory which the general as well as the soldiers manifested, and being unwilling to deprive the army of this opportunity of achieving a success, reported to the Consul that the auspices were proceeding favorably; whereupon Papirius set his squadrons in order for battle.[72]

Unfortunately, one of the Pollari spread the word that the chickens had not pecked, something that Papirius himself hotly denied. Machiavelli adds:

> And so that the result might correspond with the prognostication, [Papirius] commanded his lieutenants to place the Pollari in the front

ranks of the battle; and thus it happened that, in marching upon the enemy, the chief of the Pollari was accidentally killed by an arrow from the bow or a Roman soldier. When the Consul heard this, he said that all went well and with the favor of the gods, for by the death of this liar the army had been purged of all guilt, and that whatever anger the gods might have felt against him had been thereby appeased.[73]

In this way, Papirius too has bent Fortuna to his will, doing what he had to (including having the hapless head of the Pollari shot) in order to maintain the authority that would ensure the Roman victory, which, of course, was the end result. This too can be considered an act of self-interpellation insofar as Papirius needed the auspices to be a certain way and, respectful of that authority, he did what he had to in order to make sure that the auspices aligned with what he desired or needed to be true.

In the same chapter where he describes Papirius's actions, Machiavelli contrasts this story with a seemingly less able leader, Appius Pulcher:

Appius Pulcher acted just the contrary way in Sicily during the first Punic war; for wishing to fight the Carthaginian army, he caused the Pollari to ascertain the auspices; and when they reported that the fowls did not eat, he said "then let us see whether they will drink," and had them thrown into the sea; he then went to battle and was defeated. For which he was punished at Rome, while Papirius was rewarded; not so much because the one had been beaten and the other victorious, but because the one had contravened the auspices with prudence, and the other with temerity.[74]

In Machiavelli's telling—which I'll revisit with an alternative reading in a moment—Pulcher was not more honest than Papirius but rather more feeble. "Prudence" in this case amounts to the correct engagement with a story so that it serves its purpose, so that authority is bestowed and victory is won. In his rash actions, Pulcher destroyed the basis for belief in victory and, in so doing, ruined the basis for authorization of the Roman victory (also with predictable results).

Yet, for all his seeming praise of Papirius and denunciation of Pulcher, in telling these stories, we see that Machiavelli's discussion of these stories tells us something about how to derail the processes of interpellation—or self-interpellation—that he seems to otherwise enthusiastically promote. The story of Pulcher, although it is presented as an example of ineptness—

or, more accurately, a lack of "prudence"—also gives us information about how an authorizing structure can be unraveled. Because interpellation is ultimately a closed loop, whereby authority is projected outward and it returns in the form of an alienated and unaccountable power over us, an interference in that cycle potentially renders the failure of that cycle too evident, producing—again at least potentially—a deauthorization in its wake.[75] Another way to think about this is that in taking away the faux authority that is the result of projecting human agency onto or through the screen of some externality—whether it is the gods in the case of the Romans or the state in the case of Althusser's notion of interpellation—it becomes possible for a different form of authority or agency to appear and interfere with this system. This other authority does not come from acts of political fetishism and projection but rather from individuals and communities that have experienced the failure of that authority. In other words, this is an authority based on misinterpellation.

Appius Pulcher, in my reading, emerges as an unlikely hero of sorts in Machiavelli's stories. It's not, once again, that he is more honest than Papirius, but rather that his actions lead to the breakdown of the ideological apparatus while Papirius's actions only foment more of the same. In this way, Pulcher advances the cause of misinterpellation in a way that Papirius does not. If we can think more clearly about how those mechanisms break down, then we can find better strategies for revealing how moments of misinterpellation are not the occasional and rare exception (the one time out of ten) but rather a symptom of the generally phantasmic, circulating, and endlessly failing nature of authority and the way it is both projected and received.

We could even read Machiavelli, as I have done elsewhere, in a yet more conspiratorial light by recognizing the fact that his examples of interpellation involve not only clear manipulations and lies—so that the poses of all-knowingness and ontological grounding are exposed as frauds—but also the exposure of interpellation as being something that the Romans did for themselves.[76] In other words, by looking at the examples he supplies us with: Numa, the Roman soldiers at Veii, Junius Brutus, Papirius, and Pulcher, we see a dramatization of (and hence an improved legibility for) the fact that interpellation is a closed circuit, a projection, and a self-feeding mechanism. What in Althusser's depiction takes on the quality of being something that is truly objective (or material to use Althusser's own language) becomes in Machiavelli's telling far more visibly phantasmic, unmistakably self-created and contingent (if still material). Even the fact that he enthusiastically tells us that Numa is a liar suggests the exposure and ruination of the very system of interpellation that Machiavelli seems to ardently promote. In this reading it is Machiavelli himself who calls into question the external, seemingly objective nature of the returning authority that the Romans crave. By showing that authority does not come from the gods, nor from the state, in any kind of ontological sense, but rather comes in the form of a set of call and responses between various members of a community, Machiavelli has spun a tale that reveals not only the power of interpellation—which he appears to be all for on the surface of things—but also the vulnerability of its mechanism, the way it functions, and also, more critically, the way it malfunctions.

If we read Machiavelli in this sense, he becomes less an enthusiastic fan of lying and manipulation as a form of interpellation and becomes instead a subverter, someone who in the guise of praising the mechanism of state authority ruins it instead. To use a Benjaminian term, we could say that he allegorizes interpellation, much as Butler suggests about Althusser as well. And, in so doing, Machiavelli may make it possible for his readers to ruin such authority in turn. If Appius Pulcher is his antihero—when we read Machiavelli in this conspiratorial light—my own anti- (or un)heroes are not the Toussaints and Wellington Koos of the stories told in this chapter but the nameless former slaves, Filipino peasants and workers, Egyptian laborers, and the fruit peddlers of Sidi Bouzid.[77]

This consideration of Machiavelli allows us to see not only the way that interpellation is a closed circuit, but also the way that it is a circulation that requires ongoing maintenance in order to keep that detached authority in place (i.e., killing those who may threaten "the party line," thereby keeping the circuitry of authority closed and ongoing). Realizing this, we see the true vulnerability of interpellation. The systems of authority that are produced by interpellation are not just "there," an ongoing and permanent feature of the political landscape; they are rather the results of an active and continuing set of productions that must occur each and every day (something Althusser suggests as well, at least obliquely). Thus any break in the circuit can bring down the whole edifice of power and authority that interpellation produces (which helps explain why very often long-lasting regimes collapse very quickly). The key to such breaks comes in getting at the entire edifice of circulation and not just with particular instances of its effects.

The moments that I have looked at—Haiti at the end of the eighteenth century, the colonial world at the end of World War I, Tunisia at the dawn of the Arab Spring—are all instances when, rather than disguising the way the chickens aren't pecking (to use Machiavelli's example), the whole apparatus of chicken-based augury is rendered visible and unworkable. In this way, misrecognition is rendered impossible, at least for a time. The figures I am interested in ruin the workings of the stories that support and reproduce interpellation. Sometimes they do this by accident but sometimes they do it deliberately, even if they are not always aware of what they are doing or why. If we think of Appius Pulcher as a model for disobedience and misinterpellation, then the question to ask is what can be done to make various interpellative narratives and circuits visibly unworkable or "incredible"? What is the narrative fabric that supports the current ordering and how can it be undermined and subverted? In this way the accidental begins to shade into the deliberate and we can see that one source of counterauthority is not a new external (a new lie to replace the old) but rather the actions and decisions of an individual or a community in responding against and in spite of the interpellative forms of authority that normally order us.

Conclusion: Murdering Michael Brown

Machiavelli's analysis of classical and renaissance forms of subjectivity and authenticity can also be applied more immediately to our own time. In doing so, we can think further about the way that interpellation continues to function and dysfunction in our contemporary context. At the time of this writing I witnessed the ongoing struggle in Ferguson, Missouri—and in the United States more broadly—over the police killings of black people. In the case of Ferguson, Darren Wilson, a white police officer, shot and killed an unarmed eighteen-year-old African American man named Michael Brown. At his grand jury testimony, which was meant to decide if Wilson should be put on trial for killing Brown, Wilson described Brown as having a face like a "demon." He said he felt like "a five year old holding onto Hulk Hogan" (even though he himself is quite large in stature).[78] In other words, Wilson spoke the magical formula that gets white cops exonerated; he turned Brown into an Angry Black Man and so was not charged (furthermore the prosecutor of the case was actively raising funds for Wilson, and the grand jury was given erroneous instructions in Wilson's favor).

Although the murder of unarmed African Americans by the police is a commonplace in the United States, this particular case of blatant injustice has not gone down easily. Activists in Ferguson have been rallying for well over two years now. And, in the wake of other such incidents such as the notorious strangulation of Eric Garner in Staten Island, a new movement rose to prominence: Black Lives Matter. In Oakland, activists shut down the freeway and at one point shut down BART service to San Francisco. There have been die-ins all over the country, black brunches, protests and agitation, and lots of organizing. New faces, many young and African American, have appeared on television to comment on events. More recently the city of Baltimore exploded in rage over the killing of another African American man, Freddie Gray (and even more recently yet, his killers have also been exonerated). And countless black women have been killed too; Sandra Bland was murdered in her jail cell in Texas. Tanisha Anderson was held down by Cleveland police and died. Yvette Smith, also from Texas, was shot to death by police while she was responding to their order to leave her home. Native Americans and Latino/as are similarly targeted and murdered with impunity. Anger and frustration are high but there is also a great deal of resolve.

As I read it, the rise of Black Lives Matter is also a moment of misinterpellation, a moment when the things that most people already know—that US policing is racist, that young people of color are moving targets, that the US court system does not provide justice—become too glaringly obvious to ignore, where the fabric of ideology begins to tatter and unravel. Rather than continue to accept an interpellation of young African Americans as "thugs" and "gangsters," Black Lives Matter asserts counteridentities. The ordinary scene of interpellation, Althusser's "hey, you there!," becomes, in the American context, a fount of murder and police brutality (a subject I will revisit in detail in chapter 6). In this instance, unlike the case of Mohamed Bouazizi, the response comes not from the subject himself (Michael Brown did not kill himself; he was murdered by Darren Wilson) but from the larger community of which he is a member and, in turn, to greater reactions yet from increasingly large and numerous segments of the population.

Black Lives Matter may or may not lead to the kinds of conflagrations that we saw in Tunisia. But either way, it is another moment, another chance for the circuits of interpellation to display their malfunctioning, their basis in nothing but their own assertion and projection, in displays of violence and acts of murder. More critically, it is a moment when alternative countersubjectivities and authorities can be demonstrated and produced.

If, as Machiavelli tells us, political authority is produced by reading signs, then we can argue for another way to read them. We can read Michael Brown's murder as a sign of the failure of interpellation, of the ethereal (and hence vulnerable) quality of projected (or stolen) authority, of the violence that such authority brings to those that it rules over. If the "message" to Michael Brown—his call if you will—was "we own your body; we invented and produced your subjecthood; we can and will take your life if we choose to demonstrate that power; your subjectivity is entirely in our hands," the response to that call by Black Lives Matter has been to refuse that power and that authority, to challenge and subvert it whenever and however possible. And that's the thing about interpellated authority; once a hint of its vulnerability—indeed, its nonexistence—becomes apparent, it becomes supremely vulnerable; the whole edifice that it produces can vanish in an instant. It can also (and generally does) remain largely intact; the workings of interpellation are renewed, as already noted, every day and everywhere. This is where strategies of refusal (like Pulcher's refusal to play by the rules of the Roman civil religion) come into play. The more misrecognition becomes impossible, the better.[79]

By refusing to accept that Black Lives Don't Matter, this movement is, not unlike the Haitian ex-slaves of the turn of the nineteenth century and the anticolonial agitators of the 1910s, along with the Tunisians taking part in the Arab Spring, working to make bogus liberal rights (which in fact disguise murderous intent) into forms of authority of their own design. Here too, the emptiness of the universal serves as the site upon which the realization of alternative forms of agency and subjectivity can become legible, if only partially and temporarily. There are, once again, no guarantees, but when we think of these events as occurring in constellation (to borrow a word from Walter Benjamin) with one another, we see how one act of resistance can bolster another, how, when read in tandem, they can collectively undermine and subvert interpellated authority in a way that no one moment can do on its own. In that regard, rather than simply focus on "great moments" of resistance, we can add every other moment as well, every small act of resistance and defiance. With the weight of all such moments, the apparatus of interpellation becomes that much more vulnerable; its monopoly on authority and subjectivity becomes that much more tenuous.

CHAPTER THREE

"TIENS, UN NÈGRE"

Fanon and the Refusal of Colonial Subjectivity

In looking at the life and writing of Frantz Fanon, the paradoxes of interpellation—and the ways to resist it—are all clearly displayed for us. Fanon is, on the one hand, the acme of a radical, full-throttled rejecter of colonialism and the phantasms of liberal (and colonial) subjectivity that have held so many others in captivity. Yet, at the same time, Fanon is very much a product of the West; his refusal comes from the perspective of a universal subject on whom the universe has closed its doors. Fanon received a classic French education in Martinique and was taught and believed himself to be French (ergo, in some sense, white) until he learned (was interpellated) otherwise. In his further education as a psychologist, and in his response to the injustices of colonialism—injustices that he was a firsthand witness to in Martinique, in France, in Algeria, and elsewhere—he evinces something of the same universalist tendencies that produced colonialism and its liberal capitalist variants in the first place. How can we think about this person as being both a product and an opponent of liberal authority along with its correlates of colonialism and racism?

What in Louis Althusser's case is a purely hypothetical situation with relatively disembodied beings (Althusser readily supplies a gender but few other aspects of the subject of the "hey, you there!") becomes, for Fanon, a situation that is all too tangible and literally unbearable, an absolutely personal experience; in his case, the misfirings of interpellation became too vivid to ignore. If the various calls put out by liberal capitalist and colonial authority are always racist, always dividing along lines of class and gender, in Fanon's case this fact is not just in his face, it is his face.[1] For Fanon then, the racism of the call does not so much ruin what would otherwise be universal and true (as a liberal would probably argue) but rather reveals that the call is ruined from the outset. It's not that Fanon is denied a subjectivity and right that white people get to enjoy (so that there *are* universal subjects just as long as they are white). It is rather that racism trumps the seductions of the call that others (i.e., white people) feel so that Fanon is not permitted even to go along with the phantasm. Prevented from taking on a subjectivity he feels he was meant to enjoy, Fanon is better able to see the subject for what it is: a projection, and a production. And it is precisely on these terms that Fanon attacks not just the false universality he is trapped within but even the subject position itself. Or, perhaps more accurately, as I will argue further in this chapter, Fanon shows how by insisting on holding to the subject position as such by an act of refusal (refusing, that is, the exclusion from the universal that is part and parcel of the "call" he receives) the formation of subjectivity is further destabilized. Fanon shows how the subject position's uncertainties and shifting bases can be used to create new forms of identity that challenge and unmake the false identities that subjects are normally called to be (and especially the particular forms of subjectivity for people of color).

The falsities of universal liberal interpellation have met their match in Fanon. In a system where even saying "no" is a way of acquiescing, Fanon's refusal challenges not only his own subjective position but also the position of all subjects. His challenge is a radical one; he refuses to not be the subject of the call.[2] He insists on standing in the contradiction (Rancière would say the dissensus) that the act of misinterpellation produces in him.[3] He won't allow the slinking away or papering over (misrecognition) that often accompanies being an excluded person in the face of liberal subjectivity (that is, the moving off from the call, the acceptance of being excluded from the universal even while the universal itself remains ostensibly valid). Instead, he seeks to destroy what he calls liberalism and colonialism's—for

Fanon these are completely intertwined phenomena—"psychoexistential complex."[4] Insofar as he is interior to this position—even as he is denied and excluded—Fanon turns his disadvantage into a way to do maximum damage to what would otherwise be a prison and a trap.

In this chapter, I treat Fanon first as a subject who is himself misinterpellated (in a way that is particularly legible) and then as a critic both of interpellation and subjectivity more generally. My argument throughout will be that Fanon demonstrates a set of strategies that serves to maximally damage the workings of liberal subjectivity; he is the misinterpellated subject par excellence, the one who best fulfills the promise of "another Abraham," a figure that God didn't intend to call but who showed up anyway.

"Look, a Negro!": Fanon's Subject Position

In *Black Skin, White Masks*, Fanon recounts what could be considered his critical moment of misinterpellation. This was a moment when a young white boy in Lyons, walking along with his mother spots him and calls out (not to him but about him), saying "Look, a Negro!" ("Tiens, un nègre!"). For Fanon—at least in the way he narrates an account of this moment in *Black Skin, White Masks*—this is a shattering event, the moment when he realizes the extent to which he is not in control of his subjecthood, how he is not who he thought he was. A narrative of race and colonialism has been superimposed on and over his own sense of self, even on—and in—his own body.

Fanon tells us that up to this moment in time, he was "satisfied with an intellectual understanding of [racial] differences."[5] He goes on to write that "it was not really dramatic. And then . . ."[6] That ellipsis introduces a new doubt or question into his narrative. Following this, Fanon goes on to write, "And then the occasion arose when I had to meet the white man's eyes. . . . In the white world the man of color encounters difficulties in the development of his bodily schema. Consciousness of the body is solely a negating activity. It is a third-person consciousness."[7] Fanon makes it clear what he means by a "bodily schema." He speaks of how he experiences his own bodily movements, how he reaches across a table for a pack of cigarettes, for example. He writes, "All these movements are made not out of habit but out of implicit knowledge. A slow composition of my *self* as a body in the middle of a spatial and temporal world—such seems to be the schema. It does not impose itself on me; it is, rather, a definitive structuring of the self and of the world—definitive because it creates a real dialectic between my body and the world."[8] Thus, for Fanon, the way he moves, his own sense of occupying his body and controlling his movements suddenly becomes no longer his own; a sense of his own bodily integrity is surrendered to an alien (third) consciousness.

The encounter with the white boy in Lyon (which happened when Fanon was a student at the local medical school) culminates or produces this sense of not being who he thought he was, not even being the body that he thought he (at least) had mastery over.

> "Look, a Negro!" ["Tiens, un nègre!"] it was an external stimulus that flicked over me as I passed by. I made a tight smile.
>
> "Look, a Negro!" It was true. It amused me.
>
> "Look, a Negro!" The circle was drawing a bit tighter. I made no secret of my amusement.
>
> "Mama, see the Negro! I'm frightened!" Frightened! Frightened! Now they were beginning to be afraid of me. I made up my mind to laugh myself to tears, but laughter had become impossible.[9]

This moment has effects that are initially completely devastating. For Fanon, the false subjectivity of his liberal persona is pierced, even as it is replaced with something much more tangibly false, a persona that is completely alien to Fanon even as it is insistently him. As Fanon goes on to tell it,

> The corporeal schema crumbled, its place taken by a racial epidermal schema. . . . I was responsible at the same time for my body, for my race, for my ancestors. I subjected myself to an objective examination, I discovered my blackness, my ethnic characteristics; and I was battered down by tom-toms, cannibalism, intellectual deficiency, fetichism [sic], racial defects, slave-ships, and above all else, above all: "Sho' good eatin' [Y a bon banania]."[10]

Just before he describes this scene, Fanon engages in a language that approaches the question of interpellation, of being called to who he was: "I thought that what I had in hand was to construct a psychological self, to balance space, to localize sensations, and here [with the scene with the young white boy] I was called on for more."[11]

Expecting one kind of call, Fanon gets another instead. Although he goes on to say, "All I wanted was to be a man among other men," he feels instead that he has experienced "an amputation, an excision, a hemorrhage that spattered my whole body with black blood."[12]

Fanon's response is incredulity. How is it possible that he, the subject of discrimination, is the one who is hated? He writes,

What! When it was I who had every reason to hate, to despise, I was rejected? When I should have been begged, implored, I was denied the slightest recognition [on me refusait toute reconnaissance]? I resolved, since it was impossible for me to get away from an *inborn complex* [*complexe inné*], to assert myself as a BLACK MAN. Since the other hesitated to recognize me, there remained only one solution: to make myself known [puisque l'autre hésitait à me reconnaître, il ne restait qu'une solution: me faire connaître].[13]

It is here that Fanon epitomizes the moment of refusal that is the hallmark of the misinterpellated subjects I looked at in chapter 2 (something that I will also speak about when I discuss Ellison and Coates in chapter 6). Fanon was seeking recognition. Yet when he received the call—in this case not "hey, you there!" but "look, a Negro!" [tiens, un nègre!] and not by an officer of the law but by a white child—it had the opposite effect of securing or establishing his subjectivity.

Rather than being destroyed or reduced by that experience, Fanon resolves to remain in the contradiction that is produced from such moments of false subjectivization. In this way, it could be said that Fanon is holding onto the only thing that could be said to be authentically *his*: the self-canceling position of misinterpellation itself.

Yet, the notion of "making [him]self known" is hardly a clear or self-evident path. As David Macey notes in his biography of Fanon, this idea is complicated by the fact that Fanon is also undertaking a project of self-knowledge.[14] Rather than simply asserting his "true" self (a demand made by the universal subject he still believes himself to be), Fanon must in effect produce and create a self in response to the self that has been imposed upon him, the one that blocks any actual form of recognition. In this way, "making [him]self known" becomes quite a complex project, one that I will explore further in this and the following chapters. It suggests a mode of counterrecognition that usurps the power and authority of the caller and takes that task and power on for the subject. We can therefore see that, in this instance, Fanon's refusal may indicate something about the refusal of the misinterpellated subject more generally. Fanon, in a sense, accepts the challenge of the call as if to say "I am not who you say I am, but I will take your false forms of recognition and turn it into something of my own choosing or making."

In his response, Fanon works his way out of a trap that the moment of recognition seems to bring; hailed as a subject ("look, a Negro!"), Fanon seems to have a false choice between acquiescence (hence his initial attempt at smiling and laughter, which didn't get him anywhere) and complete rejection (akin to one of the strategies Hannah Arendt attributes to the parvenu). But, as Fanon notes, he does not have the luxury of a straightforward rejection. His recognition is forced onto him from the exterior ("an external stimulus"). He cannot actually say no to this hailing. It is done without his involvement and yet he seems to be totalized by it.

Fanon recognizes that resistance to such an impossible demand (be what you are not!) cannot come from walking away: "my blackness was there, dark and unarguable. And it tormented me, pursued me, disturbed me, angered me."[15] There is no avoiding or averting the call; Fanon is already a subject, already predisposed to turn toward the call.

Therefore, Fanon takes the subjectivity he is given as a challenge; he seeks out a deeper mode of refusal that is not merely negative but is positive and self-asserting as well. After saying (as cited above) that he wants to "be a man, nothing but a man," Fanon goes on to write, "Some identified me with ancestors of mine who had been enslaved or lynched: I decided to accept this. It was on the universal level of the intellect that I understood this inner kinship—I was the grandson of slaves in exactly the same way in which President Lebrun [of France] was the grandson of tax-paying hard-working peasants. In the main, the panic soon vanished."[16]

Since he can't abandon the universe that traps him, Fanon seeks to engage with it, not by conceding defeat and being the person he is called to be, but rather by insisting on a radical equivalency (although this may not be the right word since Fanon always insists on his racialized difference as the basis for that equivalency), a literalizing of the empty universal formulas of liberal authority. Yet this is exactly what is impossible in liberal universalism. If, as I will argue further, racism is a break in the circuitry of mutual recognition that underlies interpellation, Fanon's insistence on being a subject who is black (that is, to call liberalism on its bluff or to insist that its lie is true) is an assertion of himself as being that break. By refusing to not be the subject of a call that was never meant for him, Fanon brings down the apparatus of interpellation, including the very subject position from which he chose to do battle.

In a sense, Fanon is able to conduct this battle precisely because he recognizes the ways in which the battle over recognition involves identities that are malleable and porous, always in transition and crisis. In his comments on *Black Skin, White Masks*, Homi K. Bhabha argues that Fanon's treatment of racial identity is not rooted in a concrete and historical narrative. Instead, Bhabha writes,

> There is no master narrative or realist perspective that provides a background of social and historical facts against which emerge the problems of the individual or collective psyche. Such a traditional sociologist alignment of Self and Society or History and Psyche is rendered questionable in Fanon's identification of the colonial subject who is historicized as it comes to be heterogeneously inscribed in the texts of history, literature, science, myth. The colonial subject is always "overdetermined from without," Fanon writes. It is through image and fantasy—those orders that figure transgressively on the borders of history and the unconscious—that Fanon most profoundly evokes the colonial condition.[17]

Thus the very unreality of colonialism suggests, for Fanon, a larger unreality, that of liberal subjectivity itself. In refusing to recognize the absolute reality—and hence inevitability—of colonialism, Fanon points both to the way that power systems create what passes for reality and the way that such a false reality can be challenged (that is, he notes both the resilience and vulnerability of liberal subjectivity and authority).

For Fanon, the very question of ontology is an ongoing battle, an attempt to lay claim over a deep structural support for existing power relations. On one level, ontology is something that is denied to colonial subjects. Still in *Black Skin, White Masks*, Fanon writes, "As long as the black man is among his own, he will have no occasion, except in minor internal conflicts, to experience his being through others. There is of course the moment of 'being for others,' of which Hegel speaks, but every ontology is made unattainable in a colonized and civilized society."[18] Here, it seems as if, for Fanon, ontology is this great universal truth, and that the problem with colonialism is that it offers the colonial subject an alternative and false version of reality. Yet Fanon goes on to offer that ontology itself is a weapon against people of color. Thus it is not a foundational basis for people of color (as it is for whites) but the very means for their alternative—excluded and inferior—form of existence. He writes,

> Ontology—once it is finally admitted as leaving existence by the way side—does not permit us to understand the being of the black man. For not only must the black man be black; he must be black in relation to the white man. Some critics will take it on themselves to remind us that this proposition has a converse. I say that this is false. The black man has no ontological resistance in the eyes of the white man.[19]

Lewis Gordon discusses Fanon's opposition to ontology, the way he reveals himself, once again, to be a dangerous foe to liberal forms of authority and subjectivity:

> Fanon's critical philosophy is a reflection upon Western society as his life-world ironically situates his thought within the specific Western matrix of existential phenomenological critique. As a radical humanist, however, he stands in critical relation to ontology. He rejects all ontology that puts existence to the wayside. . . . Philosophically, then, he demands a conception of the human sciences that rejects an ontologized nature. I offer the hermeneutical significance of bad faith, premised upon human beings as fundamentally open, as a clue.[20]

If ontology is the secret basis of "there is no alternative" (TINA), a way to shore up the power and irrefutable nature of European subjecthood even as it subdues and overwrites other sorts of subjects, Fanon's refusal of this notion suggests, once again, the way he is willing and able to stand in his contradiction, choosing openness (as Gordon offers) and contingency over fixed states of being (Kohn and McBride make similar arguments).[21] Yet Gordon admonishes us not to conclude that Fanon is accepting contingency for contingency's sake. He cites Fanon himself as explaining why this is not the case. In *Toward the African Revolution*, Fanon writes,

> I shall be found to use terms like "metaphysical guilt" or "obsession with purity." I shall ask the reader not to be surprised: these will be accurate to the extent to which it is understood that since what is important cannot be attained, or more precisely, since what is important is not really sought after, one falls back on what is contingent. This is one of the laws of recrimination and of bad faith. The urgent thing is to rediscover what is important beneath what is contingent.[22]

Rather than reading this as implying that Fanon believed in some kind of ontology after all—that is, "the important" that lurks beneath all the false appearances that constitute contingency—I read this passage as offering that even as he stands in the contradiction, even as he occupies the position of the misinterpellated subject, Fanon holds on to politics; he does not surrender either to the ipseity of ontology or the potentially endless fluidity of contingency. Rather, he seeks to establish his own form of agency in the face of all he is told to be and all that he knows he is not.

Importantly, Fanon distinguishes himself from Léopold Senghor and the négritude movement of his day. He certainly feels the seductions of this movement and, indeed, he even feels it as form of alternative interpellation: "From the opposite end of the white world a magical Negro culture was hailing me."[23]

For Fanon, négritude is a strategy of embracing the identity constructed by imperialists; in some sense, it is the equivalent of what Gayatri Spivak calls "strategic essentialism."[24] He writes, "Black Magic, primitive mentality, animism, animal eroticism, it all floods over me."[25] Here, Fanon is adopting what he perceives to be the voice of négritude. He is trying it on for size. But, in the end, he rejects it because he sees it as a trap, and one of white devising: "I had tried to flee myself through my kind, but the whites had thrown themselves on me and hamstrung me. I tested the limits of my essence; beyond all doubt there was not much left of it."[26]

Fanon goes on to describe his dilemma more clearly: "Every hand was a losing hand for me. . . . I made a complete audit of my ailment. I wanted to be typically Negro—it was no longer possible. I wanted to be white—that was a joke. And, when I tried, on the level of ideas and intellectual activity, to reclaim my negritude, it was snatched away from me."[27] Thus, Fanon discovers that one can neither simply say "no" or "yes" to colonial subjectivity. As with the earlier discussion of being good or bad subjects, colonial forms of interpellation have him predetermined, whether coming or going.

Fanon also differentiates himself from Jean-Paul Sartre. He quotes Sartre's *Orphée Noir*, where Sartre critiques négritude as being a pure negative and therefore "insufficient by itself . . . a means and not an ultimate end."[28] In response, Fanon writes, "For once, that born Hegelian [i.e., Sartre] had forgotten that consciousness has to lose itself in the night of the absolute, the only condition to attain the consciousness of self. In opposition to rationalism, he summoned up the negative side, but he forgot that this negativity draws its worth from an almost substantive absoluteness."[29] In this way, neither négritude nor Sartrean philosophy escapes from the kind of absoluteness that comes from colonial/enlightenment thought. "Not yet white, no longer wholly black, I was damned. Jean-Paul Sartre had forgotten that the Negro suffers in his body quite differently from the white man."[30]

Thus, for Fanon there is no getting beyond the condition of the colonial subject; the break in the circuitry of recognition that comes from colonialism cannot be resolved or sidestepped by recourse to seeking to co-opt it (like négritude) or denying it (like Sartre). To Aimé Césaire and Léopold Senghor, Fanon is perhaps not black enough. For Sartre, he is perhaps too black, too rooted in his body and his experience. After discussing a "crippled [presumably white] veteran of the Pacific war" who advises Fanon's brother to "resign yourself to your color the way I got used to my stump,"[31] Fanon writes,

> Nevertheless with all my strength I refuse to accept that amputation. I feel in myself a soul as immense as the world, truly a soul as deep as the deepest of rivers, my chest has the power to expand without limit. I am a master and I am advised to adopt the humility of the cripple. Yesterday, awakening to the world, I saw the sky turn upon itself utterly and wholly. I wanted to rise, but the disemboweled silence fell back upon me, its wings paralyzed. Without responsibility, straddling Nothingness and Infinity, I began to weep.[32]

Here we see better the nature of Fanon's refusal. This may seem like a moment of defeat but when we consider Fanon once again as the misinterpellated subject par excellence, we can read this situation differently. Fanon's courageous act is to refuse both the essentialism of négritude and the implied transcendence of Sartrean notions (with a great deal more empathy for négritude than Sartre himself demonstrates). Experiencing himself as "a soul as immense as the world," Fanon will fight the universal—the world—on its own terms, occupying a position that he is explicitly denied. If all sides would like him to pick a side (an "authentic African," a "human being and nothing more"), Fanon refuses. His refusal is the stance of misinterpellation. He seeks not the resolution of his status but the irresolution of the very question that assigns him this status, and so his refusal goes much deeper than simple rejection (in the same way that one cannot just be a "bad"—and rejecting—subject and leave it at that). Fanon no longer seeks a transcendent humanism that lies beneath the false categories of race. Rather he seeks to reimagine himself and his circumstances in a way that offers him a role in determining what he is and what he is to become. In other words, he seeks to politicize his subjectivity, taking its very impossibility (he is a black man who has decided to act like the universal subject he was never meant to be) as a basis for altering his subject position and, potentially, the subject positions of every one who receives a call that isn't meant for them. Fanon takes on the responsibility of deciding for himself what his blackness is and means and in that way he both refuses and stands in his given subject position.

"The Negro and Hegel"

In the penultimate section of *Black Skin, White Masks,* entitled "The Negro and Hegel," Fanon further considers the condition of the colonial subject as one who desires recognition above all. He begins the section by writing (after quoting Hegel himself), "Man is human only to the extent to which he tries to impose his existence on another man in order to be recognized by him."[33] This could be said to be the essence of interpellation, the basis for the mechanisms of power and authority. Alluding to Hegel's famous consideration of the master-slave relationship, he writes that "there is not an open conflict between white and black. One day the White Master, *without conflict*, recognized the Negro slave. But the former slave wants to *make himself* recognized."[34] This language echoes Fanon's earlier point of "mak[ing him]self known." In the original French, he seeks in the first instance to "me faire connaître."[35] In the latter he writes, "Mais l'ancien esclave veut *se faire reconnaître.*"[36] In the space between being known (connaître) and recognized (reconnaître), we find the terrain of Fanon's subject position. Asserting the circulation of authority that is the basis for interpellation, Fanon writes that "if I close the circuit, if I prevent the accomplishment of movement in two directions [or recognition between the self and the other], I keep the other within himself. Ultimately, I deprive him even of this being-for-itself."[37]

Thus, this circuitry is necessary, Fanon writes, "the other is waiting for recognition by us, in order to burgeon into the universal consciousness of self. Each consciousness of self is in quest of absoluteness."[38] Yet, ultimately, Fanon concludes that this Hegelian system of recognition requires conflict. Resistance to the process is required to make desire, which in turn propels the subject forward. Thus, "Human reality in-itself-for-itself can be achieved only through conflict and through the risk that conflict implies."[39]

This, for Fanon, is where race comes into play for it allows an allocation of winners and losers in the struggle for recognition where one sort (the whites, the winners) can take on the risk of freedom without too much peril because they know that they will achieve a form of recognition that is explicitly denied to people of color. Thus, the false sense of equivalency, the universality of the liberal subject, disguises the requirement for hierarchy and domination: "The Negro is a slave who has been allowed to assume the attitude of a master. The white man is a master who has allowed his slaves to eat at his table."[40] Even the two verb forms used here "has been allowed" versus "has allowed" reveals the degree to which agency is really only possible for the white subject.

Fanon describes the freedom that was given to black slaves as "reach[ing] the Negroes from without. The black man was acted upon."[41] Here, he is presumably not talking about the Haitian slaves who freed themselves but the more ordinary means of being freed by white decree.[42] This is a kind of post hoc form of recognition.

For Fanon, such a form of externally derived freedom is not freedom at all; what is given can also be taken away (to the extent that "it" exists at all).[43] The freedom of the person of color in such cases is not the same as white freedom. It is a false dance of recognition designed to only instill recognition for the former masters. Here, the equivalency established between black and white serves only for the benefit of the latter and the appearance of a circulation masks a de facto one-way street.

Speaking very much to the peculiar subject position of the misinterpellated subject fighting within the confines of a liberal universal, Fanon writes, "The Negro knows nothing of the cost of freedom for he has not fought for it. From time to time he fought for Liberty and Justice, but these were always white liberty and white justice; that is, values secreted by his masters."[44] If the colonial subject merely takes on the values of the authority figure that appears to call her (but does not), then she is doomed to live in a false appearance of rights and justice, which is designed to deny her precisely those things; this is the nature of the liberal universal. In the face of this pseudo equality, Fanon writes that "the white man tells [the black man]: 'Brother, there is no difference between us.' And yet the Negro knows that there is a difference. He wants [a difference]."[45]

Here, we really get to the heart of Fanon's refusal. He does not want to become white even if he could do so (becoming white seems to be the only way he could ever get access to what the universal promises him). He "wants [a difference]" to remain as a black man and only a black man in the face of false universal subjecthoood. In seeking to remain black but a subject nonetheless, Fanon demands not inequality, but the rupture of the false equality that holds him or her in servitude long past the time when slavery and colonialism are formally ended. Decolonization struggles not just against such oppressive expressions of power and violence but is waged against interpellation itself.

In the face of this, and of the various false choices that present themselves to Fanon, he opts for neither "yes" nor "no" but both and, thereby, in a sense, neither. This is the stance of refusal. Fanon writes,

> I said in my introduction [to Black Skin, White Masks] that man is a yes. I will never stop reiterating that. Yes to life. Yes to love. Yes to generosity. But man is also a no. No to scorn of man. No to degradation of man. No to exploitation of man. No to the butchery of what is most human in man: freedom. Man's behavior is not only reactional. And there is always resentment in a reaction. Nietzsche had already pointed that out in The Will to Power. To educate man to be actional, preserving in all his relations his respect for the basic values that constitute a human world, is the prime task of him, who, having taken thought, prepares to act.[46]

Here we see a bit more clearly what it means to refuse, to stand in the contradiction that represents the position of the misinterpellated subject (the one who says "yes" and "no" at the same time). Fanon seeks to replace ontology and inevitability with politics. He seeks to contend with false choices by wreaking havoc with the mechanism that installs the choice in the first place. Above all, Fanon seeks to take the subordinate subject position he has been forced into and turn it against the very submission it is meant to instill in him. Insofar as blackness represents a break in the circuitry (a site from which recognition only proceeds unidirectionally), Fanon uses this break as a weapon to wield against the functioning of the entire interpellative apparatus.

Fanon concludes Black Skin, White Masks by fully embracing this subject position because it involves real risk. This is opposed to the ostensible risk in Hegelian recognition, which turns out not to be a risk at all (not a risk for the white subject who is guaranteed recognition and not a risk for the black subject either who is guaranteed to be denied recognition, receiving a grotesque mockery of it instead). The risk that Fanon takes on does not condemn him to randomness and the absence of all values. He uses the very detested bases of European society—its circulation of authority and recognition—as a way to derive values that are nonetheless not tied up with that tradition. Another way to say this is that Fanon uses the forms and consistent patterns of interpellation—the repeated grammars of address, the expected responses—as a way to engage with contingency without risking collapse. He does this even as the substance of interpellation—the built-in hierarchy, the unidirectional forms of recognition that it produces, the inherent racism of its forms of authority—is exposed and ruined.

Near the end of his conclusion, Fanon tells us, "I should constantly remind myself that the real *leap* consists in introducing invention into existence."[47] This nicely encapsulates the way that invention—really self-invention: "me faire connaître"—interacts with whatever passes for reality or lived experience ("L'expérience vécue du Noir"). His final line reemphasizes this point when he writes, "O my body, make of me always a man who questions [un homme qui interroge]!"[48] Embracing contingency and risk, Fanon allows for choice and possibility and a space, finally, for politics that is impossible so long as the game of recognition remains fixed and unalterable.

In this way, Fanon reclaims his subject position, reappropriating and repurposing it as we saw the Haitian rebels, the anticolonial subjects, and the Tunisian underclass do in the previous chapter. They too take a stance of refusal instead of mere rejection. They too attack, not just the surface of their oppression, but its roots in a form of subjectivity based on (false) universal principles. They too assert their own subaltern status as a weapon against the very inclusion that they are promised but denied by liberal forms of interpellation. But what happened in those cases through a complex mixture of accident and canniness comes here, in Fanon's case, through a kind of purposive resolve.

Fanon helps to resolve the tension described in the last chapter between the semicompromised elite subjects of misinterpellation (the Toussaint Louvertures, *ilustrados*, Wellington Koos, and Lajpat Rais of this story) and the subaltern subjects who are further removed from the European enlightenment. He shows how an engagement with European subjectivity does not have to reproduce the damned-if-you-do and damned-if-you-don't mechanisms of interpellation as it is usually practiced. Fanon's analysis of the racial politics that underlie interpellation reveals, perhaps more clearly than any other argument, how interpellation is always "getting it wrong," how, whether the subject is white or black (if we limit ourselves to this binarism), there is no real recognition going on, just a rigged system. Fanon shows that it is not a matter of "getting interpellation right;" to argue this would, once again, only be to reproduce liberal phantasm in a new guise. To think in this way still holds in what liberalism "could be" if it were not distorted by racism and so forth. Fanon fully recognizes that liberalism and its values are rotten to the core but he also sees this rot as offering a way to avoid the very traps that liberalism has set for him. If some revolutionary leaders are compromised, at least to some extent by their buy-in to enlightenment thought (in terms of how they engage with capitalism and liberal ideas of subjecthood), Fanon shows how to avoid this outcome, how to refuse absolutely. In this way, the cleavage that we could see in the previous chapter between elites and subalterns is not as inevitable, not predetermined by the arrangements between those who would resist interpellative authority.

The Politics of Misinterpellation

In thinking about resistance to colonial forms of subjectivity, Fanon begins to show us a way out of the trap of interpellation, a way to claim and hold a misinterpellated subject position. What he works out in his earlier work, such as Black Skin, White Masks, he develops further in his later writing as he continues to engage both as a writer and as a political leader in his fight against the interpellative power of colonialism. In a sense, one could argue that interpellation itself is a form of colonialism (perhaps even for Fanon the primary, or at least most intractable, form) wherein a false subjectivity is mapped onto (colonizes) a person, rendering them subjects, but for Fanon this experience is redoubled by the actual experience of colonialism so that the colonial subject suffers, as if it were a double subjectification.

In order to think about the fight that Fanon brings against such a form of colonization, we can take one final passage from Black Skin, White Masks (one that was previously referred to in part) as indicating the forward direction of Fanon's later work. Early in Black Skin, White Masks, Fanon writes, "I believe that the fact of the juxtaposition of the white and black races has created a massive psychoexistential complex. I hope by analyzing it to destroy it."[49] This could be considered to be Fanon's statement of purpose or battle plan. His talk of "analyzing" suggests a familiarity and engagement with what is being resisted. It also suggests critique and strategy. The destruction of this "psychoexistential complex"—from within and by its own tools—does not merely serve the purposes of nihilism and rage (although Fanon has often been accused of acquiescing to these goals). Rather, it serves to interfere with the interference that suppresses and reduces other forms of counterinterpellation. Removing or disturbing the edifice of false authority and subjectivization makes these other forms of address and calling not so much possible—since they have always been present—but rather able to function with a relative lack of distortion. "Destroying" the psycho-existential complex means, once again, occupying the subject position of misinterpellation, of recognizing—and thus ruining—the misrecognition that accompanies every moment of establishing interpellative authority.

If *Black Skin, White Masks* begins this task, Fanon's magnum opus, *The Wretched of the Earth*, develops it further, along with some of his other works, such as *A Dying Colonialism* and the aforementioned *Toward the African Revolution*. It is in these later works that we see more fully the political upshot of Fanon's development of the position of the misinterpellated subject. While there are times when Fanon's language of new forms of identity, liberation, and revolution can seem less helpful to our contemporary predicament insofar as they are a product of a struggle that has now morphed into much more convoluted encounters with liberal power and authority, considering his work from the perspective of misinterpellation allows us to read Fanon anew.[50] We can consider his language and program in terms of how they inflict maximal damage onto forms of identity that have otherwise survived countless upheavals, revolutions, and daily acts of defiance. Furthermore, I would add that Fanon's focus on the struggle against colonialism, while it too may seem bound by a history that is specific to his own time, is in fact highly relevant, even critical, for the current struggle because the circulation of interpellative authority continues to reproduce the patterns that Fanon himself identified at the time of his writing (once again, principally along racial lines). Here again, we can see how colonialism has never ended; it continues its operations to this very day.[51]

A Proper Rhythm

Early on in *The Wretched of the Earth*, Fanon reiterates a point that he makes many times in *Black Skin, White Masks*. He writes, "It is the colonist who *fabricated and continues to fabricate* the colonized subject. The colonist derives his validity, i.e., his wealth, from the colonial system."[52] Here again, we see the perils of recognition, how subjectivity is given in such a way as to maximize the profit and benefit of the colonial master at the expense of both the colonial subject's livelihood and even her identity. Accordingly, Fanon tells us further that

decolonization never goes unnoticed, for it focuses on and fundamentally alters being, and transforms the spectator crushed to a
nonessential state into a privileged actor, captured in a virtually gran-
diose fashion by the spotlight of History. It infuses a new rhythm,
specific to a new generation of men, with a new language and a new
humanity. Decolonization is truly the creation of new men. But such
a creation cannot be attributed to a supernatural power: The "thing"
colonized becomes a man through the very process of liberation.[53]

There's a lot to unpack in this statement. The colonial subject, via the process of decolonization itself, becomes "a privileged actor," a subject who
has the power and authority always promised by liberal theory but who has
been denied any modicum of such agency until this moment. I'd go even
further (although Fanon doesn't explicitly say this) and argue that the decolonized subject gets an agency that no liberal subject, whether colonized
or colonizing, receives (the former because of the reasons Fanon has already stated; the latter because they are acting as agents of liberalism itself, driven by its siren calls and phantasms). This idea of misinterpellated
agency is something that I will expand upon in the subsequent chapters of
this book.

Fanon also states that through the process of decolonization—which, as
I have tried to argue in the last chapter, can be itself in some sense a product
of misinterpellation—the subject acquires a "new rhythm." In the original
French, the term is perhaps yet more telling: "un rythme propre" means
something more like "a rhythm of their own," or perhaps (more loosely) "a
rhythm that is fitting for their own situation."[54] This suggests, as in the previous discussion of recognition, that the decolonized subject ceases to receive someone else's rhythms, or identities. This does not necessarily mean
(and Fanon would certainly not be the kind of writer to suggest this) that
the new subject finds their "authentic" or true self at last, buried under the
layers of colonialized subjectivity. To think that is to tend more toward the
ideas of négritude that Fanon was attracted to but did not ultimately accept.
Rather, a "proper rhythm"—which is how I would finally suggest translat-
ing the term—aligns with the subject's own particular context, with their
struggle and self-assertions, and with their political expression.

Fanon completes this thought when he argues that "the 'thing' colonized
becomes a man through the very process of liberation." Fanon's use of the
term "man" for "person" (in the original French as well) reflects the sexual

politics of his time. It also may suggest that Fanon himself was not immune to the kinds of divisions that he believed decolonization might serve to overcome. But we also see here that the "process of liberation" is itself the means by which a "proper rhythm" comes to the subject. This is another example of what I have earlier been referring to as countercircuits or counterinterpellation. This constitutes other assertions of identity and subjectivity that, although no more true or authentic than the false identities fomented by liberalism, have the virtue of coming from and through the communities in question (communities that are de facto excluded from the universal), reflecting more local, or at least anti-universal, forms of identity and agency in the process.

The Colonized Intellectual and Authenticity

In this reading, the struggle of decolonization becomes a struggle with the very "ontological" bases, by which the European has constructed colonial subjectivity. While, as already argued, this construction takes on different valences at various levels of colonized society, the factor that unites the various forms of contesting ontology is a way of coming to terms with—and moving on from—this legacy. In his chapter "On Violence," the first chapter of The Wretched of the Earth, Fanon himself brings up the specter of the intellectual or elite leader of the struggle for decolonization and the way that person is much more bought into the phantasms of Western authority and beliefs than the subaltern subject. He writes,

> In its narcissistic monologue the colonialist bourgeoisie, by way of its academics, had implanted in the minds of the colonized that the essential values—meaning western values—remain eternal despite all errors attributed to man. The colonized intellectual accepted the cogency of these ideas and there in the back of his mind stood a sentinel on duty guarding the Greco-Roman pedestal. But during the struggle for liberation, when the colonized intellectual touches base again with his people, this artificial sentiment is smashed to smithereens. All the Mediterranean values, the triumph of the individual, of enlightenment and Beauty turn into pale, lifeless trinkets. All those discourses appear a jumble of dead words. Those values which seemed to ennoble the soul prove worthless because they have nothing in common with the real-life struggle in which the people are engaged.[55]

Thus, for Fanon, the solution to the problem of the colonized intellectual's attachment to Western thought and universal ideals is to connect with their own people (that is, to choose, fashion, and love their own blackness) as they collectively struggle with the product and result of such thinking and acting. Alternative subjectivities are then a kind of group project, a counterinterpellative set of maneuvers with which to compete with the "universal" subjecthood that colonial intellectuals otherwise are forced to contend with.

There may be quite a bit of autobiographical reflection in comments like these on Fanon's part. He himself was, after all, a Western-trained intellectual who writes in French and who quotes from Sartre and Hegel and Lacan. In some ways, it could be argued that, in writing *The Wretched of the Earth*, Fanon is in part negotiating within himself the struggle with the universalism that he is a product of.[56]

Fanon goes on to list individualism as the first and most pernicious of the universal values that the intellectual must let go of. "The colonialist bourgeoisie hammered into the colonized mind the notion of a society of individuals where each is locked in his subjectivity."[57] This is indeed the product of interpellation; isolated, the colonized intellectual is picked off one by one ("hey, you there!"), "locked" in an identity that is not of his or her devising.

Individualism, and the subjectivity that it brings with it, is, of course, the hallmark of interpellation. The notion of the individual forces the subject to be what the colonizer wishes her to be. Fanon sees that with the end of individualism, we also have "the destruction of all [the colonized intellectual's] idols: egoism, arrogant recrimination, and the idiotic, childish need to have the last word."[58] Against this false—indeed "idol[atrous]"—agency, Fanon asserts that the intellectual must hear other calls, calls between and among the community. In this way he or she "will . . . discover the strength of the village assemblies, the power of the people's commissions and the extraordinary productiveness of neighborhood and section committee meetings."[59]

Fanon also states that "self-criticism has been much talked about recently but few realize that it was first of all an African institution. Whether it be in the *djemaas* of North Africa or the palavers of West Africa, tradition has it that disputes which break out in a village are worked out in public. By this I mean collective self-criticism with a touch of humor because everyone is relaxed, because in the end we all want the same thing."[60] This kind of experiential development allows the intellectual access to the "proper rhythms"—the alternative forms of calling—that come along with decolonialization and misinterpellation. As the intellectual "sheds all that calculating, all those strange silences, those ulterior motives, that devious thinking and secrecy," Fanon tells us that in this way "the community has already triumphed and exudes its own light, its own reason."[61] In other words, as the circuitry and interpellation of European colonialism recede, other forms of address (the call of the *djemaa*, the palaver) are allowed to take a more prominent role. I once again do not read Fanon as arguing that traditional forms of African subjectivity are simply meant to arise in the place of false European ones (otherwise we'd just be back with négritude once again), but rather that they provide resources; these founts of counterinterpellation serve to displace the power and centrality of European interpellation even as they also allow a positive and political project to move forward. They choose, once again, to be not the false black subjects—or other subjects of color—that liberalism tells them they are (even as they are told that they are also universal subjects), but the black subjects they themselves have become through their resistance to liberal and colonializing forms of interpellation. Their value comes not from their "authenticity," but rather from the shared and collective political and economic experiences that they encounter in the population, especially in terms of being acts of mutual resistance. By interfering with the interference of interpellation, they offer a counterinterpellation that multiplies and complicates the colonial subjects' sources of hailing and recognition.

Furthermore, if we once again think of interpellation itself as a form of deep colonization, a colonization in this case not of land but of subjects at the level of the psyche, then the anticolonial struggle mirrors an internal form of decolonization as well. The intellectual learns not the content of that struggle (since there is no "true" or "authentic" form that it takes) but rather that the form, the act of refusal itself, is a training in reconstituting the self from its colonized (i.e., interpellated) status. In this way, for Fanon, it is not so much a matter of "native (i.e., African) and authentic" versus "alien (i.e., European) and false," but rather a distinction between those notions and circuitries that produce a kind of communal empowerment versus those that do not. As already noted, for Fanon, the local and African community can exert "its own light, its own reason": ideas that are nominally European can be taken over by the decolonializing power. The struggle is, indeed, for Fanon a dialectical one and nothing is deemed either pure and original or polluting in its own right.

In an earlier writing, I argued that Fanon's calls for violence were meant not just literally—although they were often meant in that way as well—but also in the sense of standing for a dramatized break with existing thoughts and practices.[62] For Fanon, the notion—as opposed to the actuality—of violence serves to render unavoidable the break, the radical rupturing, of all existing compromising entanglements for the colonized subject. For Fanon, it often seems that for subaltern colonial subjects, violence generally serves practical ends—and probably allows them a modicum of revenge as well—but for colonial intellectuals in particular, the idea of violence forces a real break with a system that they are intimately connected to. With violence, there can be no fence sitting, no reformism or trying to have it both ways (a real and ongoing temptation for many intellectual colonized subjects in Fanon's view).

When we read Fanon as a misinterpellated subject, we can align his calls for violence with the larger function of misinterpellation itself, providing a clear and legible cessation of interpellative circuitry. As I've argued, this struggle, for all of Fanon's seeming Manicheanism, is not really about a clear demarcation. Insofar as reality itself and the source of recognition involved are caught up with European colonialism, it is, once again, not just a matter of rejection, of saying "no" to Europe and all that it stands for. The universality that Europe promotes, however false, encompasses—and even produces—the colonized subject, no matter how much they resent or resist it. And so the struggle with the universal, and with colonialism as a whole, is much messier and more intimate than the idea of a simple rejection would suggest (especially at the level of the colonial intellectual, that is to say at Fanon's own level). Violence, then, is Fanon's answer to ensure that, despite the ongoing deep entanglement that is a feature of the decolonializing struggle, there is no further temptation to hold onto false values and ideals. Violence serves to make that temptation less or even impossible.

If misinterpellation is itself a moment of rupture with given forms of subjectivity violence is an instrument in the hands of the misinterpellated subject to ensure that such a rupture goes further and deeper, becomes undeniable and unfixable going forward. For Fanon, violence is not the exclusive domain of the struggle for decolonization—clearly the colonizer engages in a lot of violence too—but the difference between these practices lies in the way that, for the colonizer, violence only serves to preserve the status quo, the papering over and misrecognition that accompany the interpellative processes of colonization. For the colonized, on the other hand, violence can be just as empty—Fanon writes that, under conditions of colonization, "we have seen that this violence . . . runs on empty. . . . We have seen it exhaust itself in fratricidal struggle"—even as it can also be generative.[63] Yet violence, in his view, can also propel and deepen a radical moment. He thus writes, "The challenge now is to seize this violence as it realigns itself," that is, to align these acts that dramatize the break with the past toward the kinds of collective and local responses that come out of the struggle against colonialization.[64]

On some level, Fanon's calls for violence are eminently practical. In the face of the extreme violence that is routine and ordinary in the practice of colonialism itself—practices that hide under the disguise of a universalism for which "violence" and "savagery" are terms reserved for the colonized subject only—Fanon's own call for violence only seeks to fight fire with fire. Thus, he writes,

> In fact the colonist has always shown them the path they should follow to liberation. The argument chosen by the colonized was conveyed to them by the colonist, and by an ironic twist of fate it is now the colonized who state that it is the colonizer who only understands the language of force. The colonial regime owes its legitimacy to force and at no time does it ever endeavor to cover up this nature of things.[65]

When it is "realigned," with revolutionary purpose, for Fanon, the violence of the colonized subject helps to expose and even elicit the brutality of the colonialist regime. It also serves, as previously noted, to force certain elements of colonized society—the intellectuals, the national bourgeoisie—either out of their collusion with the colonizer or at least to clearly declare themselves to be open enemies of the popular struggle.

Yet, along with all of these pragmatic reasons—ones that are tied up far more with the actual practice of violence—I think that for Fanon violence serves most of all as a way to address the deep hold that the psychoexistential complex has on the colonized subject as such. As Walter Benjamin argues in "Critique of Violence," violence is not just about hitting and shooting people.[66] Far more deeply, violence is about imposing false forms of agency and subjecthood onto people. The real violence of the state for Benjamin lies in the way that the state arbitrarily asserts its right over and above a population that it ostensibly serves, the way it dominates and produces ontology itself. Read in this way, the process of interpellation itself is an ultimate act of violence.

Thus, although Fanon's calls for violence can once again certainly be read literally—and I think that Fanon had no problem with actual acts of violence as such, although, as a psychologist, he was also keenly aware of the damage that such acts inflicted not only on the victim but also on the perpetrator—they can also be understood in a context in which the violence of the colonial subject can be read as a counterviolence, an engagement with and extension of misinterpellation. Fanon says, at one point,

> It so happens that for the colonized this violence is invested with positive, formative features because it constitutes their only work. This violent praxis is totalizing since each individual represents a violent link in the great chain, in the almighty body of violence rearing up in reaction to the primary violence of the colonizer. Factions recognize each other and the future nation is already indivisible. The armed struggle mobilizes the people, i.e., it pitches them in a single direction, from which there is no turning back.[67]

We can see some of the misinterpellative work that violence does for Fanon in this passage. Rather than being a purely negative and reactive feature—as it can be when it is simply spontaneous or in response to some atrocity of the colonizer and nothing more—"this violence is invested with positive, formative features." In saying that such violence constitutes the community's "only work," Fanon also alludes to the way that agency can be derived from this kind of collective action. This is, once again, not the faux agency of liberal colonialism, whereby the colonized subject literally can't do anything at all. This violence *does something*; it moves the community past its own false formations and produces new possibilities and new subjectivities for its practitioners. Whereas Fanon states in a passage just prior to the one cited above that "the arrival of the colonist signified syncretically the death of indigenous society, cultural lethargy, and petrification of the individual," through violence, the individual is drawn back into a collective, into a "proper rhythm"—and calls of its own—that is of their own action and their own devising.[68]

Another way to think about this is to say that, for Fanon, violence, whether literal or metaphorical, politicizes the subject and moves her into a different path. Critically for Fanon, violence erases the kinds of hierarchies that exist within a community and which are themselves largely the product of European interference of division and conquest:

> Even if the armed struggle had been symbolic, and even if they have been demobilized by rapid decolonization, the people have time to realize that liberation was the achievement of each and every one of them and no special merit should go to the leader. Violence hoists the people up to the level of the leader. . . . When they have used violence to achieve national liberation, the masses allow nobody to come forward as a "liberator."[69]

We see here that, as with misinterpellation more generally, for Fanon, violence can produce an anarchic response (although he does not use that particular language). Violence can remain to some extent on a symbolic level, even as he also talks about violence as a "praxis"; it is not literally true that each member of the community must engage in acts of violence but rather that the violence of the struggle itself can serve to form new communities out of the ruins of the old.[70] In these communities, once the struggle produces a sense of political agency, this is not readily surrendered back to some new figure who replaces one set of authoritative interpellations from above (i.e., colonialism) with another (i.e., some kind of internally produced elite that takes power in the name of the struggle). If we think of violence and the struggle somewhat interchangeably—or at least as being deeply mutually implicated—then we see that both are part of the process that for Fanon breaks the circuitry of colonialism, an extension of the break he himself epitomizes when he insists on asserting a subjectivity that was never intended for him.

Fanon addresses this possibility for violence quite directly when he writes the following:

> [Members of a community] prove themselves to be jealous of their achievements and take care not to place their future, their destiny, and the fate of their homeland into the hands of a living god. Totally irresponsible yesterday, today they are bent on understanding everything and determining everything. Enlightened by violence, the people's consciousness rebels against any pacification. The demagogues, the opportunists and the magicians now have a difficult task. The praxis which pitched them into a desperate man-to-man struggle has given

the masses a ravenous taste for the tangible. Any attempt at mystification in the long term becomes virtually impossible.[71]

For Fanon then, perhaps most critically of all, violence reflects his desire that tangibility and self-assertion are no longer a creation of the colonizers. In order to render the members of the colonized community agents, in order to arm them against the various seductions of power and authority that have no real basis (are the product of "a living god"), Fanon would transfer that ability to struggling people in all of their variety. If tangibility and ontology are themselves up for grabs for Fanon, capable of being produced by the most base and self-interested sources—such as colonialism—they can also be produced by individual persons acting in a collective capacity and this is, in his view, what collective acts of struggle and violence can do for a given community. This too is the upshot of refusal.

In this way, violence, for Fanon, can enforce a kind of recognition for the colonial subject after all. What is recognized is no longer the faux dead-end subjectivity offered to her by the liberal universal but rather a self-assertion in the face of that subjectivity, a recalibration of the processes of recognition more generally.[72] Here, the unbalanced and false symmetries of recognition as it is produced out of the context of interpellation becomes something else entirely, not the "resolution" of liberal forms of recognition but rather a complete break with such practices. The subject who emerges out of this process of decolonization is now recognized—or at least not misrecognized—because the colonizer has no choice but to do so (and on the terms of the misinterpellated subject herself). To cite Tunisia's former dictator Ben Ali once again, he says "I have understood you" to the Tunisian revolutionaries only after he is literally forced into such an understanding.

If we continue to read Fanon through the lens of misinterpellation, in thinking about more effective and better uses of violence, Fanon is also, thereby, thinking of more effective strategies to extend and surpass the moment of misinterpellation itself. Violence can be read as his name for the kinds of positive and agentic outcomes that result from struggle, the product of an initial act of refusal. Violence here becomes the way that misinterpellation can be turned from something accidental and occasional—at least on the surface; as I've already argued, misinterpellation in its deeper sense is built into the structure of interpellation and occurs at every moment that interpellation does—into something far more deliberate and effective just as it operates for Fanon himself.

If Fanon's considerations that a people, having engaged in violence, could prove themselves to be immune to the blandishments of new "living god[s]," new idols who could replace the old gods of colonialism, seem off the mark (given what was then to occur in Algeria, among countless other places), his reading of the possibilities for violence can be taken to mean that, at the very least, people have a fighting chance not to succumb to an endless process of authoritarian—and colonizing—interpellation. Fanon is asserting that it is possible to break the circuitry of interpellation—it is, of course, also very possible to fail to do so—no matter how much it seems to be absolute and grounded in ontology, no matter how much it seems to be fated (a subject I'll pick up again in chapters 4 and 7). In this way, Fanon gives us a glimpse of how misinterpellation can be rendered far more prevalent, far less reactive, and generally a practice that allows people to forge new paths and new—and proper—rhythms. In doing so, Fanon reminds us that we have no guarantees, that guarantees themselves are the stuff of colonialism and "living god[s]." Against the certainties that colonialism presents—the certainty of eternal rule by the French, the certainty of the futility of struggle by Algerians and Martinicans alike—we get something radically different, the absence of any sure ending (happy or sad) at all. This lack of guarantees and certainties constitutes the "promise" (if we can call it that) of misinterpellation.

Thinking about the Future

Fanon is not as bloodthirsty as he is often imagined to be.[73] He writes of a "vertigo" that comes over the revolutionary when he realizes that he is killing actual human beings.[74] Indeed, he argues that bloodthirstiness can be the unraveling of the very revolution that he seeks:

> Racism, hatred, resentment, and "the legitimate desire for revenge" alone cannot nurture a war of liberation. The flashes of consciousness which fling the body into a zone of turbulence, which plunge it into a virtually pathological dreamlike state where the sight of the other induces vertigo, where my blood calls for the blood of the other . . . this passionate outburst in the opening phase, disintegrates if left to feed on itself.[75]

Here, Fanon is distinguishing between violence per se and vengeance, a particular and, in his view, insufficient form of protest and resistance.

Fanon recognizes the ways that such forms of violence can be dangerous for a revolution. Such forms of violence simply reproduce the Manicheanism that violence more generally is otherwise a remedy for.

In his comments on the nature of revolution and, in particular, the Algerian revolution, Fanon was well aware that the formulations that he proposed might go awry, were going awry, in fact. The plan he put forward for resisting and subverting the European universal was a dangerous and narrow path. The very tools that he saw as potentially producing a real break with past practices and beliefs—violence very much included—could readily become a part of that earlier fabric, becoming part of old and bad rhythms. In the same way, Fanon's appropriation of liberal values such as freedom and agency—his seizing of these forms of address via his acts of refusal—risks, as already noted, transferring authority from old colonial gods to new ones. Fanon's goal is the proper alignment (or realignment) of revolutionary action, the achieving of "proper rhythms" and this, it turns out, is a singularly difficult task.

In his musings on the Algerian revolution in *A Dying Colonialism*, for example, Fanon recognized some of the excesses and unfortunate acts of his fellow revolutionaries. It is to Fanon's credit that he didn't become a simple propagandist, one who never admitted that anything ever did or could go wrong. He acknowledges that the Algerian fighters had done terrible things. Although he writes, "No, it is not true that the Revolution has gone to the lengths to which colonialism has gone,"[76] he also states,

> But we do not on this account justify the immediate reactions of our compatriots. We understand them, but we can neither excuse them nor reject them. Because we want a democratic and renovated Algeria, because we believe that one cannot rise and liberate oneself in one area and sink in another, we condemn, with pain in our hearts, those brothers who have flung themselves into revolutionary action with the almost physiological brutality that centuries of oppression give rise to and feed.[77]

In such considerations, we see that the risk and contingency that Fanon embraces are just that. There is, once again, no guaranteed happy outcome and, in fact, the odds may even be against the revolutionaries. Yet the tools and strategies that he offers remain valid whatever the outcome of his particular struggle, not only for open cases of opposition as was the case in the Algerian revolution, but for all forms of struggle on the individual and collective level against the usurpation of authority by interpellating—and colonializing—powers.[78]

The Voice of Algeria

Much of *A Dying Colonialism* (whose title in French is *L'an cinq, de la révolution Algérienne*, i.e., "Year Five of the Algerian Revolution") is devoted to thinking about various institutions in Algeria—the role of women, the family, radio and "the voice" of the Algerian people—and the way they can be transformed into something new and unprecedented (even while retaining some connection to the past, including the precolonial past). Some of this writing is controversial. Fanon's writing about Algerian women and the veil, for example, has come under criticism by some feminist authors, ranging from Assia Djebar to Winifred Woodhull.[79] His writing about Algerian radio is less controversial but, I would venture to say, it is especially telling about the path that Fanon would have the revolution take and—to put it in my own terms—the way that misinterpellation can be enhanced and strategized.

Under conditions of French colonialism, Radio-Alger was developed as part of the colonial apparatus. It was essentially an instrument of French propaganda, serving in particular the settler colonial population, and, as Fanon notes, many Algerian families who could afford a radio didn't actually bother to buy one. The radio itself was seen as Western technology and part and parcel of the colonial apparatus. In short, radio in prerevolutionary Algeria was a call that was not attended to, at least not by the subject population. He tells us that "Algerian society, the dominated society, never participates in this world of signs."[80] For Fanon, this began to change in the late 1940s as independent and postcolonial broadcasting stations were set up in Syria, Egypt, and Lebanon. Thus, "the Algerian who read in the occupier's face the increasing bankruptcy of colonialism felt the compelling and vital need to be informed."[81] With this need for information—which the settler population had in droves—Fanon tells us that the general Algerian populace began to perceive the need to counter the lies of the French with "acted truth[s]," that is, statements of what the resistance was doing.[82]

In this way, the question of truth itself, of what constituted facts and reality, became a contested ground in Algeria. Furthermore, by appropriating the medium of radio that had always been redolent of European power and control of information, this mechanism ceased to work in the same way in terms of how it was received by the general population. Fanon writes,

"*Because it avowed its own uneasiness, the occupier's lie became a positive aspect of the nation's new truth.*"[83]

We see here a great illustration of the way that the complex encounter with French universalism can lead to outcomes that are unexpected and novel (Fanon calls them "essential mutations").[84] This is a case of reproduction gone wrong and hence is itself a form of misinterpellation. This may be especially evident in the case of radio because it is a material object, a technology that lends itself to thinking in terms of semiotics, to the war over meaning and truth that lies at the heart of the Algerian revolution. Unchanging in its physical and technological form, the radio nonetheless offered a way for Algerians to find their own voice, their own access to speech and "truth" that had until then been the exclusive province of the colonizer. In terms of its potential for countercircuitry, Fanon writes that, thanks to the innovation of Algerian radio,

> almost magically—but we have seen the rapid and dialectical progression of the new national requirements—the technical instrument of the radio receiver lost its identity as an enemy object. The radio set was no longer a part of the occupier's arsenal of cultural oppression. In making of the radio a primary means of resisting the increasingly overwhelming psychological and military pressures of the occupant, Algerian society made an autonomous decision to embrace the new technique and thus tune itself in on the new signaling systems brought into being by the Revolution.[85]

Whereas a veritable battle raged among the urban settler intelligentsia over which papers could or would be read, for an Algerian, reading a left French paper like *L'Humanité* or even *Le Monde* was tantamount to declaring open rebellion. The fact of widespread illiteracy made the radio a far more decentralized and horizontal source of information. When the Voice of Algeria began broadcasting in 1956, the inventory of radios sold out instantly.

Part of the radicalizing nature of radio lay in the fact that, as the French started to jam the signal, Algerians began an intense process of distributing information about how to get around this signal jamming and when to listen and at what frequency. The very fact of this endeavor suggested that it was not so much the content of Algerian radio that was vital but rather the involvement, the collective action, and the politicization of everyday life (where even buying batteries became a political act). Indeed, Fanon writes that given that it became increasingly hard, and even dangerous, to listen to the radio, "claiming to have heard the *Voice of Algeria* was, in a certain sense, distorting the truth, but it was above all an occasion to proclaim one's clandestine participation in the essence of the Revolution. It meant making a deliberate choice . . . between the enemy's congenital lie and the people's own lie, which suddenly acquired a dimension of truth."[86] Fanon goes on to say that the radio signal was like the revolution itself: " 'in the air' in isolated pieces, but not objectively."[87] He also calls this a "true lie."[88] In this way, we see that the question is, once again, not of a choice between truth and lies per se but rather between a call that comes from without (a call with all of the falsities that comes along with it) versus a more horizontal and local (or at least not universal) call, a counterinterpellation meant to expose and ruin the workings of colonial subjectivity.[89] Here, Fanon borrows the language of the European enlightenment (in this case "truth") and turns it into something utterly different, not a value that affirms the universal but quite the opposite, an endeavor whose grounds of reality or truth are shifting and contingent without being any less powerful.

Similarly, as Fanon tells it, via the transmission of radio, even the French language—that ultimate instrument of French universality—was appropriated and subverted by the Algerian revolutionaries. Insofar as some of the transmissions, such as the emission "Fighting Algeria," were in French, this served to "liberate the enemy language from its historic meanings."[90] Whereas French was up until then largely the language of domination, insult, and oppression, it became another aspect of Algeria's own self-creation as it was appropriated and thus "the French language also becomes an instrument of liberation."[91]

Through these kinds of refusals and reappropriations of discourse, for Fanon, via radio, the failures of colonial interpellation were not only made more evident (as the tools of that interpellation began to become appropriated for various forms of counterinterpellation) but undeniable, another form of recognition by force. By taking on their own voice, the Algerian revolutionaries were able to "tell [the Algerian subject] *explicitly*" about the changes that were happening.[92] Rather than simply occupy the subject position of various interpellative sources, the Algerian revolution, as Fanon tells it, employed a form of self-creation, asserting itself by virtue of its own insistence on speaking and being heard, a counterrecognition of the dominant forces that it was created in response to. Perhaps most critically of all, this countercall was uttered in the same manner and by the same technology (sometimes even in the same language) as the oppressive interpellating language it was undermining. In this way, it hijacks the authority of such power and uses it to unmake and subvert what it mimics.

The upshot of this story is that, for Fanon, nothing is inherently oppressive or revolutionary; it is all in the way that something is perceived and handled, the way it is used and the way that it is engaged with. Fanon plays fast and loose with enlightenment categories like ontology that normally ground and anchor a discourse, making it mean one thing only. Instead, he politicizes the various components that make up human life: speech, action, violence, and the material world and objects that we surround ourselves with. This is a delicate balancing act and Fanon acknowledges times when it fails, when the appropriation falls back into looking too much like the unidirectional forms of agency that are the hallmark of colonialism in his telling.

We see then that the Algerian appropriation of the radio might signal a larger and more positive agenda that comes out of struggle. By its nature, the radio is not an entirely decentralized medium. It is generally a one-way signal, something to be received (the modern Internet is, of course, much more interactive). At the same time, as Benjamin indicates, radio has a radical potential based in its particular technology. Insofar as the listener has the power to switch channels or easily turn it off, radio does not command attention in the way that theater or cinema does. Given the way it empowers the listener, Benjamin writes that it potentially produces a reversal of the presumed hierarchies between broadcasters who are "in the know" and the audience who passively accepts that knowledge. Under certain conditions, Benjamin writes that radio can produce the "audience on its side, as experts. And nothing is more important than that."[93]

This possibility seems to have been borne out in Algeria over the course of its revolution. In this case, radio reveals itself to be more of a collective endeavor after all. Whereas, for the French, the radio truly was unidirectional, for the Algerians it became an instrument of their own self-assertion, their coming together as a community with a voice of their own in ways both real and imagined (with both variants being equally powerful and participatory). Here too the Voice of Algeria is a form of refusal. It is a refusal to cede language and access to the colonizing power, a refusal to slink away or not be a speaking subject in its own right. In the story of Algerian radio, we see a manifestation of the inward journey that Fanon sought in himself as well as the outward trajectory he sought for oppressed subjects of colonization everywhere.[94]

The story of Algerian radio is illustrative of a larger pattern of collective actions that can come out of struggle. It shows a forward direction for Fanon that derives from a more collective and deliberate form of misinterpellation. Fanon himself did not live long enough to see the ultimate result of the Algerian revolution. Most speculate that he would have been bitterly disappointed by the outcome.[95] Yet, as with the other stories that I have told in this book so far, the lack of a happy ending does not mean that we should cast aside any chance for a practice of misinterpellation that multiplies and extends resistance. There is no promise of happiness, only the possibility of nondetermination and Fanon achieved that much (as did Algeria, although it quickly succumbed to new forms of determination).

Even if Algeria was ultimately unsuccessful in continuing on that process, even if it succumbed to new "living gods" who replaced the old colonial rulers, the process of struggle itself was, in its very existence, a refusal of the notion that things can never be other than what they are. In addition to his own refusal to slink away from the scene of interpellation, his refusal to try to abandon his blackness in favor of a faux whiteness or to turn to a faux blackness to make peace with whiteness, Fanon adds something that is just as critical, if not more.[96] He offers, perhaps in a way that is unmatched by any other thinker or subject of misinterpellation, a fully thought-out understanding of how to enhance and multiply its effects, how best to find the "proper rhythms" and countercircuitries that collectively produce an alternative that is both viable and sustainable. He shows that misinterpellation, although it is a product and a form of failure, can be what Peter Fitzpatrick calls a "productive" failure.[97] It can allow a plethora of identities and agencies, a cacophony of calls to emerge, formed out of resistance and struggle, that is to say, out of politics. In the face of his sense of amputation by being forced to be black, Fanon responds by "assert[ing himself] as a BLACK MAN." This might be the most revolutionary (and, in some sense at least, the most violent—or counterviolent—thing he writes). As noted previously, in doing this, Fanon takes the very form of subjectivity which prevents him from accessing the universality he has been promised and refuses to cede it; instead, he turns blackness into an identity of his own devising, something that comes out of struggle rather than something that is forced onto him.

For all of this, there remains in Fanon a great deal of anxiety about the future and the direction of revolutionary transformation; even if he didn't know where the Algerian revolution would end up, he articulated many of the dangers that would ultimately befall it. As Kohn and McBride argue, Fanon fears that the acts of imagination involved in repurposing agency and subjectivity under colonial conditions threaten to undermine the very enterprise of self-determination. They write,

> The revolutionary mobilization is dependent upon two things, imagination and direct antagonism. Both of these dynamics can end up going horribly awry. The imagination of victory, or complete empowerment and solidarity, can even create the fantasy that it would be possible to return to an idyllic pre-colonial past. . . . The revolutionary struggle produced a new kind of imaginative reality in which fantasies of complete empowerment replaced the colonial fantasies of complete control.[98]

Thus there always remains the danger that with success the centrality of failure, of resisting and distorting phantasm, will be replaced with some other newer variant of interpellation, a new form of pseudo agency. This suggests once again that refusal is not a once-and-for-all act but an ongoing requirement. For Fanon, self-determination is a very thin reed, a dangerous balancing act between resistance and assertion, materiality and imagination. Still, he was willing to take that risk. Indeed, he felt that such risk was mandatory insofar as he thought it absolutely necessary to avoid—as best as one can, even if partially and temporarily—a future dominated by the phantasms of the past, present, and future.

With this reading of Fanon, I now transition from a consideration of misinterpellation as an actual practice to a more theoretical, philosophical, and literary consideration of the possibilities of misinterpellative subjectivity. In some ways, however, this reading of Fanon has already begun to set us along this path of inquiry. Fanon suggests the possibility for an enhanced process of misinterpellation, a way to further the exposure of the misfiring and misfunction of existing systems of authority and, just as critically, a way to think about what a politics of misinterpellation looks like, what kinds of new forms of life the misinterpellated subject might produce. Turning to philosophy and (in the chapters that follow the one on Nietzsche) literary and filmic figures does not mean to abandon the political nature of misinterpellation. Rather, it allows us to engage in thinking about resistance in ways that are markedly representative and hence available for the kinds of stark and dramatizing tendencies that help bring misinterpellation—and its resistant possibilities—to our attention in the first place. It thus continues, albeit in a different form, the work we already saw with Fanon of engaging with politics on a deeper, more subterranean, level, which, I would argue, is essential for any political project to move beyond the occasional or accidental forms of resistance that we usually find ourselves limited to (and by).

PART II. THE ONE(S) WHO SHOWED UP

CHAPTER FOUR

"[A PERSON] IS SOMETHING THAT SHALL BE OVERCOME"

The Misinterpellated Messiah, or How Nietzsche Saves Us from Salvation

Throughout the last few chapters, I discussed the notion of alternative forms of agency and subjectivity, those that arise when the circuitry of interpellation—of business as usual—is subverted or altered. In this, the second part of this book, I wish to discuss the nature of this other agency, of how it differs from liberal doctrines and what kinds of subjects emerge from the processes of misinterpellation. I also want to look at how such a subject can further expose—and wreck—the workings of interpellation even as she remains part of the failure of and resistance to that order. To make this argument, I leave behind my discussion of actual world events and people—the Haitian revolution, the anticolonial movement, the Arab Spring, the life and works of Frantz Fanon—and move to a more philosophical and literary (and filmic) basis (although in chapter 6 I will return to "the real world" in the form of a treatment of Ta-Nehisi Coates's *Between the World and Me*). But I want to be very clear that, in doing so, I am not trying to leave politics behind. Indeed, the value of turning to literary and filmic works (as well as philosophical ones) is that the explicitly representational nature of these texts renders the operations of representation more vivid than they are in a "real" life case. It is precisely because literature and film both concern themselves with the nature and functioning of representation that they readily lend themselves to illustrations of how ideology works (and also doesn't work), how calls are performed and received and resisted. In the chapters that follow, I will argue that the subject that emerges from misinterpellation is multiple and anarchic; the agency that comes from subjectivity is collective and decentralized. I will principally examine six literary and filmic characters: Herman Melville's Bartleby in "Bartleby, the Scrivener" and Virginia Woolf's Lily Briscoe in *To the Lighthouse* (in chapter 5); Franz Kafka's Karl Rossmann in *Amerika*, Ralph Ellison's narrator in *Invisible Man*, and Coates's narrator (himself) in *Between the World and Me* (in chapter 6); and Lars von Trier's Bess McNeill in the film *Breaking the Waves* (in chapter 7). I examine these various characters in order to think about the nature of agency and subjectivity when it has been markedly decentered and complicated by the operations of misinterpellation. Although, from the position of our own interpellation—that is, from our perspective within the realm of liberal subjectivity—these characters may seem passive, crazy, angry, and/or detached, I will argue that in fact these subjects are what agency looks like when perceived through the distortions of our own false forms of agency and subjectivity. Whereas they often seem inert and/or out of control, these subjects have choice and power in a way that other characters in the literary and filmic works they are portrayed in do not. These subjects are what emerges when the misinterpellated subject refuses to slink away or to give up the possibility of her own subjecthood, when she stands her ground and, in doing so, upends all the certainties and conventions of subjecthood in the process.

Reading these texts and films helps us to think more about the "yet more minor literature" that I referred to in the introduction. This is a practice of reading against the grain, against what the text insists it is saying, against the characters we think we are supposed to be paying attention to (or what we are supposed to think about them). In this sense, the practice of reading I am describing here is itself a form of misinterpellation, of "not getting the reading right," of misunderstanding (often deliberately) the "clear" message of the text, giving us access instead to the undertext(s) that normally would escape our attention.[1] Another way to say this is that we read against the misrecognition that text normally performs for us. Here, our attention is always on the socially peripheral characters (although they are not always peripheral to the plot); it is an attention to—and an affection for—the outcasts and losers, generally the ones whom we would never want to be but who are (nonetheless) the people who show up when a call is put out.[2] These characters, akin to that least fortunate of Abrahams discussed in the introduction, serve as stand-ins for ourselves, for our own subjectivity that is never what we want it to be (we are never the people we'd like to show up when answering the call of authority and subjectivity). Reading literature and film in this way is therefore helpful because it allows us access to an identity and way of being that we normally do everything we can to avoid thinking about (i.e., that we misrecognize).

But before I can discuss these characters and this style of reading, I must first offer up a messianic figure who makes such agency possible, a figure whose very conception allows for the kinds of subjective defiance we see in these novels, short stories, and films. In this chapter, therefore, I discuss Friedrich Nietzsche's messianism, arguing that he offers us a vision of a misinterpellated (or misinterpellating—sometimes it is both at once) messiah, one who makes our own misinterpellation apparent to us. This is no ordinary messiah, of course. Whereas most messiahs are meant to save us, as I shall show, Nietzsche's messiah abandons and betrays us. If this messiah saves us, it is only from salvation, from the sense that we need to be redeemed (that is, interpellated "correctly"). Insofar as we have seen, via Judith Butler, how, even for Louis Althusser, the roots of interpellation are theological, we require a countertheology in order to unmake the teleologies and other traps that produce our contemporary subject position. Nietzsche supplies us with such a countertheology. He allows us to fight the fire of the stealth theology that underlies interpellation—the very theology that Butler espies in Althusser himself—with the fire of a messiah who exposes and ruins that process. In an earlier writing I called this Nietzsche's "cruel messianism."[3] It is cruel because it must destroy our hope for salvation, for a whole identity that is "really" us. Without this cruelty, we might retain some hope for redemption and, if we did, we would remain subject to interpellation; the subversive potential of our misinterpellation would not be realized.

As I will show in this chapter, Nietzsche takes us through several and repeated complicated maneuvers in order to deliver us from deliverance (in the following chapters I will argue that Woolf and Ellison do the same thing). He must betray not only the formal functions of the messiah (which is relatively simple to do) but something far more entrenched; he must betray the reader's own deep and stealth (misrecognized) desire to be delivered by some authority—especially, in this case, the author him- or herself—that goes to the core of our (interpellated) subjectivity. In other words, he must betray the way the text is meant to give us an answer, the way it produces a series of expectations and unacknowledged teleologies that we ordinarily both want and obey.

Nietzsche's betrayal comes, as I will explain, via a series of moves wherein he raises our hopes for salvation, only to dash them. We find messiahs within messiahs in his work. If Nietzsche the author can't save us—he tells us repeatedly that he can't and he won't—perhaps his character Zarathustra can do so. Zarathustra acts and talks so much like Jesus, perhaps he is the textual messiah—or at least prophet—that we have been looking for in vain up till now. When Zarathustra is, in turn, revealed—as I will argue further—to fail to redeem us, Nietzsche has one last card up his sleeve. If Zarathustra can't save us, perhaps the overman can. The overman is, after all, the messiah that Zarathustra promises us. Surely this mystical and nebulous figure is the messiah at the heart of Nietzsche's work. Yet, as I will argue, even this final and deepest messiah proves to be a failure and a disappointment (as he must); this is a messiah who turns out to definitively *not* be the messiah that we thought he was, not the one whom we'd like to show up to answer our own calls for salvation. Showing up nonetheless this messiah comes and, by taking the place of the messiah we expect, he ruins messianism for us, rendering us once and for all on our own with no further hope for redemption (at least until Nietzsche starts up the whole round of hope and betrayal again).

This is the cycle that I explore in the pages of this chapter. The levels of deepening disappointment and abandonment peel back our layers of authorization and our sense of being called. In this way, Nietzsche's textual maneuvers unmake our formation as interpellated subjects. These levels represent what we must ourselves pass through as we insist on our own right to answer calls that are not (and never were) meant for us but which we respond to nonetheless; here, we cease to respond to the call of the author and respond instead to other calls, other voices (and authorities) that become apparent to us via these acts of authorial betrayal.[4]

What emerges at the end of this process is more than disappointment. It is a kind of collapse of subjecthood. What remains is the basis for the subject who can finally discover *amor fati*, the love of one's fate. When false visions of our fate and destiny (the entire apparatus of interpellation) fall away, we can discover what fate is and can be for us when we are finally and only what we are.

In the previous chapter, I described how Fanon argues that "man is a *yes* . . . but man is also a *no*."[5] In writing this, Fanon cites Nietzsche as an authority on the yes and the no and their relationship to human action and possibility. In particular he tells us that for Nietzsche "there is always resentment in a *reaction*."[6] In other words, the no produces a kind of yes and, conversely, the yes itself is connected to the no. In this entanglement, we see something that is foundational for Fanon and Nietzsche both. For each thinker there is a way that we can never be entirely free of what is being struggled against. There are desires and lures that connect the yes and the no; we are drawn in by the deliciousness of resentment, the lure of hope, the seductions of subjectivity.

If there is one difference between these thinkers—on this subject anyway—it is a question of the intensity of that entanglement and of the degree to which we can emerge from it at all. For Fanon, as we saw, we are condemned to permanent struggle but that struggle is itself a means, if not of freedom then at least of nondetermination. For Nietzsche, however, this struggle is complicated by a much higher degree of complicity with what is being struggled against. Part of this might be due to the fact that, unlike Fanon, Nietzsche does not deal with the question of race (except in ways that are generally problematic). Nietzsche's subject does not face the dead-end status of Fanon's subject of color, which leads to Fanon's turn to refusal (I'll write more on this distinction in chapter 6). The hopes and allures of interpellated forms of subjectivity play more strongly to a subject who has some chance (if only symbolically) of access to the promises that are the hallmark of liberal universalism.

Even so, in recognizing the need for "yes" as well as "no," Fanon too acknowledges something of this entanglement both in himself and in the colonial—or postcolonial—subject more generally. If Nietzsche doesn't speak directly to the experience of this subject, he nonetheless offers a way of engaging with the hidden desires that are never completely broken off from, even in Fanon's formulation.

Accordingly, in order to describe the descending levels of disappointment that are employed to reduce and disrupt the subject's complicity—at whatever level that occurs—with an interpellating authority, let me begin with Nietzsche the author. Nietzsche frequently warns his readers not to follow him too closely, not to slavishly hang on his every word. He is famous for being outrageous, off-putting. Even this performance may be intended to serve to break the reader from the habit of textual obedience.

Yet, amid his outright warnings, Nietzsche also practices a more subtle form of textual distancing, of abandoning his authority (and, in the process, his readers as well). One critical way that he does this is by figuratively dragging his readers up and down the highs and lows of his text. Throughout his writing, Nietzsche practices a kind of manic-depressive circuitry of hope and failure. Such cyclicality may reflect Nietzsche's own personality (perhaps too his own mental state), but it also suggests a rhetorical device that serves to elicit our hopes only to dash them decisively. This may be seen throughout not only *Thus Spoke Zarathustra* but also in other works such as *The Genealogy of Morals* (the other main work, along with *Ecce Homo*, that I draw on in this chapter). These authorial highs and lows, function, I will argue, as a way to elicit the readers' hopes—not just those on the surface but our deepest hope too—and ruin them one and all.

Frequently this cycle of hope and ruination occurs around the theme of messianism, as if, in speaking about the messiah, Nietzsche knows he will trigger the reader's innermost hopes for redemption (hopes that are otherwise covered over by much more ordinary desires and wishes). In terms of his messianic language, sometimes Nietzsche raises our hopes and dashes them within a single sentence, sometimes even within a single word. For example, in the First Essay of the *Genealogy*, after he describes how Christianity is the end product of the "tree trunk of Jewish vengeance and hatred,"[7] Nietzsche speaks of "Jesus of Nazareth, the gospel of love made flesh, the 'redeemer,' who brought blessing and victory to the poor, the sick, the sinners."[8] By calling Jesus the "redeemer" (with quote marks in the original German as well ["Erlöser"]), Nietzsche raises our hopes (a redeemer!) and dashes them (with scare quotes).[9] We get excited by the promise of a messiah but is Nietzsche saying that Jesus is a redeemer or not? If the scare quotes are too subtle, we see that later in the *Genealogy*, at the end of the Second Essay, Nietzsche speaks of a "true Redeemer" (without quote marks in the original or translation [*der erlösende Mensch*]).[10] The implication here seems to be that by leaving off the quote marks, we have the juxtaposition of a false "redeemer" and a real one (a redeemer full stop). Thus he writes,

At some future time, a time stronger than our effete, self-doubting present, the true Redeemer will come. . . . This man of the future, who will deliver us both from a lapsed ideal and from all that this ideal has spawned—violent loathing, the will to extinction, nihilism—this great and decisive stroke of midday, who will make the will free once more and restore to the earth its aim, and to man his hope; this anti-Christ and anti-nihilist, conquerer of both God and Unbeing—*one day he must come.*[11]

This is the height of Nietzsche's redemptory tone; surely this "man of the future" is who we are looking for, the one, finally, we want to be called or interpellated by. Surely he is the one who "really" knows who we are (and by that knowledge, the one who transforms us into the subjects we were always "meant" to be). Here, Nietzsche's own perverse negativity seems to work in his favor; after Nietzsche has shredded all of the other would-be messiahs, surely the one *he* offers is the right one. We are, therefore, maximally tempted by this form of antimessianic messianism. And yet Nietzsche complicates this moment by speaking of this figure as "this great and decisive stroke of midday." This notion (which is a recurring theme in many of Nietzsche's works) reflects back to the very beginning of the *Genealogy* when, after telling us that "we knowers are unknown to ourselves," Nietzsche compares the subject to "a man divinely abstracted and self-absorbed into whose ears the bell has just drummed the twelve strokes of noon [and who] will suddenly awake with a start and ask himself what hour has actually struck."[12] This passage encapsulates the experience of being a misinterpellated subject in a nutshell; we hear a call (in this case, the strokes of the clock), but we aren't sure if it is "for us," that is, we know it is saying something—we know that it is telling us the time—but we do not know what it is saying, how the message relates to us. Still, we hear that call and try to answer it anyway. Another way to think about this image is to say that it represents us in our current predicament; so fixated are we on "knowledge" in general that we have lost the ability to experience the present as such. We have lost the noontime hour, the present moment that we occupy.[13]

Thus, when Nietzsche speaks of "the man of the future" as someone who is "this great and decisive stroke of midday," we see that the future is, in fact, now, already here. The figure of the man of the future is only us, in all of our mundane and banal existence.[14] But insofar as we are bereft of that knowledge—the knowledge of ourselves—our actual present exists for us as a kind of mythical sublime status, a "height" that is, in fact, no height at all and a future that is only now. The figure of the man of the future serves both as a reminder of what we are promised that we can be as well as a potential way to derail such a realization (thus not that different from speaking of a "redeemer" after all). Here, Nietzsche uses the lures of futurity and betterment as a way to force us into a cruel act of self-recognition. Like a bullfighter, Nietzsche waves a red cape before our eyes (a messiah! A future!). When we lunge for it—as we inevitably do—the cape is swept away, revealing nothing underneath. But this is not a true nothing, for what we are left with is ourselves, delineated and made apparent by the absence of those things that we thought "really" made us who we are but that turn out to be nothing at all.

By simultaneously showing us the devices by which we are fooled and then employing those very same devices on us, Nietzsche is not just telling us what to beware of (although he does plenty of that as well); he is also training his readers, at least potentially, testing and tempting them to see if they can possibly break from the bad habit of seeking salvation from any source, including—or especially—from him.

In raising our hopes only to dash them, Nietzsche does indeed leave us disappointed but such a response—as well as the cruelty of the author that is required for this kind of disappointment—is in fact a prerequisite for the reader to learn how not to be led along by any authority, even as anti-authoritarian an author as Nietzsche himself. Were Nietzsche to simply say "rely only on yourself!" we would be in effect gaining our self-reliance by fiat, by authorial command.[15] This would only reconfirm the way we need some external source (an authority) to tell us what to do. For us to really read and think—and act—on our own, we first need to be broken as obedient subjects. Indeed, in disappointing us so deeply and cruelly, Nietzsche is challenging not just our beliefs but our subjectivity too; by doing so much damage to our basic beliefs and motivations, he is in effect remaking us as disappointed subjects. In other words, he is bringing on our experience of misinterpellation, calling our attention to the fact that we are not the person that we'd like to be when we receive the call of law and subjectivity, even as we are the person who shows up anyway.

Perhaps this discussion helps to illuminate what Nietzsche means when he writes in the *Genealogy of Morals* that, "as regards my *Zarathustra*, I think no one should claim to know it who has not been, by turns, deeply wounded and deeply delighted by what it says. Only such readers will have gained the right to participate in the halcyon element from which it sprang, with all its sunniness, sweep, and assurance."[16] Reading this through the lens of an author who seeks to disappoint his readers (an antimessianic messianism or an anti-authoritarian author[ity]), the "halcyon element" that Nietzsche promises is only available after one has been "deeply wounded" by Zarathustra (and "delighted" too). When we have been so wounded, we recognize that the halcyon heights are in fact not heights at all; they are, once again, just where we are, here and now, ourselves after we have been put through the wringer by Nietzsche's textual contortions (achieving what Nietzsche calls that great "noontime"). Here, we can already begin to see how Nietzsche is trying to lead us toward "*amor fati,*" toward a self-recognition that surpasses all the false forms of recognition that he battles if only because it is not so much "true" as simply present and available, a quality not shared by other aspects of subjectivity that come through the usual channels of interpellation.

Betrayed by the Prophet

By a similar token, and as already noted, Nietzsche's great prophet Zarathustra is also depicted as someone who promises a lot and delivers nothing. As with Nietzsche himself, Zarathustra often warns his disciples not to trust him and also tells them not to follow too closely in his path. Quite famously he tells his followers at one point, "Now I bid you lose me and find yourselves; and only when you have all denied me will I return to you."[17] This kind of straightforward claim of abandonment—or request to be abandoned—is fraught insofar as it seems to promise a payoff in the end (if you abandon me, then you'll *really* get something good out of me). The kind of teleological guarantee this implies, wherein you must pass through something terrible in order to get redemption, is redolent of the very kinds of false salvations that *Thus Spoke Zarathustra* is so deeply opposed to. But, as I'll argue further, it is not quite that simple; Nietzsche seems to be telling us that if we deny him now we will get him back but perhaps in a form that we would never expect or ask for (or even want). Read through the lens of misinterpellation, this passage suggests that Nietzsche *will* deliver a messiah but one of a very peculiar—and quite possibly undesirable—sort. (It is certainly undesirable from the standpoint of our interpellated subjectivity.)

Furthermore, in the way that Nietzsche depicts the actions of Zarathustra, we see him practicing the same cycle of promise and abandonment as the author does himself. While he promises plenty, Zarathustra delivers less than nothing; he actively takes things away.[18]

We see this perhaps most clearly in a chapter called "On Redemption." There, Nietzsche offers us a vision of his prophet who, coming upon a group of afflicted people, is asked, like Jesus, to heal them:

> When Zarathustra crossed over the great bridge one day the cripples and beggars surrounded him and a hunchback spoke to him thus: "Behold, Zarathustra. The people too learn from you and come to believe in your doctrine; but before they will believe you entirely one thing is still needed: you must first persuade us cripples. . . . You can heal the blind and make the lame walk; and from him who has too much behind him you could perhaps take away a little . . ."
>
> But Zarathustra replied thus to the man who had spoken: "When one takes away the hump from the hunchback one takes away his spirit—thus teach the people. And when one restores his eyes to the blind man he sees too many wicked things on earth, and he will curse whoever healed him. But whoever makes the lame walk does him the greatest harm: for when he can walk his vices run away with him—thus teach the people about cripples."[19]

This may seem cruel (and it is) but Zarathustra explains—however cryptically—why he won't be saving anyone.[20] He offers that if he takes away the "hunchback" (or whatever other affliction) he takes away the person's "spirit." That is, by saving these people he would be confirming them in their self-hatred; removing—or fixing or adding—something makes them other than they were, hence confirming that they really *are* the horrible people they imagine themselves to be; they really do need salvation to become something other than what they are.

Here we see an added dimension to interpellation that might not otherwise be legible to us. When the subject receives her identity, she is also able to drop what feels like her bad, prior sense of self. Saying she "really" is the subject of the law—that is, whom the law intended to call—suggests that she really isn't something else, something infinitely worse (at least for privileged subjects; as already noted, for Fanon, and other colonized subjects, this works in reverse).[21] Even if the identity that comes with law is at times bad or subordinated, it remains caught up in a network of identity, which promises a superlative kind of redemption. A subject may be bad or lowly now—a criminal, a troublemaker, or what have you—but the law, in recognizing her, allows her access to its own sense of progress and betterment.

Subject to the law (interpellated), she is, she seems, part of something bigger and more hopeful.

Zarathustra does more than turn down these people's wish to be interpellated into a better, different identity; he destroys their basis for doing so. Taking on the guise of a messiah—a life that is parallel to the life of Jesus—Zarathustra initially raises the hopes of the people. In saying "heal us," they are also saying "call to us; give us an identity that is not our own." In this way they are participating, consciously or not, in the circuitry of interpellative authority, just as Machiavelli describes. These subjects (or would-be subjects) may be thinking that, finally, the messiah has come; finally, they can be rid of their afflictions and become their "true self." By saying no to this request, Zarathustra is shattering not just the immediate hope that he elicits in his followers but even the hope for such a hope. What happens when the messiah—or at least prophet—comes and goes and does nothing? What are these people supposed to think or do next? This is an exact reversal of the scene Kafka invokes us to imagine between God and the "other Abraham" who answers the call to sacrifice. Here, it is the deity who is "wrong" and who exposes the failure of the subjectivities being created and produced. If the Subject (that is, the divine origin of subjectivity) is in this case the one ruining the process of subjectivization, it becomes less a matter of how to respond (i.e., what does this other Abraham do when he shows up?) but a matter of whether any response at all is possible. Here, Numa's trick of externalizing authority, the basis for the circuitry of interpellative authority more generally, is ruined at its very origin. Here also we can see just how subversive Nietzsche really can be.

Indeed, rather than saving them, Zarathustra identifies with the afflicted people when he tells them, "The now and the past on earth—alas my friends, that is what I find most unendurable; and I should not know how to live if I were not also a seer of that which must come. A seer, a willer, a creator, a future himself and a bridge to the future—and alas, also, as it were, a cripple at this bridge: all this is Zarathustra."[22] If he is a "cripple at this bridge," a fellow nontraveler, as it were, what does that tell us about where Zarathustra is heading? What does it say about the possibilities for any kind of future, something different than what already is? And, above all, what does this do to our own hope, we readers who were reading this book expecting and hoping that Zarathustra would fix all of our problems and save us from being ourselves?

Betrayed by the Messiah

If the author and the prophet Zarathustra cannot save us, there is one last and final hope in this text. The ultimate prophesized figure in *Thus Spoke Zarathustra*, and therefore the key figure to contend with, is, as already mentioned, the overman (the *übermensch*). Zarathustra is, after all, not the messiah and never claims to be; he plays John the Baptist to the overman's Jesus. There is thus a perpetual distancing of the future in this book; even the one prophet who really can speak to the future—Zarathustra—defers to yet another and more distant figure, the overman himself. Thus, for example, shortly after he tells his disciples to deny him—in a typical distorted mimicry of the life of Jesus—Zarathustra tells us, " '*Dead are all gods: now we want the overman to live!*'—on that great noon, let this be our last will."[23]

Here again, we see an evocation of "that great noon." And here too that moment seems impossibly distant, future even to Zarathustra himself. But what, and when, is the overman? What does this figure do for and to us and how are we to respond to it?[24]

One of the most telling passages in *Thus Spoke Zarathustra* in this regard may be found in the preface when Nietzsche describes the encounter between a tightrope walker and a jester (in German, *Possenreißer*, literally, "joke ripper").[25] At this point in the narrative, Zarathustra, having descended from the mountains, has been preaching to a group of townspeople, speaking to them of the overman and also the last man. The latter figure represents the person who *thinks* they already are at the end of history (like the Hegelian liberal subject, the person who assumes that they are correctly interpellated) and therefore is ultimately distant from "that great noon." The people, mocking Zarathustra, say, "Turn us into these last men! Then we shall make you a gift of the overman!"[26] The whole time this has been happening, a tightrope walker has been preparing a performance; he seeks to walk across a tightrope that has been stretched above the audience's head between two towers. Such an act is the figuration of a sentence that Zarathustra said a bit earlier in the preface: "Man is a rope, tied between beast and overman—a rope over an abyss."[27] Nietzsche goes on to say of this that "what is great in man is that he is a bridge and not an end [evocative of his line, already noted, that he is a "cripple at this bridge"]: what can be loved in man is that he is an *overture* [*Übergang*] and a *going under* [*Untergang*]."[28]

The incident proper begins when the people, perhaps wearying of his metaphors, say to Zarathustra, "Now we have heard enough about the tightrope walker; now let us see him too."[29] Nietzsche goes on to write, "And all the people laughed at Zarathustra. But the tightrope walker, believing that the word concerned him, began his performance."[30]

In this way, the tightrope walker is misinterpellated. He thinks he is being called to perform but, like Kafka's Abraham, he is not the right one at the right time. Perhaps because of this disrupted form of hailing, his passage over the rope is similarly disturbed; the tightrope walker's attempt to get to the other side is suddenly and violently interfered with when "a jester . . . jumped out and followed the [tightrope walker] with quick steps."[31] Nietzsche goes on to write:

> "Forward, lamefoot!" [the jester] shouted in an awe-inspiring voice. "Forward, lazybones, smuggler, pale-face, or I shall tickle you with my heel! What are you doing here between towers? The tower is where you belong. . . ." [W]ith every word he came closer and closer; but when he was but one step behind, the dreadful thing happened which made every mouth dumb and every eye rigid: he uttered a devilish cry and jumped over the man who stood in his way. The man, however, seeing his rival win, lost his head and the rope, tossed away his pole, and plunged into the depth even faster, a whirlpool of arms and legs.[32]

Here, Nietzsche, who is ever prone to tricks and jokes—he is in effect himself a *Possenreißer*—is playing a trick on the reader once again, but a grotesque, glaringly obvious trick. In all the talk of being "overcome" by some future figure (the overman himself) we see a gruesome figuring of this outcome as the jester bounds over (i.e., "overcomes") the tightrope walker, sending him hurtling to the ground.

Such a reading raises a question: Is it possible that this horrible and grotesque figure is himself the overman? Is this what a cruel messiah does for us, jumping over our head and killing us in the process? Is that really what overcoming means? And, if that is the case, why would we ever want to follow such a messiah? Shouldn't we prefer the nihilism and self-loathing of contemporary morality to this awful and quite permanent fate?

Yet Nietzsche provides us with several reasons not to make so hasty a judgment. For one thing, the fate of the tightrope walker, although surely dire, is not bereft of virtue. As he lies dying by Zarathustra's side, the tightrope walker has this exchange with the prophet.

"What are you doing here?" [the tightrope walker] asked at last. "I have long known that the devil would trip me. Now he will drag me to hell. Would you prevent him?"

"By my honor, friend," answered Zarathustra, "all that of which you speak does not exist: there is no devil and no hell. Your soul will be dead even before your body: fear nothing further."

The man looked up suspiciously. "If you speak the truth," he said, "I lose nothing when I lose my life. I am not much more than a beast that has been taught to dance by blows and a few meager morsels."

"By no means," said Zarathustra. "You have made danger your vocation; there is nothing contemptible in that. Now you perish of your vocation: for that I will bury you with my own hands."

When Zarathustra had said this, the dying man answered no more; but he moved his hand as if he sought Zarathustra's hand in thanks.[33]

Here, the tightrope walker gets a kind of redemption after all. Zarathustra, true to form, does not perform any miracles. He does not save the man's life, nor does he bring him back from the dead. All he does is to take away some of the mythologies that had kept this man trapped in a cycle of self-loathing and fear. Zarathustra thus dismisses the ideas of hell and the devil as well as the hope for redemption that such ideas contain or conceal. When he tells the man that he has "made danger your vocation," he is referring to the danger of a life that has no guarantees, a life that is not presupposed by our ideas of good and evil and a "redemption" that is nothing of the kind. The job of being a tightrope walker epitomizes the dangers we all face, whether we realize it or not. By personifying that danger as a figure in the text, the tightrope walker illuminates something about the human condition more generally. While the tightrope walker himself may remain in the maw of nihilistic beliefs at the end—we have no idea since he doesn't say anything—we see that his body at least, or his hand, anyway, moves as in thanks, to show gratitude to the prophet for the redemption that he actually has always had but didn't consciously know about (as opposed to the redemption that he was hoping for).[34]

And, in a way, the man has been redeemed not only by Zarathustra but even by the "overman," the jester that overcame him. Throughout *Thus Spoke Zarathustra* we have the repeated line "[a person] is something that shall be overcome" ["Der Mensch ist etwas, das überwunden werden soll"] and the jester has done just that.[35] In doing so, the jester prevented the tightrope walker from trying to cross to the other side; had he allowed him to do so, the tightrope walker would have believed once again in "redemption," in striving to cross the bridge rather than accept his status as a "cripple" upon it. He would have been a goal rather than a way and, in so doing, lost the most basic aspect of what salvation—if we dare to call it that—really consists in, namely, the state of not being saved.[36]

Here again, we see that overcoming does not represent so much an act of futurity but, on the contrary, it eliminates any idea or hope of the future. The jester prevents the tightrope walker from having any future at all (by killing him); he denies the shining future, the safety and knowledge promised by the lure of the other end of the rope. Or perhaps more accurately, he does show the tightrope walker the future; the true future, as we see once again, is only here and now, the noontime hour that we deny at our true peril (and, by the same token, the future—now made present—as death). The tightrope walker may have died but by implication he was spared a much worse fate: he was able, at least potentially, to live the last minutes of his life in the now (the noon hour made all too tangible and present in the form of the ground he came hurtling down to). He is able to have a realization—or a dramatization—of his mortality and his own agency whereas the last man, the figure that had been just promoted by the townspeople, lives on but in such a state of delusion that it is as if he didn't live at all.[37]

Who Is the Overman?

In this consideration of the overman as jester, Nietzsche may have one more trick up his sleeve (if not many more). Much further along in the book, buried in part 4 of "On Old and New Tablets," Zarathustra says, "There are many ways of overcoming: see to that *yourself!* But only a jester thinks: 'Man can also be *skipped over.*' "[38] Such a line chastises us for even thinking that an unpleasant creature like the jester could actually be the overman; here again, another false prophet is exposed. We are taunted (or at least I am) for taking the figure of the overman too literally; the joke turns out to be on us.

But, as is typical of Nietzsche, even jokes have their purpose and even an exposed fraud like the jester has his uses as well. In this case, the figure of the jester tells us something about the figure of the overman (even as we are pointedly told that this is *not* the overman). The jester reminds us that just because the author himself suggests that someone or something is the overman doesn't mean that it is. It instructs us not to trust even the author of the text that tells us not to trust in what other people say. The very prank-ishness of the figure of the jester suggests the prankishness of the figure of the overman itself more generally (and maybe of the author as well). Maybe the joke is on us, but what is the joke?

As I read this, the jester serves not so much to *be* the overman but to take its place, ruining it in the process and returning us to our own position. In this way the reader, like the tightrope walker, comes crashing down from her halcyon expectations. Like Zarathustra, who takes the place of Jesus for the hunchback, the jester occupies the space where the overman might or should have appeared. In doing so, he blocks the possibility of the overman actually showing up and, in this way, saves us from this truly awful and ut-terly false fate (that is, the fate of becoming something new and better, the fate of self-hatred and nihilism).

In other words, the jester (and not the overman) is the misinterpellated messiah; he is definitely *not* whom we asked for. He is the last person we want to see. He is weird and terrible and no redeemer (not even a "redeemer") at all. Yet the jester is the one who shows up; he is the one who "overcomes" us and, in his actions, the tightrope walker (and via his example, the reader as well) is left to his/our own devices, freed from fear and the dread of being who he is/we are.[39] In this way, the jester has allowed—albeit only for an instant—the tightrope walker to have his experience of *amor fati*. He loves not the fate that is promised, the fate that twinkles alluringly on the other side of the bridge, but the mundane and ordinary fate that always was, the fate that was here all along.

In this way, the jester models the reader's own potential acts of misinter-pellation, our own showing up where we are not expected or wanted. Giving up on being called to what we think we are supposed to be, we can be what we are (*Ecce Homo*, Nietzsche's "autobiography," is subtitled "How to be what you are").[40] We can recognize that we are, like the jester, the one who shows up when we are called.

Nietzsche may himself suggest this alternative reading of the jester when he references him a bit later in the text in "The Other Dancing Song." There, he speaks of "you malicious leaping belle! Now up and over there! Alas, as I leaped I fell."[41] Here, once again, Zarathustra seems to be identifying not with the overman but with the victim of his leaping, with "the cripple at [or in this case under] this bridge." Zarathustra goes on to say, "Oh, see me lying there! You prankster [*Übermut*: literally, high or overly spirited], suing for grace. I should like to walk with you in a lovelier place."[42] As with so many things in Nietzsche's writing, this could be read several ways. On the one hand, we see the possibility that even Zarathustra longs for "redemption," for a kinder, sweeter relationship to a messiah, for a salvation that is total and fulfilling (like that which Jesus promises). On the other hand, perhaps instead, he is referring to the kind of actual redemption that he espies. A "lovelier place," depending, on how one reads it, could also mean, once again, this place, the place where we already are, made lovelier by our recognition and acceptance of it. In this case, Nietzsche may be showing us how even for Zarathustra such a place may be elusive, even as it is absolutely tangible, already here and now. Perhaps the jester is a coconspirator, a kind of spirit guide in his own way for Zarathustra's endless searching. He is an antimessianic messiah, a figure we couldn't possibly want or ask for but who comes anyway and does something that we could never have asked for (but which is nonetheless necessary for our ability to accept ourselves as such).

This figure thus serves to prevent Nietzsche's own work from becoming a final and ultimate obstacle against the choice of *amor fati*. If we say "yes to all of life so long as it's Nietzsche's version of it," we have merely substituted one kind of nihilism and self-denial for another.[43] We must say yes to our life, not his, and so even Nietzsche himself must be removed as a possible source of salvation, leaving us truly on our own, abandoned and without hope. This is where the figure of the overman comes in. As I see it, the overman is the final instrument in Nietzsche's arsenal to draw out our last hope for "redemption." When this figure is itself finally "overcome," we are returned to ourselves, to *amor fati* once and for all.

Summoning the Messiah

The overman is not the messiah we were asking for, and the call to summon him is similarly not the kind of call we seek or are used to hearing. If we slightly adjust the call to include people other than men, Zarathustra's repeated saying "[A person] is something that shall be overcome" is a very different statement than "hey, you there!" For one thing, this call is not directed at the person in question (perhaps recognizing that the person in question is in fact in question, not an object of address but a moving target). Instead, it is generally addressed, conveyed to everyone (and to no one).

Similarly, this call alters the directionality that is normally implied by the calls of interpellation. Whereas God the Subject's call and the "hey, you there!" of the police officer summon the subject, in this case it is the messiah who appears to be summoned. This in and of itself is not that unusual; under the context of interpellation, we call for messiahs all the time (we call, that is, for the one who calls to us). Yet, in this case, the summoning doesn't bring the messiah but the opposite; it banishes and ruins the messianic, leaving the bystander (who was neither the subject nor the source of the call) broken—at least for a moment—of her hope for redemption.

Furthermore what this call conveys is not, as first appears, an announcement of the annihilation of the human race, nor its replacement with a much better set of beings (the ones whom we have always wanted to be). Instead, this call cancels itself out, as it were, "overcoming" itself even as it is being expressed. If for Nietzsche the future is actually the present and our dreams for redemption are actually dreams for ourselves, "overcoming" means the cancellation of our interpellated identities—along with our phantasms of halcyon heights and bright futures—in favor of whatever emerges once that overcoming takes place. In other words, overcoming means being misinterpellated. The "shall" in the sentence "[A person] is something that shall be overcome" is less a confident prediction of the future than a sign that this overcoming is possible, that it has in a sense already happened and is just a matter of us recognizing (or ceasing to misrecognize) this. As is typical of Nietzsche, this call does not make us into something but unmakes what we are not. "[A person] is something that shall be overcome" could therefore be said to be the call of misinterpellation itself, a statement of its ongoing possibility.

Nietzsche (and Us) without the Overman

Such a reading of the overman (and the call that "summons" him) leads us to a basic question: What does Nietzsche's philosophy mean or do without the overman as that figure is normally read? Doesn't this figure loom as the centerpiece to his work? Here, we confront the ultimate disappointment in Nietzsche's text. But it is a disappointment that he prepares us for all along. The overman's ultimate gift to us—his final cruelty, if you will—is to not exist. If he did, we would be right back where we started, facing a perfect savior who is ultimately better than we are and confirming our own self-hatred.[44] In fact, however, the figure of the overman *does* take us back to where we start—not where we *think* we are but where we actually are: to the noontime hour, the stroke of twelve.

For those of us who are waiting for a messiah to deliver us from ourselves, Nietzsche has this to say: "Cursed I call those too who must always *wait*;

they offend my taste: all the publicans and shopkeepers and kings and other land- and storekeepers. Verily, I too have learned to wait—thoroughly—but only to wait for *myself*."[45] The overman is the figure by which we come to wait for ourselves, that is, a figure that finally exhausts us in our eternal waiting for the call of interpellation. By failing to appear, by failing even to exist, except as a figure of our own expectation, the overman is that final false horizon or lure that—unlike the usual lures of Christianity and philosophy or even the lures that Nietzsche himself packs into his works—returns us to ourselves, to the here and the now.

In this way, however paradoxical it may be, we can say that the overman "saves" us after all (we could say that, Jesus-like, he sacrifices his own existence for ours with the difference that he never actually exists—even in the text—at all). And perhaps we do not have to read quite so hard against the text as might be expected from such a reading. When Nietzsche tells us that the subject is put on earth to be overcome (and by the overman), we can read that as saying that the idea of the subject has to be overcome and the overman is that figure by which such overcoming can be achieved (paradoxically by overcoming the figure of the overman itself). Once the idea has been canceled out, what remains is the ordinary, actual life that we lead minus its superstructure of phantasm. This is the self that we always are but cannot be aware of (cannot "know") so long as we are preoccupied and dazzled by the spectacle of hope and authority that constitutes much of our reality.

Insofar as Nietzsche's project is fundamentally antimetaphorical—using metaphor to defeat metaphor—the one greatest metaphor of all, the idea of the subject, is his main target. The long strange journey of Zarathustra and the messiah that he looks to is required to achieve the undermining—or overcoming—of this phantasm. Insofar as the reader is utterly implicated in the phantasms of subjectivity and interpellation, Nietzsche must assume a hostile audience; he must win us over to ourselves by guile, by deceit and treachery. He must be a cruel author who in turn produces a cruel messiah so that the "kindnesses" that have led us to the trap of identity can be finally overcome. And, once again, in so doing, he (re)produces us as subjects who are meant to be disappointed.

If misinterpellation means accepting and recognizing failure, then we see that we must be held to that failure. As Nietzsche shows, recognizing failure cannot be an easy task, a matter of "if you agree that you are failed as a subject then you can have everything that you ever wanted" (that is, failure that is only in fact a disguised teleology). Real failure is what it sounds like: ugly, bitter, and sad and Nietzsche has both the cruelty and the compassion to force us to remain in the face of that failure until we've finally give up and love our fate. What Fanon endured in his own struggle with his subjectivity, Nietzsche asks of everyone.

And, furthermore, lest we think that we can realize the nonexistence of the overman once and for all and be free of the whole matter, Nietzsche warns us over and over that these cycles of highs and lows do not ultimately resolve but are themselves the fabric of our lives. We will always be tempted by the overman (why wouldn't we be?) and we will be required to be disappointed by his nonexistence not once but over and over. Like Trotsky's notion of continuous revolution, for Nietzsche as well, there can be no end, no final redemption, just a moment of rest ("a cripple at this bridge") as we prepare to begin the cycle of phantasm and disappointment all over again.[46]

Nietzsche and Amor Fati

Having shown how Nietzsche tricks and manipulates us, abandons and betrays us, let me turn the focus of this chapter to the result of that abandonment, the kinds of subjects, agencies, and authorizations that emerge once interpellation has been broken or reduced. Key to this analysis is a better understanding of Nietzsche's conception of amor fati and the related notion of eternal recurrence. These concepts define our state of emergence out of the false loves and fates that interpellation produces in us. They represent a kind of radical presentism that is itself indicative of the anarchic subjects that we have always been but haven't recognized—or, rather, have misrecognized—given our subjection to interpellation. It is my hope that this discussion of the nature of subject when she is free from interpellation—however temporarily—sheds more light on one of the most complex questions in Nietzschean philosophy: the political upshot of his work.

It often seems that this endlessly paradoxical thinker has a central paradox that structures all of his writing; here is a person who calls for authenticity and will—in however complex and subversive a manner—and yet the whole idea of amor fati seems hopelessly passive. If we love our fate, doesn't that mean that we have to accept the world as it is? Doesn't that condemn us to a life that is entirely depoliticized, returning us to the subject position that the misinterpellated subject rebels against in the first place?

Clearly, this is a "rhetorical" question: I have already begun to suggest how this is not necessarily the right way to read Nietzsche. As I read him, *amor fati* does not mean loving what passes as fate; it does not even mean loving a future state (as the word "fate" usually implies to us); instead, *amor fati* means loving the present, accepting it, and, from that position, rearticulating and reconceptualizing the subject position itself (as Fanon does as well, including by his own consideration of Nietzsche).

As with so many other terms ("future," "halcyon heights," "redeemer"), for Nietzsche the idea of fate is a lure. We read it through the lens of our interpellated subjectivity and it seems out of our control, futuristic, beyond us. But Nietzsche employs this term to trick us back into the present. Knowing that his readers are profoundly teleological creatures (or at least seekers of teleology), Nietzsche takes advantage of this to trick us into its opposite. We are back with the bullfighter and her cape; "fate" as a future term is revealed to be empty and in that emptiness we encounter (perhaps) what fate really is, the only thing it could be: the present, the noontime. The present is the only thing that is determined, that is what it must be, what we must make our peace with and what, above all, we must love.

This idea of fate could be called, for lack of a better word, the positive— or even anarchist—agenda in Nietzsche. Now that we have seen how he strips us down to the bottom of our subjecthood—relentlessly, cruelly, and lovingly all at the same time—we can turn to what emerges in the aftermath (but even the word "aftermath" is not quite right; this is not a temporal stepping forward, it is rather, once again, a kind of radical presentism, something that happens only right here and right now, not "after" anything). In this way, and with this kind of temporality, we can discover who we are when we aren't hell-bent on "really" being the person that the law or other authority figures call for.

Loving the Present

Perhaps one of Nietzsche's most well-known invocations of the idea of *amor fati* comes in the section entitled "Why I Am So Clever" in *Ecce Homo*: "My formula for greatness in a human being is *amor fati*: that one wants nothing to be other than it is, not in the future, not the past, not in all eternity. Not merely to endure that which happens of necessity, still less to dissemble it—all idealism is untruthfulness in the face of necessity—but to love it."[47] Here, we see once again that *amor fati* is at bottom a temporal attitude wherein one wants all (and only) what is. This is a deeply antimetaphorical and antitranscendent form of thinking. For Nietzsche, wishing or believing the world to be other than it is, having recourse to idealism for the future and regret and *ressentiment* for the past, traps us in a false and terrible temporality (I would argue it traps us in an archist temporality as well, a sense of time that demands big moments, big rescues, and big futures). We cannot live in the here and now—we don't even recognize that we do—when we desperately want to be somewhere else and at some other point in time, or even to escape time altogether.

The idea of *amor fati* ties in very closely with Nietzsche's notion of eternal recurrence, a concept that is also expressed perhaps most clearly in *The Gay Science*. There, in a section entitled "The Greatest Weight," Nietzsche asks,

> What, if some day or night a demon were to steal after you into your loneliest loneliness and say to you: "This Life as you now live it and have lived it, you will have to live once more and innumerable time more; and there will be nothing new in it, but every pain and every joy and every thought and sigh and everything unutterably small or great in your life will have to return to you, all in the same succession and sequence—even this spider and this moonlight between the trees, and even this moment and I myself. The eternal hourglass of existence is turned upside down again and again, and you with it, speck of dust!" Would you not throw yourself down and gnash your teeth and curse the demon who spoke thus? Or have you once experienced a tremendous moment when you would have answered him: "You are a god and never have I heard anything more divine." If this thought gained possession of you, it would change you as you are or perhaps crush you. The question in each and every thing, "Do you desire this once more and innumerable times more?" would lie upon your actions as the greatest weight. Or how well disposed would you have to become to yourself and to life *to crave nothing more fervently* than this ultimate eternal confirmation and seal?[48]

In both the case of *amor fati* and eternal recurrence, Nietzsche has essentially done an end run around both religion and metaphysics. Nietzsche is saying that even if we do live other lives both in terms of the great span of time and space—that is, if we live our lives over and over again and in multiple planes of existence—he advocates that at each of these points, we choose to be exactly what we already are here and now. In this way we have no way to escape from ourselves; our self-loathing is no longer facilitated by having a better alternative version of ourselves either in time or in space. So armed, we could face the shining messiah of the future—the Subject itself—and turn our backs.[49]

In terms of how the concepts of *amor fati* and eternal recurrence are related, perhaps we can say that *amor fati* is the name that this choice looks like from the subject's position while eternal recurrence is Nietzsche's name for the life-affirming choice when viewed from the perspective of eternity. Within the bonds of time, we employ *amor fati*, that sense of being trapped between the past and future, with the past consisting of things we have done and wish we hadn't and the future being characterized by things that we wish we could do but almost certainly won't, because of the dead hand of the past. In this way, we come to love what we actually—and only—are. Outside of this sense of time and fate, taking a broader and philosophical view, we must seek out eternal recurrence of the same, ensuring that any chance to wish ourselves to be other than we are is thwarted, ruined, and abandoned (thus returning us to the requirement, or at least possibility, for *amor fati*).[50]

For Nietzsche this kind of realization does not come easily. As noted, it requires giving up on all the hope and promise that come with religion's promise of an afterlife and metaphysics's promise of a noumenal self who is infinitely superior to the merely human creatures that we are. The entirety of *Thus Spoke Zarathustra* depicts Zarathustra as constantly struggling, and failing, to love his fate, to love who and what he is, and to be present with himself. It is not even clear that at the end of the book Zarathustra has truly accepted this realization, despite Nietzsche's—and Zarathustra's—own claims to the contrary (this point can be debated; Nietzsche is a master of complex and uncertain conclusions).[51]

Even if these states of acceptance are realizable, however, there is a paradoxical quality to both *amor fati* and eternal recurrence that suggests further complications of Nietzsche's war on metaphysics, especially in light of the previous discussion of Nietzsche's engagement with misinterpellation. To truly choose the now implicitly means to choose not only "even this spider and this moonlight between the trees, and even this moment and I myself" but also seemingly the *ressentiment*, the self-loathing and the paralysis that comes along with this saying "yes."[52] To say "yes" to life means, in part, saying yes to saying no (as Fanon also suggests). The transformation that seems to be promised by a turn to *amor fati* appears, at least to some extent, to be a trick. Even this final out, this escape from our self-loathing, is taken away from us. Why would Nietzsche promise (or seem to promise) a solution to our self-loathing, our being trapped in time, if even this trap and this loathing must be accepted? Is this possibly even worse than a formula for passivity? Does it force us not only to duly accept what is but to *love* it?[53]

How One Becomes What One Is

By way of beginning to address such questions, I would suggest that for Nietzsche, *amor fati* implies not only being a subject—which we already are—but also choosing to be one, which is something quite different, perhaps a form of self-recognition or even self-interpellation (in a way that is markedly unlike the way that the Romans self-interpellated in Machiavelli's description of them). Choosing to be a subject does not mean that we passively accept all that happens to us (although, in the next chapter I will look at a character—Melville's Bartleby, the Scrivener—who seems to do exactly that; as I will argue in that chapter, as long as we see the misinterpellated subject as passive, we continue to misrecognize the intense passivity that marks our own subject position). Rather, it suggests that we finally are able to choose our subject position—in the ruins of its usual form—but with the caveat that these choices are limited and contained by what we "are," the entirety of those forces, endogenous and interior, historical and phantasmic, that make us up. Rather than having one neat and clean subjectivity as interpellation demands (what we "really" are), for Nietzsche, we give ourselves over to the anarchy of our subjectivity. This, and only this, is what we can love.

That may seem to embrace passivity after all but a short digression to Thomas Hobbes (with critical help by one of his best readers, Samantha Frost) may help explain how this is not the case. As Frost notes, it is often said that Hobbes's materialism condemns him to pure determinism, which in turn threatens the much-heralded notion of "free will." I have no interest in saving free will—a concept that I think, like the liberal universal it partakes in, is rotten to the core—but I think Frost's answer to the people who worry about determinism tells us something about Nietzsche as well. Frost cites a passage from *On Liberty and Necessity* where Hobbes discusses the determination of a pair of dice. When rolling dice, it seems that they simply must roll the way that they roll. It seems as if their outcome is predetermined, fated, and we, in turn, must simply passively accept their outcome. Yet Frost cites Hobbes as writing "the posture of the parts of the *hand*, the measure of *force* applied by the caster, the posture of the parts of the *table* and the like" all serve separately and together to "determine" what is rolled.[54] The upshot is, as Frost puts it, that "Hobbes's determinism is so complex as to not be determinable."[55] Thus while Hobbes argues that the will is not free, this doesn't mean that we are robots (in one of my favorite sentences in critical thinking, Frost writes that, given the nondeterminability of outcomes, "the specter of a crude political behaviorism can settle back down").[56]

Bringing this back to Nietzsche, we can say something similar. For Nietzsche our subject position is a reflection of a vast complex of forces. In a sense we cannot say that we are "called" to anything but are rather massively overdetermined by infinite forces and events (in a way that is remarkably similar to Hobbes's reading of human subjectivity). But the way the subject position is produced is so porous, so multiply determined, so indecisive—so anarchic—that it is impossible to say that it is passive or determined in any tangible way at all. Amor fati means loving and accepting the mess that we are. It is choosing and acting from this subject position; it doesn't mean that we must construct a new true self out of the ashes of false interpellation. Rather, it means to love the ashes and the failure, the whole deal. While it becomes much harder to say where one person begins and another ends, and while this subject is impossible, something that no one could ever wish to be, this is what we have to work with. What the misinterpellated subject finds, via the process of amor fati, is herself, her crazy quilted, weird, multiple subjectivity that shows up when the call is made. Whether she wishes to be this person or not, this is who is here and this is the only possible position from which anything like agency—although not any agency that we normally recognize—is available.

The Subject Who Showed Up

We can see some of this argument emerging out of Nietzsche's direct writings on subjectivity, in particular in his text Ecce Homo. At one point, Nietzsche responds to an imagined question about why he attends to so many matters that appear utterly trivial in the guise of discussing human potential, which seems to be about much greater sets of concerns. His answer is telling:

> It will be said that in doing so I harm myself all the more if I am destined to fulfill great tasks. Answer: these little things—nutriment, place, climate, recreation, the whole casuistry of selfishness—are beyond all conception of greater importance than anything that has

been considered of importance hitherto. It is precisely here that one has to begin to *learn anew*. Those things which mankind has hitherto pondered seriously are not even realities, merely imaginings, more strictly speaking *lies* from the bad instincts of sick, in the profoundest sense, injurious natures.[57]

In other words, everything that we think is important and great turns out to be a set of lies (Nietzsche goes on to list notions such as "God," "Soul," "virtue," and also "all questions of politics [as we usually understand it], the ordering of society, education[,]" and so forth).[58] Instead of these false goals, what matters for him are those aspects of life that adhere much more closely to the self (hence "selfish"). These things—"nutriment, place, climate, recreation, the whole casuistry of selfishness"—are what actually constitute our life. These things are not organized into a unity but express a more chaotic version of the self, as much exogenous as endogenous to our person. Yet, as already noted, these things are generally overshadowed or eclipsed by our self-loathing and our hope for redemption and being other than what we are. Even if that self-loathing remains when we have opted for *amor fati*, the turning of our attention to our subjectivity as such is deeply significant. When we recognize ourselves, as we recognize Zarathustra, as a "cripple at this bridge," we may remain entranced by visions of the future to some extent—we can never really be free of that habit for Nietzsche as is also the case with Walter Benjamin whom I read very much as a kindred spirit—but we also will spend a bit more time looking at our actual surroundings, at that which makes up the great complex and anarchic mess that we are.

Indeed, for Nietzsche, we must love *all* of this messy self that we are, warts and all, including the part of us that hates and denies our self. Thus, still in *Ecce Homo*, after Nietzsche speaks of "*how one becomes what one is*," he goes on to write,[59]

That one becomes what one is presupposes that one does not have the remotest idea *what* one is. From this point of view even the *blunders* of life—the temporary sidepaths and wrong turnings, the delays, the "modesties," the seriousness squandered on tasks which lie outside *the task*—have their own meaning and value. They are an expression of a great sagacity, even the supreme sagacity, even the supreme sagacity: where *nosce te ipsum* [i.e., "know thyself"] would be the recipe for destruction, self-forgetfulness, self-*misunderstanding*, self-diminution, -narrowing, -mediocratizing becomes reason itself. Expressed morally: love of one's neighbour, living for others and other things *can* be the defensive measure for the preservation of the sternest selfishness.[60]

Here, we begin to see more clearly what the payoff of *amor fati* may be, why it is vital that we don't give up *even* our self-loathing (that, in fact, we must come to love it along with our fetishism, our self-delusion, and all the rest). This is part of us too, a part that is at odds with other parts of ourselves and hence reflects our lack of internal harmony, our failure to be a unified being. To accept this part is necessary because our self-loathing, as well as our "self-forgetfulness, self-*misunderstanding*, self-diminution etc." preserves within itself the very self that it seeks to annihilate. Like Fanon once again, our yes is also a no and our no is also a yes. This is certainly a disappointing message from the perspective of a self that longs for salvation. It is even disappointing for a self who is sick of being sick of herself because it means we can't shed the parts of ourselves that we do not like. Here, Nietzsche offers us therefore a double betrayal; both our aspirational self and even the self we think we will become when we give those aspirations up—a self that is equally false, equally fetishistic—are betrayed ("only when you have all denied me will I return to you"). Instead we just get ourselves, our boring, mundane, troubled and multiple fleshy selves that we have never wanted to be. This may be the ultimate argument for why every moment of interpellation is also a moment of misinterpellation: not one of us, as we are, is who we would like to be when we receive the call of subjectivity but we are, each and every one of us, the one who showed up anyway. *That* is our fate, the only fate we can have (or love).

The Anarchist Nietzsche

To conclude this chapter and to begin looking at the literary and filmic examples that exemplify a misinterpellated form of reading, let me turn briefly to an explicit consideration of the politics that comes from this turn to Nietzsche. As may be obvious by now, I think that a Nietzschean politics is also an anarchist one but it is anarchist in a very unique and critical sense. If anarchism normally concerns itself with communities, with the distribution of power among members of a society and the way that the burdens and pleasures of politics are widely shared, Nietzsche's anarchism concerns itself with a deeper anarchism, the anarchism of the subject (and a misinterpellated subject at that). I think this is critical because, in a sense, if each of us remains "us," that is, interpellated subjects—whether privileged or not, at the center or at the periphery of power and authority—we retain within ourselves a fragment of the oppressive system that forms us. An anarchism based on such subjects will tend (as often happens) to reproduce exactly what is to be avoided: archism, centralized modes of subjectivity, hierarchy, and dominant forms of political and social authority. As I will explain further in the conclusion, we need to be anarchist "all the way down," down to our very psyches, in order to avoid reproducing archism over and over despite our greatest intentions to the contrary.

Reading Fanon and Nietzsche in tandem helps us to resist that tendency down to the level of the individual, the level where such power tends to establish itself most intimately and intractably. If we think, once again, of Plato's analogy between the city and the soul, we can see that anarchism cannot stop at the city; it must involve the soul as well. With Fanon we see a way to turn the bitterest—and most deeply internalized, even psychological—forms of refusal into a basis for resistance. With Nietzsche, we add a sense of what the subject that emerges from misinterpellation looks like. This is an anarchist subject in the true sense of the word; their very being has been decentralized. Rather than having one core and centralized subject, each of us becomes many voices, many overlapping and mutually entangled "selves." Thus, when Nietzsche famously writes in the *Genealogy of Morals* that "There is no 'being' behind the doing, acting, becoming; the 'doer' has simply be added to the deed by the imagination," we can see that when he speaks of the absence of a "doer" he is not suggesting that we are merely empty beings who have no subjectivity at all.[61] Rather he is pointing to the multiple heterogeneous and garrulous selves that constitute what each of us "is." The "deed" is the result of some infinitely complex process, one that is so multiply determined as to be effectively undetermined, at least as far as we are concerned. We act and speak, not because we are possessed of "free will" and clearly determined core selves that guide our every move, but rather out of our own internal complexity. We act not because but despite the presence of this Doer (with a capital D in this case) that purportedly organizes and commands our internal life.

As such, we can still speak of the anarchist subject as a subject or agent in the sense that the deed still gets done without the centralizing organization of a Doer. Just as anarchist communities are not one voice but can and do manage to make decisions and act in concert, so too do anarchist subjects—that is, the subjects that we are when we are not actively subject to interpellation—go through life making various decisions despite a great deal of internal complexity. This is not a situation where the decision to cross the street or not will require endless internal check-ins and discussions. As Walter Benjamin offers as well, there is an anarchism of everyday life in which countless decisions are made and actions engaged in that do not involve centralized modes of authority in any way (although we tend to think that we require such modes in order to act at all, hence giving credit for our own cohesion and agency to an outside and alien source). The same is true for the anarchist subject; here too there is a form of effectiveness that is not nullified by the absence of a centralized and interpellated form of subjectivity. On the contrary, the absence of such an archist presence allows the subject her fullest and most complex form of expression. This in turn allows her to act in concert with other anarchist selves in ways that broaden and deepen the possibilities for an anarchist politics.

In the chapters that follow, I will explore the consequences of being this subject. Because our subjectivity is so deeply connected to archism, to interpellation and externalized forms of authority, it is easier to imagine an anarchic form of subjectivity via literature and film (and philosophy and political theory, as this chapter on Nietzsche and the previous chapter on Fanon have attempted to do). As previously noted, the explicitly representational nature of these media allows us to think about the construction of the subject, the way the subject appears to herself as well as to other people. The next three chapters will show different facets, different forms of politics that result from misinterpellated—and anarchist—forms of subjectivity as well as different strategies for that exposure.

The following chapters are distinguished from one another by their focus on different aspects of misinterpellated subjectivity. Each serves as a model for how to turn an aspect of misinterpellated subjectivity into a form of resistance in keeping with the larger notions conceptualized by Fanon and Nietzsche. In the following chapter, I look at two authors, Melville and Woolf, to think about modes of resistance that follow from the way the misinterpellated subject is hardly noticeable. Without ceasing to be meek and nearly nonexistent, the characters in the works I will look at exert a tremendous, even irresistible power. In chapter 6, I focus initially on the failure and incoherence of the misinterpellated subject, that is, the power that comes from being a decentralized (and hence "unsuccessful" subject). Here I will look at Karl, a character from Kafka's *Amerika*. Insofar as this failure is not an option for subjects of color—because they are "understood" and typecast, regardless of their internal makeup—in the second half of the chapter

I look at works by Ellison and Coates to further explore the Fanonian model of refusal. Finally, in chapter 7 I will look at the way inner plurality can itself be turned into a weapon against interpellation (and even against the original "Subject" that is the source of interpellative authority in the first place) by looking at the case of Bess McNeill.

In each of these chapters, there are also other forms of calls, forms of counterinterpellation, that rival and undermine the calls that I looked at in part I. I already looked at one such call in this chapter with Nietzsche's "[a person] is something that shall be overcome." The other calls I will look at in the following chapters are all based on different sets of strategies and contexts. They express not one single way to fight misinterpellation, but (as if fitting) a plethora of ways. Collectively, these chapters attempt to answer Butler's question that I reversed in chapter 1: "how to make the possibility of becoming a 'bad' subject [less] remote and [more] incendiary than it might well be?"

CHAPTER FIVE

"COME, COME!"

Bartleby and Lily Briscoe as Nietzschean Subjects

In the readings that follow, I look at instances of various literary characters who, in some way or another, accept "who they are" in a way that other characters in their respective narratives do not (paradoxically, as I have been suggesting, they do this by denying any solid or unified sense of themselves, by accepting—even choosing—their failure to be a unified subject). As previously noted, these characters do not look terribly heroic, at least when viewed from the perspective of our own interpellated forms of subjectivity. In fact, few of the "subjects"—if I may be permitted to continue to use that term for these characters; "objects" might be a better term—in the chapters that follow seem like someone you would want to emulate, let alone choose to be. (Ta-Nehisi Coates, a living author and a subject of his own book, is an exception to everything that I will be saying here.)[1] And that is precisely the point; these characters are who we don't want to be but actually are. Like the other Abraham that Franz Kafka describes in his story, these characters are the ones who answer a call that was not meant for them. No one would ever want to know, much less *be*, these sorts of characters but they are the ones who show up anyway and, in doing so, they radically change the scene where they appear.

In thinking about such subjects, turning to literary and filmic examples helps to express some of the complexities of misinterpellated subjectivity in a way that might otherwise be more difficult or even impossible to convey. As Maria Aristodemou writes in her book *Law, Psychoanalysis, Society*, whereas culture in general can "perform the function of ideological fantasies," literature, which normally serves to paper over—or misrecognize—the gaps in our subjectivity, is also a means by which to resist the production and depiction of such subjects (that is, to reveal the very gaps it is normally meant to hide).[2] As previously noted, because literature is clearly and visibly "untrue" (manifestly representative), it allows us to explore and think through other untruths—those that have been given the quality of truth and reality—in ways that defy and get around attempts at enforcing existing subject positions. As the exploration of Niccolò Machiavelli in chapter 2 suggests, insofar as the ubiquity of misinterpellation generally only comes to our attention via moments of dramatization—such as we saw in the historical examples also considered in chapter 2 and in Frantz Fanon's life and work in chapter 3—dramatization itself is a function of literature. In literature (and film) we can find a way to rework the symbolic economy—an economy that is normally meant to produce obedient and properly interpellated subjects—into something quite different.

My argument in the rest of the book will be that the authors I treat—Herman Melville, Virginia Woolf, Franz Kafka, Ralph Ellison, Ta-Nehisi Coates, and Lars von Trier—allow the dramatization of the failure of interpellation to appear to us, to render it visible, if not completely unavoidable. The fact that these characters are often read as losers, as boring and quiescent, or as angry or crazy could be read as a sign that people are not easily shed of their belief in interpellative subjectivity.[3] If the reader scorns the alternative forms of agency—or really, as I will make more clear the *only* forms of agency that are actually possible—that these stories present, it may amount to scorning and missing the chance to be something other than what interpellation determines, thereby giving up on what Kafka called a "hope . . . that is not for us."[4]

By reading in a misinterpellated fashion—via the methods of a yet more minor literature—the reader can not only become attuned to the misinterpellated characters in these novels, books, and films, but, perhaps more important, she can also learn how to spot misinterpellation more generally, under more ordinary circumstances and within her own self. Reading through the lens of misinterpellation helps to attune the reader to a way of resisting the hegemony of interpellation and other externalized forms of identity and authority. In seeing the (sometimes spectacular, other times quite ordinary) failure of these characters, the reader may see her own failure to conform, her own inability to be what she most desperately seeks: to be some other, redeemed sort of subject.

Let me then turn then to two such characters in this chapter: first Bartleby and then Lily Briscoe. They both engage in Nietzschean modes of subjectifying (and antisubjectifying). Bartleby, I will be arguing, is not passive at all; he does more than any other character in the story. And Woolf in particular emerges as a writer who is willing—as Nietzsche was himself—to disappoint us, to save us, once again from salvation and leave us bereft, forced to be exactly what we least expected or wanted in ways that leave us profoundly affected. What unites these characters—and hence is the focus of this chapter—is the way that the antiheroes in question, Bartleby and Lily Briscoe, respectively, fly under the radar, appear meek and useless, and, above all, *harmless* even as they do immense and spectacular damage to the apparatuses of interpellation that oppress and overwrite them, along with everyone else.

Bartleby's Preferences

Melville's "Bartleby, the Scrivener" has received a lot of academic attention in recent years, notably from figures like Giorgio Agamben and others who are attracted to the way the character of Bartleby says "I would prefer not to" when asked to do certain tasks.[5] For Agamben, this statement models the idea of what he calls "inoperativity," a refusal to do what is asked, a noncooperation with the phantasms of capitalism and sovereign politics. I have a somewhat different reading of this figure. As I see it, Bartleby is not so much inoperative as he is operating along a different calculus, that is, he is misinterpellated. He looks and, perhaps at first glance, acts, as we'd expect an interpellated subject to act but in fact his actions disguise a separate agenda, an entirely different approach to relationality, subjecthood, and instrumentalism, which uproots and subverts the ordinary world that he enters into. As I read him, Bartleby is a figure who exemplifies the Nietzschean form of subjectivity; although he is normally read as being completely passive, as saying "no" to everything, I think, he epitomizes instead what it looks like to say "yes" to his own self, to his own sense of agency and even his own mortality, all of which is to say that he says "yes" to *amor fati*. As such Bartleby both serves as a kind of (Nietzschean) messiah in the text—a messiah who is utterly unwanted by the other characters in the story and who is ignored as much as possible—and an indicator of what a post-messianic subject might look like (that is, one for whom the messianic rescue becomes utterly redundant). Although he appears to be passive to the point of vanishing, Bartleby is, as I will argue, the only actual agent in the text "Bartleby, the Scrivener."

In Melville's short story, Bartleby is hired by the unnamed narrator to work in an office where legal documents are copied by hand, sometimes several times over. Needing new help, the narrator employs Bartleby, whom he initially describes as a "motionless young man."[6] Bartleby begins quite well, copying faithfully and carefully whatever is handed to him. It is only when the narrator asks Bartleby to do anything else (read his copies to make sure there are no errors, run errands, and so forth) that Bartleby gives his famous response "I would prefer not to."[7]

The narrator is astonished that Bartleby won't do as he is asked, assuming that he is, like his other employees, a part of the ordinary functions of capitalism where the employees do—or at least pretend to do—what their boss asks of them. The narrator says,

> I looked at him steadfastly. His face was leanly composed; his gray eyes dimly calm. Not a wrinkle of agitation rippled him. Had there been the least uneasiness, anger, impatience, or impertinence in his manner; in other words, had there been anything ordinarily human about him, doubtless I should have violently dismissed him from the premises. But as it was, I should have as soon thought of turning my pale plaster-of-paris bust of Cicero out of doors.[8]

The comparison between Bartleby and the bust of Cicero is telling; there is something deeply objectlike about Bartleby, something not quite human. Indeed, there seems to be some affinity between Bartleby and this (and other) object(s). Later in the story, while enduring one of the narrator's many attempts to reason with him, Bartleby is said to have "kept his glance fixed upon [the] bust of Cicero," as if engaged in mutual material recognition and support.[9] As the story progresses, Bartleby becomes increasingly objectlike. Eventually he refuses to even continue to copy anything—saying he would "prefer" not to—and then refuses to leave when the narrator tries to get rid of him.

Even before this moment, Bartleby is odd; he seems to live only off of cookies ("Ginger-nuts") and he spends much of his time barely moving, if at all. As the narrator notes, "One prime thing was this—*he was always there*—first thing in the morning, continually throughout the day, and the last at night" (it seems that Bartleby sleeps—or at least passes his entire evenings—in the office).[10] In this way, Bartleby shares the immobility of the bust of Cicero, along with other objects in the office. He cannot be bribed, threatened, or cajoled. Eventually, despairing of getting rid of him, the narrator actually moves his offices, leaving Bartleby behind. Yet he cannot escape Bartleby so easily. The new occupant of the office complains to him that Bartleby still won't leave and the narrator has to go back and plead with him to leave (unsuccessfully, of course). Eventually Bartleby is arrested and sent to prison. Even in prison, a place that is ultimately about forcing people to the will of the state, Bartleby is intractable. The narrator visits him there and learns that he would "prefer" not to eat and sees him finally dead, now truly and only an object at last.

At the same time, the connection to the bust of Cicero also suggests some very human qualities about Bartleby as well so that we can't just presume that Bartleby is merely a material object and leave it at that. Cicero was an advocate of stoicism, a principled form of resistance that offered, as we see with Bartleby himself, a kind of imperviousness to fortune. No matter what comes Bartleby's way, he accepts the results. He accepts, and even causes, his own death as I will discuss further in a moment. All of the violence, the intimidation, and the subjectivization that normally pertain to human agents fail to move Bartleby. If Bartleby was only an object we could just say that he is not one of us; Bartleby is strange and other, so his experience offers us no sense of our own ability to resist. Who would want to be like Bartleby? But because Bartleby exists on the margins between subject and object and because his position exposes the way each of us is similarly situated, he deeply subverts the interpellated order. For all of his passivity and near invisibility, Bartleby causes havoc and an unraveling of interpellative authority perhaps precisely because, appearing to do virtually nothing at all, he fails to perform his false identity and, in that way, also fails to drown out the quieter voices of the subject that he actually is.

In the normal sense of things—that is, according to the world of phantasms of authority and interpellation that we live in—Bartleby seems crazy; his preferences doom him to an early and sad death. But if we think of him through the screen of a Nietzschean misinterpellated messiah—like the jester, a figure we'd never ask for and one we certainly don't want to be—we can see him according to a different calculus. It is true that Bartleby shows up in answer to a call—the call for a new copier—but it soon becomes equally clear that the caller and the callee are working with two utterly different modes of operation. Bartleby may have appeared to answer the narrator's call but we soon realize that he is speaking an entirely different language. His claim "I would prefer not to" can be read, through a Benjaminian lens—one that is extremely compatible with a Nietzschean one—as the voice of the text, the voice of the objects that we normally fetishize. For Benjamin, when we use any means toward an end, we are acting as fetishists because our ends are, by definition, idolatrous, false projections much like interpellation itself. Only when we achieve what he calls "pure means"—that is, means that have been severed from those ends—can we act in a way that subverts the fetishism and violence we participate in.[11] As such, Bartleby can be seen as engaging in a conspiracy, cooperating with the fetishized objects he encounters in a joint rebellion against the identities and uses that everything and everyone is otherwise subordinated to.[12]

Bartleby's apparent passivity is not quite the same, I think, as Agamben's notion of inoperativity. Bartleby is operable; for one thing, as we see, for a short period of time, he faithfully copies all that is presented to him (although he won't do anything else; one might say that he "works to rule"). But we might read his operativity in this case as something other than compliance. Rather than seeing him as faithfully rendering the text to be an object of the law's scrutiny—recall that he refuses to check that the copies are accurate; he doesn't really seem to care about what the company he works for actually does—we can see him as instead simply engaging in acts of further representation, making more objects, more texts, more co-conspirators for his resistance. Thus, unlike as with Agamben's reading, not only does Bartleby not cooperate with his orders (not operate), he, like the other objects he joins in rebellion or conspiracy with, actively works to unmake the power of interpellative phantasm in a way that is very "operational" indeed. In fact, his actions subvert from deep within the heart of capitalism, on Wall Street itself.[13]

Another critical difference between Agamben's notion of inoperativity and misinterpellation comes from the kinds of temporality that each way of thinking works with. Agamben requires the total breakdown of the subject before that subject can act whereas I see that breakdown as having already occurred (or, more accurately, that subject was never not broken down in the first place). There is a certain teleology in Agamben—as Jessica Whyte points out in *Catastrophe and Redemption*—wherein he sees the subject as passing through a catastrophe in order to become redeemed after all.[14] From a Nietzschean (and misinterpellated) position, this guarantee of ultimate redemption—no matter how much has been suffered along the way—threatens the kind of true failure and true disappointment that are required for the resistance to interpellated forms of subjectivity (it suggests an occult teleological approach that Nietzsche is resolutely opposed to). Accordingly, Bartleby operates with no guarantees of any sort. In a sense, his "redemption," such as it is, comes from his refusal itself rather than what that refusal produces or leads to.

If Bartleby is some kind of messianic figure, he certainly does not act in the way we'd expect. He draws no attention to himself and barely speaks. He literally does nothing (or nearly nothing). But he does not leave the people he has encountered unchanged. The narrator says that Bartleby "not only strangely disarmed me, but in a wonderful manner, touched and disconcerted me."[15] Representing the possibilities of resistance as he does, he is nonetheless never recognized as any kind of threat (the narrator holds a continuous and deep amount of trust in Bartleby for all the ways he drives him crazy). Because his affect is not that of one who resists—he is not angry; he does not seem resentful—he is allowed to act in ways that deeply unsettle and disturb the ordinary operations of capitalism and he manages to do this right under the noses of the capitalists (the narrator included). Bartleby responds to the waves of interpellation that go back and forth between subjects—all the calls to copy this, answer this, expand his work responsibilities, and so on—with forms of defiance that seem mild on the surface but that are highly subversive and toxic to the workings of the normative order. Eventually Bartleby's actions leave the realm of normalized comprehensibility altogether; he can no longer be read in any way as acting in accordance with the authority of ordinary law and social propriety. It becomes clear to the narrator that Bartleby is unique and disturbing—hence his desire to narrate his story for the rest of us—but at this point, it's too late, the damage to "normality" is done.

Bartleby's rebellion is infectious. At one point, the narrator begins to notice that both he and the other employees begin to take up Bartleby's language, in particular the term "prefer." It comes to a comical pass when the narrator tells one of the other employees (named "Turkey") that he too has started using "that" word.[16] Turkey, completely unconscious of his use of the term, insists that he doesn't know what the narrator is talking about. Finally, Turkey gets it. He says,

"Oh, *prefer?* oh yes—queer word. I never use it myself. But, sir, as I was saying, if he would but prefer—"

"Turkey," interrupted I [the narrator], "You will please withdraw."

"Oh certainly, sir, if you prefer that I should."[17]

The narrator concedes that when another employee ("Nippers") uses the term as well, "he did not in the least roguishly accent the word 'prefer.' It was plain that it had involuntarily rolled from his tongue."[18]

Here, it seems even the objects that are our bodies, our tongues very much included, collude with this subversion of our conscious—and complicit—minds. Bartleby's objecthood seems contagious: the narrator describes himself as turning into "a pillar of salt" upon first encountering the firm and placid denials that Bartleby offers.[19]

If Bartleby's preferences are contagious, the narrator's own form of communication is far less successful. To Bartleby's tendency to prefer, the narrator engages in acts of assumption. After initially telling Bartleby that he simply must leave, the narrator goes home and enters into a reverie—one that is enabled by being far from Bartleby's presence—wherein he congratulates himself on having handled Bartleby's exit so well (in fact Bartleby doesn't leave, as it turns out). The narrator thinks to himself, "I *assumed* the ground that depart he must; and upon that assumption built all I had to say."[20] But the next morning he realizes that "that assumption was simply my own, and none of Bartleby's. The great point was, not whether I had assumed he had quit me, but whether he would prefer so to do. He was more a man of preferences than assumptions."[21]

This contrast is very telling; the narrator's mode of engagement with others is to assume, an act of projection that is hegemonic and normativizing. Bartleby's power comes from the fact that he does not assume but rather prefers, that is, he does only what he wants (or doesn't want) to do, and he never bases his behavior on what he thinks others must or should do. Another way of saying this is that Bartleby shows how to operate and resist in a world where our very subjectivity is dictated to us, along with virtually every accompanying aspect of behavior, action, and even thought. Bartleby says no a lot because he has a lot to say no to. But saying he "prefers not to" does not occlude but rather establishes and enables his ability to make other choices (other preferences).

What none of the characters in this story understand, not even the narrator, is that Bartleby's preferences mark an entirely different attitude toward life and a Nietzschean one at that. He says no to the false selves that would be mapped on him on behalf of the self—or selves—that he actually is. This gives Bartleby access to the same messy, anarchic riot of subjectivity that we see Nietzsche identifying with, the same self that is both objective and subjective, the self that is not just itself but has many overlapping aspects and influences. It may be that we see Bartleby as utterly passive because his acts of *amor fati* are screened for us via the "normal" interpellated perspective of the narrator. Like the fallen tightrope walker in *Thus Spoke Zarathustra*, Bartleby does not cling to a life animated by hopes and phantasms (perhaps Bartleby never had or needed such hopes; Melville doesn't say). He can give up all desires, even the desire to live, because he has, in effect, accepted his objecthood, his material existence. He has altered what counts as salvation, what one looks for out of life, not just for himself but potentially for all those whose life was affected by his example. In this way Bartleby enjoys a form of subjectivity, even an agency, that no other character in the story enjoys.

In thinking about the other forms of salvation offered by Bartleby, it is worth thinking more about when he becomes a corpse. Normally we think of a corpse as being "past saving," but in a different sort of thinking—a different view of subjectivity/objectivity—this might not be the case. In *The Origin of German Tragic Drama*, Benjamin tells us that the corpse is in some sense the "salvation" of the human being. He writes,

> And if it is in death that the spirit becomes free, in the manner of spirits, it is not until then that the body too comes properly into its own. For this much is self-evident: the allegorization of the physis can only be carried through in all its vigour in respect of the corpse. And the characters of the *Trauerspiel* [the "mourning plays" the baroque dramatists wrote] die, because it is only thus, as corpses, that they can enter into the homeland of allegory. It is not for the sake of immortality that they meet their end, but for the sake of the corpse.[22]

For Benjamin, the corpse is the body when it is free of projections, that is, free of the soul and of the false subject as well. The corpse is the body when it is abandoned by ends, a pure means that is only what it is (and hence "saved" in this more limited, less phantasmic sense). The fact that a corpse is horrifying, that no one wants to be one, is what allows this caesura in the projection of interpellative subjectivity (no more "hey, you there!"). Burial can banish this corpse—potentially allowing a return to phantasms of interpellative subjectivity about the person that this "really was"—but it can perhaps also recognize the corpse as such, hence Zarathustra's offer to the tightrope walker to bury him with his own hands (in chapters 6 and 7, we will see other versions of subversive burials).

Much the same dynamic can be seen with Bartleby. When he is a corpse, the distance between Bartleby's humanity and his objecthood vanishes; he enters into the "homeland of allegory," a zone that is inherently resistant and subversive to the phantasms of authority and personhood we normally subscribe to.

If Bartleby's death itself suggests an alternative view and model of life, his actions while alive are even more threatening to the operations of power and phantasm. When we see how Bartleby was so easily misperceived as operating within the spectrum of human actions—that is, as an interpellated subject—we see some evidence once again that every act of interpellation cannot but be misinterpellation at the same time. Whereas behavior generally conforms to expectations—wherein the "right" person turns around and meekly accepts her subjectivity—Bartleby is so out there, so outlandish in his failure to be a subject, that we can't miss his disobedience (unless we want to). Even the fact that he acts so objectlike reveals the way we are all connected, whether we like it or not—and we don't—to all the objects that form our context, to things and to one another in ways that we can't shut out (even though we try).

Bartleby shows us how this is so. Simply by demonstrating an alternative version of subjectivity, Bartleby shakes the confidence of interpellation to the core. Bartleby shows that there is another way to respond, not with phantasms but preferences, statements put out into the void, operations according to his own judgment. He does this not entirely on his own but in conjunction—or conspiracy—with "other" objects, with the texts he writes, with the bust of Cicero, with the wall he stares at, with his own body, even with the tongues of his fellow employees.

In this way, we can think of Bartleby as somehow "saving" us from interpellation, an example of a Nietzschean messiah (or antimessiah if you prefer). It is Melville himself who alerts us to the possibly sacred character of Bartleby. Characteristically the narrator misreads the theological implications of Bartleby, arguing that he is "predestined from eternity" whereas, as we have seen, Bartleby follows no ends at all, escapes from teleology and determinism.[23] Somewhat more accurately, the narrator goes on to say that "Bartleby was billeted upon me for some mysterious purpose of an all-wise Providence, which it was not for a mere mortal like me to fathom."[24] In this sense, the narrator is perhaps closer to guessing at Bartleby's messianic function (or dysfunction?); he cannot understand what it is but he recognizes a higher or divine hand in its operations (an operation in which unfathomability is not just a question of the nature of the act but its point as well). Bartleby, like an agent of divine violence—Melville calls him "inscrutable"—seeks to return truth to its unfathomability, to make what seems crystal clear, but is actually false, return to its nothingness, much like interpellation itself, and to live his own life in the path of being something impossibly complex: himself.[25]

At the very end of the story, after Bartleby has already died, the narrator offers a rumor that he heard that prior to coming to work for him, Bartleby worked at a "dead letter office," burning the mail whose recipients could not be found.[26] This suggests, perhaps more than anything else, the way that Bartleby is a figure of misinterpellation, perhaps a misinterpellated messiah. The narrator seems to connect the newly made corpse of Bartleby to his former station in life, stating, "Dead letters! Does it not sound like dead men?"[27] Never quite realizing Bartleby's true power and function—nor his threat to the established order—the narrator misrecognizes the connection that Bartleby has to writing, to letters and to acts of representation. He writes of the endless burning of dead letters by Bartleby's former office, saying that

> by the cartload [these letters] are annually burned. Sometimes from out of the folded paper the pale clerk takes a ring—the finger it was meant for, perhaps, moulders in the grave; a bank-note sent in swiftest charity—he whom it would relieve, nor eats nor hungers any more; pardon for those who died despairing; hope for those who died unhoping; good tidings for those who died stifled by unrelieved calamities. On errands of life, these letters speed to death.
> Ah, Bartleby! Ah, humanity![28]

For the narrator, the fact that these letters, these callings and being called made manifest in texts, do not get delivered is tragic. Think of all the fingers who died without a ring, the recipient of charity who did not get what she wished for! But as Zarathustra already demonstrated, charity itself can be a great curse, a desire for the salvation and hence the unmaking of the self.[29] Instead, Bartleby offers that we should celebrate those dead letters, those "successful" acts of misinterpellation where the false calls are intercepted, failed to be delivered to their "intended" recipient. It is perhaps an act of mercy on Bartleby's part to his fellow "letters" (of both the human and nonhuman variety) to burn them. In doing so, he takes these objects out of the false economies of human intentionality, of phantasms and ends. Bartleby is returning these letters to ashes, to pure means that, like corpses, can no longer have such intentions written over them. The narrator begs for "pardon for those who died despairing; hope for those who died unhoping" but what he doesn't realize is that this pardon, and this hope, has already been granted by Bartleby. An unexpected and unwanted messiah, Bartleby shows up anyway. Like Zarathustra, he takes away all of our hopes and wishes, leaving us finally alone, able to act as we might ourselves "prefer," if we can only come to recognize this very possibility.

The final thing I wish to stress about Bartleby is that if we think of him as a messiah (a decidedly "weak" one in the Benjaminian sense), what is critical is not so much what happens to him or what he does but what effect he has on other people.[30] His "agency," if that is what we are going to call it, comes in terms of how others hear or don't hear him. In fact, the power he puts out is never his but ours, his interlocutors. It has always been ours, in fact. Bartleby doesn't tell us that we have this power; he just offers us an opportunity to figure that out for ourselves. But his presence is hard to ignore, hard to paper over with the usual mumblings and incantations of frenetic capitalist interpellation. He infects and complicates and alters our lives and this—and only this—renders him, in effect, messianic. But ultimately what is critical about Bartleby is that, having visited us, he ensures that we don't need any further messiahs (or if there are more messiahs, they wouldn't be any different or do anything differently than he did). Bartleby is the epitome of the messiah who comes and goes and does nothing in between, but that nothing, that "slight adjustment," to cite Benjamin once more, changes— at least potentially—everything.[31]

It's Not about the Lighthouse: Lily Briscoe

If Bartleby, for all his passivity, entices via his strangeness, Lily Briscoe, the unlikely heroine—or at least survivor—of Virginia Woolf's *To the Lighthouse* does not even do that. Living in the shadows of her friend, Mrs. Ramsay, Lily seems the least appealing and least interesting character imaginable.

She is not even all that strange or weird, just very humdrum. And yet, as I will argue further, Lily is, very much like Bartleby, the one agent in her novel, the only person who can avoid being totalized by her subjectivity once again not despite but because of the way she slips under the radar, barely registering as a person at all. I read *To the Lighthouse* as being an exercise in Nietzschean (or Woolfian) disappointment whereby Woolf raises our expectations about the possibility of "real" subjectivity and then, drawing out that hope, dashes it decisively. This has the effect of allowing us to experience the failure of interpellated subjectivity—or to have that failure dramatized to us—and to get a peek at the kinds of identity that such subjectivity usually obscures or overrides.

Woolf's novel lays out various types of possibilities for the subject. We have a character (Mr. Ramsay) who is clearly meant to be exposed as a patently false subject, a pompous non-self-aware person. We have a character (Mrs. Ramsay) who offers an initially more promising type of subjectivity, one that seems more "real" both because she is so attractive and so ephemeral (hence seeming to acknowledge the artificiality of subjects on the one hand, even as her example promotes the delights and tangible experience of subjectivity on the other). Finally, we have a character (Lily Briscoe) who seems to be a failure to the point, once again, of almost not being a subject at all.

Moving through these characters in the novel allows us to experience the failure of the subject in a tangible way; we could not appreciate Lily's failure without first encountering the hopes and possibilities that come through and with the other characters, only to be exposed and ruined in the end. Woolf's novel serves to produce an intense state of disappointment in us, the reader. Yet when viewed through a Nietzschean lens, this disappointment allows once again what Peter Fitzpatrick calls a "productive" failure, a set of insights and experiences the reader would not otherwise have access to.[32]

Subjectivity shimmers and promises in this novel, not unlike the Lighthouse with which it seems to be intimately related for Woolf. The very title of the novel promises some kind of encounter: wherever the novel is headed, it seems that it will end up going "to" the Lighthouse. This promise is repeated by the characters in the very beginning of the novel when Mrs. Ramsay, the erstwhile, but not ultimate, protagonist tells her son—presumably after being asked if they can go to the Lighthouse—"Yes, of course, if it's fine tomorrow."[33] Shortly after, Mr. Ramsay enacts the crushing disappointment of such a promise, saying quite brutally, "But . . . it won't be fine."[34] This proves to be a prophetic statement. Indeed, nothing turns out "fine" in the novel: neither the weather nor the lives of the people who inhabit it. This short back and forth between Mr. and Mrs. Ramsay sets up the larger structure of the novel itself: promise followed by disappointment. Yet what is not yet present in this initial episode, what will emerge over the course of the text, is a third option, one that denies neither the promise nor the disappointment but grows out of the encounter with each (and which forms, I would therefore argue, the actual object of the "to" that is the first word of the novel's title). This other option is the very messy—and anarchic—alternative form of subjectivity that we see with Lily, the misinterpellated subject and unlikely heroine—or, perhaps more accurately, antiheroine—of the novel.

"All Their Flamingo Clouds and Blue and Silver"

In *To the Lighthouse*, there is a lot at stake in things that seem quite trivial on the surface. The initial quick call and response between the Ramsays concerning the chance of going to the Lighthouse is laden with deep emotion and passion. The Ramsays' son James's response to his father's pronouncement of doom is a barely repressed violence. Woolf writes, "Had there been an axe handy, a poker, or any weapon that would have gashed a hole in his father's breast and killed him, there and then, James would have seized it. Such were the extremes of emotion that Mr. Ramsay excited in his children's breasts by his mere presence."[35]

Such a violent response on James's part indicates that we are already not merely speaking about whether a particular family (the Ramsays) will go to a particular place (the Lighthouse) on a particular day (tomorrow). Rather, we see that there is a great burden put on these seemingly mundane statements. They bear an enormous representational weight, speaking not only to activities and plans but also to an entire set of hopes and wishes, desires and fulfillments. Not just the physical world but the psychic one too seems implicated in these statements (and, furthermore, these two worlds seem to be mutually implicated in a very profound way). Somehow, it is conveyed—not directly, for that would ruin the effect—that the Lighthouse represents a promise of concreteness, of fullness and wholeness and resolution of self. The Lighthouse, it seems, is the source of interpellation; the stand-in or personification of God in this novel (and hence, following Althusser, the "original Subject").

In terms of the various characters and their response to the hopes and dreams illuminated by the Lighthouse, Mr. Ramsay serves in the novel as the voice of standard Western rationalism and—by extension—imperialism (Woolf speaks of the children as encountering an atmosphere of "chivalry, of the Bank of England and the Indian Empire, of ringed fingers and lace").[36] Mr. Ramsay is described as embodying his harsh logic and antimagical thinking in his very person. He is "lean as a knife, narrow as the blade of one."[37] Furthermore we are told, "he was incapable of untruth; never tampered with a fact; never altered a disagreeable word to suit the pleasure or convenience of any mortal being, least of all his own children."[38]

Mr. Ramsay is a philosopher by profession. When she ventures to ask what he writes about, Mrs. Ramsay is told that his work deals with "subject and object and the nature of reality." She is told to "think of a kitchen table . . . when you're not there" when she thinks of his work.[39] In response, Mrs. Ramsay,

> with a painful effort of concentration . . . focused her mind, not upon a silver-bossed bark of the tree, or upon its fish-shaped leaves, but upon a phantom kitchen table, one of those scrubbed board tables, grained and knotted, whose virtue seems to have been laid bare by years of muscular integrity, which stuck there, its four legs in air. Naturally, if one's days were passed in this seeing of angular essences, this reducing of lovely evenings, with all their flamingo clouds and blue and silver to a white deal four-legged table (and it was the mark of the finest minds to do so), naturally one could not be judged like an ordinary person.[40]

Although Mrs. Ramsay is (perhaps excessively) charitable toward her husband, we can see a critique at the basis of this description. For all of his "objectivity" (as it were), Mr. Ramsay is arguably the character in the novel who is most out of touch (least conspiring) with the material universe as well as his own subjectivity; he is the character who best embodies the false conceit that human beings are utterly in control of themselves, of their own subjectivity, as well as their relationship to the objects of the world and the fabric of reality.

It might be said that Mr. Ramsay effectively avoids the pervasive magic of the world (the "flamingo clouds and blue and silver") in favor of a "phantom" reality, a kitchen table that is only imagined and that, in its stark nonexistence ("laid bare by years of muscular integrity") displaces and replaces the world that is actually lived in.

Mr. Ramsay is exceedingly transparent; it would be easy to see that he is not who he thinks he is. And yet he is formally the most privileged subject in this novel. He is the father, the head of the family; he has the full interpellative power of the state and the academy, of his class, gender, and race behind him. Yet the reader can readily see that this pose is empty, that Mr. Ramsay is not "really" who he is said—or called—to be, that, in fact, he is in some sense nothing at all, a mere cipher (and an angry one at that).

"It Is Enough!"

Mrs. Ramsay herself, on the other hand, seems to have a much more engaged relationship to both herself and the world about her than her husband precisely by avoiding his assumptions and projections. Mrs. Ramsay is open to the way that the world and other people enchant and seduce us; she allows external influence to wash over her, to accept a far more fluid form of subjectivity that seems to come from multiple and varied sources. This can be seen most clearly in terms of Mrs. Ramsay's various encounters with the Lighthouse. Mr. Ramsay, the purportedly fully and successfully interpellated subject, has no time for magic or the Lighthouse (although by the end of the novel, he too very much wants to go and visit it). It's almost as if Mrs. Ramsay knows the true path of interpellation; unlike her husband, she is open to its ephemeral—because unreal—nature. She knows how to make subjectivity work, how best to receive the full promise of interpellation without reducing it to a cipher as her husband does. Perhaps more accurately, she seems to know, at least to some extent, that the "emperor has no clothes" but this does not prevent her from fully taking advantage of the lures and promises of interpellation nonetheless.

We can see the way that these questions of subjectivity, magic, and the material world are all intermixed in the novel by looking at the first viewing of the Lighthouse. This occurs while Mrs. Ramsay is walking to town with "the atheist" Charles Tansley, one of her husband's students and acolytes. Although Tansley shares his mentor's skepticism and sense of mastery over the material world, he nonetheless is strongly affected by—and doesn't or can't resist—the lures of the Lighthouse, the effect its beauty and light have on his own self and sense of mastery over his personal boundaries.

At the first appearance of the Lighthouse, Woolf writes, "Mrs. Ramsay could not help exclaiming, 'Oh, how beautiful!' For the great plateful of blue water was before her; the hoary Lighthouse, distant, austere."[41]

As they walk further, things begin to change from an aesthetic appreciation to something far more profound. As if unleashed by the appearance of the Lighthouse, the stuffy, pompous Tansley becomes increasingly drawn toward Mrs. Ramsay and possibly toward the world itself: "Under the influence of that extraordinary emotion which had been growing all the walk, . . . he was coming to see himself, and everything he had ever known gone crooked a little. It was awfully strange."[42]

Seeing Mrs. Ramsay at the top of a set of stairs, having an ordinary conversation with a local merchant, Tansley is transfixed by the sight of her. "Suddenly, in she came . . . stood quite motionless for a moment against a picture of Queen Victoria wearing the blue ribbon of the Garter; when all at once he realized that it was this: it was this:—she was the most beautiful person he had ever seen."[43] Mrs. Ramsay suddenly comes forth to him, in the same way that the Lighthouse appeared to her moments before. The "atheist" Tansley is overcome by her. Reading this through a Nietzschean lens—at least when he is in his seductive, transcendent mode—it could be said that Tansley sees the shining beautiful subjectivity of Mrs. Ramsay as it is mediated via the Lighthouse. She appears to him in a way that leaves no doubt that she is the epitome of fulfilled personhood; transcending the narrow insistence on rationality that Mr. Ramsay and Tansley share—an assumption that is so easily pierced as false—this seems to be the "real thing." She is even equated with Queen Victoria(!) who, if not the Subject in an Althusserian sense, is certainly the subject for Britain during her reign.

There is an even more intense example of the effect of the Lighthouse later that evening. The Lighthouse is lit as evening begins to fall and Mrs. Ramsay has a rapturous experience of its beauty and power.

> Losing personality, one lost the fret, the hurry, the stir; and there rose to her lips always some exclamation of triumph over life when things came together in this peace, this rest, this eternity; and pausing there she looked out to meet that stroke of the Lighthouse, the long steady stroke, the last of the three, which was her stroke, for watching them in this mood always at this hour one could not help attaching oneself to one thing especially of the things one saw; and this thing, the long steady stroke, was her stroke.[44]

This merger of herself with the light culminates to the point where she feels

> as if it were stroking with its silver fingers some sealed vessel in her brain whose bursting would flood her with delight, she had known happiness, exquisite happiness, intense happiness, and it silvered the rough waves a little more brightly, as daylight faded, and the blue went out of the sea and it rolled in waves of pure lemon which curved and swelled and broke upon the beach and the ecstasy burst in her eyes and waves of pure delight raced over the floor of her mind and she felt, It is enough! It is enough![45]

In her claim that "it is enough!" we see the rapturous possibility that is promised by interpellative subjectivity; Mrs. Ramsay is fulfilled, complete, and whole (enough!). Such a realization, in its very intangibility, is exactly what Mr. Ramsay is denying himself by his refusal to read the world in a way that does not conform to his own predeterminations. Mrs. Ramsay, on the other hand, encounters the Lighthouse with much greater promise; she offers us fulfillment, ecstasy, and perfection, a genuine encounter wherein we are, however temporarily, completed. And, in her better grasp of interpellation, Mrs. Ramsay also seems—but only seems—to answer the point that the subject is never unified, not purely internal but a mixture of exogenous and endogenous forces. Mrs. Ramsay seems to take all of that in stride and become a subject just the same (perhaps you could say because and not despite of the amorphous nature of subjectivity).

"The Red Fresh on His Lips"

This possibility of subjectivity is so alluring, so potent, that, as Woolf portrays him, even Mr. Ramsay isn't completely immune to its lures. For all his bladelike existence, we see a softer side of Mr. Ramsay at various points in the novel. One of his old friends, William Bankes, notes wistfully that although "the pulp had gone out of their friendship" and "repetition had taken the place of newness" between them, still "his affection for Ramsay had in no way diminished; but there, like the body of a young man laid up in peat for a century, with the red fresh on his lips, was his friendship, in its acuteness and reality, laid up across the bay among the sandhills."[46] This, of course, is not Mr. Ramsay's own thinking but it suggests that some kind of affection, some connection outside of himself survives intact even despite his formal denial of the world's power over him. Thus Mr. Ramsay's mastery over the world—over reality itself—is mercifully not complete. He's shown to be open to learning from and connecting with the more ephemeral forms of subjectivity that Mrs. Ramsay engages with and is hence perhaps not a lost cause after all.

In his own mind, Mr. Ramsay ruefully acknowledges to himself that the material and exogenous world has a power to resist his mental conquest of it. He frets at one point about whether he can know—and thus command—all forms of knowledge in the world, which he pictures as a series of letters of the alphabet from A to Z (he feels himself to have reached the letter Q and that "very few people in the whole of England ever reach Q" but then he worries about getting to R, that is, to himself, and beyond).[47]

Mr. Ramsay also worries that "the very stone one kicks with one's boot [shades of Samuel Johnson] will outlast Shakespeare," suggesting more of the resilience of material things, their independent power from his own consciousness (and the consciousness of human beings in general).[48] Going further along in this mode, he thinks,

> Who will not secretly rejoice when the hero puts his armour off, and halts by the window and gazes at his wife and son [who are indeed close by at this moment, even as he looks "into the hedge, into the intricacy of twigs"], who, very distant at first, gradually come closer and closer, till lips and book and head are clearly before him, though still lovely and unfamiliar from the intensity of his isolation. . . . Who will blame him if he does homage to the beauty of the world?[49]

At the end of the first night of the novel—a night that presages a passage of many years, Mrs. Ramsay's untimely death and Mr. Ramsay's definitive retreat from the world, the certainty that he will never make it to "R"—Mr. Ramsay has a brief, but critical encounter with the magic of reality, one that he shares with his wife.

The Ramsays have retreated to their bedroom to read and get ready for bed. At dinner that night, Mrs. Ramsay could tell that Mr. Ramsay had grown irritated and anxious about the question of how his own books would be received, whether they would have a lasting impact or would be quickly forgotten. Mrs. Ramsay, thinking past these preoccupations, says to herself, "There is something I want—something I have come to get."[50] As she is thinking this, and falling deeper into a reverie, there is a transformation in the room, not unlike the one affected by her seeing the Lighthouse for the first (or second) time.

At first, a snatch of a line from a book comes to her, something that had been said earlier that night at dinner: "The China rose is all abloom and buzzing with the honey bee."[51] These words "began washing from side to side of her mind rhythmically, and as they washed, words like little shaded lights, one red, one blue, one yellow, lit up in the dark of her mind, and seemed leaving their perches up there to fly across and across."[52]

As this is happening, lines of poetry come to her seemingly unbidden:

And all the lives we ever lived
And all the lives to be,
Are full of trees and changing leaves.[53]

Mrs. Ramsay "did not know at first what the words meant at all."[54] Mr. Ramsay is similarly entranced: "Their eyes met for a second; but they did not want to speak to each other. They had nothing to say, but something seemed, nevertheless, to go from him to her."[55]

At this point Mr. and Mrs. Ramsay are both reading and are surrounded— quite physically, it seems—by poetry. Lines of poetry appear to enable the connection they are experiencing (even as this connection is itself conveyed to us via text). As with Charles Tansley's revelation earlier that day, Mr. Ramsay thinks amid this swirl of poetry and text that "[Mrs. Ramsay] was astonishingly beautiful. Her beauty seemed to him, if that were possible, to increase."[56] What was earlier that day "still lovely and unfamiliar from the intensity of his isolation" becomes transformed into what seems to be a real appreciation, an experience of his wife such as she is (or appears to be, anyway).

The fact that it is poetry that allows or even produces this moment seems to be telling; in poetry there is some kind of gesture across the gulf between words and objects (or subjects). In the way that Woolf portrays it here, it seems that there is redemption even for Mr. Ramsay (insofar as everything has indeed "gone crooked a little").

As if reflecting this new role and power of language, the chapter—and the night—ends with a kind of wordless struggle between the spouses. Mr. Ramsay looks at Mrs. Ramsay and she knows that he is thinking how beautiful she is. Mrs. Ramsay thinks,

Will you not tell me just once that you love me? . . . But . . . she could not say it. Then, knowing that he was watching her, instead of saying anything she turned, holding her stocking, and looked at him. And as she looked at him she began to smile, for though she had not said a word, he knew, of course he knew, that she loved him. He could not deny it. And smiling she looked out of the window and said (thinking to herself, Nothing on earth can equal this happiness)—

"Yes, you were right. It's going to be wet tomorrow. You won't be able to go." And she looked at him smiling. For she had triumphed again. She had not said it: yet he knew.[57]

In a way, Mrs. Ramsay has turned the tables on her husband. Mrs. Ramsay uses words—the very tool of Mr. Ramsay's trade—without actually speaking them, to deny him the power over language and reality that he ordinarily feels himself to have. Mrs. Ramsay is triumphant because she seems to have had an experience of and with her husband despite his every attempt to exert control over himself and his situation.

It seems that this then is the acme of interpellation. Woolf could be read—at this point, but, of course, the novel is not done—to be saying that subjectivity is real but its reality is one that is always mediated, never quite our own. This could be seen as a rebuke of classical understandings of personhood—such as is represented by Mr. Ramsay—wherein each isolated individual controls their identity full stop. Because Mrs. Ramsay is open to the fact that she is interpellated in a way that Mr. Ramsay is not, she accepts the external nature of her own subjectivity—perhaps we could say she ceases, at least to some extent, to misrecognize this fact—and, in that acceptance, thrives and animates even her recalcitrant husband. In other words, she accepts her role as a woman, a wife, and a mother—however exceptional and unique she seems—as determined by the norms and principles of interpellation. She seems to say "yes" to all of that.

In such a reading, Mr. Ramsay is an undeserving beneficiary, it would seem, of the magical power of interpellation that gives, if not truth, then something more wonderful than truth, fulfillment, and joy. While Mrs. Ramsay may offer a critique of some positivist version of personhood, what she is offering is not failure and therefore not misinterpellation. Her path promises instead success and a fulfillment that is imperfect but gratifying (it is enough!). Here, we see the full seductive glory of all that liberalism promises (especially in its more unorthodox guises).

Time Passes

If the novel ended there, Woolf might yet be a great critic of some aspects of liberal subjectivity: the narrow, patriarchal, imperialist forms that it takes. She would raise critical points and expose the vulnerability—and pomposity—of a model of subjectivity that is patently and evidently false (i.e., Mr. Ramsay's). But Woolf would remain within the umbrella of liberalism nonetheless because she would be showing how interpellation can actually work. She would be showing how the subjects produced via interpellation can be true, or true enough, anyway. She would be showing how we can "really"—or pretty close to "really"—be what we are called to be (as Mrs. Ramsay is herself).

Furthermore, although she clearly would be stretching and complicating the concept of what it means to be a woman, if the novel ended at this point, Woolf would still be limiting her endorsement of feminism by remaining within the bounds of understanding women—as already noted—as being at one with nature and as a necessary support, even salvation, for her husband; she would be bending but not breaking the bounds of the options for women offered by interpellated forms of subjectivity.

Yet Woolf has quite a trick up her sleeve; she does not take this path and she does not throw in her lot with Mrs. Ramsay. It is here that she demonstrates a strong parallelism with Nietzsche, a penchant for raising our hopes and then dashing them, seducing us and then disappointing us in the process. If we think that we can really be and succeed as liberal subjects, even if we have to shed some of its less attractive aspects—patriarchy, imperialism—many of us will sign on then and there. As readers of Woolf, we are immediately alerted to the falsities of Mr. Ramsay's approach. He is clearly the one who is most deluded. But how can we resist the siren call of Mrs. Ramsay? In her beauty, in her endless knitting, her concerns, and her clear and vulnerable humanity, she seems to be the one with all the answers. She looks like the redeemer that we are looking for in this novel ("it is enough!").

I noted something similar in the reading of Nietzsche's *Zarathustra*; Nietzsche easily and readily exposes many of the false forms of messianism he decries, that of philosophy and certain modes of Christianity. Yet surely we can trust Nietzsche himself with his own beautiful and merciless prose? If he is the one who shows us what not to believe, surely we can trust him and believe everything he tells us?

In the case of both Nietzsche and Woolf, this is the moment for a second, and much deeper, act of betrayal or disappointment. For Nietzsche, it will be recalled, this is when he brings out the overman, only to have that messiah too fail to arrive or redeem (except insofar as he does arrive and "redeem" in the form of the unexpected and unwanted jester). Woolf makes a similar move in her treatment of Mrs. Ramsay. For all the promise of love and connection and fulfillment offered via the figure of Mrs. Ramsay, everything seems to be unmade by the section that follows the first "day" of the novel (a middle section entitled "Time Passes"). Here, we get the description of one long—years long, actually—night that follows Mrs. Ramsay's triumphant moment. As we discover, it is not Mrs. Ramsay who holds the key to subjectivity after all. At the very least, she, along with her approach, does not survive to the end of the novel. In a brutal act of bracketed annihilation, Woolf writes, "[Mr Ramsay, stumbling along a passage one dark morning, stretched his arms out, but Mrs Ramsay, having died rather suddenly the night before, his arms, though stretched out, remained empty]."[58]

In this long night described during the middle section of the novel, various ephemeral objects, the air, even the house itself seem to come to life. The more solid objects within the house similarly take on a fully independent existence from the human characters, indeed seemingly coming to life at their expense; not only does Mrs. Ramsay die but so does her daughter Prue, something else that we are told within another pair of brackets in the text. And a son, Andrew, dies as well. Woolf writes of all of this mortality that "loveliness and stillness clasped hands in the bedroom, and among the shrouded jugs and sheeted chairs even the prying of the wind, and the soft nose of the clammy sea airs, rubbing, snuffling, iterating and reiterating their questions—'will you fade? Will you perish?' "[59]

Tantalizing us with images of fulfillment and completion in the first part of the novel, Woolf now seems to shut the door on the very possibilities that she raised earlier:

> It seemed now as if, touched by human penitence and all its toil, divine goodness had parted the curtain and displayed behind it, single, distinct, the hare erect; the wave falling; the boat rocking; which, did we deserve them, should be ours always. But alas, divine goodness, twitching the cord, draws the curtain; it does not please him; he covers his treasures in a drench of hail, and so breaks them, so confuses them that it seems impossible that their calm should ever return or that we should ever compose from their fragments a perfect whole or read in the littered pieces the clear words of truth. For our penitence deserves a glimpse only; our toil respite only.[60]

Here, as we saw in Bartleby too, there may be a material conspiracy afoot; the objects of the house conspire against the human resident's hubristic notion that they control their own subjectivity. If "the night before," poetry magically seemed to connect the Ramsays to reality, to life itself, during this longer, darker night, these more mundane objects do something far different; they seem to announce the distance between human subjects as they wish to appear and what they actually are (or perhaps more accurately, they point to our death, to what life is when it is denuded of magic).

If the Lighthouse seems to be—at least in the way the novel's characters respond to it—the great interpellator, an original Subject not unlike Althusser's reading of God, the minor objects of the house (the pillows, curtains, chairs, and so forth) conspire to ruin any certainties that interpellation might produce; perhaps it takes a material uprising to ruin and subvert a material operation, to make the failure that is inherent in interpellation more visible to those who (otherwise) respond to its call.

Up till this point in the novel, we seemed safe in thinking that if we could only get "to the Lighthouse," if we could see the world and the Lighthouse itself, as having an independent power over us—rather than merely serving as instruments of human whim as Mr. Ramsay does—we would be recognized and whole. If only, that is, the externalities that we project back onto ourselves were real—or if not quite real, then at least suitably ephemeral and dreamy—like Mrs. Ramsay herself, just "real" enough to do the trick, then we would be saved from being "who we are."[61]

Yet Woolf is not the kind of author or thinker who affords us such an easy conclusion. Just as Mrs. Ramsay herself is done away with, so too is the hope that she represents. If she promises something beyond herself, an openness to the interpellation that forms her—and hence offering a more "honest" sense of her identity, conceding her lack of autonomy without conceding her basic completeness—her own untimely death indicates the limits of such a viewpoint. It offers that she (and we) remain all too mortal, hemmed in and subject to powers that not only are not under our control but also, in some ways, constitute forces that have nothing to do with us at all. Whether bewitched by magic or not, we are still "us": we can't be more than that no matter how beautiful and alluring—or not—we may seem or wish to be.

It's Not about the Lighthouse

As the novel develops, it is not Mrs. Ramsay but Lily Briscoe, a seemingly minor and irrelevant character in the first part of the novel, who shows us another path.[62] In my reading that is refracted via Nietzsche, Lily is, as already noted, the misinterpellated and ultimate protagonist of *To the Lighthouse,* one whose entry is unheralded and unexpected (even, to some extent, unwanted). Lily is one of the many figures who hover around the Ramsay family. In the first part of the novel, when Mrs. Ramsay is going from triumph to triumph, Lily is largely an object of pity: "with her little Chinese eyes and her puckered-up face, [Lily] would never marry; one could not take her painting very seriously; she was an independent little creature, and Mrs. Ramsay liked her for it."[63]

For her own part, throughout the first part of the novel, Lily is in awe of Mrs. Ramsay; the latter's beauty, the seeming perfection of her large and boisterous family, are all things that Lily thinks she should have or at least envy. Mrs. Ramsay thinks to herself that Lily would be best off marrying William Bankes (who seems singularly unattractive). It is part of Mrs. Ramsay's nature to wish "happy endings" for one and all (and it is she who effectively decides what counts as happiness). Lily is aware of this and also knows that in fact, like everyone else in the novel, William Bankes is smitten with Mrs. Ramsay herself. Yet none of this seems to bother Lily (or at least not visibly at that point in the novel; later we find out that it bothers her very much). Woolf writes of Lily that she "saw [William Bankes] gazing at Mrs. Ramsay [and thought it] was a rapture. . . . Such a rapture—for by what other name could one call it?—made Lily Briscoe forget entirely what she had been about to say."[64]

For all her observation of human interactions—albeit at some remove—Lily is more interested in representation per se, in the mechanics of communication, especially through painting. She is depicted as painting throughout the novel (in two separate but epic sessions corresponding to the first and third—and final—part of the novel, the latter of which is called "The Lighthouse"). For Lily, the frustration of painting comes from trying to communicate what she thinks in her head onto the canvas:

> She could see it all so clearly, so commandingly, when she looked: it was when she took her brush to hand that the whole thing changed. It was in that moment's flight between the picture and her canvas that the demons set on her who often brought her to the verge of tears and made this passage from conception to work as dreadful as any down a dark passage for a child. . . . "I'm in love with this all," [she thought] waving her hand at the hedge, at the house, at the children. It was absurd. It was impossible.[65]

In the first part of the novel, Lily's painting seems unfinished to her. She observes, she responds, but somehow there is a lack of correspondence between her internal vision and the world about her. In a sense then, she shares with the other characters in the novel, at least to this point, the notion that the world ought to conform to one's own apparently internal sense of self, that is to say, to a phantasmic form of subjectivity that we usually identify as our "self" and then project (back) out.

Yet, even in the first part of the novel, Lily stands out exactly because she is a misfit and out of her element, because she does not really feel like she belongs here and is allowed to do so by the Ramsays—it seems—out of pity and patronizing views rather than genuine friendship. For all of her near invisibility, Lily wants to love, to feel the passions that others feel, but her own disconnection from the world will prove to be the secret to her success (or, perhaps more accurately, her—productive—failure). Lily's interest in representation as such—her fidelity to modes of depiction that may or may not obey her dictates or even offer her any benefits at all—becomes the means by which she avoids remaining determined by her wishes and projections. One could say that, as a failed artist, Lily is also able to access her failure as a subject; she has a sense that parts do not always cohere, that beauty and dazzle are not the same as truth, and that there is no inherent destiny or telos that demands that, in the end, we all will be complete and whole subjects (or at least those of us who rate such a happy ending).

In the last part of the novel, after the long passage of night that divides the book in two, Lily is initially bereft, without the firm guidance and assuredness of Mrs. Ramsay. She finds herself at a complete loss: "What did she feel, come back after all these years and Mrs Ramsay dead? Nothing, nothing—nothing that she could express at all."[66]

Lily remains very unconventional in the last part of the book. Mr. Ramsay, now a widower and much older and sadder, wonders at one point why Lily is looking at the Lighthouse and not at him. At that moment, "there issued from him such a groan that any other woman in the whole world would have done something, said something—all except myself, thought Lily, girding at herself bitterly, who am not a woman, but a peevish, ill-tempered, dried-up old maid, presumably."[67]

But it is not Lily but Mr. Ramsay himself who is the ultimate loser of this novel. In this, the second "day" of the novel, a party is finally going out to the Lighthouse; Mr. Ramsay, his son James, and his daughter Cam. As they make their way to the Lighthouse in a sailboat, Lily stays behind to do her painting. The novel splits into two as it were, alternating between telling the story of the Ramsay expedition to the Lighthouse and Lily's experience of painting (itself juxtaposed to her earlier act of painting in the first part).

In going to the Lighthouse, Mr. Ramsay seems to be fulfilling the great unmet wish of Mrs. Ramsay, first expressed in the opening lines of the novel. But James, the Ramsay's son, is implacable. He still burns with a hatred against his father for his statement on that day so long ago that the weather would not be "fine" (as well as many other moments when his father was aloof and inhuman). James hates his father and begrudges him any attempt at resolution or conciliation. Mr. Ramsay, in any event, seems beyond all that. He is "a desolate man, widowed, bereft."[68] While Mr. Ramsay has his nose in a book, his son seethes, and his daughter tries to make peace. Finally as they get to the island we have this scene where the adult children are both watching their father:

> They watched him, both of them, sitting bareheaded with his parcel on his knee staring and staring at the frail blue shape which seemed like the vapour of something that had burnt itself away. What do you want? they both wanted to ask. They both wanted to say, Ask us anything and we will give it to you. But he did not ask them anything. He sat and looked at the island and he might be thinking, We perished, each alone, or he might be thinking, I have reached it. I have found it; but he said nothing.
>
> Then he put on his hat.[69]

This scene vaguely parallels the scene at the end of the first day between Mr. and Mrs. Ramsay where there is a demand for saying something—in that case, "I love you"—which is not given. In this case, far more clearly than in the earlier situation, it is evident that these characters are desperately trying to understand and control the world beyond their minds; they seek to understand their father, to make him ask questions, to know who he is and to be acknowledged and recognized by him. He, in turn, insists on retaining his island like fortitude; he withholds his recognition and with it, the promise of fullness that both he and his wife represent, albeit in very different ways.

After all the buildup, there is something curiously anticlimactic about the Ramsays' arrival at the Lighthouse (in the end, we don't even get to see them set foot on the island; rather, James is captured midair as he springs for the rocks on shore). We have finally come "to" the Lighthouse but we seem to be nowhere different than where we began. There is no big revelation here, no discovery (except a small act of kindness wherein Mr. Ramsay does praise James's sailing skills for getting them over a rough patch of sea).

For a book that sets itself up as a journey, where even the question of being able to go to the Lighthouse is so fraught that it sets the other events of the book in motion, we seem to have stalled, to remain very much where we are. This is very much in keeping with Nietzsche's own way of thinking about subjectivity, of how to "become what one is," but without similarly recognizing—much less embracing—this impasse as such at least as far as Mr. Ramsay is concerned. These are failed subjects—cripples at this bridge—indeed, but they do not even realize that, having come to the origin of the promise that animates them, and finding nothing, they have the option to go another way. This, I would argue, is the same fate that would have met the tightrope walker, had the jester not "overcome" him and prevented him from reaching the other side (the "Lighthouse" he was heading toward).

Contrast this anticlimax with the experience of Lily, who, even as this event is transpiring, is busily trying to paint or capture the journey to the Lighthouse that has just been completed. As usual, she is at a remove, representing an experience rather than actually participating in it.

Even as she feels the loss of Mrs. Ramsay, as she is painting, Lily becomes more critical of her dead friend, including the role that she had sought for Lily herself. She notes of Mrs. Ramsay's beauty that

> beauty was not everything. Beauty had this penalty—it came too readily, too completely. It stilled life—froze it. One forgot the little agitations; the flush, the pallor, some queer distortion, some light or shadow, which made the face unrecognisable for a moment and yet added a quality one saw for ever after. It was simpler to smooth that all out under the cover of beauty.[70]

Here we see something of a critique of Mrs. Ramsay's approach to life. Mrs. Ramsay wanted everyone to be married, to conform to social norms, to be happy, smooth, and complete (once again as she understands such things). Lily allows herself a moment of smugness thinking about the couples that Mrs. Ramsay set up who ended up having marital problems. We may see this as an act of betrayal on Lily's part but it could just as easily be a warning against taking too many of Mrs. Ramsay's beliefs at face value. It also might reflect the absence of Mrs. Ramsay herself; dead, she can no longer police other's thoughts, she can no longer "smooth" things over with her beauty and grace.

Lily's concern about her painting, about getting everything just right, parallels this concern over propriety, emotions, and her feelings about others. She thinks to herself "so much depends . . . upon distance: whether people are near us or far from us; her feeling for Mr Ramsay changed as he sailed further and further across the bay. . . . He and his children seemed to be swallowed up in that blue, that distance."[71] Disharmonies in her thinking about Mr. Ramsay threaten the harmony of the painting too: "Was it, she wondered, that the line of the wall wanted breaking, was it that the mass of trees was too heavy? She smiled ironically; for had she not thought, when she began, that she had solved her problem?"[72]

Lily's concerns about the harmony and structure of the painting are further reflected in her concerns about her own future. What would become of her? What would become of her painting? She frets that it will end up "rolled up and stuffed under a sofa" as she might herself live the rest of her life alone, unloved, dusty and forgotten.[73] Here, we see echoes of Mr. Ramsay's own fretting about whether he would ever reach "R" or how his own books would be received after he died.

All of these concerns show that Lily too remains in contention with the idea that there is a proper and necessary way to be a subject; she feels a failure as a woman, as a friend, and as an artist.

Yet unlike the anticlimax of the Ramsay expedition to the Lighthouse, Lily has a much more intense experience, a revelation that concludes the novel.

> Quickly, as if she were recalled by something over there, she turned to her canvas. There it was—her picture. Yes, with all its greens and blues, its lines running up and across, its attempt at something. It would be hung in the attics, she thought; it would be destroyed. But what did that matter? she asked herself, taking up her brush again. She looked at the steps; they were empty; she looked at her canvas; it was blurred. With a sudden intensity, as if she saw it clear for a second, she drew a line there, in the centre. It was done; it was finished. Yes, she thought, laying down her brush in extreme fatigue, I have had my vision.[74]

Here, Lily resolves her struggle, at least for this moment, at least potentially. In a flash, she abandons her sovereignty over her own subjectivity just as she seems to abandon any attempt to control her painting ("there it was—her picture"). Mr. Ramsay is, we are told, "melted away into a blue haze."[75] Her painting will end up in the attic, destroyed, and she herself will one day be a mere corpse (like Bartleby). In this moment, Lily becomes a Nietzschean subject. She accepts (and indeed loves) her fate; she accepts the mess of it all, the "greens and blues, its lines running up and across, its attempt at something."

Reflecting this kind of transformation, Lily's painting, which up till then seemed to demand a perfect situating, becomes completed simply by adding a single line, a "slight adjustment," to cite Benjamin once again, that delivers her vision, an assertion of her newly found agency (more accurately, the agency that was always hers but which was swallowed up in so much more).[76] The anguish that she feels when she tries to conform, when she tries to love as she feels she should—an anguish that brings all the self-hatred and contempt that she has long internalized—gives way at this moment to a kind of peace, a reconciliation to and with herself in all her messy and failed subjectivity.[77] The line that she draws is perhaps not the point; it merely serves as an opportunity for Lily to accept, to cease to struggle for answers in a painting—and, by extension, a universe—that has none to offer. One more line and it's done; now she can stop worrying about perfection. Or perhaps the line is a negating one, crossing out the possibility for perfection and even a sense of completion, making her painting "finished" in the much more denuded, smaller sense that she simply isn't going to work on it any further.

In this way, we can see that *To the Lighthouse* is not actually about the Lighthouse after all (just as her painting is not about that last line). The Lighthouse is a chimera that seduces us with its promise of completion and redemption but which delivers nothing of the kind. The structure of the novel reinforces the way that the Lighthouse serves as a false messiah in the text. Against the obvious errors of Mr. Ramsay and his attempt to assert a subjectivity that is real on its face, Mrs. Ramsay appears to be the answer (even for Mr. Ramsay). Her approach appears at first glance to be the antithesis of his. Where he is brutal and callous, clearly wishing to dominate the world and assert himself by fiat, Mrs. Ramsay appears to be at peace with the world, wishing only to be part of it and to participate in its magical effects. Yet, from a Nietzschean (and Woolfian) perspective, Mrs. Ramsay is, if anything, more problematic than her husband because she offers the appearance of self-acceptance, of *amor fati*, whereas in fact it is really only more of the same self-hatred and denial in a deceptive guise (where fate is a future and a "not here"). In the end, the seductions of Mrs. Ramsay are far more dangerous, ultimately more archic, than her husband's because they threaten to make the impossible and incredible actually appear to be workable.

In her own way—as Lily Briscoe experiences quite viscerally—Mrs. Ramsay can be as hegemonic as her husband; her own phantasms, while they seem gentler and more connected than her husbands, remain phantasms, remain her own attempt to control and dominate a form of subjectivity that is in fact wildly anarchic and rebellious. Worse yet, because her phantasms seem to acknowledge their own phantasmic quality, they seem to have looked the lack of truth—or lack of it—in the face and stared it down. There is no recourse with Mrs. Ramsay because she is like the fetishist described by Freud (and rearticulated by Wendy Brown): "I know [I am a fetishist] but still. . . ."[78]

Lily Briscoe, who clearly feels the same allures as the Ramsays—including the allure of the Ramsays themselves—is the only one who truly experiences the failure of her subjectivity. This is not the glamorized "failure" that Mrs. Ramsay encapsulates but a much more bitter and unattractive failure, a failure that no one would actually want to claim for themselves (whereas I could see a lot of people saying "if Mrs. Ramsay is what failure looks like, count me in!"). For all her attempts to get the painting right, to be a "real" woman, to respond as she thinks a person ought to respond, Lily is a failure in a bleaker, less romantic, and more disappointing sense. And this failure is her salvation (a salvation from salvation, once again). She fails to be who she—and Mrs. Ramsay—thinks she is supposed to be and, in this way, shares a perspective usually relegated to objects; she accepts that she and/or her paintings will end up in an attic, that she will die and that her painting will never be perfect (never be "real"); she gives up on this shining future and, in doing so, gains her present, her "noontime."

We see here the value of Woolf's construction of the novel. Were we to directly access Lily's failure at the end of the novel without the initial setup, we wouldn't recognize it for what it is; we wouldn't be able to appreciate what we have given up in the process. It is only by tempting us, first with the subjectivity by fiat of Mr. Ramsay, then with the much more seductive magical subjecthood of Mrs. Ramsay, that Woolf can demonstrate a new and different form of misinterpellated identity by contrast. As with Nietzsche, we must be tempted and then betrayed—and not just once but repeatedly—in order to break us, at least potentially, at least for this moment, from our subservience to interpellation.

"Come, Come!"

As for what emerges as a result of Lily's failure to be the subject she feels she has been called to become, Woolf perhaps best captures the complexity of an anarchic subjectivity in a different writing, her beautiful and enigmatic work *Orlando*. In that work she writes of Orlando's own subjectivity (one that moves across time and gender, one that is many beings at once). Toward the very end of that novel, Woolf writes that Orlando calls out to herself, saying "Orlando?" Here, the call is turned inward, the circuitry of interpellation becomes shrunk down to a party of one. But that party is itself vast:

> For if there are (at a venture) seventy-six different times all tick-ing in the mind at once, how many different people are there not—Heaven help us—all having lodgment at one time or another in the human spirit? Some say two thousand and fifty-two. So that it is the most usual thing in the world for a person to call, directly when they are alone, Orlando? (if that is one's name), meaning by that, Come, come! I'm sick to death of this particular self. I want another. Hence the astonishing changes we see in our friends. But it is not altogether plain sailing [using the same metaphor we see in *To the Lighthouse*], either, for though one may say, as Orlando said (being in the country and needing another self presumably) Orlando? still the Orlando she needs may not come; these selves of which we are built up, one on top of another, as plates are piled on a waiter's hand, have attach-ments elsewhere, sympathies, little constitutions and rights of their own, call them what you will (and for many of these things there is no name) so that one will only come if it is raining, another in a room with green curtains, another when Mrs. Jones is not there, another if you can promise it a glass of wine—and so on; for everybody can mul-tiply from his own experience the different terms which his different selves have made with him—and some are too wildly ridiculous to be mentioned in print at all.[79]

Orlando may seem to be an exceptional person (she is ageless, she changes her gender, she travels through time) but Woolf is connecting her here to all of our experiences. Whereas she, like Nietzsche, forces the reader to en-counter her own self, in Woolf's eyes—and in Nietzsche's as well—that self is much more complicated, much more interesting and problematic than one might think. Indeed, it may help to explain why the reader is so ready, desperate even, to change her identity when she realizes that her internal identity itself is always in flux, never settled on one thing. Unlike the phantasmic identities that liberalism seeks to supply us with—to insist that this is "really" what the subject is—these separate identities have a mind and will of their own. They might not come when they are called. They might have other things to do (as some of the Abrahams did in Kafka's telling when God called to him/them). All of that has to be worked out (or not). In the anarchy of each subject's individual selves, there are no guarantees, no "plain [or smooth] sailing"; each subject will have to work out how she will function, who will answer her call to herself (and under what circumstances). Yet if the ease and certainty of liberal subjectivity is being sacrificed—at least the ease and certainty that is promised but never actually delivered—the subject can take solace in her own internal diversity, in her struggles and disagreements. Rather than to seek to artificially unify the self, Orlando shows how to benefit from each subject's variety and complexity, how to make the subject's anarchic subjectivity work, not so much for her as with her. For, in a sense, each of us is an us and, as I will be arguing in the next chapter, that collective and overlapping sense of "usness" is perhaps the one thing that everyone really does have in common.

And furthermore, it bears repeating that this anarchic "us" is the only "self" that the subject will ever be. Even if the liberal subject *were* better than the anarchic subject (and I would strenuously argue that it is not; it is a harbinger of racism, misogyny, class warfare, and nihilism), it doesn't matter because it isn't real. It is a set of phantasms and misrecognitions and so, by definition, the subject can never actually have it. But fortunately the choice is not between a false subjectivity that can never be achieved and an awful multiplicity that no one would ever want. Nobody wants to be that self because each subject is drawn to the lies of liberal universality but, as the case of Lily Briscoe shows (and Bartleby, too, in his own way), there are pleasures and promises in embracing the misinterpellated self too. And, what for both of these minor characters appears to be a set of small and narrow victories is, in the hands of a figure as spectacular as Orlando, quite seductive in its own right, awash with joy, brashness, and a full engagement with and acceptance of life in all of its complexity and beauty (and pain).[80]

In order to aid us in this greater possibility of subjectivity, Woolf adds yet another call to our list of possible appellations. To Althusser's "hey, you there!" and Berlant's "wait up," we now see "come, come!" as a call that suggests both interpersonal and intrapersonal aspects. Whereas, in this case, "come, come!" is a call to all the subjects and objects that form the entity known as Orlando, it also shows the possibility of how to move from an internal form of anarchism to an external one as well, an anarchism between and not just within persons. Either way, "come, come!" is an invitation without any kinds of strictures; it does not command so much as entice and negotiate (and, as we saw, sometimes resorts to bribery—"if you can promise it a glass of wine"). "Come, come!" is a kind of recognition of our lack of control over one another and even our selves. In this sense it is a much weaker call than "hey, you there!" but it serves the purposes of misinterpellation far better insofar as it invites the complexities of personhood/personhoods that are normally masked by interpellation and all that comes along with it.

Conclusion

In looking at these two characters, Bartleby and Lily, we see that often it is the most despised and the lowliest of creatures who have the most to teach us. Zarathustra understood this when he came to the hunchback and his ilk and saw that he himself was one of them ("a cripple at this bridge"). The misinterpellated subject is, almost by definition, going to appear in a way that is deemed unattractive, lowly, or inferior (Orlando may be an exception, but then she is exceptional in many, many ways). This subject often appears to be passive, sad, and broken. This is because she has experienced a catastrophic failure, an encounter that is required as a precondition for *amor fati*. If you love yourself too much as you think you are or want to be— that is, according to interpellation—if you are too devoted to your role as a good citizen, an obedient subject, a beautiful and desirable person, a winner, a billionaire, if, that is, interpellation is working too well for you, it is that much harder to recognize that you too are broken and hobbled. The misinterpellated person stands for everyone—hence, messianic in her own peculiar way—but she can't take that journey for each individual subject; each one must travel this bitter journey on her own, even as she does it in community with others, those other failed subjects each subject already is (and has always been).

And, for these two characters in particular, as previously noted, the very fact of marginality, of near or total invisibility and "flying under the radar," permits these characters to exercise their unique (and lonely) agency against what otherwise looks like insurmountable odds. Bartleby does next to nothing but he undermines subjectivity in the heart of capitalism. Lily sits there and paints and yet she effectively wins a struggle with a character that is ten—perhaps a hundred or a thousand or even a million—times her equal in normative terms: the formidable, beautiful, and magical Mrs. Ramsay. Whereas any direct attack on capitalism or privilege would be met with swift and fierce counterattack, these characters succeed by failing. Unnoticed, they are able to subvert from deep within the system that oppresses them.

CHAPTER SIX

"CONSENT TO NOT BE A SINGLE BEING"

Resisting Identity, Confronting the Law in Kafka's *Amerika*, Ellison's *Invisible Man*, and Coates's *Between the World and Me*

In the interest of imagining what exists, there is an image of Michael Brown we must refuse in favor of another image we don't have. One is a lie, the other unavailable. If we refuse to show the image of a lonely body, of the outline of the space that body simultaneously took and left, we do so in order to imagine jurisgenerative black social life walking down the middle of the street— for a minute, but only a minute, unpoliced, another city gathers, dancing. We know it's there, and here, and real; we know what we can't have happens all the time.—FRED MOTEN AND STEFANO HARNEY, "MICHAEL BROWN"

When it comes to the authority and credibility created by interpellation, the question of whether the caller "really" knows whom they are calling seems especially acute when it comes to matters of law and policing. It seems desirable to think that the police know what they are doing and whom they are accusing, even as in many communities, it is quite clear that they do not. Especially when it comes to catching and punishing criminals, a great deal of the law's legitimacy and authority come from the belief (if it is held) that the police, part of what Louis Althusser calls the repressive state apparatus, or RSA, tends to dispassionately and carefully collect evidence and, on that basis, accuse the right person of a crime. Of course, there are many times when the police have been wrong, often horribly so. In the United States, the cases of Michael Brown in Ferguson, Missouri; Eric Garner of Staten Island, New York; Freddie Gray of Baltimore, Maryland; or Sandra Bland, in Waller County, Texas—all unarmed black men and women who were murdered by the police—come to mind immediately. So do the disproportionate killings of Native Americans by police; the endless harassment, abduction, and imprisonment of Latino/as by Immigration and Customs Enforcement (ICE); and innumerable other forms of legally sanctioned violence. The annals of law are replete with such "errors." The police have also, of course, had many instances of "success," moments when the person who was accused turned out to actually have committed some crime or other. The reputation of the police—and hence the law more generally—is based on the presumption that the times they get it "right" far outweigh the times they get it "wrong," hence the ongoing authority of the law at least among those communities and individuals that benefit from the political system the law and its enforcing agents serve to support, that is, white people, rich people, and so forth.

Yet to think about whether the police, or the law more generally, ever "gets it right" presumes that the very nature of accusation obeys some basic, empirical logic, that it is aligned with reality in a way that affords the law the ability to know the truth and act accordingly, at least most of the time. This is, in other words, to accept the basic premise of interpellation, to believe that the law hails or accuses—as I will further argue in this chapter, they amount to the same thing—the right person "most" of the time (nine times out of ten).

Yet, as Walter Benjamin tells us, the law is incapable of "getting it right," not only because the hailer never "really knows" the subject but also because the very agents of communicating and executing that "rightness"—the police, the jailers, security forces in general and so forth—are themselves a separate and violent force of their own.[1] In Benjamin's view, the police are not the same thing as the law. They represent instead the limits of the law's power to enforce what it believes to be its right and purpose. Even if the state believes itself to be bound by the "rule" of law, the police show, in effect, the lie of the law; they are its weakest link. Benjamin writes,

> The "law" of the police really marks the point at which the state, whether from impotence or because of the immanent connections

within any legal system, can no longer guarantee through the legal system the empirical ends that it desires at any price to attain. Therefore, the police intervene "for security reasons" in countless cases where no clear legal situation exists, when they are not merely, without the slightest relation to legal ends, accompanying the citizen as a brutal encumbrance through a life regulated by ordinances, or simply supervising him . . . [the power of the police] is formless, like its nowhere-tangible, all-pervasive, ghostly presence in the life of civilized states.[2]

For Benjamin, the police represent a problem of temporality; the will of the law has to be made manifest at some specific point in time and this is the very point at which that will is revealed to be other than the law imagined or declares itself to be (not "really" what it wanted or thought). The police are that element of random violence that shows up the larger violence of the law more generally (an example of what Benjamin calls "mythic violence"). Instead of being all-knowing and in charge, the law operates from a position of desire, a desire to hail and control all of us, which falls to the police to put into effect.

Above all, what the police do for the law is to accuse. If we recall the notion, discussed in the introduction, that as subjects of the law we are already guilty, even before the hailing—as Judith Butler points out—then we all, to some extent or other, stand ready to be accused. Although for Butler, Althusser's model of God as the Subject is primary in his account, let us not forget that the figure he principally uses to advance a theory of interpellation is that of a police officer ("hey, you there!"). Through the hailing and accusation of the police, the law performs its power over its subjects in ways that go way beyond matters of solving crimes; as we have seen, it serves as the very basis of the subject's identity.[3] Yet, here again, as the tangible and material expression of the desire to hail and control, the police demonstrate a weakness at the core of the law itself. In practice, it does not matter as much *who* is accused, as that *someone* is accused. And, furthermore, as I will discuss at much greater length in this chapter, that someone, certainly in the United States, which is the focus of this chapter, is often as not a person of color.

Accusation is the way that the law tries to show that it is invaluable to its subjects (because it catches criminals, because it executes justice, because it "really knows" who we are). It thus serves as a mechanism by which we submit to law's rule, to its desire. Wrong accusation happens all the time, not because, or at least not only because, the police sometimes make mistakes in calculation, but because the realization of law's desire must always be screened through actors who, whether inadvertently or not, demonstrate the violence behind that desire; they serve as the law's—or, really, the citizenry's—"brutal encumbrance." In this way, the point of accusation is never to know but to project (or assume) knowledge and authority, along with an accompanying underlying threat or even actuality of violence (as a way for the law to "jut manifestly and fearsomely into existence," as Benjamin puts it).[4] Here, the law—via the police—dominates according to a calculus that has nothing to do with the formalities of the rule of law; they express the secret truth beneath the law's apparatus of power that Machiavelli reveals to us as well, that the law is empty, devoid of any authority except its own self-promotion.

To better understand the way that interpellation itself is inherently a form of accusation—that is, a form of address that occurs within a preestablished field of guilt—as well as to think about how that accusation can be undermined or challenged, in this chapter, I turn first to a reading of Franz Kafka's novel *Amerika* (whose original title in German is *Der Verschollene*, sometimes translated as "The Man Who Disappeared"). In this book, questions of accusation and interpellation are revealed to be—as so much is in Kafka's subversive and allegorical style of storytelling—instances in which the phantasms of law and authority are more legible as such than is usual. In particular, Kafka's telling reveals the unexpected vulnerability of law. Far from seeing the law through its instrument of the police as absolute and omniscient—the accuser behind the call "hey, you there!"—we see that the law is a hair's breadth from acknowledging its failure (that is, acknowledging the one thing it cannot acknowledge). We can also see the law's participation in the very randomness and arbitrary rule that it purports to protect its citizens from but subjects them to via its own agents. In this case, Karl Rossmann—the hero of *Amerika*—precipitates that failure with a failure of his own. Karl's failure as a subject—his inability to be that which the law requires of him—provokes or exposes the law's own failure in response. Without a stable and knowable subject to control—and accuse—the law itself becomes unsure, even weak. As its own desires and its own violence become more legible in the face of Karl's inability to play his part—as the accused, as guilty, as subject—the law's pose of authority wavers and crumbles accordingly.

Here we see once again how the law needs its subjects more than they need it; it needs the subject's recirculation of authority to project itself onto whereas its subjects—as I have already begun to argue in preceding chapters—have alternative forms of hailing, as well as alternative modes of subjectivity, to draw upon. It's not that the subject doesn't want the law. Very often even subjects who suffer horribly at the law's hands continue to desire its recognition (as we see in many of the cases examined in this chapter). Even refusal of the law is never absolute.[5] At the same time, the subject does not *require* the law in the way that the law requires the subject. Kafka's narrative is useful because it allows us a glimpse of the operations of law without the veneer of naturalness and authority that it is usually accompanied by (that is to say, in telling his story, Kafka helps to strip away misrecognition, leaving misinterpellation in its place). We can see in the example of Karl Rossmann's failed subjectivity a way to think about law where the relationship between identity, guilt, and innocence does not follow the usual script and where decisions about justice and subjectivity can devolve to the community and individuals in whose name law is nominally—but only nominally—performed.

Yet, as I will argue further, there are ways in which Karl's resistance is not available to every would-be subverter of law. Karl may be an alien in *Amerika* but he is European and white; his situation is not the same as it would be for an African American, as it was in real life for Michael Brown, Eric Garner, Freddie Gray, or Sandra Bland.[6] In some sense, African American targets of law are not "allowed to fail" in the same way that we see with Karl (and, as I will show, Kafka himself was well aware of the status of black people in the United States as well as the way they were treated by white authorities and vigilantes alike).

Accordingly, in the second part of this chapter, I return to the question of racial identity and universalism explored in chapters 2 and 3, to show that categories of guilt and innocence do not follow a uniform pattern.[7] As the situation in Ferguson, Missouri, and elsewhere in the US—at the time of this writing—demonstrates, guilt can be ascribed to individuals (Michael Brown) or to entire communities (in this case, African Americans), regardless of what the individual says or does. Interpellation not only accuses in this case; it also kills in response to the explicit forms of guilt that agents of the law project onto black and brown bodies.[8] For other people and communities, this guilt is more underground; for those communities who are held in privilege (white communities, the affluent), guilt is effectively suspended, even as it remains a potentiality for anyone who lives under a system of interpellated law.[9] If interpellation accuses everyone: for some, this accusation has far more serious implications than for others. Although for white subjects the accusation inherent in interpellation lies mainly at the level of a potential—and hence to some extent depends on the subject's response—for many people of color, their own response is irrelevant. There is literally nothing that they can do (at least as isolated individuals) to ward off the violence of the state.

Insofar as the person of color's experience of the law and interpellation is therefore utterly different from that of white subjects, different strategies and different modes of resistance are required. Accordingly, and focusing principally on the condition of black subjects in the United States, in the latter part of this chapter, I turn to a reading of two other texts—Ralph Ellison's Invisible Man and (more briefly) Ta-Nehisi Coates's Between the World and Me—in order to think about these other strategies, other forms of resistance to the accusation that is inherent to being black and brown in America.[10]

In all three writings, I focus on an encounter between the police and a figure in the text (Karl's encounter with a police officer in Amerika, and the murders by police officers of Tod Clifton in Invisible Man, and of Prince Jones in Between the World and Me). Here, we revisit Althusser's classic moment of "hey, you there!" with other renditions. Whereas for Karl, the failure to cohere as a subject is enough to call interpellative authority into question, in the readings by Ellison and Coates, we see that the law is not interested in the character of the subject at all (both men are said to be exceptional, brilliant, and physically beautiful). Accordingly, in both Invisible Man and Between the World and Me, the response to these murders by the author/narrators follows a script closer to what Fanon suggests than Kafka. Rather than resisting by failing, these authors demonstrate an enhanced strategy of refusal.[11] Both of these author/narrators refuse the opaque and superimposed identities that they receive from the law—that is, they refuse the unique form of accusation inherent in their hailing as it pertains to those with black and brown bodies—and turn instead to forms of identity and blackness that compete with and supersede such imposed subjectivities. Here too, refusing the false subjectivity that is imposed on black bodies, as well as other bodies of color, does not reveal the "true" subject underneath. Rather, it allows the subject a chance, but only a chance, not to be what they are otherwise determined to be. This strategy obviously does not save or protect the murdered subjects in these books but it does offer an absolute refusal of the dance of subjectivity that Karl can play at and win—or at least not lose—but which is denied to black and brown subjects from the outset. These authors suggest the power of losing hope—hope for inclusion, hope for a "rule of law," hope for a truly capacious liberal universalism after all—not in order to retreat from the world entirely (although the narrator of *Invisible Man* seemingly does just that) but rather to see what forms of identity and politics emerge when universal ideals of hope and progress have been abandoned once and for all.

Going to Amerika

Kafka's *Amerika* is a sprawling book that was never completed and that seems pointedly not to "go" anywhere (much like *To the Lighthouse* in that sense, even though both depict a frenzy of movement nonetheless). Whether it is intentional or not—with Kafka, it is always hard to know—the very aimlessness of the book is itself a kind of commentary on the usual novels of success about America. Rather than setting himself up as an authentic and independent subject—the ideal that liberal subjectivity in general and its US variant in particular subscribe to—Karl Rossmann seems to be a lost soul, someone who seems incapable of "being himself" or avoiding the entrapments and subjectivities of others.

If this is true of the novel generally, it is even more true and clear in the case of Karl's own encounter with the law. In a scene that roughly parallels and anticipates but ultimately subverts and upsets Althusser's description of the scene of interpellation, Kafka shows how when Karl meets a police officer, things go in unexpected and undesired (from the law's perspective) directions. The context for this scene, which comes deep into the novel, is that Karl, a young immigrant from Europe who initially had a great chance at success (due to a rich uncle) only to completely blow it, has fallen in with two very unhelpful "friends," Delamarche and Robinson. These two characters seize on Karl as a source of money, clothing, and opportunity. They give him nothing but treachery, lies, and manipulation in return.

In the previous chapter, entitled "The Robinson Affair," Karl finally seems to have started a life of his own. He manages to evade Delamarche and Robinson and gets a job as a elevator boy in a fancy hotel. He begins what he and the reader assume will be a long ascent to autonomy, to being a "self-made man." But then Robinson comes to the hotel, drunk and demanding money from Karl. The scandal about Robinson's intrusion, along with some false accusations by some of Karl's rivals in the elevator-boy business, causes Karl to lose his job. He accompanies Robinson, who in the interim has been beaten up and now has a terrible hangover, in a chauffeur-driven car, to be paid for by Karl, of course.

The chapter that begins with the scene with the police officer is the first chapter that has neither a number nor a title in the current form of the novel (due probably more to the fact that it wasn't finished rather than anything deliberate on Kafka's part). Here, Karl and Robinson are dropped off by the chauffeur in front of the apartment where Delamarche has been living with/ sponging off an opera singer named Brunelda. As they arrive, Robinson insists that Karl pay the chauffeur something extra for all his troubles. Karl is at this point entirely out of money. He begins to leave the car and these terrible so-called friends behind. As this is happening, Kafka describes the coming of the police officer: "Just then a policeman on his rounds through the street looked down at the man in shirtsleeves [i.e., Karl], sized him up, and halted. Robinson, who had also noticed the policeman, cried out stupidly from the other window [of the car] 'It's really nothing, nothing at all,' as if one could shoo away a policeman the way one shoos away a fly."[12]

In this instance, the police officer does not say anything (not the "hey, you there!" that Althusser imagines). But he hardly needs to; he has "sized [Karl] up," extending his authority, as is the habit of the police, outwardly to announce his power. His physical presence is felt intensely by everyone present (including Delamarche who has revealed himself from his balcony and who comes down to join them): "The policeman held his little black truncheon in front of his chest and waited quietly, with the great patience that policemen must always demonstrate, whether they are carrying out their regular duties or lying in wait."[13] The police officer's truncheon alone speaks volumes about the source of his power, the underlying threat of violence that it manifests. At that point, Karl decides to take his leave once again. He is not leaving the police officer per se but rather Robinson and Delamarche. Despite being completely innocent, not only in the sense of not having committed any crime, but also of any tangible form of identity that he can be called to, Karl is interpellated nonetheless. As he tries to slip away from the scene, Delamarche tries to stop him "but he himself [i.e., Delamarche] did not have to intervene since the policeman held out his truncheon and said, 'Stop!'" (i.e., "hey, you there!").[14]

"What's your name" [the police officer] asked, sticking his truncheon under his arm and slowly pulling out a book. . . . "Karl Rossmann," he said. "Rossmann," said the policeman, who was doubtlessly repeating the name merely because he was a calm and methodical individual, but Karl, who was encountering American authorities for the first time, saw in this repetition a sign that he was considered somewhat suspect. And things certainly did not look good for him.[15]

For all of his inexperience, Karl is correct; the repetition of his name is part of the ritual of "sizing him up," calling him by his name and putting him in his place.[16] The police officer asks Karl to show him his papers, which Karl does not have. Kafka writes, "This was surely only a formality, for if you don't have a jacket [Karl had to surrender his when he was fired from the hotel], you probably don't have identification papers either."[17] Karl doesn't therefore answer but the police officer persists, asking him whether he has any income and getting in response Karl's story of being fired from his hotel job.

"And you were let go without a jacket?" asked the policeman. "Well yes," said Karl; so in America too, the authorities make a point of asking questions even when they could see perfectly well for themselves. . . . Karl had a great desire to run away and hide somewhere instead of having to listen to more such questions. And the policeman even asked the question that Karl had most feared, and probably because of the unease with which he had anticipated the question, he responded more carelessly than he might otherwise have done.[18]

Karl feels the ring of authority tightening around him. He fears that the police officer will discover the hotel he was fired from (the Occidental) and take him there, and that "hearings would be held to which his friends and enemies would be summoned."[19] The ever treacherous Delamarche takes the police officer aside to tell a story of how Karl took advantage of him—whereas in fact it was quite the opposite—how "he [i.e., Karl] had no idea . . . about conditions in America, having just come from Europe, where they couldn't find any use for him either."[20] Delamarche goes on to say that "we took him along, let him live with us, explained everything to him . . . believing despite all the sins to the contrary that we could still manage to turn him into a useful person."[21] Here, Delamarche, a singularly unsuccessful, but nevertheless highly motivated subject, seems to be colluding with the police officer to see how Karl might best be brought under control, rendered into a knowable subject of the law.[22]

At this point, Karl is effectively on trial, not so much for whatever he may or may not have done—he actually hasn't done anything but draw the police officer's attention somehow—but for his very being. While this discussion is going on, Karl finds himself increasingly physically hemmed in by spectators—mainly porters who have come up to listen and watch the spectacle—so that he "could no longer have retreated a single step and whose ears were continually engulfed by the babbling voices of the porters, who did not so much speak as thunder in an English that was absolutely incomprehensible and may have included a smattering of Slavic words."[23]

In this case, the scene of interpellation is transformed from a simple statement ("hey, you there!") to an entire spectacle. Yet, this performance does not have the usual desired effect. Karl, because of his indeterminate personhood, his lack of certainty about who he is and what he wants, does not readily lend himself to the kinds of subjectivities that are the stuff of liberal identity. In some sense, he is the recipient of the police officer's baleful attention exactly because he does not readily fit into any taxonomies of the law; the officer has sized him up but still doesn't know what to make of him, and this exposes the extent to which interpellation is a kind of correspondence between predetermined categories, as Butler implies too, and persons (so, for example, the police officer might determine that Karl the person corresponds with the category of "criminal" or "deadbeat" or "vagrant").

Karl's very vagueness is both a protection and a weapon against such a procedure. If we are all guilty as subjects before the law, in Karl's case, it becomes very hard to determine the nature of that guilt. How do you blame or connect this figure to any kind of identity when he is so nebulous and ill formed? How do you accuse such a person when there is no sense that he belongs to any categories of activity or personhood whatsoever (so that, to paraphrase Nietzsche, there is no "doer" behind the "deed" and, actually, in this particular case, little-to-no deed either)?[24] Rather than serving to produce Karl's subjectivity via an operation of ideology, the effects of law only terrify and alienate him.[25] In his experience, the words and attitudes that are ordinary parts of the operation both of law and everyday life become menacing. Here the words of the officer are filled with threat and the very language of the porters becomes a kind of incomprehensible babble.

Perhaps even more to the point, recalling once again that Althusser's tale of interpellation is narrated largely from the position of the subject and not the police officer, we can see that Karl's failure as a subject also involves a failure on his part to project any real authority "back" onto the police officer. In his naïveté, Karl cannot see the false projection of the law's authority, only its tangible expression as an imminent—and visible—threat of violence. Accordingly Karl offers no phantasmic desire for authority that he can alienate, no all-knowingness that he ascribes to the law, and no way to externalize his desire for law (so that he can receive it in the form of an interpellation). He thus does not play his part in the circuitry of call and response. The law, as a result, has nothing to say; the police officer, as the agent of the law, literally does not know what to do with Karl. Karl offers no clear, determinable "you" to shout "hey, you there!" to.

As if to confirm the ambivalence of the situation, the police officer gets contradictory statements about Karl from Delamarche and Robinson. After the police officer announces his intention to take Karl back to the hotel to find out why he was dismissed, Robinson claims that Karl was not dismissed at all and that in fact he had left his jacket behind simply to help Robinson get home. At this point, doubt over Karl's identity and subjectivity become even more indefinable:

> "But is that really true?" asked the policeman in a wavering voice. "And if it's true, why does the boy pretend he was dismissed?" "You should say something," said Delamarche [to Karl]. Karl gazed at the policeman, who was meant to keep order among these strangers who could think only of themselves, and some of his general worries passed over to Karl. He did not want to lie and held his hands tightly clasped behind his back.[26]

The police officer starts off by knowing nothing about Karl when he first sees him and he knows even less as the interview goes on. As noted, his voice "wavers" as he hears the conflicting stories about what Karl is up to. Giving up on projecting authority, eventually he just resorts to violence, trying to physically grab Karl. As he does so, he says to Karl that "if we go on like this, we'll never get finished," testifying to the way that the police officer sees this encounter as a teleological process that will lead to a culmination (a "finish," but not in the same sense that Lily Briscoe "finishes" her painting).[27] Here, the police officer is following a kind of script, seeking to bend the world to the law's will. When the world does not lend itself to such bending—when, that is, the officer encounters a subject as unformed and subversive as Karl—he continues to follow that script but the disconnect between the phenomenon he is witnessing and the way he is meant to taxonomize this particular subject's behavior becomes more and more evident. The missing bit of the puzzle—a belief on Karl's part in the power of the law and his own consequent and resultant subjectivity—being absent, the whole performance is cut short, arrested, as it were.

When the police officer tries to grab Karl, the latter, taking advantage of the fact that the porters have been called back to work and thus ceased to press in on him, starts to run away. The policeman yells, "Stop him!" and "continu[ed] to emit the same cry at regular intervals" while running "in a powerful silent stride."[28]

Other police officers join the chase and Karl is finally only saved by the intervention of Delamarche who hides him from view while the policemen run along "their steps sound[ing] like steel striking stone."[29]

Like most things in this vague and ambiguous novel, there is no clear resolution to this story. The police officers lose Karl but it isn't clear that they ever "had" him in the first place. We are never told why the first police officer stopped him, what indicated to him that something was awry (except perhaps that Karl was in his shirtsleeves at the time). Instead of the law's pose of knowledge and clearly predetermined categories of behavior, we see instead that when faced with an aporia such as Karl we get just the desire to control, to "understand" and categorize. As previously noted, even before he speaks, the police officer is shown holding "his little black truncheon in front of his chest," demonstrating his power and even his potential for violence—as well as his desire to dominate and accuse—as a precursor to any question of his being able to discern the "innocent" from the "guilty."[30]

The distinction between the way the police officer engages with Karl and Karl's own response is perhaps best highlighted by a passage that comes in the middle of the chase scene. While he is desperately trying to run and hide, with the police in hot pursuit, Karl notes ruefully that "the policeman always had his goal before him and never had to think, whereas for Karl the running itself was of secondary importance, for he had to consider everything, choose among various options, and then choose all over again."[31] While this passage is formally just a commentary about how someone being chased has to make decisions that the chaser doesn't—they only have to follow the person being chased—it also suggests something larger about the nature of the would-be interpellator versus the subject who resists that interpellation. Whereas the police officer always knows what to do— follow the script, apply the categories, react accordingly—Karl, who is not so easily categorized, has to make endless decisions.[32] Failing to coalesce as an interpellated person whose choices have all already been made, he must therefore choose over and over again; his identity is always in flux and there is nothing predetermined about him.

We see then that the very pose of knowledge that underlies the authority of the law limits choice. It is the "knowledge" of a decision tree; if the subject does A, you do B, if they follow that with C, you do D, and so forth (this is very much like the kind of knowledge that we see Mr. Ramsay expressing as well with his "Q" and his "R"). Paradoxically, this constriction of choice on the part of the police also may help to explain the frequent lapses from the formal script that the police often engage in, a move into implicit violence (which we see suggested by the police officer's truncheon in this case) or murder (as with the case of Michael Brown). There seems to be a "script beyond the script" at work here, a response that is not formally part of police procedure but that occurs too regularly to be any kind of true lapse. This is still a script; it still accuses and it still "knows." It is almost uniformly violent and racist. Yet this kind of improvisation serves to paper over the glaring gap between the discourse of rule of law and its practice on the ground level, to render it misrecognized (at least for privileged subjects).

In the contrast between the police officer and Karl, we see two clearly distinct approaches to law and subjectivity, the one restricted and controlled, the other responding to context and the moment, unpredictable, maybe even free (if we can use such a loaded term). Devoid of any counterprojection, the pose of law—the authority produced by attributing the power to call to certain bodies—becomes visible as being just that, a pose, a to-do list devoid of ultimate purpose (except for phantasmic ends that are, in fact, extraordinarily elaborate).

What may initially seem like a disadvantage for Karl—it certainly does seem so while he is being chased—can be read instead as imparting a kind of power or agency on his part. In a sense, for all his weakness and inchoate nature, Karl is acting in a way that is more in keeping with who he is as opposed to who he is supposed to be. Rather than being falsely organized, Karl acts through and out of his disorganization. He thus acts so as to maximize, rather than disguise, his internal complexity and, in this way, acts as "himself" in a way that no one else in the book can (with the caveat that "himself" is, as with Justine in Berlant's analysis in chapter 1, only a denotation and not a complete identity). For this reason, Karl acts in ways that read as pathetic failure from the perspective of interpellated authority but that yet ultimately succeed in freeing him, both from his "friends" and from the police.

What's more, thanks to Karl's intervention, we see more clearly now how the police officer's way of thinking and acting limits and actually disempowers him, how he is trapped within his own falsely mediated form of subjectivity. The police officer in Amerika cannot act and think on his own. Accepting his own seemingly unproblematic personhood—he's the person who calls other people's personhood into being—the police officer is only what he is told to be.[33] All of his other qualities, whatever they may be, are forgotten, ignored, or superseded, and so he has a lot less of the contingency and unscripted creativity to draw upon from his own anarchic interiority. In this way, the strength of the law, its pose of authority, is revealed to be its vulnerability and limitation. Far from a pose of all-knowingness, we see that the law actually knows nothing at all; it is the epitome of the practice we saw with Bartleby's narrator: all assumption and projection without preference. In such a state of affairs, there is no question of the law getting it "right" or "wrong." Rather, the law's desire (its assumption), it seems, is to run its course, to move the way it moves, over and over again wherein different figures come in and out of view but the law itself never ceases to work its patterns.

Revisiting the Scene of Interpellation

In order to demonstrate the degree to which Kafka's novel subverts the standard concept of interpellation and, in particular, the interpellating power that we normally attribute to the police, to the army, and other agents of legal authority, let me directly compare Kafka's scene of interpellation with Althusser's and note the differences between them. In both cases, the police officer's call—whether said aloud in Althusser's telling or implied by their attention and presence in the case of Amerika—is, as already noted, not necessarily based on some evidence that the subject of the call is actually guilty of a crime. As previously discussed, for the law, we are all guilty to some extent or other, already subject to law before we are called to our legal identity. But in the case of Althusser's telling, what really matters is not the question of guilt—since that is presupposed—but rather the effect of the call: the person turns and "by this mere one-hundred-and-eighty-degree physical conversion, he [or she] becomes a *subject*." In Kafka's version of this story, there is no such response. The individual—Karl in this case—does not coalesce as a subject of law. Karl feels hemmed in, trapped; words seem to him to become like "thunder" and he is isolated despite being surrounded by many other people. When the police officer decides to cut to the chase and grab him, Karl doesn't submit; instead he grows increasingly confused and frightened and eventually runs away. Rather than conform, he fails to become the subject that he is intended to be.

In terms of what we can learn from or apply to contemporary politics, thanks to Kafka's intervention, we can say that, in the face of the law's monstrous desire for obedient subjects, Kafka offers one way to resist: namely, to fail to become a successful subject of the law. Guilty or not, intended or not, Karl fails, and spectacularly so, to become a subject. Just as Kafka himself (in Benjamin's eyes) succeeded at failure—a failure, that is, to coalesce as a phantasmic author, as someone who passed along false truths and doctrines in such a way that they became palatable and natural to the rest of us—his characters fail as well.

If Karl had responded to his moment of interpellation with defiance or rebellion, he would have brought the entire violent force of the law onto his person (it will be recalled that the narrator in "Bartleby the Scrivener" said the exact same thing about Bartleby). He would be destroyed and, in the process, returned to a category that the law *can* contend with: the rebel, the renegade, the one who must be eliminated or contained or "rehabilitated." Instead, Karl responds by first shrinking into himself and then, when he seemed to have no choice, to flee, successfully escaping the police. Karl thus adds to our understanding of different models of resistance to the authority of law (as Bartleby and Lily do as well in their own way). Of course, had he been caught, Karl would have been subject to a great deal of legal misery and violence. But one also gets the feeling that Karl—just like Bartleby when he was himself in prison—could never become a "proper" legal subject; he is too amorphous, too ambiguous, too failed to ever do so.

The Theater of Oklahama: The Failure after the Failure

At or near the end of *Amerika*—at least at the purported end for this unfinished book—Karl ends up joining the so-called Theater of "Oklahama"—Kafka's misspelling of the US state is consistent throughout—a seeming resolution to the aimless wandering of the rest of the book. This theater promises to hire everyone who applies for a position. As Karl's friend Fanny tells him (she has already been hired by them): "It's the largest theater in the world. . . . Though I've never seen it myself, some of my co-workers who've already been to Oklahama say it's almost limitless."[34] In a sense, the Theater of Oklahama is a parallel world to our own. Infinitely large, it seems possible that everyone who wants to can work there, reproducing reality in a new, theatrical—and therefore explicitly representational—guise. Although it doesn't refer to law per se, this depiction of the Theater of Oklahoma suggests at first glance that perhaps Kafka sought some better, different form of interpellation later in his book, a different, distinctly legible representational subjectivity—it is a theater after all—that might serve as an alternative to the endless desires and powers of law, to the drudging misery and subservience of "Amerika."

This would be a tempting conclusion to draw but keeping in mind Kafka's tendency to celebrate failure above all else—and in a way that fits very much with the kinds of disappointing moves I already noted with Nietzsche and Woolf—allows for a different, misinterpellated, reading. Indeed, I read Kafka, just as I read Nietzsche and Woolf, as drawing out this final hope in order to, once again, betray and ruin it. Like Mrs. Ramsay, the Theater of Oklahoma is seductive but misleading; the real and possibly effective disappointment begins when it too is revealed to be false.

The Theater of Oklahoma is not all that it appears to be. When Karl first approaches the recruiting offices of the theater he is greeted by a celestial scene:

> In front of the entrance . . . was a long, low platform on which hundreds of women, dressed as angels in white robes with large wings on their backs, blew long trumpets that shone like gold . . . each stood on her own pedestal, which however was not visible, for it was completely covered by the angels' long billowing robes.[35]

The appearance of heaven is belied by the crafting Karl espies, the hiding of some objects (the pedestals), and the generally ersatz nature of these "angels." Fanny, who is herself employed as an angel, tells Karl that later on men come and dress like devils, standing on the same pedestals for a presumably different effect. The sight of these angels and the sounds of their trumpeting initially raises expectations for the people who come to see them but ultimately they are let down. Kafka writes of some members of the audience coming to see this spectacle that "though they marveled at the spectacle, one could see that they were disappointed. They too must have expected that there would be an opportunity to find employment, but this trumpet-blowing merely left them confused."[36]

Furthermore, the Theater of Oklahoma is distressingly similar to the very world that Karl is always trying to escape from. When he talks to the theater's recruiters about actual employment, he is told, "As you'll have noticed from our poster, we can make use of everyone. But we have to know the prior occupation of each individual so that he can be assigned to the right position, where he can make use of his expertise."[37] In other words, the Theater of Oklahama is a near or exact replica of the world Karl has already experienced (i.e., Oklahama and Oklahoma are quite nearly identical). All of the problems that he has in Amerika more generally will be reproduced in the theater. The Theater of Oklahama, then, can be said to provide the function Nietzsche conceives of for eternal recurrence; even if we are presented with the possibility of a "better world" that can solve all of the problems in the current one, Kafka, like Nietzsche, sees to it that this world is an exact duplicate of our current one so that we have no choice but to "choose" the world that we already live in. If Karl were able to escape this life, it would mean that *amor fati* would be denied to him and, by extension, to us, the readers of this story. In this way, Kafka effectively shuts the door on any "successful" resolution to the question of Karl's identity.

There are a great number of ways that the Theater of Oklahama replicates the failures and problems of America. For example, the fact that Karl has no papers continues to haunt him. More pointedly, he finds himself dealing with an all-too-familiar bureaucratic mind-set. He gets sent first to one office and then another, each time not being quite what they had in mind.

Things become comical—indeed Kafkaesque—when he is sent to a booth specially designed for those who graduated from a European middle school. When he sees the man who is there to deal with applicants he "was almost startled by the resemblance between this man and a teacher who was probably still teaching at his vocational school at home."[38] Here, we see more evidence that for Kafka, the representation of the world Karl aspires to may be so close as to be indistinguishable from—and certainly no better than—the world he has already been subjected to (that is, this world).

By summoning this magical alternative of the "Theater of Oklahama" only to expose it as failed, no different from what it is meant to redeem us from, Kafka raises the dazzling promise of redemption only to dash it, Nietzsche (and Woolf) style. He suggests the possibility of a real subjectivity—however paradoxical it may be that this reality comes in the form of a theater—only to show, in small glimpses and hints, that this alternative has no reality after all (and, by extension, neither does the "real" world that is formed by interpellation). In this way, Kafka repeats the lessons we learned from the ruination of Mrs. Ramsay (or, the overman, or even, in Kafka's own telling, the story of Abraham); the Theater of Oklahama is no true escape but a return to the same state of failure that Karl already occupies.

Yet, for all of this, not unlike Lily Briscoe and her painting, Kafka's treatment of the Theater of Oklahama shows us that representation is a double-edged sword; it can serve either to mask the failures it portrays or to highlight that failure. Just as Lily finally accepted her painting in all of its "greens and blues," so too does the Theater of Oklahama offer Karl a way to see that the world he seeks is "already here." Here the "representation," the theatricality of a duplicate world that is actually a theater, serves mainly to highlight the absurdities and phantasms of the world that we normally take for granted or naturalize (i.e., misrecognize). In this way, this Theater of Oklahama offers Karl a chance to realize or not—the outcome is up to him—the extent of his own misinterpellation.

"Negro"

For all the ways that Karl "succeeds by failing" there is one sense in which Karl nonetheless has privileges that he himself is only dimly aware of. Karl is not only privileged through being white—with vast consequences for the way that the law treats him—but also via class (recall his rich uncle). As is all too obvious, both in our own time and the time that Kafka was writing *Amerika*, the scene of interpellation works very differently for people of color (and poor people in general; when those two categories intersect, as they often do in the United States, discrimination and state violence only intensify).

While *Amerika* doesn't directly treat the question of the condition of black people in America/Amerika, Kafka himself was clearly aware of the problematic racial politics in the United States; he knew that racism formed the chief backdrop of the "real world" that Karl is always trying to escape from. In writing *Amerika*, Kafka was very influenced by a book called *America: Today and Tomorrow*, written by a Hungarian Jew named Arthur Holitscher. That book contains a photograph depicting a lynched black man surrounded by grinning whites with the title "Idyll aus Oklahama" [sic] (Idyll in Oklahoma). This suggests a much darker source and meaning for the "Theater of Oklahama" (and, as we see, Kafka even kept the same misspelling of Oklahoma as Holitscher in his original text).[39]

Kafka's engagement with the racial violence of America may be reflected in a pervasive sadness that suffuses the book but it is occasionally hinted at in the text itself. Perhaps most critically, when asked by the theater agents for a name, Karl says that he is called "Negro." When, in other words, he gets a chance to rename himself, Karl identifies himself as being outside of the conventions of white subjectivity altogether.[40]

Perhaps, by calling himself this name, Karl is registering his protest even against the theater and the way it will inevitably reproduce the bigotry of the world it represents. Yet Karl's identification with black Americans may even go further than that. There is evidence that Kafka intended to have Karl be executed at the end of *Amerika* and even possibly lynched. Responding to a 1915 entry in Kafka's *Diary*, Michael Löwy writes,

> It is possible, therefore, that Karl Rossmann was destined to end up like the black man of that image. Considering the more lenient formulation in Kafka's *Diary*—that Karl would be executed, but that he would be "more pushed to the side than hurled to the ground"—one could also imagine an ending that would serve as the counterpart to the first chapter: driven by his sense of justice to defend a black man threatened by lynch laws (as he had tried to defend the stoker) [in the very beginning of the novel], Karl Rossmann would be "pushed to the side" [presumably lynched himself] by the lynchers.[41]

If this is true, it suggests that even an author as subversive and complex as Kafka can succumb to false equivalences at times. Of course, it is possible for white people to be lynched, but the equation of Karl as "Negro" and sharing this violent fate with black Americans suggests a blurring of racial identities that does not square with the lived experience of black people in the United States or elsewhere (to cite Fanon).

Even making this equivalency may mark Karl's privilege, and perhaps even Kafka's own as well. Karl can try on race as a kind of empty signifier because he doesn't experience race in the same way that a black person does, or people of color more generally. He can get away with failure and incoherence because he is white.[42] He is afraid of the police when they stop him, to be sure, but not in response to some kind of history or pattern that any black person in America knows all too well.

Neither Michael Brown, Eric Garner, Freddie Gray, nor Sandra Bland were afforded such the luxury to fail as a subject; they were marked from the beginning by the color of their skin, by the history of racist policing in the United States. It doesn't seem that there is anything that these people could have done or not done to avoid being targeted and murdered. None of them seem to have had a choice other than death (not even crying out that he couldn't breathe in Garner's case). In such a situation, does their own misinterpellation, the fact that these subjects were not who the police said that they were (not demons, not "thugs," but human beings), offer them any tools to resist state violence?

The Black Subject and the Universal

Here we come, to some extent, to a difference between the RSA and the ISA (the ideological state apparatus) in Althusser's account. There is projection and there is counterprojection. The police have their own fantasies and ideas about race and class, and this heavily shapes the way that the police "manifest" the law. Whereas with Karl the police officer's voice may "waver" and be uncertain, with Michael Brown, Eric Garner, Freddie Gray, or Sandra Bland, they "know" whom they are dealing with in a way that leaves out a response (saying "Don't shoot!" or "I can't breathe" doesn't have any effect). In a way, Karl on the one hand and Brown, Garner, Gray, and Bland on the other represent opposite ends of the spectrum of ideology. In Karl's case, the mismatch between projection and failure is so extreme that it cannot help but be visible. In the case of the murdered black subjects, racism and a history of police violence make that failure completely invisible; it is masked—misrecognized—by a universal that denies systematic or institutional racism in order to be able to practice those very things (more on that paradox when I get to an analysis of Ellison's *Invisible Man*).

It's true that this is more than a "white cop, black victim" story. For one thing, other people of color are also disproportionally murdered by the police. Furthermore not all the murdering cops are white. For example, one of the police officers charged in Freddie Gray's murder in Baltimore is an African American woman. And in Coates's narrative, the officer who killed Prince Jones was black himself. Similarly, it is undoubtedly true that not all police are personally racist and not all of their victims are unarmed; not all of them refrain from shooting back (some even shoot first). But none of this changes the way that the RSA is violently and structurally racist, infused by an accusation against black and brown bodies that cannot be denied by recourse to the formal rejection of racism in statutory law. To think otherwise is to deny the key and critical insight Marx makes in "On the Jewish Question" that when a state formally disavows itself of some quality (religion in that essay, racism in the current situation), it allows that operation to flourish and even be presupposed precisely through this act of disavowal.

The violence against black and brown people in police shootings, in the neo-slavery of mass incarceration, in the gulags run by ICE for undocumented immigrants who have been seized without any legal rights whatsoever, and in innumerable other cases and circumstances serves as a backdrop to any analysis of interpellation. Any thoughts of resistance must take this reality into account.

Invisible Man

One author who thinks seriously about the predicament of people of color, and, in particular, black people in the United States is Ralph Ellison. As I read it, Ellison's novel Invisible Man can be read, just as Woolf's and Nietz-sche's works, as an exercise in repetitive disappointment. The unnamed black narrator goes through a series of highs and lows as he navigates the racist landscape of America. The contrast to Karl in Amerika is striking. Karl starts out with the world at his disposal (his rich uncle) and he ruins every-thing by his inchoate nature. The narrator of Invisible Man, on the other hand, is eager to succeed; he very much wants to fit in, is only too happy to be interpellated. The iterations of hope and betrayal Ellison subjects his narrator to—and, through him, the reader—include a historically black college (modeled on the philosophy of Booker T. Washington) where the narrator is a promising student, only to ruin his reputation and standing by taking the white benefactor of the college on a ride to the former slave quarters and a raunchy bar (the outcome of which is the narrator's expul-sion and ruin). He later joins "the Brotherhood"—a rendition of the never explicitly named American Communist Party—which also promises the narrator redemption but proves itself to be utterly uninterested in black lives, in Ellison's telling, and seeks mainly to dominate wherever and how-ever it can. This experience too ends in expulsion and ruin.[43]

The book begins and ends with the narrator telling us that he lives in a "hole," a secret room that is nonetheless warm and full of light. The nar-rator retreats from the world he tried to join and tells us, from the very first sentences of the book—which is narrated retrospectively—that he is "invisible . . . because people refuse to see me."[44] The narrator seems to have abandoned the world and retreated into himself, offering—it would appear—nothing but retreat as a form of resistance, avoiding the calls of au-thority and the law (as well as alternative calls from black nationalists, com-munists and others) simply by disappearing. Here, the notion of invisibility seems to be upended; rather than using invisibility as a strategy—as I have argued Bartleby and, especially, Lily Briscoe do—the narrator appears to consider invisibility to be a trap, a denial of his humanity.

And yet the fact that the author narrates the entire story from this position suggests that he has not entirely given up on the world, nor has he given up his voice. He has a story to tell and a point to make (and the hole he retreats to is not dark but brilliantly illuminated). His tale of invisibility makes the narrator very visible in fact. Indeed, the very title *Invisible Man* suggests a paradox insofar as the color of the narrator's skin makes him, in a sense, all too visible, only not as a subject. This is a version of Fanon's shock when the young white boy in Lyon says, "Tiens, un nègre!" The fact of his skin color marks the narrator as a kind of unsubject, or at least a person burdened with a form of subjecthood that is not of his own devising (and far more so than is the case for someone designated as a white subject, like Karl).

Paradoxically, Ellison's narrator sees interpellation rendered visible, in a sense, by the very invisibility that it projects onto him. Like other misinterpellated subjects discussed in this book, the narrator cannot be the subject that he thinks he is called to be. But in his case, his "failure" to be such a subject gives him no power insofar as no active form of subjectivity is demanded or expected of him. It is here that Ellison's narrator may find a form of power after all, as a nonsubject, as an "invisible man" who, for all the way he feels the allure of liberal—and even communist—forms of subjectivity, nonetheless ultimately refuses to be that subject (or those subjects). Like Karl, Ellison's narrator also fails to be the subject he is called to be. But in his case his failure is complicated by aspects of his identity that are determined by the color of his skin. In his relations with both the establishment at his college as well as "the Brotherhood," the narrator's racial identity constricts his choices and even his identity in a way that Karl does not experience.

Accordingly, as already noted, the path for the narrator is not failure but refusal. By repeatedly refusing to be the subject (or unsubject perhaps) he is told that he inexorably is and must always be, the narrator evades and subverts this determination. As with Fanon, his refusal is more than just saying "no," a rejection of white supremacy, communist forms of universalism—at least as Ellison sees it—and other forms of determination. In a very Nietzschean sense, the narrator's refusal is also, as I will argue further, saying "yes" to all that he (also) is when other aspects of subjectivity are made available to him, when he neither acquiesces to nor abandons (slinks away from) the scene of his interpellation. (This is a question that I will return to at the very end of this chapter.)

The narrator's act of refusal can be seen quite clearly in the aforementioned case where the narrator witnesses a police officer murdering his colleague and friend Tod Clifton. Clifton is also a member of the Brotherhood and a fellow African American. The narrator describes Clifton as "very black and very handsome."[45] Clifton is someone that the narrator very much looks up to; his fiery defense of communism (which is never named as such) and his opposition to a Garvey-like figure called "Ras the Exhorter" steels the narrator in terms of his own views. Even as the author begins to experience serious doubts about the degree to which the Brotherhood really has the interest of black people at heart, the fact that Clifton, a strong and beautiful black man, is so deeply devoted to the cause helps to assure him that his loyalties are not misplaced. Yet, as the novel progresses, Clifton himself becomes disenchanted with the Brotherhood and switches over (unbeknownst to the narrator) to Ras's African nationalist movement.

At the point in the narrative where we encounter the run in with the police officer, the narrator spots Clifton on the street selling "Sambo" dolls on Ras's behalf, a way to belittle black people who submit to stereotypes, who allow white people to determine who they are and how they behave.[46] The narrator gets very angry and spits on the dolls. He starts to call to Clifton, saying "you, you!"[47] Just after this, Clifton, seeing a police officer coming over, packs up his dolls and leaves.

This "you, you!" speaks volumes about the narrator's relationship to Clifton. This is yet another kind of calling. As already noted, the narrator looks to Clifton to justify the fact that he can remain in the Brotherhood (which has its own kind of universal) as a black man when blackness is clearly not part of what the Brotherhood values. "You, you!" is hence at least in part a cry of betrayal; seeing Clifton engaging with Ras suggests that Clifton has adopted a different model for his identity, abandoning the narrator in the process (leaving him alone in his own version of blackness, as it were).

A further, richer, possibility emerges in a passage just after this when the narrator asks himself, "How on earth could [Clifton] drop from Brotherhood to this in so short a time? . . . It was as though he had chosen . . . to fall outside of history."[48] As Silindiwe Sibanda notes in *Invisible Man*, the term "Brotherhood" is almost always accompanied by the article "the" preceding it, indicating the American communist party. Leaving out the "the" in this passage suggests, at least possibly, that a different kind of brotherhood is being established, a notion that is reinforced a bit later after Clifton is killed and the narrator is surrounded by white cops and white spectators, stating that "I was the only brother in the watching crowd."[49] It is possible, as Sibanda also suggests, that while he was seeking one kind of brotherhood (i.e., "the Brotherhood") the narrator found another; in his unspoken bond with Clifton, and through Clifton's beauty and magnetism, the narrator was able to fall in love with blackness, with a subjectivity that stood in opposition and even defiance to the "Brotherhood" that "Brother Jack," the white leader of the party, offered to him.[50] Clifton's move to African nationalism suggests he took on yet another version of brotherhood (and blackness as well) but in this case, the narrator is excluded and cast out, hence the cry, "you, you!," which simultaneously recognizes that abandonment and seeks to restore the connection that was lost (i.e., both "what have you done?" and "it's still you!" at once).

In addition to the relational aspects involved in this other reading there are temporal consequences as well. The idea of "falling out of history," the move that the narrator sees Clifton as having chosen in his abandonment of the Brotherhood, might appear to be a very bad thing indeed (for the narrator at that particular moment it does appear to be bad but he will change his mind quite soon). Yet falling out of history can also be read as falling out of the kinds of eschatologies and teleologies that the Brotherhood promotes and engages with; in the "brotherhood" that emerges between the narrator and Clifton, another kind of temporality might emerge as well.

Whatever possibility there is for reconciliation and brotherhood (with a decidedly lowercase b) is however ruined in the next scene where Clifton meets his fate at the hands of a police officer. After Clifton leaves with his dolls, the narrator stumbles on Clifton and the same police officer again a bit later. At a bit of a remove, he sees the policeman pushing Clifton, and Clifton responding by hitting the policeman. At that point:

> Between the flashing of cars I could see the cop propping himself on his elbows like a drunk trying to get his head up, shaking it and thrusting it forward—And somewhere between the dull roar of traffic and the subway vibrating underground I heard rapid explosions and saw each pigeon diving wildly as though blackjacked by the sound, and the cop sitting up straight now, and rising to his knees looking steadily at Clifton, and the pigeons plummeting swiftly into the trees, and Clifton still facing the cop and suddenly crumpling.[51]

The narrator asks himself if he is to blame for Clifton's death. He asks "Why had he resisted the cop anyway? He'd been arrested before; he knew how far to go with a cop."[52] It occurred to him that Clifton's anger at his—that is, the narrator's—own actions might have motivated him to strike out at the police, costing him his life. All the anguish and pain, the possibility but then the withdrawal of "brotherhood" may have done Clifton in.

After Clifton's murder, the narrator pushes such thoughts aside, along with the different forms of relationality they might suggest. He throws himself into planning a large funeral for Clifton. Unable to contact the central leadership, he and the Harlem district office of the Brotherhood plan the funeral, making signs that read:

BROTHER TOD CLIFTON
OUR HOPE SHOT DOWN[53]

The narrator gives a speech before a large crowd at the funeral. He intends to give a political speech, abstracting from Clifton's murder and directing the crowd in the way that he knows the Brotherhood would expect and desire. At the time of the speech, however, a mood takes him, along with the rest of the crowd, propelled, it seems, by an old man singing an old spiritual and another man accompanying him by blowing through a horn. Ellison writes,

> Something deep had shaken the crowd, and the old man and the man with the horn had done it. They had touched upon something deeper than protest, or religion . . . all were touched; the song had aroused us all. It was not the words, for they were all the same old slave-borne words; it was as though he'd changed the emotion beneath the words while yet the old longing, resigned, transcendent emotion still sounded above, now deepened by that something for which the theory of Brotherhood had given me no name.[54]

After successive failures to be an interpellated subject in a variety of modes—as an acolyte of Booker T. Washington, as a member of the Brotherhood, even as an ordinary black man living in Harlem—the narrator hears another kind of call. This is a countercall, a reminder of his past. It brings him not so much to "himself" as such—it should be clear that there is no "himself" in the usual sense of the term to be had; the narrator has nothing but his narration to hold him together—but rather to a position of relative nondetermination (so he is "himself" in the same way that Justine is "herself," not a coherent and singular self at all). As the narrator states, the "slave-borne words" of the song are not the point; rather, it is a suggestion of alternate callings, other histories that serve as a counter to and underminer of the calls that he has been answering (or trying to) for most of his life.[55] Perhaps through this music, the kind of "brotherhood" that was emerging between the narrator and Clifton is once again hinted at. Losing Clifton, the narrator may have thought he had lost his connection to or love for blackness (of Clifton's, of his own, and of that of his community) but he can see that such a connection remains.

Accordingly, in his speech, the narrator reiterates his own version of blackness as well as showing what choosing to "fall . . . out of history" might look like. Rather than submitting to the subjectivities, the false futures and ends that the Brotherhood promised him, the narrator begins with a statement that evokes Zarathustra when he tells the tightrope walker "all that of which you speak does not exist: there is no devil and no hell. Your soul will be dead even before your body: fear nothing further."[56] In a similar vein, the narrator says:

Do you expect to see some magic, the dead rise up and walk again? Go home, he's as dead as he'll ever die. That's the end in the beginning and there's no encore. There'll be no miracles and there's no one here to preach a sermon. Go home, forget him. He's inside this box, newly dead. Go home and don't think about him. He's dead and you've got all you can do to think about you.[57]

Attesting that "there'll be no miracles," the narrator is speaking to the lack of supernatural or phantasmic qualities in human lives. In general, the subject is, as we have already discussed, never who he or she is said to be. But this is perhaps especially true for a subject of color insofar as she or he is that much more distant from being the perfect subject the universal says she or he is. There is a temptation (the narrator feels it) to compensate for this state of affairs by turning the murdered subject into a superhuman hero of his own, a martyr that would be reinforcing the temporal narrative set by Brother Jack. Had he revisited Clifton's life in supernatural or miraculous terms, the narrator may have sought redemption in the story of his murder, raising Clifton to the status of a universal subject after all—perhaps in defiance of the white world's denigration of him.

Yet Ellison, like Woolf, resists such a turn while also revealing a distinctly Nietzschean tendency (or perhaps Nietzsche is anticipating Woolf and Ellison; there is no necessary directionality in these associations). The move toward making Clifton into a superhuman martyr is a trap because it reproduces, as I'll describe further, the very teleological determinations, the doctrines of redemption and futurity, that keep people of color trapped in their roles in the first place. In refusing to speak of him in this way, the narrator is trying to depict Clifton as something other than the hero that a "political" (i.e., interpellating) speech might offer. He further says, "His name was Clifton and he was young and he was a leader and when he fell there was a hole in the heel of his sock and when he stretched forward he seemed not as tall as when he stood. . . . His name was Clifton and he was black and they shot him. Isn't that enough to tell? Isn't that all you need to know?"[58] The narrator goes on to describe the way Clifton's blood flowed after he was shot, how his blood "gleamed a while, and, after a while, became dull then dusty, then dried."[59] He also describes how Clifton is shut up in his coffin ("Now he's in this box with the bolts tightened down").[60]

Attesting to the materiality of Clifton's now-dead body, the circumstances of his corpse, is a way to attend—as with Bartleby once he was dead, or the tightrope walker, as he lay dying—to the ways that the body itself, the holes in one's sock, the trickling blood, undermine and prevent the subject from being the salvational figure that interpellation promises (and demands of) them; these material things resist the way that a human being is organized and even colonized as a subject.

At the end of his speech, as if to ensure that disappointment is the main takeaway from his speech, the narrator says, "Forget him. When he was alive he was our hope, but why worry over a hope that's dead? So there's only one thing left to tell and I've already told it. His name was Tod Clifton, he believed in Brotherhood, he aroused our hopes and he died."[61]

This is not the speech the narrator intended to give but it is what he has to say. After the speech is over, Ellison writes,

> The crowd sweated and throbbed, and though it was silent, there were many things directed toward me through its eyes. At the curb were the hearse and a few cars, and in a few minutes they were loaded and the crowd was still standing, looking on as we carried Tod Clifton away. And as I took one last look I saw not a crowd but the set faces of individual men and women.[62]

This scene—and the effect the narrator's speech has on the audience—is evocative of an entirely separate description written by Assia Djebar in her novel *Children of the New World*. In that book, set during the Algerian revolution, Djebar describes a character, Youssef—a would-be revolutionary—who witnesses a demonstration against French rule marked by a large group of people carrying a series of green flags representing Islam. Djebar writes,

> Youssef, whose only true love was for this shifting reality, this flood tide of wretchedness, would continue his tale. Then his jaws would tighten and he'd add, "Of course, they were simple rags, bits of sheets patched and sewn by the women for their luminous songs." "Filthy rags!" the police yelled, giving their first warning that they [i.e., the flags]'d have to disappear. The flags kept moving forward.[63]

Here, we see that Youssef's insight that the green flags are merely sheets does not dispel its power. Indeed, it is only as a sign that has been denuded, exposed as "what it really is" (i.e., sheets) that the flags can be something other than what they usually are taken to be, a symbol that magically unites—and interpellates—a community under its aegis. Exposed as being misinterpellated (and misinterpellating), the flag ceases, however briefly, to convey an overarching signification that determines and controls those that it purportedly only represents. Seeing the flag in all of its materiality suggests a way to recognize the anarchic possibility of this community, a way to see it as complex and multiple rather than as being presupposed and ordered by one single sign even as the sign continues to signify, continues to point to a location and a movement. This is, once again, a bit like the metaphor of the matador and the red cape discussed in an earlier chapter; here, too, a sign is presented: the flag! And then it is "exposed" for what it is: just sheets! And, in the gap or emptiness created between what the flag is supposed to convey and the community that is denoted by its sign, we see the possibility of a fuller anarchic expression of community, one that follows from the disappointment that is conveyed by the flag's exposure (the absence of what it is felt to signify even as the referent remains) and which could perhaps not have been expressed in its full complexity (at least not as readily) without that exposure.

In *The Origin of German Tragic Drama*, Benjamin explains how something similar was done with the figure of Jesus in certain literary renditions. He tells us that the German baroque dramatists, who are the subject of that book, turned Jesus—quite inadvertently—from a mystical figure into an everyday person (to put it in his own words, how "the symbolic becomes distorted into the allegorical").[64] He writes that these plays are full of "examples of birth, marriage, and funeral poems, of eulogies and victory congratulations, songs on the birth and death of Christ, on his spiritual marriage with the soul, on his glory and his victory."[65] In so doing, Benjamin writes that "it is an unsurpassably spectacular gesture to place even Christ in the realm of the provisional, the everyday, the unreliable."[66] Insofar as Christ is not just another symbol but *the* symbol, the ur-Subject who sits at the origin of the mechanisms of authority and interpellation, to render him of all figures from a symbol to an allegory—in Benjamin's terms—suggests a "spectacular" assault on the heart of false projections of authority.

While this instance may indeed be spectacular, it helps to model other, more humble, examples as well (including Djebar's). It shows how to turn a part of the economy of interpellation into something subversive and dangerous simply by treating it as an ordinary part of (unheroic) human life, rendering it back into the everyday anarchist materiality and temporality from which it is drawn.

In *Invisible Man*, the narrator's funeral speech that is said over, Clifton's coffin achieves a similar effect. By focusing on Clifton's body, his sock, his blood, his confinement in his coffin, the narrator interferes with Clifton as an object of interpellation—what the Brotherhood might presumably have desired him to be—and instead allows a glimpse of the anarchic multiplicity that lies beneath the surface of that representation. By rendering Clifton into an unhero, the narrator refrains from engaging in a kind of political language that reproduces those forms of representational hegemony that he is constantly struggling with (as is his audience). Even as he does so, however, the narrator also continues to insist on the beauty of Clifton's face and body, even if dead. He tells the audience, "His name was Clifton and he was tall and some folks thought he was handsome. And though he didn't believe it, I think he was. His name was Clifton and his face was black and his hair was thick with tight-rolled curls—or call them naps or kinks."[67] If Clifton helped the narrator to love blackness by loving this beautiful black man, he is expressing both the loss of that body and the fact that he remains both black and beautiful as a way for both himself and his audience to love themselves as such (as black people) rather than as they are told to love themselves (as subjects of the law which offers a different kind of blackness).

In supporting the theme of "our hope shot down," the narrator is expressing rage and despair but, when read in a Nietzschean vein—and a misinterpellating vein at that—we can see something else afoot in this slogan. Without ceasing to attest to the brutality of police violence, and the racist system that such violence supports, the phrase, "our hope shot down" also suggests moving beyond—and away from—hope, moving beyond those promises of salvation (i.e., hope) that keep black and brown subjects bound to a system that truly offers them nothing of the kind. "Our hope shot down," then, has a more positive (or at least less negative) connotation in terms of being a way not to remain trapped by the false choices that the narrator initially sees himself as facing.[68] The refusal that it signifies is thus not purely negative but has creative and constructive aspects as well. The kind of blackness or brotherhood or sisterhood that the narrator may be discovering, the same blackness that Fanon "asserts . . . as a BLACK MAN," becomes possible or visible perhaps only, or at least especially when hope (for "Brotherhood," for liberal subjectivity, for universality) has been shot down.

For this reason, I do not read the narrator's turn to true "invisibility" (that is, his retreat into his warm, bright "hole") as an abandonment of politics nor of the visible blackness that he often seems to regard as his burden. As he reminds us near the beginning of the text, there is much in politics that occurs below the surface that remains valid, potent, even dangerous. Several times in the novel, the narrator recalls his grandfather's dying words to him when he was much younger. In a statement very reminiscent of Scott's "hidden transcript," the narrator's grandfather tells him,

> "Son, after I'm gone I want you to keep up the good fight. I never told you, but our life is a war and I've been a traitor all my born days, a spy in the enemy's country ever since I gave up my gun back in the Reconstruction. Live with your head in the lion's mouth. I want you to overcome 'em with yeses, undermine 'em with grins, agree 'em to death and destruction, let 'em swoller you till they vomit or bust wide open."[69]

The narrator is not quite sure what to make of his grandfather's words. He always took his grandfather to be utterly passive. But as he becomes increasingly alienated from the Brotherhood—his funeral speech for Clifton is the last straw, both for himself and the leadership of the Brotherhood—he sees the virtue of what might be called "visible invisibilities," strategies of hiding in plain sight and taking advantage of one's nonpresence and nonrecognition.[70] Thus invisibility presents itself to him as a double-edged sword; on the one hand, it serves as a source of unwilled nonrecognition that he suffers at the hands of other people. On the other hand, it serves as a way to subvert and conceal the narrator's own attack on that very same system of recognition and interpellation (in the spirit of his grandfather).

The narrator notes that, after his speech, the crowd separates into "the set faces of individual men and women." Although it remains unclear whether these selves become legible as individuals only to the narrator or to all of them as well, this image could be taken even further. Those "set faces" are themselves masks that suggest unitary subjects when what they convey— what lies behind those faces—is multiple. The narrator's refusal, the way he will not render Clifton into a hero, and the way he takes a symbol and shows it to be merely a cipher for something far more complicated but also far more human break apart the kinds of belief systems that normally organize a community under some overarching sign (like a flag). His actions render visible and available the anarchist plethora that this community has always (also) been even as it still remains a community, bounded by a common blackness that the narrator may just now be learning to make his own.

Given the forms of refusal that he practices, Ellison's narrator can be read as an example of a Fanonian-style refusal of his own rejection. In neither case is a demand being made for full inclusion. Both Fanon and Ellison recognize the dead end of liberal subjectivity (even as they both attest to the lures of such subjectivity, despite there being "no hope"). Instead, what they offer is a refusal to be the failed, false subjects that liberal interpellation offers to black bodies (this could also be considered to be a "failure to fail," at least in the way that liberal subjectivity demands of them). Both Fanon and Ellison's narrator say in effect, "that isn't me." But rather than assert some "true identity" in its stead, they stand in the failure of that failure (akin perhaps to Marx's negation of the negation but I think somehow quite different).

Rather than try to shove themselves in to get a place at the table, they simply refuse to leave the scene of their rejection. They refuse to be misrecognized, papered over, ignored, and folded into a universal subjectivity in ways that deny them precisely what they are promised by the universal. Not willing to be *that* failed subject, they elect a deeper and more radical failure by their act of refusal; both Fanon and Ellison assert their insistence on being black *and* subjects at the same time (and thus a very different kind of black subject than what interpellation itself offers). This is not the failure of Karl, which seems to come naturally to him. This is a purposeful failure (not unlike Wall's "purposeful misunderstanding"), one that must struggle to assert itself as constituting an option when all options seem already determined and limited.

The critical difference between Ellison's narrator and Karl is that Karl can respond to law; he can resist it by failing (or not, as is the case for so many white subjects). Ellison's narrator, however, is not afforded this privilege. He can only refuse the call of the law.[71] His refusals are multiple; he refuses to give the speech that he knew he was supposed to give; he refuses to ascribe to a universalism that denies him his value; he refuses to cater to expectations, even of the crowd (although it is quite possible that the crowd heard whatever they expected or wanted to hear; misrecognition runs deep). Instead he focuses on what Nietzsche would call the "noontime," the here and the now, the dripping blood, the casket in front of him, the foot that had a sock with a hole in it within the casket, Clifton's physical beauty and, in so doing, the narrator's refusal opens him up to a completely different form of failure. Rather than asserting the failed self that is offered to bodies of color in America, his refusal produces a deeper failure, one that leads to far more radical (I would say anarchist) outcomes.

Destroying the Black Body

In *Between the World and Me*, Ta-Nehisi Coates similarly faces the reality of police officers killing black people. In the case of Coates, there is not even the disguise of fiction involved. In a book written to his fifteen-year-old son as a kind of open letter—at least as a form of literary device—Coates narrates his own life and the world as he perceives it. In his book, Coates describes the murder of his friend Prince Jones, who was shot and killed by a police officer who followed him by car for many miles until the officer confronted him and ended his life.[72] As with the narrator in *Invisible Man*, Coates too describes the murder and its outcome in very physical terms. He describes being at Jones's funeral where he feels alienated and distant from the general tone of the service. Whereas the talk at that service was of forgiveness, and the soul, Coates focused on Jones's physical—and murdered—body and his own anger. He writes,

> Forgiving the killer of Prince Jones would have seemed irrelevant to me. The killer was the direct expression of all of his country's belief. And raised conscious, in rejection of a Christian God, I could see no higher purpose in Prince's death. I believed, and still do, that our bodies are our selves, that my soul is the voltage conducted through

neurons and nerves, and that my spirit is my flesh. Prince Jones was a one of one, and they had destroyed his body, scorched his shoulders and arms, ripped open his back, mangled lung, kidney, and liver. I sat there feeling myself a heretic, believing only in this one-shot life and the body. For the crime of destroying the body of Prince Jones, I did not believe in forgiveness.[73]

Coates employs the term "destroying [his, her, or my] body" quite often in this text. It is a way to remind us that murder is not a metaphysical activity but a very tangible one, that what is being lost is not, after all, an ephemeral subject (not just hope) but an actual body, a site that is animated by so much more than could ever be captured by a single, coherent name or term.

In contemplating the loss created by the murder of Jones (the destruction of his body), Coates writes,

The plunder was not just of Prince alone. Think of all the love poured into him. Think of the tuitions for Montessori and music lessons. Think of the gasoline expended, the treads worn carting him to football games, basketball tournaments, and Little League. Think of the time spent regulating sleepovers. Think of the surprise parties, the daycare, and the reference checks on babysitters. . . . Think of soccer balls, science kits, chemistry sets, racetracks, and model trains. Think of all the embraces, all the private jokes, customs, greetings, names, dreams, all the shared knowledge and capacity of a black family injected into that vessel of flesh and bone. And think of how that vessel was taken, shattered on the concrete, and all its holy contents, all that had gone into him, sent flowing back to the earth.[74]

Here too Coates engages in antiheroic language. He discovers in Jones an immense and collective—and I'd once again say anarchic—set of actions, objects, desires, and thoughts, all of which was laid to waste by Jones's murder. Here, in a way that is not dissimilar to Ellison's narrator, Jones is returned back into the community that sustained and formed him; his boundaries are not clearly delineated, he is not the (supposedly) autarkic liberal subject he is told to be.

In speaking of Jones in this way, Coates is offering a form of counterinterpellation. In warning of the "destruction of the body," he seeks to render Jones unheroic, unavailable to teleological and salvational narratives. He wishes to make animate and complex what has been robbed from black people via the facts of state violence and narratives of loss. A bit later in the book, Coates speaks of slaves in the precise way he speaks of Jones, rendering the reality of their existence via the details and diverse aspects of their material existence. He tells his son that

> slavery is not an indefinable mass of flesh. It is a particular, specific enslaved woman, whose mind is active as your own, whose range of feeling is as vast as your own; who prefers the way light falls in one particular spot in the woods, who enjoys fishing where the water eddies in a nearby stream, who loves her mother in her own complicated way, thinks her sister talks too loud, has a favorite cousin, a favorite season, who excels at dressmaking and knows, inside herself, that she is as intelligent and capable as anyone.[75]

Resisting the kinds of redemptive narratives that recoup the experience of slavery for some better teleology (the same narrative that would ask forgiveness for a cold-blooded and racist killer), Coates writes further to his son that "the enslaved were not bricks in your road, and their lives were not chapters in your redemptive history. . . . Enslavement was not destined to end, and it is wrong to claim our present circumstance—no matter how much improved—as the redemption for the lives of people who never asked for the posthumous, untouchable glory of dying for their children."[76] This point is critical because the idea of "dying for a reason" folds the destruction of the body into the very teleological order that kills black and brown people in the first place. Resisting these narratives, fighting the material production of an ideology of interpellation with materiality itself, Coates is providing a counternarrative of his own. Like Ellison, he invites what I'd call a misinterpellated reading into a script that otherwise seems tragic and doomed.

In his own descriptions of Jones's physical beauty, Coates may not require this as much as the narrator of *Invisible Man* may have done in order to love and choose and determine his own mode of blackness. Yet, by alluding to it at several points in the book, Coates does assert a form of identity that has nothing to do with liberal or white conventions (either of beauty or of subjectivity per se). It is, once again, to assert an alternative form of blackness.

There is something highly subversive about this other kind of blackness. Just as the in the story that Assia Djebar tells us the French police see the green flags of Islam as being nothing more than "filthy rags!" (hence missing their greater and more radical significance), the alternative blackness Coates presents similarly looks to the outside (interpellating) world as just the same blackness that they have always (mis)recognized and which they count upon to keep the black subject down.[77] In this way, a form of subversion and refusal hides in plain sight; it is both visible and invisible at once.

For all of this subversive possibility, the black subject is never out of danger in America. Coates's discussion of Jones's death is not the only instance in which he comes up against the violence that the state and the white community more generally poses to black people, his own self very much included. In his narrative, Coates describes his own brush, not so much with the police per se as with the general interpellating power of white citizenry in the United States. When a white woman expressed anger that his son (then much smaller) was dawdling while walking along in a movie theater on the Upper West Side of Manhattan, Coates snapped at her, evoking in turn a white man who came to the woman's defense saying, "I could have you arrested!"[78]

In saying this, the white man is letting Coates know exactly where he (i.e., Coates) stands in the legal order. Although not himself a police officer—at least not that we know of—the white man evokes the power of the law, his own ability to interpellate Coates, and, thus, a version of "hey, you there!" and "tiens, un nègre!" all in one. Coates says of this, "I came home shook. It was a mix of shame for having gone back to the law of the streets mixed with rage—'I could have you arrested!' Which is to say 'I could take your body.' . . . I had forgotten the rules, an error as dangerous on the Upper West Side of Manhattan as on the Westside of Baltimore."[79] For Coates, it is precisely when he believes himself to be safe, that he can survive and even thrive in a white-dominated world, that he is in the most danger because his subjectivity, such as it is, never ceases to invoke an implied and omnipresent threat of violence and destruction.

His response to Jones's death as well as his own encounters with the law commit Coates to a path of refusal and struggle. After noting that his son is named Samori after Samori Touré, the nineteenth-century founder of an Islamic empire in Guinea, who fought (and died) struggling against French colonialism, Coates goes on to say, very much in the spirit of Fanon, that struggle has its own meaning:

Perhaps struggle is all we have because the god of history is an atheist, and nothing about his world is meant to be. So you must wake up every morning knowing that no promise is unbreakable, least of all the promise of waking up at all. This is not despair. These are the preferences of the universe itself: verbs over nouns, actions over states, struggle over hope.[80]

Here again, as with the narrator in *Invisible Man*, hope turns out to be a chimera, part of the cruel package wherein hope and redemption ensnare black people in a false unsubjecthood in the name of an all-inclusive and all-loving universal that is nothing of the sort. Coates too evokes the universe but he does so in order to defy what the universal normally entails: "verbs over nouns, actions over states, struggle over hope." Here, in refusing one set of values, Coates is endorsing other ones. In this way, Coates's own refusal is not a form of despair, but it is not a form of hope either. His refusal is a step away from teleology and determinism, a step toward life and subjectivity in its most intimate, complex, intertangled, and material aspects. Coates offers an assertion, as with Fanon, of a subject position that is recognized as impossible but nonetheless still insistently refuses to not be (thus once again offering a "yes" and a "no" at the same time).

"Consent Not to Be a Single Being"

We can see a bit more of the political implications in both Coates's and Ellison's texts by considering a 2013 interview with Fred Moten (along with his fellow radical writer, Stefano Harney). In that discussion, Moten offers us a way to think about calling and narration—that is, the way authority is handled and (re)distributed—that doesn't automatically seek to replace or override the anarchic, but simply recognizes it. In this sense, it is comparable to what is achieved by Woolf's "come, come!" or even the form of relationality that is possibly evident in the call of "you, you!" that the narrator of *Invisible Man* makes to Clifton (even as it is wrapped up with a lot of despair and pain as well). In the interview in question, Moten effectively contrasts two ways of engaging with relationships of authority. He first offers a traditional—and interpellative—approach, describing how, as a teacher, he comes into his classroom when students are already having multiple and varied conversations. He interrupts those conversations with a "call to order," presumably to allow the "real" (i.e., authorized) conversation to begin. Moten writes,

> My position, at that moment . . . what I'm supposed to do is to call that class to order, which presupposes that there is no actual, already

existing organization, happening, that there's no study happening before I got there. . . . I'm calling it to order, and then something can happen—then knowledge can be produced. That's the presumption.[81]

In fact, Moten concedes that his call to order is not a beginning but an interruption—as all forms of interpellation are—and, in a sense (therefore), also an accusation. It is tantamount to saying, "I don't and I won't recognize your own conversations as legitimate. I know better than you; you must abandon those conversations in order to bolster my own authority over you." This is the stance of the law as well.

A bit later in the interview, Moten contrasts this call to order with another form of address. Speaking of the singer Mavis Staples, he describes one particular song of hers as having a radically different form of address:

If you listen to the Staple Singers' "I'll Take You There," it's got one little chorus, one little four-line quatrain, and then the whole middle of the song is just Mavis Staples telling the band to start playing. "Little Davie [the bassist] we need you now." . . . Then the verse was like "somebody, play your piano." That's the whole middle of the song. That's the heart of the song. Not the damn lyrics. It's just her saying "play," and they're already playing.[82]

Moten concludes by saying, "And that's not a call to order. It's an acknowledgment, and a celebration, of what was already happening."[83] As such, this other kind of address has an entirely different relationship to what it engages with. Rather than telling the audience who it is or what it ought to be doing—an interpellation, a call to order—this form of address simply acknowledges what is already happening in all of its diversity and complexity; it acknowledges an existing context that the call itself is not external to but part of, that which it is recognizing, even bringing together, by its act of calling out.

We see a bit more of the political stakes involved in this form of address when Harney adds to this concept, calling the Black Panthers "a revolution in the present of already-existing black life."[84] In his view the call for this kind of radical blackness does not inaugurate anything new per se but calls attention to realities and complexities that interpellation is dedicated to stamping out. Yet this other form of calling *does something*. As with the examples of the Black Panthers, it draws on existing networks and agencies but, through the call itself, that attention can crystalize these things into an effective and powerful form of resistance; the call in this case can be a catalyst for what already is to recognize itself as such (or cease to misrecognize itself). Hence such a call is not as passive as it might seem. It is not simply saying "there you are," but something more like Woolf's "come, come!"; it engages, negotiates, galvanizes, and celebrates what is already there but it also clarifies. Such a move politicizes the subjects in question; it produces a positive form of refusal which may not have been there before, at least not in the active political form that it becomes via the call itself.

In a sense, these statements by Moten help us to better understand—with some help from Djebar and Benjamin as well—what the narrator of *Invisible Man* and Coates are doing when they describe their murdered friends; avoiding a language of redemption and heroism, they too acknowledge what is already there, permitting their audiences in turn to similarly acknowledge what they are and what they have suffered and lost. It is a way to remind them that their bodies, their blackness is *theirs*, not as a unitary and inalternable "fact," but as a set of choices and recognitions. They show that blackness— and their subjectivity more generally—doesn't belong to or come from the "recognition" of the state. Such a view serves to alter and subvert forms of identity they seem to simply describe (by focusing, for example, on physical attributes, skin color, hair texture, etc.). By refusing the language of interpellation, they interrupt the normal and teleological flow of black subjectivity, permitting other blacknesses, other subjectivities, temporalities, and events to become visible and possible.

In his interview, Moten also offers a line from the Caribbean author and poet Édouard Glissant that I think is especially potent as a misinterpellating call: "consent not to be a single being."[85] I think this phrase richly illuminates the strategy I discuss here. Elsewhere, Moten writes about engaging with his students about such a call, stating that

> pretty much everybody I know is driven to dissent from such a movement [i.e., to permit the undermining of interpellated, singular subjectivity], where consent is inseparable from a monstrous imposition, but . . . me and my students [were] primed, nevertheless, to be drawn, against ourselves, to the rail, to the abyss, by the iterative, broken singularity it hides and holds, by the murmur of submerged, impossible social life—that submarine, excluded, impossible middle passage into multiplicity, where pained, breathlessly overblown harmonic striation, from way underneath some unfathomable and impossible to overcome violation, animates ecstasies of chromatic

saturation, driven down and out into the world as if risen into another: impossible assent, *consentement impossible*, *glissment impossible*, impossible Glissant.[86]

Here, Moten also speaks of "not represent[ing] the ones who become multiple; it just asks you to join them."[87] Such a "submerged, impossible social life" is precisely the anarchic community that each being is together and separately (once again without, in this case, ceasing to be black). Perhaps this sounds a bit like the doubled selves that we see with Luce Irigaray's understanding of female subjectivity (the call "to be two") and maybe there is some similarity in that, although the anarchic subjects I discuss here are far more than "two" in terms of their interior identity (although there is nothing to preclude the female subject in Irigaray's thought to be "two" even as she is also many).[88]

Part of the power of the call to "consent not to be a single being" comes from the fact that it contests liberal universality on its own terrain. It uses the language of consent, which is a mainstay of liberal theory, but in this case consent becomes a weapon against its own ideology; it serves to undermine the very presuppositions that form the liberal subject in the first place and expose the anarchist subject(s) that can dwell beneath and alongside with this subject. This call could, of course, be a call to all persons, all subjects of the universal, but I think that the fact that it comes from within the context of black and Caribbean (and, more particularly, Francophone) political and aesthetic thought is telling. It derives from the same general geographical milieu as the Haitian revolution itself; it thereby imports all of that history, all of that refusal and struggle into the present call. It could be thought of as the antidote to that original, interpellating call that sparked it all, the French revolution's "Men are born free and equal in rights."

In this way, the call to "consent not to be a single being" can be said to be the positive face of refusal. It is a form of refusal expressed as a form of consent. To "consent not" shows how the refusal is not purely negative, how in saying no to one thing (being a single being), it is saying yes to something else (being multiple, being anarchic, being black or some other kind of identity).

Conclusion: Conspirators, Not Allies

As we have seen throughout this book, the black subject has to face not only the false subjectivity of the universal, as the white subject does, but a second false subjectivity, the opaque subject that Fanon discovered when he was hailed by that white boy in Lyon with "tiens, un nègre!" If all subjects want to be the higher, better, truer self that liberal universality promises—as well as some variants of left universality too as Ellison shows us—the black subject encounters another self that isn't them either but in this case this is not a subject they would want to be. This, then, complicates the notion of the misinterpellated subject as "the one who shows up," because the one who shows up—from an external perspective, from the position of the police, for instance—isn't "really" the black subject either. For her then, the lures of the universal are tempered with the anguish of being this other being. The question of who shows up to answer the call then involves multiple layers of being. The call to "consent not to be a single being" disallows both the universal subject and the false opaque subject that shows up, or responds to, the call "tiens, un nègre!"

Bearing Moten's concepts in mind, and thinking about the unique context of the black subject—although I think other people of color have related, if not identical situations—in contrasting and also relating Karl Rossmann, Ellison's narrator, and Coates's own self-narration, we see both some common ground and a great deal that isn't common at all. There are different forms of challenges, different strategies, different outlooks for these narratives. This contrast is further evidence that it is pointless to keep looking for a left universal (as Frank Wilderson III argues that Gramsci does), some unifying structure that joins everyone into one big, happy human race.[89]

If there is one thing that all of these narratives share, it is an intense allergy to—or ineptness for—redemptive solutions, to false commonality and overarching and compelling analogy. In the face of law's violence in the form of the police, instead of calling for universality (or "Brotherhood"), I would call for a counterinterpellative conspiracy. From their different positions in the "universal"—the white subject on the "inside" and the black subject on the "outside," which is, however, still very much inside as well—these various subjects can take advantage of these differences in order to collectively conspire against interpellative authority as a whole, coming at it from different directions, as it were.

Anarchism can never be more than a set of co-conspiracies precisely because it does not subscribe to the universalism that liberalism does.[90] Under the universal, everyone is all "the same," even as people are ordered and rendered in a hierarchy that is impregnable because it is un- (or mis)recognized. Archist politics stem from that unifying, totalizing vision. Under such a universal, everyone can be "allies," working together on a presumed common cause. And leftists often adopt this language too in ways that duplicate the very universality that they purportedly oppose (if they do). From this perspective, it seems that we can really be a "we," a unity that speaks if not with one voice, then with voices that are understood as commensurable, equivalent (e pluribus unum: the words on the US dollar say it all). All the de facto inequalities that such an alliance covers over are presupposed, preserved in the very stance of denying—or even struggling against—their existence.

Without that universal, however, when one "consents to not be a single being"—that is, not be "one" at all, not a single iteration of a universal that reproduces itself in each separate self—a much more complicated picture emerges both on the collective and individual level. Rather than say, as liberals do, that this means that we are all fundamentally the same, regardless of race or gender in all of its variety, sexual orientation, class, ability status, and so forth, I would say this view of the subject means exactly the opposite; we are all very, very different, not only from one another but even from and within ourselves. As noted in chapter 4, each one of "us" is itself an us, a complicated and protean subject and so any politics that comes from this position is also inherently anarchist. Just as anarchism rejects the organization of society into a single harmonized unity, so by extension must it reject the organization of selves into unitary subjects. The same logic applies in both cases.

This doesn't mean that we should all embrace some extreme form of individualism. That stance generally presumes an archic subject who is one singular and unique being who competes with—in the (Ayn) Randian formula anyway—and ultimately triumphs over other selves through the violence of capitalism. To think this ignores the way that these selves overlap and don't have clearly distinguished boundaries. Accordingly, thinking about the anarchy of the subject doesn't involve dissolving intraconnecting forms of identity such as race or gender (to do so, of course, would be to return each person to the false equivalencies—and secret hierarchies—that liberalism makes in the first place). As discussed in this and previous chapters, race is an integral, even central part of that complex and multiple array of factors that make each person a person, as are gender, sexuality, disability, and other forms of identity. As the narratives of Ellison and Coates attest, being black in America offers a lesson in identity that is impossible to escape, even if one wanted to believe in what Coates calls the "Dream" (the fantasy of being white or without a racial identity at all, which is more or less the same thing in his view).[91]

Instead of looking for alliances and equivalences then, for struggle contained within a narrative of redemption (and, hence, teleology), I think it would be far better for individuals and groups to seek out conspiracies with other individuals and groups, even forming conspiracies among and within each "self/us" at the same time. An alternative term to conspiracy that I've seen used is "accomplices," which has a common sense of working outside and against the law and other forms of interpellative authority.[92] I think both terms are equally helpful. The kinds of conspiracies that I am talking about here allow different groups—however those are considered—with different histories and different subject positions to conspire together even as they conspire separately as well. "Individualism" under such a context takes on a very different valence and meaning; it recognizes both the ways that subjects overlap and are interconnected and the ways that they don't. It offers a much more complicated and dynamic vision of community, of how subjects are together and alone, than the autarkic model that we inherit from John Locke.[93]

Under current conditions, anarchists are no more immune to issues of racism and gender privilege and hierarchy than anyone else; many women and anarchists of color have directly experienced this in dealing with the larger—generally white- and male-dominated—anarchist community. It's not that an increase in misinterpellation will magically sweep all forms of racism and privilege away—just as it wouldn't sweep away race and other identities—but it would make it more difficult to practice these hierarchical sorts of behaviors because the very idea of a privileged position from which to view other positions becomes much more difficult without the full-bore force of the universal backing up and presupposing such assumptions. Without a working universal, individuals and groups are left much more to their own devices and, as such, one could see something more like a real conspiracy—that is, a temporary and shifting set of relationships—emerging rather than having recourse to a readily available common humanity (which, in my view, is always a prelude to more interpellation and archism).

If interpellation is always an accusation, one with different connotations for people of color than for white people, then Ellison and Coates show a way to turn that accusation around; through their acts of refusal, they show us not how to disengage and retreat from interpellating power, but rather how to get in closer, to do maximal damage from the impossible position of the black subject. What they offer is neither a formula for certain success nor a happy ending—for that is the kind of promise or guarantee that comes from universalism—but a different vocabulary, a way to speak and act that doesn't reiterate the accusation that forms their subjectivity in the first place.

One related and final question that I would like to address here is whether we can speak of these acts of refusal or resistance as being any form of *amor fati* insofar as the "fate" that people of color are being asked to love seems distinctly and especially unlovable. It is one thing, perhaps, for Zarathustra to call himself a "cripple at this bridge" (especially when he is actually able bodied) but there seems to be no election, as I have shown, for the subject of color, no trying on of roles to see what works and what doesn't. Does it add insult to injury to say that the subject of color must not only accept and choose their fate but also love it?

One way to think about this question is to argue that the "fate" these figures have chosen to love is *not* based on the self given to them by interpellation but rather on a self that is precisely defined in opposition to and defiance of such a self (so a very different kind of fate as well). The courage of Fanon's refusal, of the refusal that we also see Ellison and Coates practicing, comes, as I've stated before, in insisting on neither conceding to nor leaving the scene of interpellation, not slinking away and permitting the ongoing work of misrecognition to maintain the status quo. This, too, is a kind of *amor fati* in the sense that these subjects are actively producing and creating the self that is to be loved; this is the moment when Fanon decides to "assert [him]self as a BLACK MAN," when he takes on his impossible situation and makes it into something radically different and of his own making.[94]

Moten and Harney also help us to think about *amor fati* in the context of race in this regard. In a separate writing, thinking about the words and opinions of Michael Brown, they note that in a Facebook post from a few days before he was murdered, he wrote "if i leave this earth today atleast youll know i care about others more than i cared about my damn self."[95] Adding to this and speaking in his voice, as it were, Moten and Harney add: "Go on call me 'demon' but I WILL love my *damn self*."[96] This assertion of self-love in the face of all that happened to Michael Brown as both a living and a dead subject can itself be read as an act of refusal. This is a positive and productive form of refusal which is opposed to false liberal statements of universal equality and human rights wherein value is awarded only from the outside, from interpellation itself (and when that value is not the subject's to control regardless of what they do and say). Moten and Harney's radical assertion—"preference" may be a better word—of *amor fati* does not rely on anyone else, and certainly not on any state or social authority to be valid or recognized. In this way it gives nothing to the state; it doesn't feed it back the recognition that the state itself requires but bypasses it entirely, indicating alternative sources of value and judgment in the process. I also think this statement captures the way that refusal is both a "no" and a "yes," an act of refusal and also, in a very different way an act of love.[97]

But do such acts of refusal necessitate a complete rejection of the interpellated form of blackness that these authors contend with? Another somewhat different way to think about the question of *amor fati* and the subject of color would be to say that in loving themselves, these authors are even loving the dead-end subjectivity that they have been given by interpellation. To say this may be more in keeping with a Nietzschean approach to subjectivity in which one must say yes to everything, even (or especially) to selves that one does not want to be. But if these authors are saying yes even to their interpellated form of subjectivity, that subjectivity becomes something else in doing so. Perhaps there is no original difference between the "amputated" self that Fanon found himself in possession of and the created self he chose to be or between the invisible man and the subject at the end (and beginning) of Ellison's novel who is bathed in warmth and light. Perhaps in loving the first self, these authors have discovered or produced the second.

The words Moten and Harney associate with Michael Brown may even suggest something along these lines; saying "I WILL love my *damn self*" might accept that damnation while still refusing to be condemned to being just one thing. Perhaps the stance of refusal, refusal to slink away, refusal to not be the kind of subject they are promised to be, is also a stance of retrieval. In this case, the subject retrieves from a false and externally imposed form of subjectivity a subjectivity that they could not only live with but could love. This is a subjectivity that gives a position from which to act; it is in full flux and maximally open to its own internal anarchy, creativity and possibility. In learning to love their own blackness, they show how blackness itself is not (only) a mode of interpellation ("tiens, un nègre") but the means by which that subjectivization can be contested, on its own terms and terrain.

Whichever way one thinks about the subject of color and her relationship to her own selfhood, we can see perhaps most clearly how *amor fati* is not a passive acceptance of what must be but rather an active engagement with the world. The act of engaging in *amor fati* makes it possible for the subject to become an agent, even, or perhaps especially, a subject of color who despite all the blandishments of the liberal universal is meant to be excluded and depoliticized, that is, "loved" in a more universal and hence highly inegalitarian and violent way. Refusing that kind of love, these subjects suggest other ways of being both alone and together wherein the primary form of recognition is not accusation but rather acknowledgment (but also a kind of mustering). As such, the pathways to resistance and conspiracy become that much clearer while the entombing love (which, as Nietzsche reminds us, is actually a form of deep hatred) of liberalism becomes that much more disrupted and exposed.

CHAPTER SEVEN

"I CAN BELIEVE"

Breaking the Circuits of Interpellation in von Trier's *Breaking the Waves*

Throughout this book, I have argued that interpellation is a circuit; it is projected from one site—usually, in this case, the state—and received by individuals who then become legal subjects. These subjects in turn, in obeying, and—at least to some extent—in absorbing this subjectivity, project that authority back out to the "origin" from which it was received.[1] The actual story of this circularity is clearly more complicated than this model suggests; as I've argued, it differs from group to group, from individual to individual. For some (Mrs. Ramsay, or the Wall Street narrator of "Bartleby"), interpellation is a true circuit; for others (Frantz Fanon, Ralph Ellison, Ta-Nehisi Coates), it can function as a dead end disguised as a circuit. Either way, the circuitry of interpellation is a key aspect of how global liberalism functions (among other systems) and this circulation of authority, akin to what Fanon calls the "psychoexistential complex," is what I have been trying to trouble, to show how and that it is resistible in the pages of this book.

In this final chapter before the conclusion, I engage in one more literary (actually filmic) analysis, this time focusing on Lars von Trier's *Breaking the Waves*. Von Trier is a complicated figure, to put it mildly. His politics—especially his gender politics—are controversial and always at issue.[2] Yet in *Breaking the Waves*, von Trier has given us a character—Bess McNeill (played brilliantly in the film by Emily Watson)—who demonstrates, I think, what a definitive break in the circuitry of interpellation might look like. I say that with a great deal of trepidation because what Bess chooses to do as a result of that break is not something that anyone would ever want to do; as I will describe, she allows herself to be raped and murdered as part of an attempt on her part to save her husband's life; in her own view, and seemingly von Trier's as well, she sacrifices her own life—and in the most horrible way possible—for her husband. It is difficult in Bess's case to see where agency ends and madness begins.

But the point of a misinterpellated character is not for us to want to be them or to approve of them. I've already amply demonstrated that these are generally people we don't want to be and, in a way, the horror of Bess's experience especially disallows any tendency to romanticize or heroize such a figure. Bess, on the one hand, shows, in a very tangible way, the dangers and suffering of the path of resistance, the price that must be paid for taking on the role of misinterpellated subjectivity but, by the same token, she also shows the joy of that subject position, the possibilities of freedom from determination and moving into a space of radical contingency and subjective (and intersubjective) anarchism. Therefore, even if she is not a role model for our own behavior, Bess's example may still open the viewer up to the possibility of a misinterpellated politics for herself or himself.

For this reason, in this chapter, I present Bess as a case study to speak directly to some of the central issues—particularly the theological ones—that animate this book. If, as Louis Althusser tells us, even if inadvertently, God is the Subject, the origin of interpellation, then, as I have tried to show at various points in the text, a break in the circulation of interpellation—that is, a way to maximize misinterpellation—must begin with this God. Bess directly interferes with the circuitry of divine interpellation, as I will argue further, by talking not only as herself but also as God. In doing so Bess reveals yet again the anarchic subject that we all are; somehow Bess and God are able to share the same interior space, to speak from the same mouth and with the same voice—although God has a deeper resonance, and a stronger Scottish accent than Bess does—even as they are separate, at least to some extent, from one another. By speaking with God's voice, Bess bypasses the false images of God that serve to reinforce interpellation, as everyone else in her village does, and produces instead a Nietzschean—and Benjaminian—God, a messiah that leaves her largely to her own devices. Bess epitomizes, therefore, a particularly effective strategy for how to resist the God of interpellation (the Subject), how to replace that God by myriad local and personal Gods who interfere with the interference that the original Subject produces.

By giving one part of herself its own voice and consciousness, Bess makes it impossible for a singular interpellated subjectivity to colonize her. Now that she is no longer "one" but "two" entities ("consent not to be a single being!"), Bess McNeill has armed herself against ever being reunified, falsely settled and reformed by some external being that was never herself. Furthermore, and, relatedly, it is critical to note that, rather than answering a call from God—or at least the perception of such a call—Bess's God answers *her* call (at least most of the time). It is *she* who is, in some sense, the one doing the interpellating or at least minimizing the degree to which she herself is being interpellated. The fact that she does all of this, not only with some random aspect of her subjectivity but with God, the ur-Subject—or at least a plausible approximation of such, a deity who answers to the name of God—suggests that this is another "unsurpassably spectacular gesture" (to cite Benjamin again) against interpellation and fetishism more generally. Bess uses the power and authority of interpellation as a weapon against itself and, in the process, radically interrupts its circuitry. I thus would add this final strategy to the strategies that I have discussed in the previous two chapters in order to give a fuller picture of what resistance looks like and how to maximally subvert and upend interpellated forms of subjecthood.

This may seem like a very cruel and rough terrain upon which to build a project of resistance and misinterpellation, yet I think its resonance with the other stories I've been looking at, its direct engagement with theology, and, perhaps most of all, the way it dramatizes and clarifies the concept of breaking circuitry—so that even the title of the film does some of that work—suggests that the story of Bess McNeill offers us important resources for any endeavor to maximize the interference and ruination that misinterpellation can bring.

Let me therefore turn to an analysis of the film in order to highlight these arguments. In what follows, in addition to recognizing the horror of the ordeal that Bess puts herself through, I will explore the way that Bess's relationship to her own God offers her some unexpected and even unlikely benefits. Bess is at once a split subject, divided between herself and the God that she ventriloquizes, and, at the same time—just like Bartleby, Lily, Karl, and Ellison's narrator—the only individual agent in the film. Somehow—and my task will be to try to make sense of this—Bess's submission to this simultaneously harsh and forgiving deity allows her to love her fate (*amor fati*). I will argue that Bess's God allows Bess herself a degree of contingency and risk that is denied to the rest of the characters in the film. The other characters in the film are subsumed to phantasms of transcendence—whether of a theological or secular sort—to teleologies that predetermine their actions, to assumption and interpellation in all of its potency. They submit to a bad fate, to an unavoidable and empty form of life. For all the horror and woe that Bess is submitted to in this film, she alone lets us see what fate can be when it is not projected but chosen, that is, when it is loved.[3]

A God of Her Own

Bess lets us know early on in the film that both she and the audience are in on some kind of joke. After an initial scene where she defends the fact that she is marrying an outsider (named Jan, played by Stellan Skarsgård, a staple of von Trier's films) to a group of xenophobic church elders in her northern Scottish village, Bess faces the camera with a knowing smirk. Bess, who can't seem to keep a straight face while intoning platitudes about being good, has nonetheless managed to fool the elders, at least up until that point. She is told by the minister that when she cleans the church—which she does all the time—she doesn't do it "to be well thought of on earth but of love for God in Heaven."[4] The joke that Bess lets us in on is that God exists only via her own belief, that, in some way, God is hers and hers alone.

It is worth spending a few moments—especially for those who are not familiar with the film—to describe the basic plot, to understand the context in which this peculiar relationship between Bess and her God emerges. After an initial honeymoon, during which time Bess is ecstatically happy, Jan has to return to work on an oil rig where he spends months at a time. After he leaves, Bess is despondent (we are told that she has had bouts of mental illness in the past). At some point, she can't take it anymore. Even though she is told that Jan will be home for a visit in a matter of days, Bess wants him right away. Praying, she asks God—and as God she answers herself—to bring him home early. God asks her "are you sure that's what you want?"

and she affirms that it is. Soon afterward Jan arrives. He is sent home early because he has been horribly injured and, it turns out, he is paralyzed. At first, Bess feels a mixture of terror and ecstasy. When the local doctor tells her how gravely injured he is, Bess can only say "but he's alive!" She delights in her power, the fruits of her prayer.

Quickly, however, she regrets her decision. The dark side of Jan's injury becomes all too apparent. Paralyzed, he can no longer have sex with her. He tells Bess that he is dying and only her love can save him. He defines this love as having her have sex with other men and then telling him about it. Bess eventually complies, never willingly, but with an increasing determination; her sense of guilt of having "caused" his accident is a major motivator, along with her love for him. Bess's belief in her own God is reinforced by her sense that each time Jan almost dies, she saves him by performing a sexual act—or trying to—outside their marriage. At the end of the film, Jan is truly dying and so Bess determines that she needs to move to extreme measures. She visits a boat just offshore with horrible and dangerous men on it not once but twice. She goes there seeking her own sacrifice for Jan's sake. The first time, she becomes afraid and flees but she goes back a second time, costing her her life and miraculously saving Jan's in the process; at the end of the film, he is not only alive but also can walk again.

In each instance Bess's key interlocutor is her personal God; this God is the one she turns to for answers, for comfort, and for advice (all of which she gets in varying, not always satisfactory degrees). What we learn over the course of this film is that Bess's God is both entirely contingent—it is produced via Bess's own acts of speaking as God—and yet very real. It isn't until the very last moment of the film, after Bess is already dead, that we see what appears to be an undeniable miracle—church bells ringing in the sky—which seemingly settles the question of whether Bess is simply crazy or has access to the true deity (although, as with many things in von Trier's films, one can never be perfectly certain of anything).

The central question to think about in terms of Bess as a character in this film is the nature of her belief. How is it possible for Bess to believe in a God that she has seemingly invented? How are we, as viewers, in turn able to believe in a God that appears to be simply a manifestation of schizophrenia or megalomania—or both—on Bess's part?[5]

Perhaps the best way to think about this question is to look closely at the nature of the relationship between Bess and her God, to see both the benefits and costs of what this relationship affords and to think about whether this relationship serves a pathology or, on the contrary, a kind of mental health—taking this term mainly in the Nietzschean sense—that is otherwise absent in this film. Bess's belief—and God's contingent existence along with it—produces no guarantees, no safety for her. Indeed, as already noted, Bess is subjected to torment and ultimately an untimely death at least partially due to her belief. Yet, in a sense, Bess's belief in God saves her nonetheless. Her belief saves her from believing in the God of her community (God the Subject, the God of the Presbyterian Kirk). It saves her from having to be someone that she isn't (a fate no one else in the village can avoid).

This other God—the God that isn't Bess's own—is a transcendental and perfect deity that judges everything in creation. In the face of such a God, the members of the community have become a set of hardened creatures who have effectively surrendered their will to an exterior being (one who is, however, of their own invention, a projection of their fears and anxieties). The patriarchs and, it seems, particularly Bess's grandfather, who is the main village leader, live in the certainty—belief almost seems too weak a term for what they have—of a very specific set of Godly judgments in terms of how they live their lives. God serves as a reservoir for presupposed, assumed categories of behavior and action. Everything is already known and nothing further can happen (anything that does happen for these villagers seems inevitably to be a threat or a catastrophe). The villagers' lives are, accordingly, very spare. The grandfather proudly tells Bess's husband, Jan, that the church of their village has no bells, a testament to the way that they allow no frills of any kind. The villagers therefore bear all the hallmarks of interpellation; in von Trier's treatment the effects of that circuitry are very stark and hard to miss.

So confident are the villagers that they have God's approval that the members of the community are able, in a sense, to speak on God's behalf. At the funeral of one member of the community that they disapprove of, the village minister says that he "consign[s him] to hell." In this way, God's will returns to them as a kind of ghostly vehicle for their own authority, however distorted it may be. Speaking on behalf of God, they in effect become God, although not in a way that offers them any choice or power. As I will argue further, although it seems very much like these villagers are submitting to fate, to a destiny that is determined by some transcendent being—and which is hence completely out of their hands—in fact they are submitting only to their own anxieties and projections, that is, to the circuitry of interpellation in its uninterrupted guise. Their power is entirely derivative of a phantasm of their own production, one that they are too tightly bound by to see as anything but an inevitable force or fate to which they are themselves, therefore, consigned.[6]

This attitude toward God and the relationship that results from it could not be more different than the one that Bess experiences. As already noted, while the village minister speaks on behalf of God, Bess speaks *as* God. The minister assumes that he knows what God wants and acts, and speaks, accordingly. When Bess talks to God, God talks back to her. Rather than being a phantom of authority as God is for the villagers, God for Bess is a very actively engaged force, an agent who is not purely imagined and obeyed but spoken to, pleaded, and even argued with.

Speaking as God and to God allows Bess an element of surprise. In this way, she gains access to what is not already determined; she doesn't know what God is going to say in advance.[7] As God tells her, "Remember to be a good girl, Bess. Remember, I giveth and I taketh away." Sometimes God is very stern with her, condemning her for being bad, but other times God is kind and forgiving, allowing Bess her own decisions and her own voice.

In speaking as God with her own voice, Bess manages to pull off a miraculous form of self-production that would not otherwise be possible. Her speaking as God creates a double maneuver. First, she submits to God, apparently to the God—that is, "the Subject"—of her community, to being "good" and all that this entails. This appears to be a complete surrender of her will (and, at times, as I'll show further, her God does act the part of that transcendent deity). But Bess's apparent submission contains within itself the spark of rebellion (or conspiracy); the very sense of fate and inevitability that comes with a belief in a transcendent God is effectively broken by her own pose as God. Or, rather, "God," the voice that Bess speaks with, gives her the power and courage to defy God, the deity—and Subject—that oppresses her. In this way, this other God produces a break in the circuitry of interpellation. As with the earlier discussion of Machiavelli and the way the Romans invoked gods to serve their own purposes, if Bess did not believe in this second God, if God were not true for her, she would not be able to circumvent the power that holds her; she would only be the self that has been created—or called for—by her community. But unlike the Romans, Bess is unable to manipulate this God for her own purposes. She is truly subject and suffers as much as she benefits from her relationship with the deity. Her God is not an externality like it is for the

Romans but an internality, something that comes from herself and so represents not her unified and common purpose, a means of interpellation, but rather a way to resist the externalities that everyone else in her village obeys without question.

In this way, Bess benefits from the same kind of situation that we saw with Nietzsche. In his case, the prophets and messiahs he writes about collude against our reading of God, rendering God—as well as any other messiahs that might speak for God—unavailable as a site for projection and "redemption." In Bess's case, it is even more extreme; God is in this case colluding and conspiring with Bess against God.

As I will show further, during those moments when God does not speak to her—that is, when God does not answer her call to speak—Bess is completely bereft, albeit resolute in her belief. The God who speaks through her, then, is a critical co-conspirator, a particular and local God that allows her to break with the transcendent and universal God. In the process, Bess is able to break with one kind of destiny or fate, with the certainty of who she is and what she must be and do, in favor of another (Nietzschean) form of fate.[8] Using God against God as it were, Bess circumvents or "breaks" her bondage to an absolute moral value that she simply can't live with, which would otherwise have broken her as it has broken nearly everyone around her. Critically, so long as part of what constitutes "Bess" is "God," she becomes unavailable for the kinds of totalizing and unifying identities that have taken over her fellow villagers. Bess has effectively taken the ur-Subject (indeed, the Subject) and used it as a basis to resist its own subjectification.

For this reason, we can say that although Bess certainly appears to be crazy for much of the film—she has a history of mental illness, as already mentioned, and she is threatened with institutionalization during the process of the film—she can be read as the only truly sane person in the film. It is everyone else who is following phantasms posing as reality, projections and anxieties, and the rest. Thanks to her relationship to God, Bess can be said to be the one with access to, if not reality, a realistic view of the unreality that surrounds everything and everyone as well as a way to resist it.

Accordingly, in her own unique way, Bess becomes a Nietzschean subject; she is relatively undetermined, able to make choices and judgments thanks to the God that has broken her free, if not once and for all—for, as already noted, that is not possible—then at least each time she is tempted by the possibility of being a "properly" interpellated subject.[9]

In order to understand the radical break that Bess's speaking as God affords, let me spend more time describing the circuit that is produced between Bess's own sense of her self and the kind of other self that God becomes for her. On the one hand, we can consider Bess's act of talking to God as an entirely solipsistic gesture; there is a way in which her conversations with God are also a way for her to talk to herself, to think in the Socratic sense of having a conversation with oneself. Perhaps she is just a crazy megalomaniac after all, taking this internal conversation to an extreme. But, of course, this is not quite a conversation only with herself and that makes for a critical difference. This God acts in ways that exceed Bess's own agency; for one thing, it has a supernatural power over the world that extends Bess's psyche beyond herself in a way that produces a strange admixture of will and chance. Furthermore, as already noted, this God is completely unpredictable, not merely a projection of what Bess might expect or want her own personal deity to say and do. For all of the power it displays, Bess's God is an authority figure only in a limited sense. Unlike the God of the villagers, as already noted, this God allows, indeed I would go so far as to say produces, Bess's own agency, her own independent judgment and decision.

Bess's God then combines the function of sanctioning deity with that of co-conspirator or accomplice (as will be shown further). Very often, Bess's conversations with God are a kind of negotiation or struggle over questions of morality and her own identity and independence.

For example, after Jan's accident, horrified that she might have caused it by her desire to have him back home right away, Bess has the following conversation with God. Worried about her transgression, she asks God, "Are you still there?" and God answers, "Of course I am, Bess, you know that." "What's happening?" Bess asks. "You wanted Jan home," God replies, seemingly confirming that Bess is responsible for Jan's accident. "I've changed my mind," Bess answers. "Why would I have asked for that?" "Because you are a stupid little girl" is God's response. "Your love for Jan has been put to the test." "Thank you for not letting him die," she says, finally. "You're welcome, Bess," is God's answer.

In this exchange, we see God being critical but also affirming that Bess's decisions are primary (and, as noted, giving them a supernatural influence over the world). God often tells Bess that she is stupid or bad but there is—*very much* unlike with the other God—a kind of forgivingness and understanding to this deity, a recognition of Bess's own position as being valid in and of itself. Like Benjamin's depiction of a God who postpones Judgment Day perpetually via a "tempestuous storm of forgiveness" that offers a space for human agency, Bess's God too pulls back a bit from omnipotence, leaving room for Bess's own response.[10]

Bess's God's mixture of sanction and support ebbs and flows over the course of the film. At times, her God seems to be merely a vehicle for Bess's own neurosis and her feelings of guilt and complicity (this is when we are most tempted to consider her to be crazy). In such instances, God serves to rationalize Bess's own wishes and compulsions (they aren't always easy to separate in Bess's case). For example, at one point God says to her "prove to me that you love [Jan] and I'll let him live." After this, she tries in earnest to have sex with another man and finally somewhat succeeds with a man on a bus (this, after Jan had muttered something about "back of the bus" while he was slipping into unconsciousness and, seemingly, a swift death). Here, God appears both as judge and as torturer; he is putting Bess through a trial and, in the process, serving as an extension of Jan's own twisted desires.

Yet after this incident occurs and Bess feels terrible about herself, she says to God "forgive me father, I have sinned." God's response to that is "Mary Magdalene sinned and she's among my dearly beloved." It is moments like this when Bess's God is at its most subversive; here is God encouraging Bess to break the law of God; God is judge and friend, tormenter and co-conspirator, all at once.

The effect of God's dual nature ultimately reinforces Bess's own decision even while offering an alternative basis for the source of that decision, giving her a sense of power and authority that she would otherwise not possess (and, in the process, protecting her from forms of externalization that would have the opposite effect). Ultimately, what could be said to be "broken" in this film is precisely the circuit by which shame and punishment propel the lives and characters in this Scottish village. God is what allows Bess to break this circuit. Here, the punisher becomes something else too; no longer the source of an endless continuity, God becomes the break itself, short-circuiting the neurotic repetitions that otherwise are the stuff of life. From a Lacanian perspective, you could say that Bess's God serves as a "little other" (or perhaps "un other") that allows her to break with the "Big Other," taking its position in the psyche and ruining it as a site of judgment and determination. In that way, Bess can experience the collapse of her own (false) subjectivity insofar as the Big Other, the internalization of the source of the call, is no longer present or available.

As a result of this short-circuiting, her God gives Bess a sense of her deep responsibility for her choices, something that is not available to the other villagers insofar as they are all both guilty and accused (as all subjects of interpellation are to one degree or other). Bess is guilty too, of course—her God reminds her of this ceaselessly—but in her case, her guilt does not totalize her; indeed it is what prods her toward her own agency.

Bess's newfound responsibility and agency could be said to be the source of the supernatural powers that God exercises on Bess's behalf. Insofar as her inner life is projected outward, God enables and requires Bess to have her choices be both meaningful and consequential. At one point, amid her attempts to have sex with other men, she asks God, "Am I going to go to hell?" and God says, "Who do you want to save, yourself or Jan?" As always in this complicated relationship, this is not a clean question or a pure choice. God is manipulating Bess even as she is being offered a set of options. But what is clear is that Bess's decisions matter; she can, in effect, affect the world through her choices.

When one steps outside of the complex trio of Bess/God and Jan, one sees a lot more compulsion than choice. In light of what she has been doing, Bess's few friends—principally her friend (and sister-in-law) Dodo and Dr. Richardson, who is caring for Jan—definitely do think that she is going crazy. Her friends tell her that she must be out of her mind to listen to Jan and that she should move on with her life. Dodo says, "You are disappearing into a world of make-believe and it worries me."

Yet von Trier undermines the notion that Bess is crazy, both for her friends and us, the film viewers, whenever Bess's inner fantasy manifests itself in the actual world. As previously noted, every time Bess has sex, or tries to, with another man, Jan is pulled back from the brink of death. This is the case even, or especially, after she dies. At the end of the film, after stealing away Bess's body—to save her being consigned to hell by the villagers—and giving her a burial at sea, Jan is woken up by his friends to find that giant bells are ringing in the skies, a rejoinder to the fact that the village church rejects bells as sinfully ornamental. As already noted, this final image may serve as a kind of ultimate proof that Bess is not crazy, that her God is God at least for her, at least for Jan, but in a way that makes it much harder for the outside viewer to disagree. Now that we "know" that Bess's

God is real, we must revisit all of our assumptions about Bess throughout the film.

The Benefits of Belief

The tension between Bess's God being subjective, local, and intermittent versus being transcendent and all powerful never gets fully resolved in the film. Even the bells in the heavens at the end of the movie are subject to doubt; is this a joke on von Trier's part, a miracle that is so over the top as to call itself into question (as if he said "you want a sign from God? Here's one you can't miss!")? Yet, despite this unresolved tension, Bess's relationship with God produces results that are both critical and tangible, if not "real" or authentic in universal or objective terms.

For one thing, her relationship with God—along with her love for Jan that is deeply and psychically intertwined with it—is itself what Bess sees as her greatest accomplishment. In a conversation with Dr. Richardson, she tells him, "God gives everyone something to be good at. I've always been stupid but I'm good at this." Dr. Richardson, bitter and jealous of her steadfast love for Jan—he loves her himself—and still worried that she is in fact descending into madness, asks her, "What's your talent? Surely it is not being screwed by men you never met before?" Bess's serene answer is "I can believe."

Here, belief itself is the miracle for Bess, far more than the bells in the sky or the fact that Jan can be brought back from paralysis and death; it is the breaking of the circuit that frees her. Against the suffocating belief of the villagers, Bess's belief is accomplished in the full face of doubt and anguish; it is a belief that brings little comfort but it still has its compensations: it is, to return to the language of Bartleby, a belief based on preferring rather than assuming. Believing in God (preferring to believe, that is), Bess comes to believe in herself—her messy, anarchic, multiple self (there's even room for a deity in there)—even as she ultimately sacrifices herself in the process.

When Bess says "I can believe," she is offering a very different kind of call than the calls to interpellation. Rather than summoning anyone, she is calling to herself, as it were; she is giving herself permission to believe in what is unbelievable, her own ability to "not be a single being." "I can believe" is an acclamation of Bess's own impossible situation, a self that is not one, a multiple self where the subject and its source of authority—the

Subject—share one body and one personhood. Under such a setup, this authority is not what it usually is; it is not a power over Bess, nor is it the external sign for who she "really is." Rather, saying "I can believe" means that Bess acknowledges the way that authority is shared and disseminated; there is no certain origin in her case but only a conversation (and sometimes an argument). Belief is the solvent that allows Bess to be multiple beings, to immunize herself from colonization by the Subject, to be all the things that she is.

Critical to Bess's belief is the role that God plays in its construction and maintenance. Here it is not quite right to say that this is Bess's belief and hers alone. Her belief is a unique product of the conspiracy between Bess and her God. Even while granting Bess a supernatural power in the world, God is always putting her belief to the test. Almost immediately after her claim that "I can believe," where she seems almost arrogant about this ability, God disappears on her. She calls out to God and there is no answer. Making awful, animal-like sounds, she sobs out, "Father, where are you?" Apparently abandoned by God, she is left radically alone. In the wake of this abandonment, one disaster follows another in swift succession. During this time she finds out that Jan has signed papers to have her committed and that she can never see him again. She is also formally excommunicated by her church (and told off by the minister in front of the whole congregation in the most humiliating way possible). After this, the local boys pelt her with rocks and call her names. By this point, Bess is starting to really look crazy. A large lock of hair escapes from its hairpins and sticks out forlornly, and her makeup is smudged, her clothes are ripped and dirty.

Amidst all of this, Bess goes to a ship that is docked in the harbor where she will ultimately be murdered. She is warned that there are bad men on the ship and it seems that it is for exactly this reason that she goes to them. Her first encounter is horrible. Despite her resolve, and completely terrified, she grabs one of the men's guns and manages to escape. The second time she goes to the boat she has lost all hope, but perhaps not the shred of belief that sustains her. While traveling on a small boat that takes her back to the ship, and contemplating what is sure to be her doom, she says aloud, "Father, why aren't you with me?" "I am with you, Bess, what do you want with me?" is God's reply. "Where were you?" she asks. "Don't you think I have other people who want to talk to me? There's this silly little thing called Bess who wants to talk to me so my work's been piling up a bit." "But you're with me now?" she asks. "Of course I am, Bess, you know that," God says. "Thank you," she says. With that, Bess goes to the ship with new resolve.[11] Mercifully, we are spared Bess's torment and we see her next being loaded into a police boat to be rushed to the hospital where she dies shortly afterward.

By seeming to abandon her but showing that in fact she was never truly alone, God has, once again, shored up Bess's own decision. To call Bess "autonomous" would be ridiculous. She sees herself as completely interconnected with Jan and acts at his behest (she says that she doesn't even always have to talk to Jan, that they are spiritually connected, and, at one point, she even speaks as him as she often speaks as God). As already noted, even Bess's own "self" is not clearly one, unified being. Her boundaries are not clearly set and her agency is both fluid and shared.[12] In this subject there is Bess and there is God and it isn't always easy to see where one ends and the other begins. Once again, this God, it seems, is at once everywhere and particular to Bess ("There's this silly little thing called Bess who wants to talk to me"). God seems to abandon Bess after her testament to her powers of belief but then returns at her moment of greatest trial. It seems that, even as Bess is being raped and murdered, God is right there with her; this God experiences what she experiences and suffers what she suffers. In this way, perhaps her suffering is a bit more bearable as she is not alone—she is not a single being—and never could be.

Belief and Sacrifice

It is one of the perversities of Lars von Trier's mix of brilliance and misogyny that Bess can be said to have escaped from a certain form of doom only to be brutally raped and murdered, something that she apparently chooses for herself even as she seems compelled by forces beyond her control. What can we make of the fact that Bess chooses to use her hard-fought and miraculous freedom, her "breaking" from God and fate, at least in one form, only to sacrifice herself for the sake of her husband? How can we think about the way that she has voluntarily, if that is the right word, given herself over to be raped and tortured and ultimately killed? Here, I think it is worth once again noting that escaping from determination does not guarantee good or "authentic" results but only results that are not predetermined.

Indeed, Bess's situation epitomizes the hazards of finding one's own way without the strong guidance of existing codes of conduct. Freed up from the constraints of her family and village, from the determination of interpellation, Bess enters a period of tremendous confusion. Deciding that she can't be a "good girl"—as her God always demands of her—and especially when God, albeit temporarily, stops talking to her, Bess decides that she must be bad. She tries to dress the part with a short, revealing skirt and high heels. But she doesn't occupy this subject position any better than she does in her attempt to be good. When, as already noted, local boys throw stones at her and call her names, she seems completely confused. Once again, she comes up against a set of judgments and expectations and cannot conform to them.

The degree to which Bess is left to her own devices is quite radical. Whereas one would normally consider the ability to talk to God to be a way to bypass all the doubts and insecurities that plague Bess—although even Jesus had his moment of doubt at Gethsemane—her God does not offer that kind of support or certainty. On the contrary, her God talks to her but does not quite tell her what to do. Her God only reaffirms the way that Bess is alone in her decisions (although, as already noted, she is alone, but not abandoned, for where she goes, her God goes with her). To have God be present and speaking but not determining her decisions means that there really is no one, no all-knowing force, no external power that will decide for her. Since Bess's God leaves no room for that other deity (the Subject) Bess is, like Nietzsche's tightrope walker, faced with a messiah who does nothing (or not much), ruining that position as a site of possible salvation. Bess truly must make her own decisions with no hope for rescues or transcendent revelations.

The fact that she is on her own also affects the way we think about Bess's sacrifice. When we compare her actions to Abraham's—at least in the normal rendition of the story, not Kafka's—there are critical differences. Insofar as Bess replaces God the Subject with a God of her own, it is not her child that gets sacrificed but Bess herself. The demand by God the Subject becomes replaced by a demand that Bess puts onto herself, with the agreement—but not the requirement—of her own God. Whereas, in the case of Abraham, the sacrifice was never meant to actually occur—so that the other Abraham's interference doesn't save Isaac's life so much as alter the pattern of the demand—in the case of Bess there is once again no "Big Other" to rescue her, no mercy to dispense. Bess suffers and dies. The sacrifice is completed.

What Bess's God does do is to give Bess some peace of mind as she goes through with her sacrifice. I see the role of her God as being once again akin to that of Zarathustra as he speaks to the tightrope walker who has tumbled down to the ground and is about to die. As with Bess, death seems inevitable at this point. Recall this exchange in *Thus Spoke Zarathustra* between Zarathustra and the tightrope walker:

> "What are you doing here?" [the tightrope walker] asked at last. "I have long known that the devil would trip me. Now he will drag me to hell. Would you prevent him?"
>
> "By my honor, friend," answered Zarathustra, "all that of which you speak does not exist: there is no devil and no hell. Your soul will be dead even before your body: fear nothing further."
>
> The man looked up suspiciously. "If you speak the truth," he said, "I lose nothing when I lose my life. I am not much more than a beast that has been taught to dance by blows and few meager morsels."
>
> "By no means," said Zarathustra. "You have made danger your vocation; there is nothing contemptible in that. Now you perish of your vocation: for that I will bury you with my own hands."
>
> When Zarathustra had said this, the dying man answered no more; but he moved his hand as if he sought Zarathustra's hand in thanks.[13]

Bess's God, by letting her know that she wouldn't be going through her ordeal alone, similarly takes away a source of terror from Bess, the terror of the transcendent and the universal, the terror of a bigger, greater judgment that will follow. Both Zarathustra and Bess's God make sacrifices—the sacrifice of the tightrope walker, the sacrifice of Bess herself—less a matter of obedience and more one of choice. If there is no "Big Other," just a "little other" like Zarathustra or Bess's God, then action is no longer couched in a "you must or else" kind of format, that is, in the language of interpellation. Sacrifice under conditions of interpellation does not come from choice but from perceived necessity, from absolute power and transcendence (from the universal). Without these guises, the tightrope walker and Bess are both allowed to do what they will do (just as Kafka's "other Abraham," devoid of a predestined script, is allowed to do what he does, whether God the Subject likes it or not). As already noted, in the wave of his hand, the tightrope walker seems to be thanking Zarathustra for teaching him that his sacrifice and his death were not in vain; he was sanctified, not by God or the Devil but rather in the face of their absence. And the same goes for Bess; her sacrifice, horrible as it is, is her own. It may not have been voluntary—at least not in the way we understand that term—but it occurred within the realm of her own agency, the space produced by her disconnection from mandated, interpellated forms of authority.[14]

The Amor Fati of Bess McNeill

If we step back a bit from the film as such, we can think more broadly about the implications of Bess's release from the circuits that normally dominate our lives, the effect that her God has on her and the other characters in the film. As I see it, in her conversations with God and in the decisions and actions that result from such conversations, Bess can be considered to be yet another model for the Nietzschean practice of amor fati.

In "loving her fate," we see again the complex engagement with a sense of agency and destiny in Nietzsche. Even though, as already noted, it would seem as if it is the villagers, and not Bess, who submit to fate, the villagers submit only to their own phantasms of what God demands of them. Indeed, rather than saying that they practice amor fati, one can say that they hate their fate; their God is an externalization of that hate, a messiah who punishes—and accuses—them endlessly for the fact of their belief (and projection). They remain fully bound within the self-defeating circuitry of interpellation (and, by extension, so is their God). Wishing their own annihilation, the villagers receive it by the daily acts of self-denial and subjection to a deity that reflects and grants their darkest wishes (when Bess's grandfather tells Jan that the village has no bells, he says so with an almost obscene joy; he takes pleasure at his own deprivation, at denial itself).[15]

For Bess, as with other figures in this book, loving her fate means loving what she is and does when she is not constrained by interpellation, when she allows herself to experience the contingency of her own selfhood. Here, she is not merely bound by her own anxieties and the constraints of self-fulfilling prophecies; she is open to herself and to what is unexpected and unpredictable. It is by breaking the circuit that Bess finds that she has a fate after all, not a future but a present one as we also saw with Nietzsche; this is the fate of the noontime. This fate is no less binding than that which the other villagers face but her realization of it nonetheless grants her a freedom and agency that she would not otherwise have had.

And it could even be said that Bess's God is also included in this act of amor fati. By breaking off from transcendence, by reducing itself to being a deity that is part transcendent and part local, this God escapes from being the kind of terrible projection that we normally receive when we think about

God as Subject. In a strange way, even as her God has saved Bess from "salvation," Bess in turn saves God from being a deity who always and only hates and accuses (i.e., interpellates). By sharing her fate, by partially merging with her, Bess's God avoids playing the role of the avenging messiah and becomes instead a misinterpellating messiah, one who once again does little or nothing but changes everything.

We see here that Bess's conspiracy with her God is mutually beneficial. God allows Bess her own thought and her own judgment and, in turn, Bess allows God a chance to reduce itself, to avoid a perfect transcendence and universality and, along with those things, the trappings of a God who is nothing but a judge, a hater of creation. We see here too then a kind of "virtuous circuitry" where the unhappy interdependence of caller and callee that comes with interpellation is replaced by a form of mutuality. This is a co-conspiracy rather than a union or an alliance. Whereas in the latter, everyone knows their place and what they can and cannot do from the outset, within the bounds of this conspiracy, all of that is up for grabs, contingent and anarchist, subject to interpersonal politics, struggle and mutual forms of recognition.

Bad Boundaries

In this way, Bess's relationship to God demonstrates one answer to the problem of authority. As noted in chapter 2, in his discussion of Numa, Machiavelli shows (depending on how we read him) how we must project authority outward in order to be able to believe in it. This, as I argued there, is the impetus for interpellation and for archism more generally; we feel that authority has to come from beyond and return to us in order for us to be able to obey it, or believe in it, at all. Recall that Numa lied about the source of his laws because he felt that the Romans were not able to trust themselves as a community (and not one another either), and so any law of clearly human origin would be too weak to be effective. By externalizing that law, Numa sets off the cycle of interpellation, of promoting a law and a source of authority that has no true origin (in fact, it has a false one). The state and the law that is produced as a result of such deception is therefore eternally anxious about its own right to exist and violent as a result of that anxiety.

In the absence of the possibility that we can just "throw" off such authority—because to think we can leads us to the delusion that we are truly authentic, not interpellated at all—Bess illustrates how that outward projection and inward reception can both be broken, interfered with by a different relationship to externality. Bess's version of externality is not quite other to her. It is and isn't part of her; it is "outside" but also very much within the boundaries of her subjectivity and, as such, it offers a sense of how that subjectivity can be reconsidered, experienced differently without giving up on the possibility of agency that liberalism promises but ultimately makes impossible.

Here again, the call "I can believe" tells us something vital about the relationship with externalities. Giving herself permission to believe, Bess becomes not the subject but the author of her belief. By taking advantage of the fact that she is not a singular being, Bess's "outside" can still be found within—or "inside," if you prefer—the bounds of her subjectivity. In this way, she keeps her forms of authorization (or self-authorization) "in house," as it were, perpetuating Numa's act in a way that does not create false—and universal—projections but remains a part of the complicated site that is Bess McNeill. Bess can thus "believe" in a way that is not cynical or false. But part of the reason that she can believe in her God is that her God resides within her; she knows and believes in this God just as she knows and believes in herself more generally. No leap of faith is required here, only an openness to an interiority that is potentially vaster and more complex than any one of us realizes.

In this way, in Bess's case, her very unboundedness (or bad boundaries), her failure to be the subject that she is supposed to be, is the reason that she can escape from the bondage that holds the rest of the village in thrall. Another way to say this is that Bess's openness to her own anarchic, merged, and collective subjectivity is a weapon that she uses against the subjectivity that interpellation would otherwise give her. Bess is like Appius Pulcher—at least in my conspiratorial reading of Machiavelli—ruining interpellation, breaking with the external Subject in order to allow other forms of being to get acknowledged, to serve as a basis for her own complex forms of agency.

In response to her failure, her God responds with a failure of its own. Bess's God, as already noted, creates a space for Bess's own decision by failing to be a transcendent, all-knowing being without at the same time collapsing into Bess's subjectivity. Were God too much beyond her, too clearly a universal deity, Bess would be reduced, as her covillagers are, to a fearful, dutiful shell (paradoxically one that obeys her own projections). Were God too clearly a being of her own creation, Bess might have nothing to believe in. In a sense, her belief in God serves as an ideal technique to enable *amor fati*. If Bess cannot quite come to love herself, she can love a God that both is and is not an extension of that self (and thereby love herself, and her fate, after all). And, if Bess cannot quite trust herself (the concern that animated Numa above all), she *can* trust a God that is so intimate and yet holds itself aloof from a full merger of selves.

Conclusion

The portrayal of Bess in *Breaking the Waves* presses us to ask interesting, disturbing, and important questions. What would an actual choice look like if we weren't determined and burdened by normativity and faith of the more ordinary kind? How can belief serve us in a way that doesn't simply return us to the endless cycles of projection and obedience? What does it mean to be "oneself," when we are—not just Bess, but all of us—complicated beings who are the product of an infinite number of confluences, influences, overlapping jurisdictions of personhood and identity? Perhaps the most critical question it gets us to ask is what are the benefits of the kinds of self-determination Bess demonstrates in light of the fact that her end is so awful, so caught up in a larger pattern of violence against women, the rape culture and questions of consent and even madness? What is the payoff, finally, of being a misinterpellated subject, if it doesn't protect us against such bad outcomes?

This final question is something that we can ask of just about any of von Trier's films; his readiness to portray women in modes of self-destruction and surrender—but also empowerment and imperviousness to men—colors his films and disturbs and complicates any attempt to draw purely laudatory (or entirely negative) conclusions. There's no way to disentangle the problematic portrayal of women in von Trier's films with Bess's own actions. Instead this ambiguity—or maybe complicity is a better term—adds itself to the larger complications of Bess's story. That Bess did something awful and unthinkable does not take away from the fact that, having broken with one God, she commits to another.[16]

From the villagers' position, they probably think that Bess "got what she deserved," ended up like a prostitute, raped and murdered. She tells her mother as she is dying that "I'm sorry I couldn't be good." But from a misinterpellated subject position, Bess's end has an entirely different meaning; it speaks to the dangers and perils of self-determination, yes, but it also speaks to the power of choice. Perhaps most critically, Bess has inverted the traditional Abrahamic notion of sacrifice insofar—as already noted—it is not God who calls to her but she who calls to God. Thus, what could be read as just a boilerplate story of interpellated identity gone awry—young woman succumbs to temptation and dies for it—can be reread, through the screen of misinterpellation, the "yet more minor literature," as a very different story, with a very different political point.

Although Bess seems strangely passive, responding to the demands placed on her by others—first the villagers, then Jan, and finally God—as I've been arguing in her case, as well as in the case of Bartleby, this is what agency looks like when read from the perspective of interpellated subjectivity (i.e., our own perspective). Bess is, in fact, the only active agent in the movie, the one who changes and unmakes everything (at least potentially, at least temporarily). Her apparent megalomania may thus simply reflect her unique condition (if no one else is going to be a subject then it really is all about her!). What we might read as an act of utter submission is, in another register, an act of defiance, a marker of the way that Bess has escaped from one fate and delivered herself to another. I think Bess is not so much a model to emulate (God forbid!) so much as someone to learn from. She shows that it is possible to circumvent and subvert the cycle of projection and servitude that dominates so much of life under conditions of interpellation.

In my view, the Scottish village Bess lives in is a model for the whole world; it is merely the tip of the interpellative iceberg. We are all, to some extent or other, trapped by our teleologies, by our beliefs and our projections. Despite the talk of liberal individuality and so forth, none of us are the subjects we are promised to be; we are not self-determining, not agents, and, most important, not political, not determining our own lives both separately and together. Strangely enough, it is in her own division as a subject, the personhood that she shares with God, that Bess shows us what an individual might look like. Whereas the Scottish villagers—and hence the rest of us—seem to receive their "individuality" from a common source (God as Subject) and hence are not individuals at all, Bess, the divided subject, gets her own individuality from no one but herself. Forced to contend with a God who shares her personal space, she must form herself in response to her deity, by marking out those places and acts that are only hers—however complicated and overlapping that designation may be—encountering the vastness of her interior complexity as a result.

In her own actions and beliefs, Bess shows us another way; she fights the fire of an oppressive theology with the fire of a countertheology of her own. From her deepest flaws, her madness, her codependency, her bad boundaries, and her convictions, she creates a kind of self-rescue in the form of a God that doesn't control her, even as she doesn't control God. Her power comes in the form of her failure; her weakness becomes the source of her greatest strength.

Even if she is crazy and self-destructive—we can never quite rid ourselves of that doubt—Bess has also achieved that rarest of states: the ability to make a choice. That such a choice is impossible does not deter her. The device of talking to and as God breaks apart the constraints of agency and individualism as we normally understand these things and allows Bess access to forms of decision and judgment that would not otherwise be present to her. I find myself earnestly wishing that she'd made a different decision but Bess was willing to live—and die—with her decision and so, apparently, was her God.

The fact that such a momentous form of rebellion—or, more accurately, conspiracy—could hide in plain sight, could be misread as conforming to the power of the universal and its laws, suggests further evidence that we need to be better attuned to reading the world through the lens of misinterpellation. We need to be able to spot the Lily Briscoes and the Bartlebys; we need to acknowledge Ellison's narrator and Bess McNeill and not just in fiction and film but in the world as well (and Ta-Nehisi Coates, for one, may help us to do that). If every moment of interpellation is also a moment of misinterpellation, then we are all, to some extent or other, one of these characters. Even if our conspiracies aren't always legible, even to ourselves, we always have that rabble of competing, contesting selves, that overlapping and infinitely complex anarchic subject that is "really us" to draw upon.

I imagine that for many viewers, the heavenly bells that ring at the end of the movie announce a "happy ending." Bess is vindicated. Jan knows that she died for him. The local and subjective God that Bess follows is revealed to be the true God after all. I don't see things that way, however. I see the bells ringing in heaven as being both an act of mourning—mourning Bess's loss, mourning her choice and her sacrifice and even perhaps all that her God has suffered along with Bess in her ordeal—and of celebrating. But what is being celebrated is not the revelation of the "true God," the ur-Subject, after all but rather the failure of this God to erase Bess's own subjectivity. She has inoculated herself even against this ultimate subject, and as such, she is beyond that God's reach; she has a God of her own. The one piece of indisputable optimism that I discern from this film—and hence a reason to think more about the possibility for extending and enhancing the status of misinterpellated subjectivity—is simply the fact that we are not fated in the way that we think we are. We are fated, to be sure, and we must love that fate, but in our loving it, our fate is revealed to be other than what we imagined it to be and that is very good news indeed.

CONCLUSION

The Misinterpellated Subject: Anarchist All the Way Down

In this book, I argued for a mode of reading wherein what are ordinarily perceived as irrelevant, useless, or even awful characters can be reread as subverters and conspirators, where the seemingly least agental figures in texts and films—either because they seem to be ruled by compulsions they can't control, or a fatal mousiness or passivity—turn out to be the only actual agents, the only "selves" in the representational worlds that they occupy. This kind of reading flies in the face of the assertion that the authority who interpellates "really" knows the subject that she hails/creates. My contention is that interpellation inevitably gets it wrong; it renders subjects—in all of their multiplicity and anarchic complexity—manifestly unknowable by projecting onto them a single unitary self that, being false, offers nothing to "know" at all. Reading in a more subversive vein is not so much a way of switching things around—so that the losers are winners and the winners are losers—but rather involves rethinking the very rules of the game, how status is assigned, and how individuals are ranked and valued. As previously noted, I think of this mode of reading as a "yet more minor literature"—a nod to Deleuze and Guattari—another sign that reading can be a political act, a way of seeing and interpreting the world around us that doesn't simply replicate norms and circumstances of our present condition.

And this mode of reading through a yet more minor literature (reading through misinterpellation is another way to say it) need not reside only in the treatment of texts and films. In reading works of fiction and nonfiction alike, the reader could be said to be training (as Nietzsche certainly trains his readers) for larger—and distinctly political—applications of that reading style to the world that surrounds us. Insofar as interpellation is not something that happens merely in books and films but also in the actual world, insofar as it structures our political lives as well as our very selves, reading via misinterpellation can become a much wider practice as well. We can begin to read the world around us—other persons and even our own selves—through the lens of misinterpellation so as to retrieve or make visible the subjects (or objects) that we are beneath the subjects that we are told to be. In this way, we may be able to find new and subversive possibilities in Hobbes's famous adage to the reader in *Leviathan* to "*Read thy self*" as well as the world around us.[1]

This, it is critical to repeat, does not mean that through such acts of reading we will discover our "true" selves underneath the façade of interpellated forms of subjectivity. If Nietzsche teaches us anything, it is to be highly suspicious of any claim for truth or authenticity. All of the writers and thinkers that I have looked at in this book—Fanon and Kafka, Woolf and Melville, Ellison, von Trier, and even (despite writing nonfiction) Coates—effectively reject a sense of the authentic in favor of a deeply complex and generally submerged sense of individuality. Each of these authors in their own way offer an antiheroic (unheroic might be a more accurate term) portrayal of the subject. They locate the subject not in projections and phantasms of redemption and progress, but rather in the mundane, in daily rituals and in conversations, in overlapping forms of consciousness that connect rather than separate one subject from another, in scraps and pieces of selfhood and in multiple modes of being and seeing and acting. In so doing, these authors have offered us subjects who lend themselves to being read via the screen of misinterpellation.

And we once again do not need to limit ourselves to works of fiction. The historical examples that I looked at earlier in the book—the Haitian revolution, the "Wilsonian moment," the origins of the Arab Spring, and the life and experience of Fanon—can also be read through a misinterpellating lens. We can read them as "failures," as subjects who could not bring themselves, ultimately, into the universal, or as subverters of that universal. In the latter case, we turn the very failure that normally serves as a form of interpellating accusation into a measure of resistance, a different—and more radical—way to read the same phenomenon.

In this book, I discussed many forms of calling. There are those calls that seek to dominate fairly overtly ("hey, you there!"; "tiens, un nègre!") and ones that seem harmless and even good but project that domination nonetheless ("men are born free and equal in rights"). The latter category, because insidious, may be even more pernicious than the more straightforward sorts of calls (such a form of calling reminds me of Mrs. Ramsay: alluring and seductive but ultimately also a vehicle for more hegemony and colonization via interpellation). There are also calls to sacrifice such as when God calls out to Abraham. All of these are calls that follow the logic of interpellation, of external forms of authority being visited upon certain individuals in order to promote some desired political outcome, some perpetuation of power. There are also myriad calls that are not discussed in this book but that make up the stuff of everyday life. There is, for example, the claim "it's a girl!" (or "it's a boy!"), something that Judith Butler discusses, which is uttered upon a baby's birth to usher "her" or "him" into the world of language and set gender and sex roles.[2] "Tiens, un nègre!" is also arguably a call of this kind; it is a daily ordinary expression of power. Coates's experience of being told "I could have you arrested" is another version of this kind of call. Technically, these are not calls from a higher authority (although if a doctor is the one saying "it's a boy!" or "it's a girl!" there is clearly some authority structure in place). Yet, even so, such calls perpetuate existing power structures; they promote gender and racial hierarchy; they put people in their place telling them who they "really" are (the current discussion of "microaggressions" is another version of such a form of calling). In this way interpellation is more than a relationship between government and people or God and human actors; it is between everyone, a series of hierarchical enactments where power comes down from on high and then gets redistributed in subsequent layers.

This book has been about resisting and subverting that power and also about paying attention to what emerges when that power is lifted, however temporarily. In the face of calls to dominate, I have looked at calls of resistance, ranging from "wait up!" to "[a person] is something that is to be overcome," and from "I would prefer not to" to "come, come!," "I can believe," and "consent not to be a single being." These are all very different forms of calling, as might be appropriate to an anarchist strategy of resistance. The one aspect that these various calls may be said to share is their failure to presuppose anything about the subject in question. "Wait up!" could be said to be interpersonal (although not necessarily), one subject calling out to another in a way that is mutual and doesn't make any claims about who one is waiting for. "Come, come!," certainly in the way Woolf portrays it, is much more intrapersonal (although here too that is not always necessarily the case). This is a call to one's various selves, to a person's entire anarchic interiority to see who, and what, shows up. Nietzsche's call—Zarathustra's repeated statement to his disciples—"[a person] is something that shall be overcome"—sounds like a command and even a prophecy; on the surface, it has some of the familiar trappings of an archist, interpellating statement (the use of the word "shall," for example, which sounds very deterministic; the usual English translation of "der Mensch" as "man"—including in the translation that I use in this book—makes it sound even worse). Yet, upon examining it more closely, it seems that the idea of overcoming does not involve transcending so much as canceling out the false subject that we are told to be, exposing in this way the anarchic subject that is usually eclipsed by such a way of being.

Glissant's "consent not to be a single being" has a similar ring of interpellation but, as already noted, it uses that language to undo itself (as Glissant's poetry and writing do more generally). So these statements act somewhat as wolves in sheep's clothing, or, more accurately, sheep in wolves' clothing: they subvert and undermine what they appear to support.

Bartleby's "I would prefer not to" is probably the most famous—or infamous—of the calls I have considered here. It is a deceptively simple statement but one can see its complexity by asking whether it is even a call at all. Who is Bartleby addressing when he says this? The answer seems to be whoever he is talking to but, rather than projecting anything—that is, assuming—Bartleby is simply stating his own agenda (or lack thereof as may be the case). He is, in a sense, calling himself, or perhaps uncalling himself from the louder, more aggressive calls that one usually responds to.

These calls also correspond with different strategies of resistance that I have discussed in these pages: strategies based on invisibility and innocuousness (which disguise tremendous power and agency), strategies of failure (which unmake the "successes" of the interpellated subject), strategies of refusal (both of the ontologies produced by racist forms of interpellation and, relatedly, of the exclusion and diminishment that such ontologies produce), and strategies of disincorporation and multiplicity (as Bess Mc-Neill demonstrates).

There are myriad other strategies, of course as well; those who read with an eye for misinterpellation will readily find these other alternatives for they are not a rare thing but are practiced on a daily basis. Indeed, as Walter Benjamin informs us, we all practice a high degree of anarchism in our daily lives, as when he writes in "Critique of Violence" about "peaceful intercourse between private persons."[3] Such interactions, he tells us, occur without the interference of law, without oaths, and without contracts. There is, therefore, no externality involved beyond the subjects involved, no promises, no casting toward an empty future as a guarantee of desired outcomes.

Every day, then, we are engaged in these kinds of countercalls: calls to one another and calls to ourselves. In the normal state of affairs, these other kinds of calls are not seen or read as a threat to interpellation. This is just "life," in its mundane and unimportant sense. Yet, as I have suggested in this book, this same "life" is a resource to draw upon to resist those other "important" and "real" calls that we are normally bombarded by. A misinterpellated reading of daily interactions, as well as alternative political practices, is attuned to these other calls. When brought into focus, these calls—not unlike the misinterpellated characters that I have looked at in this book—no longer go unnoticed. They interfere and compete with the interpellating calls and (therefore) call into question the mastery that interpellation claims to have over each and every one of us.

A misinterpellated form of reading (a "yet more minor literature"), then, can have very real political consequences; it is part and parcel of a larger anarchist politics and I would say that it is a critical one insofar as, so long as we remain interpellated subjects—at least on the surface of our being, a kind of settler colonization of the self—we can never allow our actual anarchist selves their full political expression either as individuals or as members of a larger community. Even the most anarchist collective cannot protect itself from archism when archism is built into the very subject identities that compose that group. To be anarchist we must be, I think, anarchist "all the way down," not just in our political practices and the way we treat one another, but even in ourselves, in our innermost lives and identities.[4]

In terms of that much-discussed "us" and "our" that I keep referring to, I hope it is clear that "we" is muddied by each person's anarchic interiority. "We" is also a set of versions of us within more versions of us, a plethora of beings that cannot easily answer to one name. And, as previously discussed too, this "us" does not readily meld together people with different identities and histories. People of color, as I've tried to show, have never had access to the liberal—or even left—universal afforded to white people. Neither have women and queer people, transgender people, or poor and working-class people had access to their privileged counterparts' universality. "Us" in this case can never mean "all of us under one overarching unity of humanity" or some other such universalist conception.

Speaking of us in political—and external—terms can only mean that medley of various communities and persons that constitute what Rancière calls "the part that has no part." Such an us can only be a shifting and moving set of conspiracies.[5] In the same way, to speak of "us" as interior to the subject can never be a united coherent being or even an alliance. Whether intrapersonal ("come, come!") or interpersonal ("wait up!")—although these two terms could easily be switched—this "we" or "us" is far more unstable and shifting than anything that those terms normally summon (or call) forward. As Fred Moten tells us, this we or us can only be considered as a way of acknowledging what already is, a mutual recognition of selves and identities that are never singular even as this call transforms, radicalizes, and sets into motion a different politics and a different way of being.

If "we" can't be one (either as individuals or as collectivities), this doesn't condemn us to inaction and chaos. To think this way is to continue to read, think, and act according to an archist or interpellated model. In such a view, the alternative is never possible (in Margaret Thatcher's words, once again, "there is no alternative"). All the chaos and arbitrary rule of liberal universalism is projected onto anarchism and other practices of resistance, making them seem both unachievable and undesirable. But to switch that lens around and read against this way of thinking does not mean jumping into an abyss or setting off a free-for-all à la Mad Max. It means recovering and recognizing what already is. It means hearing and responding to other calls that are also, and already, being made. It means conspiring together and apart against the overwhelming sense of archist subjectivity.

As previously stated several times, in my view, the politics of misinterpellation is a politics of anarchism. Perhaps more accurately, misinterpellation is a critical element of anarchist politics, one that could well serve that larger movement. Anarchism has a dark history of racism and sexism and, yes, archism (because archism can hide, viruslike, even in the most committed of movements and individuals if the individuals in question remain subjects of, and colonized by, interpellation). An anarchism that is informed by misinterpellation offers a politics that I think has the most to offer the kind of decentered, multiply subjected, shifting conspiracies that I am describing—and advocating for—in the pages of this book. This is a politics that gives up on guarantees and the false promise of a happy ending. It is a politics that isn't already sure of what is going to happen. It is a politics that seeks to defy projection with acknowledgment, assumption with preference. Such a stance is maximally open to whoever shows up to answer calls that do not stem from interpellation ("wait up!"), however much we might wish for someone better.

A Hopeless Politics?

By way of ending this book, to get down to the critical question of political possibility, one question that I keep coming up against when thinking about this project is that of appeal. We seem to live in a particularly scary time (although there definitely have been scarier times) when the world liberal order seems to be falling apart even as neoliberalism, the core of the liberal projects is more entrenched and more in control than at any other point in human history. Fascism is (re)emerging all over the world: in the US, in Europe, in Israel and Russia and Turkey. Fascism is what happens when liberalism's kinder, gentler face no longer gets the job done. In light of this, it seems that people are more likely than ever to hope for the kind of solidity and safety that liberal subjectivity offers. Isn't this a bad time to be calling for anarchism and subversion? But scary times are also times when other possibilities become much more likely, when the masks of liberalism are weakened and its violent fist is exposed. The rise of Bernie Sanders in the US and Jeremy Corbyn in the UK, while neither of them are that far to the left, show that fascism is not the only possibility. If fascism shows the true face of liberalism, then its advent suggests a time when other possibilities are also more readily apparent.

More specifically, in terms of the arguments of this book, even if times were better and more secure, are people really going to want to break themselves down into their component parts? accept despair? give up hope as a way toward a different politics?[6] Why would anyone want to do that? Surely there have been plenty of awful political systems that dealt out plenty of hopelessness and despair already. My main response to such points is that the despair and hopelessness that I am discussing here are not absolute emotions, but only reflect the loss of the promise that liberalism offers and which it uses to keep us bound up within its false universality; it is just the sorrow the bull feels (I imagine) when it is revealed that there is nothing beneath the red cape. The question, to stick with this analogy for a moment, becomes will the bull stay fixated on that cape and keep missing (misrecognizing) the emptiness that the matador is revealing each and every time? Will the bull just reexperience that pain and loss over and over, or is it possible to do things differently? That is a version of the fundamental question I am trying to raise in writing this book.

As for the seemingly depressing nature of misinterpellation itself, in fact, there is plenty of joy and power in this form of resistance, as I hope the stories I have considered in this book suggests. I chose nonetheless to dwell on the sadder stories (Lily Briscoe instead of Orlando) because I didn't want to glamorize what I'm talking about, I didn't want to make it seem like you can simply trade one set of seductions for another (although Orlando suffers plenty and her seduction, I think, is of a completely different kind than the siren songs of liberal universalism; her seduction is to what is rather than what is not). My insistence on discussing failure as a bitter, disappointing experience is largely a matter of attempting a form of discipline—a training— as I've indicated in earlier chapters, to guard against the ways that archism reasserts itself at virtually every juncture. My insistence on the ordinariness of the subjects I treat is also a way to better expose and understand the anarchism of everyday life, the way that no moment and/or place and/or person is uniquely authorized or privileged (the pose of archism). It also serves as a way to assert that ordinariness itself is an unlikely but powerful basis from which to resist the blandishments of liberalism.

Anarchism always faces a challenge in combatting archism because archism will always promote itself as being better, flashier, funner, and easier. It promises, as I've argued, surefire guarantees in life—wholeness and fulfillment, even immortality (of a sort). Anarchists will often be seduced by these shiny, empty promises, adopting archist practices in the midst of their anarchist politics and dooming them to failure (and not the kind of failure I've been talking about in this book but rather the failure that means loss, nothing, reabsorption into capitalism and state power). So if this book seems stern and asking too much, making the politics I advocate seem too far out of reach, I would respond by saying that the politics of anarchism are completely in reach; each of us is living it every day of our lives whether we realize (recognize) it or not (misrecognize). Furthermore, to say that we must seek the anarchization of our own subjectivity doesn't mean that anarchists can't continue to create an anarchist politics and community in the more ordinary sense: the anarchist living spaces, demonstrations, organizing, conspiring, prefiguring, and troublemaking that anarchists have always been good at. Seeking to be anarchist "all the way down" doesn't preclude the "upper" or exteriorized reaches of that politics, it only asks that those politics be coordinated with an eye toward subjectivity, toward all that misinterpellation can do for a given political community, and the forms of resistance and refusal that it makes possible.

Here's my final pitch: we all know what happens if we don't resist the lures of liberal universalism and the subjectivities that it interpellates us to be. We get more of the same: more racism; more violence; more misogyny, homophobia, biphobia, transphobia, and sexism; more class warfare; more ableism; more hate; more lies (unless the planet itself is murdered and then I guess everything just stops). We can't truly fight or resist these things when our very persons are products of and colonized by violent forms of power and authority. In the face of that inevitability, perhaps it is time to think about fate differently, not as something that we are stuck with and can't change, but rather as a marker for our present circumstances, for what we actually are while we are doing and being (and wanting to be) something else. From that new position—the position of the misinterpellated subject—I wager the question of what is possible and what is impossible radically changes. Isn't it time to make liberalism impossible instead of anarchism? Isn't it time to say to liberalism, TINA (there is no alternative): you have had your time, now it's time to move aside for another way of life and politics that you've always coexisted with and drowned out with your frenzy and your greed and your hate? If the alternative to the alternative is liberalism or fascism, then I think there is an alternative (sorry, Margaret Thatcher) and the misinterpellated subject helps point the direction of where that alternative is, how it works and how it might be brought more clearly into the world.

NOTES

1 When I taught this text to my class in the Kent Summer School for Critical
   Theory, it was suggested that all the different Abrahams in the parable are all
   aspects of the one "real" Abraham that God intended to call, that the diversity
   of responses represented the diverse aspects of Abraham's interior life even as
   one privileged part of him did just what the "real" Abraham was supposed to
   do.

2 Kafka, "Abraham," 40 (German), 41 (English).

3 Kafka, "Abraham," 41.

4 Kafka, "Abraham," 43.

5 Kafka, "Abraham," 43.

6 Kafka, "Abraham," 43–45.

7 In this regard, I think that whereas the move from liberalism to neoliberalism is dramatic and critical, in terms of misinterpellation at least, what is
   true for the historical practice of liberalism is just as true for neoliberalism.
   If, as Wendy Brown argues, neoliberalism has made a new *homo economicus*,
   this subject too is a form of interpellation and, as such, is similarly subject to
   misinterpellation. See Brown, *Undoing the Demos*.

8 This term, much beloved by economic conservatives, was often used by
   Herbert Spencer and later popularized by Margaret Thatcher. More recently,
   Donald Trump has a newer version of TINA; he constantly repeats "there is
   no choice" as if the repetition itself were a basis for removing any chance of
   thinking or acting differently than he does.

9 Sarah Burgess suggested something further too: that the structure of address
   itself, that is the form of the claims being made, might themselves contain
   some radical potential.

10 I am grateful to Sarah Burgess for the idea of acting "as if."

11 I owe Bonnie Honig this insight and also the idea of this mode of reading
   serving as another version of Deleuze and Guattari's "minor literature."

12 In *The Practice of Everyday Life*, a book that I see as being highly related to Scott's
   work, Michel de Certeau discusses "la perruque" (the wig) which is an action

undertaken by the underling, which seems to be on behalf of the owner/boss but is in fact entirely for itself. One example he offers is a personal love letter written on company time and via company technology. See Certeau, *Practice of Everyday Life*, 24–28.

13   Scott, *Domination and the Arts of Resistance*, 81.
14   Scott, *Weapons of the Weak*, 317.
15   Scott, *Weapons of the Weak*, 317.
16   Scott, *Domination and the Arts of Resistance*, 95.
17   Scott, *Domination and the Arts of Resistance*, 77.
18   One example Scott provides of the strategic use of dominant ideology is that of prisoners who, through their grievances to the prison system, seek to expand their own power (or, conversely, to diminish the arbitrary power that the prison guards have over them) by a seemingly obsessive concern for the minutiae of the laws that govern them. One could read this as a weird subservience on the part of the prisoners or one could read it as an oppressed group using the only tools at their disposal, employing the ideology of the state as a weapon against it. In the case of prisoners, this course of action is, of course, only moderately successful. It depends on the willingness of the state to follow its own rules (or, by the same token, its reluctance to admit that its laws are a sham—an admission that would weaken a liberal state's authority by revealing it to be nothing but tyranny).

Scott also gives the example of a more successful example of struggle when he discusses how "quietly and massively, the Malay peasantry has managed to nearly dismantle the tithe system so that only 15 percent of what is formally due is actually paid." *Domination and the Arts of Resistance*, 89. Examples such as these offer that there is a power (or counterpower, depending on how one wants to define things) that makes real change possible even under the veneer of compliance and passivity (as Scott notes, the Malay authorities play along with the charade of tithing, once again, in order to deny the degree to which they have been outmaneuvered by their own populations).

19   See Honig, *Emergency Politics*, 128.
20   See Roberts, *Freedom as Marronage*.
21   In thinking about accommodation versus outright opposition, Georges Sorel makes a critical distinction between the "political strike" and the "general strike"; the former is a negotiation with a power that does not ultimately threaten that power system while the latter represents a real break with existing power structures (and Walter Benjamin very famously takes up that same distinction as well in his "Critique of Violence"). See Sorel, *Reflections on Violence*, and Benjamin, "Critique of Violence." Most of what Scott analyzes comes closer to the former than the latter (although, as he also tells us, the former can also lead to the latter, something Sorel himself does not account for).
22   Sometimes these two states overlap, as my example of the Haitian revolution will further illustrate. It is therefore not a matter of modern versus premodern societies. I'm definitely with Latour in saying that "we have never been

modern" (certainly not modern in the way we think that we are). See Latour, *We Have Never Been Modern*.

23 See Locke, "Of the Conduct of the Understanding," 32.

24 See, e.g., Benjamin, *Arcades Project*, 25 (in the *Exposé of 1939*). See also Cohen, "Benjamin's Phantasmagoria," 207.

25 I forthrightly confess to being a former fan of Bravo television programs myself. I don't want to suggest I do not feel the draws of the fetishism I am criticizing (I don't think anyone can fully escape it and people who say they do are sometimes the biggest fetishists of them all). Sometimes I loved the *Real Housewives* shows uncritically and with great relish (and zero irony); sometimes they made me almost physically sick with their full-bore and maniacal commodity fetishism. Sometimes (actually often and quite horribly) I felt both sensations at once.

26 Benjamin, *Arcades Project*, 4 (*Exposé of 1935*).

27 I don't think that anyone really uses the actual term "false consciousness" anymore—perhaps with a very few exceptions—but many of us subscribe to some version of the idea nonetheless.

28 By the same token, it offers that no one, not even the most ardent leftist, has access to some truth that makes them invulnerable to the lures and seductions of capitalism and interpellation. I also will argue further in the book that often our class, race, gender, and other markers of identity give us very different and far-from-uniform outcomes in terms of how we respond to interpellation and misinterpellation.

29 See Gordy, *Living Ideology in Cuba*.

30 For all of this circularity of authority, I will argue that for people of color—as Fanon shows quite clearly—interpellation can be a de facto dead end.

31 I am grateful to Sarah Burgess for pointing this out to me.

32 Scott, *Art of Not Being Governed*, 324.

33 Scott points out E. P. Thompson's critique of Althusser, for example, in *Weapons of the Weak*, 42.

34 This insight comes from Bonnie Honig.

35 Jennifer Culbert cites Povinelli in a paper that she presented at the Western Political Science Association in 2015. The paper is entitled "The Banality of Evil: Cruddy Stuff That Happens on the Bus."

36 In my earlier book *Textual Conspiracies*, I argued for the idea of "recognizing misrecognition," that is to say recognizing the way that we do not recognize our own reality. In thinking of Althusser, I would add a new version of that phrase, recognizing the way that we misrecognize specifically the workings of interpellation (or, to put it another way, recognizing the way that we fail to see misinterpellation).

37 George Shulman pointed this out to me. I look forward to his new book on the crisis in genre, which explores some of these questions as well.

38 Badiou, *Communist Hypothesis*, 209.

39 I am indebted to George Shulman for this insight.

40 In speaking of "already" being failures and the like, I do not mean to invoke
    the often-used term "always already." Like many scholars of my generation
    (and many of those who are younger too) I've often used that term but I have
    to confess to never quite liking it. Now I understand a bit better why. To
    say that we are already failures doesn't mean that we are always already fail-
    ures because our failure is meaningless unless it becomes apparent to us, ex-
    pressed in actual time rather than as an ongoing potential. Rather than a kind
    of timeless now (which is what the term "always already" has generally evoked
    for me), I am interested in a much more ordinary and, indeed, banal form
    of time (the same kind of time I think Nietzsche is interested in). In order to
    make our misinterpellation more than a potential or occasional accident, we
    have to think about actual moments, ruptures in the fabric of the false endless
    temporality that liberalism offers us (and which I worry that "always already"
    often reproduces in the guise of opposing liberal temporality).

41 Culbert, "Banality of Evil."

42 Benjamin, "Franz Kafka," 798.

43 See Deleuze, Guattari, and Brinkley, "What Is a Minor Literature?"

44 I see Bonnie Honig's book Antigone, Interrupted as an example of reading a nom-
    inally tragic figure through a misinterpellating lens. Honig reads Antigone not
    as the tragic heroine that she usually is considered to be but as a conspirator,
    in particular with her sister, the much-overlooked Ismene. In Honig's treat-
    ment, Antigone is a political figure who turns mourning itself into a political
    and subversive act.

45 For a good understanding of this other kind of failure, see Halberstam, Queer
    Art of Failure.

46 This insight comes from Sarah Burgess. In a previous book, I did try to think
    about the "event" of the Haitian revolution and misinterpellation as being
    somewhat overlapping categories. See Martel, One and Only Law. It's not quite
    true that for Badiou an event comes out of "nothing" insofar as we always
    have the option for Badiou of being faithful to the events that have already
    occurred. See Badiou, Ethics, 47.

47 In my view there are a number of people who write about parties—not always
    without ambivalence—in ways that do not necessarily fall into this category.
    One is Alain Badiou, who, in his reading of Maoism, sees Mao himself as a
    pivotal figure who used social movements outside of the party in order to
    destabilize the party and render it unable to completely trump the society it
    claimed to represent. See Badiou, The Communist Hypothesis. Relatedly, there is
    Sylvain Lazarus, who rethinks Leninism itself via what he calls Lenin's "satu-
    ration," a change implicit in the end of the formal practice of Soviet commu-
    nism. See Lazarus, Anthropology of the Name, 25. Another writer who makes an
    important contribution to this version of Leninism is Jodi Dean, whose recent
    work on crowds and the party offers that the role of the party is to stand in for
    the Big Other (in Lacanian terms) and thereby disable other candidates from
    taking on that role. Here, the party doesn't so much "represent" the people as

it prevents others from representing them instead. See Dean's *Crowds and Party* and also the end of *The Communist Horizon*. Another writer is this vein is George Ciccariello-Maher. See his *We Created Chávez*.

48 See Dean, *Crowds and Party*.

49 Among anarchist writers, Scott himself lends some support to a reading of misinterpellation as a viable explanation for why revolutions happen. At one point in *Domination and the Arts of Resistance*, he discusses how uprisings may involve some form of misreading. He asks: "How is that subordinate groups . . . have so often believed and acted as if their situations were not inevitable when a more judicious historical reading would have concluded that it was? It is not the miasma of power and thralldom that requires explanation. We require an explanation instead of *misreading* by subordinate groups that seem to exaggerate their own power, the possibilities for emancipation, and to underestimate the power arrayed against them" (79).

In speaking of misreading, Scott is anticipating—I think anyway—the possibility of misinterpellation itself. His notion of misreading helps us to understand why, under conditions of dominance in general, revolts nevertheless still occur. Here again, we can see the workings of ideology and the way that it can be resisted and upturned. The kinds of political authority that normally are associated with liberal capitalism are essentially a shell game; if every worker actually stopped working (Benjamin's—and also Rancière's—theory of the General Strike in a nutshell), this power would completely collapse. Misreading is a way for would-be insurrectionaries to be able to bridge the gap between the general impression of the impossibility of resistance and the fact that, once they begin, insurrections can take on a life of their own, benefiting from precisely all of the hidden forms of resistance that Scott catalogs in his books. Misreading allows what cannot be done to be done and, once it is done, it becomes much less impossible.

50 Foucault, "Truth and Power," 121. Actually though, I think even this metaphor can lead us to falsely believe that "cutting off the king's head" is all we have to do. As I will try to show the archism of the king goes deep within each of us so it's not just heads that we have to worry about.

51 Formally, of course, Plato seeks to overcome the anarchy of the city and soul alike but I read him, through the excellent work of thinkers like Jill Frank, as perpetuating a conspiracy in the text against such an (interpellating) outcome.

1. From "Hey, You There!" to "Wait Up!"

1 Althusser, "Ideology and the State," 116.

2 Althusser, "Ideology and the State," 116. The imagination of this scene is clearly context specific and also specific to the type of person who imagines themselves in this position. When I was teaching Althusser at the Kent Summer School in Critical Theory, one of the students in the class, Silindiwe

Sibanda, said that as a black woman she never would have turned around if she heard the voice of a policeman, or any man for that matter just calling out "hey, you there!"

3 Althusser, "Ideology and the State," 118.

4 Althusser, "Ideology and the State," 117.

5 Althusser, "Ideology and the State," 118.

6 And in the case that it isn't, the police always have their monopoly on violence to fall back on, although, as Althusser makes clear, if they relied on only this, they wouldn't hold on to power for long. I am indebted to Richard Westerman for his comments about RSA and ISA and other helpful suggestions.

7 Althusser, "Ideology and the State," 118.

8 Althusser, "Ideology and the State," 121.

9 Althusser, "Ideology and the State," 121.

10 Althusser, "Ideology and the State," 121.

11 Althusser, "Ideology and the State," 121.

12 Althusser, "Ideology and the State," 122.

13 Althusser, "Ideology and the State," 122.

14 Althusser, "Ideology and the State," 122.

15 Bonnie Honig points out that this works in the same way that Rosenzweig discusses the miracle; it looks like a unidirectional experience (i.e., the human being witnesses the miracle) but it actually depends on a response (Hobbes says much the same thing in his own consideration of miracles).

16 For the purposes of simplicity, I henceforth refer only to the state, but the link with the ruling class should never be forgotten for Althusser.

17 Similarly, it is possible for there to be exchanges of subjectivity between the state and the subject—at least some subjects, anyway—so that some people become politicians and leaders and then leave those posts, returning to "private life." Such interchanges only reaffirm the deep anchoring of individual subjectivity in the state.

18 Althusser, "Ideology and the State," 123.

19 I don't think that Althusser's use of the term "recognition" is the same thing as Hegel's. Althusser's use of the term "misrecognition," at least, is part of the status quo while the Hegelian concept of recognition is radical and potentially shattering of subjectivities, as least in terms of how he is read by many contemporary scholars.

20 Althusser, "Ideology and the State," 118

21 Althusser, "Ideology and the State," 116.

22 Althusser, "Ideology and the State," 124.

23 It is for this reason that I have chosen the term "misinterpellation" rather than "misrecognition." In a talk that I gave on this subject, Costas Douzinas pointed out to me, quite accurately, that this is more a visual than an auditory phenomenon. In this sense recognition seems to be the dominant aspect of interpellation but insofar as Althusser uses the term "misrecognition" for a

cog in the workings of interpellation, it is not possible for me to appropriate the term to describe its own unmaking.

24 At the same time, there is a way in which interpellation cannot avoid misinterpellation. As Bonnie Honig notes, in Austinian terms, interpellation is a performative with perlocutionary force; it must be subject to misfiring as one of its conditions of possibility. Therefore misinterpellation can never be ruled out and interpellation will always exceed intentionality.

25 See Rancière, "On the Theory of Ideology."

26 Dolar, "Beyond Interpellation," 76.

27 Dolar, "Beyond Interpellation," 76.

28 Dolar, "Beyond Interpellation," 76.

29 Dolar, "Beyond Interpellation," 77.

30 Dolar, "Beyond Interpellation," 77–78. I would agree with this, although, as I will be arguing later in this chapter, Dolar's failure of the subject is not utter enough; it is only partial.

31 Dean, *Crowds and Party*, 79.

32 Even when, later in the book, I discuss the nature of our subjectivity, I hesitate to discuss it in terms of actuality or reality.

33 Dolar, "Beyond Interpellation," 77.

34 Richard Dienst concedes that interpellation must fail, arguing that "ideology can miss." Dienst, *Still Life in Real Time*, 141. He goes on to say "Althusser's concept can only be made rigorous by Derrida's postulate of misdirection, which operates at a different level from the Lacanian/Althusserian postulate of misrecognition. At this level, ideology must be conceived as a mass of sendings or a flow of representations whose force consists precisely in the fact that they are not perfectly destined, just as they are not centrally disseminated. Far from always connecting, ideology *never does*: subjects look in on messages as if eavesdropping, as if peeking at someone else's mail (this is also always the route of desire, which as everybody knows by now, never comes)." Dienst, *Still Life in Real Time*, 141. To Dienst's argument that interpellation works in effect by (or despite) missing, I would simply add that this does not challenge misrecognition so much as bolsters it. I would also say that the power of misinterpellation comes from the way that it makes the fact of missing too obvious to ignore (misrecognize).

35 Butler, *Psychic Life of Power*, 106.

36 Butler, *Psychic Life of Power*, 107.

37 Butler, *Psychic Life of Power*, 109.

38 I should note here that even the question of "becoming" a subject at all (whether good or bad) may keep some of the aperture of interpellation intact and that misinterpellation may offer ways to make one even "worse" (i.e., more subversive, more resistant) than even a "bad subject."

39 Butler, *Psychic Life of Power*, 110.

40 Butler, *Psychic Life of Power*, 114.

41 Butler does not directly reference this, but the connection between original sin and the kinds of guilt we find in Althusser is easily made.

42 Butler, *Psychic Life of Power*, 118. Although, as I will argue in chapter 6, guilt and accusation are not the same thing and that, ultimately, it is accusation and not guilt per se that is the problem.

43 Butler, *Psychic Life of Power*, 119. For Butler, guilt is the mechanism that controls the whole operation of interpellation. The subject is already guilty, (therefore) already subject to law, already ready to turn. We can see some evidence for this in Althusser's choice of narratives: the subject is hailed by a police officer; the subject is therefore suspect, ready to admit her failure to obey, even as that very act serves as the basis (at least allegorically) of her obedience. Of this complex mixture of guilt and obedience, Butler writes, "Prior to any possibility of a critical understanding of the law is an openness or vulnerability to the law, exemplified in the turn toward the law, in the anticipation of culling an identity through identifying with the one who has broken the law. Indeed, the law is broken prior to any possibility of having access to the law, and so 'guilt' is prior to the knowledge of the law and is, in this sense, always strangely innocent" (108).

44 Butler, *Psychic Life of Power*, 108.

45 Butler, *Psychic Life of Power*, 120, cited from Dolar, "Beyond Interpellation."

46 Butler, *Psychic Life of Power*, 121.

47 Butler, *Psychic Life of Power*, 127.

48 Butler, *Psychic Life of Power*, 127.

49 Butler, *Psychic Life of Power*, 128.

50 Butler, *Psychic Life of Power*, 128.

51 Butler, *Psychic Life of Power*, 128.

52 I discuss the problem of turning to love as a solution to various political conundrums in *Love Is a Sweet Chain: Desire, Autonomy and Friendship in Liberal Political Theory*. In general, I find that often when a thinker turns to love as a solution, they are, in effect, smuggling in (not always deliberately) all of the hierarchies and occult sources of authority—very much including theological ones—that the concept is meant to dispel. In my view, many thinkers evoke love when they have given up on politics.

53 Butler, *Psychic Life of Power*, 129.

54 Butler, *Psychic Life of Power*, 129.

55 For Benjamin there is, of course, an "outside," namely, God and the force of divine violence, but we cannot have any access or claim to this force (it merely opens up a caesura in which we can operate) so for all intents and purposes, we must act as if, indeed, there is no outside, as far as we are concerned.

56 Benjamin, "Letter to Gershom Scholem on Franz Kafka," 327.

57 See Ferguson, *Sharing Democracy*.

58 Berlant, *Cruel Optimism*, 133.

59 Berlant, *Cruel Optimism*, 130. This is cited from the Gaitskill.

60 Berlant, *Cruel Optimism*, 130.

61 Berlant, *Cruel Optimism*, 286n12. Berlant also takes from Althusser the notion of misrecognition, saying that it "describes the psychic process by which fantasy recalibrates what we encounter so that we can imagine that something or someone can fulfill our desire. . . . To misrecognize is not to err, but to project qualities onto something so that we can love, hate, and manipulate it for having those qualities—which it might or might not have" (122). She also writes that the two girls "love whatever they can (mis)recognize as love" (129).

62 I am grateful to Anita Sokolsky for pointing this possibility out to me. She, along with many other faculty and postdoctoral fellows, gave me invaluable feedback at a workshop on this chapter held at Williams College in March 2015.

63 Benjamin, "Critique of Violence," 246.

64 Not all other forms of introjection are necessarily better or different than "hey, you there!" There is Judith Butler's own discussion of the statement, "it's a girl!," announced at birth. See Butler, *Bodies That Matter*, 232. As Bonnie Honig notes of this, such a statement isn't meant to be refused (even though its accuracy is as fragile as any other form of interpellation). Furthermore, as she notes, this is not addressed to the baby but to the parents who are the presumptive enforcers of a sexual ordering. It means effectively "you are to raise this child as a boy (or a girl)."

65 Eagleton, "Ideology and Its Vicissitudes," 216–217. I am grateful to Christian Thorne for bringing this passage to my attention.

66 Of course some people are perfectly happy with their false hailing. They feel it to be a perfect fit and wouldn't change it for anything. Why would a rich, white, cis-gendered, and able-bodied heterosexual man, for example, buck the system that privileges him so well? One of the toughest questions I ever got when I gave a version of this chapter as a talk was effectively "if I'm lucky enough to be privileged by interpellation, why would I want to challenge the status quo?" (somewhat akin to the character in *The Matrix* opting to take the pill that got him to forget the truth and go back into fantasy). Yet even the most privileged persons, I feel, are not a lost cause. Insofar as they too are falsely hailed and insofar as their acceptance of their false identity is, as I show in chapter 4, a form of intense self-hatred (not to mention hatred of others, which I don't think they have as much of a problem with) that is aggravated and not resolved by normative forms of subjectivity.

2. *"Men Are Born Free and Equal in Rights"*

1 Most famously this is demonstrated by Gayatri Chakravorty Spivak's essay, "Can the Subaltern Speak?"

2 This raises an important point, namely, whether misinterpellation is itself generally "leftist." What if the world was dominated by left politics and forms of address (if only!)? Would misinterpellation then be something that an alienated right wing latched onto for subversion of their own? I think the answer has to be

no because, as I see it, the difference between the left and the right, or at least between anarchism and archism is, ultimately, the difference between seeking the failure of phantasm versus seeking the phantasm itself. Insofar as misinterpellation will always be hostile to phantasm, it generally will tend to serve left- rather than right-wing purposes, at least those left-wing movements that were interested in undermining phantasms of identity and authority (and in this way become, to cite Benjamin again, "*completely useless for the purposes of fascism*" in this way). See Benjamin, "Work of Art in the Age of Its Technical Reproducibility," 252. This is not to say that misinterpellation only serves left-wing causes (I think in practice it is more of a mixed bag) but rather that, on the whole, misinterpellation is a phenomenon that benefits the left more than the right.

3 In *The One and Only Law: Walter Benjamin and the Second Commandment*. In that text, although I did discuss the question of misinterpellation to some extent, my focus was more on reading the Haitian revolution as a Badiouian event (or even *the* Badiouian event). As I said in the introduction, I am not sure that Badiou's idea of the event and the idea of misinterpellation are necessarily in conflict. Yet, in shifting the focus from the event to misinterpellation, I do see a very different way of reading what happened (and why).

4 See de Gouges, "Declaration of the Rights of Woman and Citizen." Of this, Jacques Rancière writes, "Women could make a twofold demonstration. They could demonstrate that they were deprived of the rights that they had, thanks to the Declaration of Rights. And they could demonstrate, through their public action, that they had the rights that the constitution denied to them, that they could enact those rights. So they could act as subjects of the Rights of Man in the precise sense that I have mentioned. They acted as subjects that did not have the rights that they had and had the rights that they had not." Rancière, "Who Is the Subject of the Rights of Man?," 304. The question of qualifying the supposedly universal rights in the Declaration reminds me of George Orwell's *Animal Farm* where, for example, one of the sacred rules of the animal revolution was "no animal shall sleep in a bed" to which it was later appended "with sheets." See Orwell, *Animal Farm*.

5 Wall, *Human Rights and Constituent Power*, 17.

6 James, *Black Jacobins*, 91.

7 Of course, the Declaration *was* radical for its time, but certainly not radical in any contemporary sense and certainly not actually promulgating the universalism that it purported to.

8 James, *Black Jacobins*, 120.

9 James, *Black Jacobins*, 120.

10 James, *Black Jacobins*, 281.

11 James, *Black Jacobins*, 281.

12 L'Ouverture, *Mémoires*, 84.

13 Scott, *Domination and the Arts of Resistance*, 97. Charles Taylor discusses a similar practice in revolutionary France where violations of law were said to done "par l'ordre du roi." Taylor, *Modern Social Imaginaries*, 127.

14 See Fick, *Making of Haiti.*

15 James, *Black Jacobins*, 156.

16 Scott writes, "The moment we insist on the importance of the hidden transcript [that is, those collective acts of resistance and subversion that constitute the entire history of subordinate/dominant relations as explained in the introduction] to the social production of charisma, it seems to me that we restore the reciprocity that is at the center of this concept. As sociologists are fond of pointing out, the relational character of charisma means that one 'has charisma' only to the extent that others confer it upon one; it is the attribution of charisma that establishes the relationship." *Domination and the Arts of Resistance*, 221.

17 George Ciccariello-Maher makes a similar point in his book *We Created Chávez*, in relationship to the rise of Hugo Chávez in contemporary Venezuela. See Ciccariello-Maher, *We Created Chávez.*

18 While Toussaint himself may qualify as subaltern, I am taking the liberty to use the term to refer to those most excluded and most outside of most understandings of power and access.

19 Dubois and Garrigus, *Slave Revolution in the Caribbean*, 18.

20 James, *Black Jacobins*, 81.

21 Dubois, *Avengers of the New World*, 102–103. The original text comes from Parham, *My Odyssey*. The last sentence is from Dubois and not the original.

22 Fick, *Making of Haiti*, 168.

23 I am struck, for example, at how the Russo-Japanese war tends to be cited as the first time that a European power was defeated by a non-European power. Leaving aside the entire history of invasions of Europe by non-Europeans throughout much of Europe's history, in modern terms, the Haitian revolution precedes the Russo-Japanese war by over one hundred years. For more information about the silencing of the Haitian revolution, see Trouillot, *Silencing the Past*, and also Fischer, *Modernity Disavowed.*

24 See Manela, *Wilsonian Moment.* I am indebted to Keally McBride for bringing this book, and the event it describes, to my attention.

25 Manela, *Wilsonian Moment*, 7.

26 Manela, *Wilsonian Moment*, 4.

27 Manela writes that in terms of non-European peoples and their own movement toward self-determination, Wilson "envisioned them achieving it through an evolutionary process under the benevolent tutelage of a 'civilized' power that would prepare them for self-government" (25). He also notes that point five of the Fourteen Points speech is not all that meets the eye. It does call for the resolution of colonial claims "based upon a strict observance of the principle that in determining all such questions of sovereignty the interests of the populations concerned must have equal weight with the equitable claims of the government whose title is to be determined" (40). But Manela points to the language here; he speaks of the "interests" of colonial people rather than their own expressed desires, leaving room, he suggests, for questions about

who determines what those interests are. He also notes that speaking of the "equitable claims" of the colonizer makes them a vested partner in any future negotiations (40).

28 Kohn and McBride, *Political Theories of Decolonization*, 22.

29 Manela, *Wilsonian Moment*, 5.

30 Manela, *Wilsonian Moment*, 5.

31 Manela, *Wilsonian Moment*, 13.

32 Manela, *Wilsonian Moment*, 90.

33 If I were to criticize one thing of Manela's otherwise excellent book, it is his nearly exclusive focus on political leaders. He often speaks of how various leaders in the countries that he studies sought to elicit popular support for their causes. No doubt, this is how these leaders thought but to speak in this way suggests a largely passive population, and if the Haitian example is a guide, populations tend to be far more radical than their leaders. Many of the leaders of the movements that Manela looks at, from Sa'd Zaghlul of Egypt to Mahatma Gandhi of India, start out themselves as liberals and become radicalized over time. But surely the vast majority of these populations did not have a similar transformation; they were not liberal to start with and did not become liberal at the end. Yet it is here that the question of misinterpellation becomes most pertinent, for it suggests a change in thinking of not just one or two people but large numbers of people, leading to an intense radicalization from below (as the case of Haiti once again attests to).

34 Guha, *Elementary Aspects of Peasant Insurgency in Colonial India*, 1.

35 Guha, *Elementary Aspects of Peasant Insurgency in Colonial India*, 3.

36 Guha, *Elementary Aspects of Peasant Insurgency in Colonial India*, 4

37 Guha, *Elementary Aspects of Peasant Insurgency in Colonial India*, 4.

38 Ileto, *Pasyon and Revolution*, 4.

39 The movement that they took part in was generally a nonelite phenomenon; Ileto tells us that, among the movement leaders, José Rizal was "one of the few popular martyrs who belonged to the *ilustrado* class" (50). Megan Thomas paints a more complicated picture of the relationship between the *ilustrados* and the "subaltern," or indigenous Filipino, community (beginning even with the meaning and history of the term "Filipino"). See Thomas, *Orientalists, Propagandists and Ilustrados*, 16. See also Anderson, *Under Three Flags*; Mojares, *Brains of the Nation*.

40 Ileto, *Pasyon and Revolution*, 12.

41 Ileto, *Pasyon and Revolution*, 12.

42 Ileto, *Pasyon and Revolution*, 12.

43 Manela, *Wilsonian Moment*, 142.

44 Manela, *Wilsonian Moment*, 142.

45 Manela, *Wilsonian Moment*, 142.

46 Manela, *Wilsonian Moment*, 142.

47 As Kohn and McBride show, the connection to liberal theory outlived the "Wilsonian moment" itself. They state, "At the 1955 Bandung conference,

the delegates endorsed the right to self-determination as well as a broader human rights agenda. Subsequent narratives of decolonialization used terms that were often in sharp repudiation of the liberal ideas that accompanied conquest and became influential. They value identities, religious beliefs, and territorial connections that had been specifically devalued or denied by the colonizing powers. The content of the narrative had to provide a clear break with the narratives of progress in order to make it clear that the tools of political action had indeed changed hands." Kohn and McBride, *Political Theories of Decolonization*, 24.

48 Bouamoud, *Bouâzizi ou L'énticelle qui a destitute Ben Ali*, 47.

49 Bouamoud, *Bouâzizi ou L'énticelle qui a destitute Ben Ali*, 47. All translations from this book are my own.

50 Bouamoud, *Bouâzizi ou L'énticelle qui a destitute Ben Ali*, 51.

51 Bouamoud, *Bouâzizi ou L'énticelle qui a destitute Ben Ali*, 52. In the original French, it is "Pauvre Mohamed! Il pensait vraiment être dans un État de droit et des institutions. Là, plutôt que de l'écouter, on le chasse [literally hunt] comme un chien."

52 Bouamoud, *Bouâzizi ou L'énticelle qui a destitute Ben Ali*, 52. In original: "Ach'hadou ann lê Ilêhê illa l'Lah."

53 Bouamoud, *Bouâzizi ou L'énticelle qui a destitute Ben Ali*, 52.

54 Bouamoud, *Bouâzizi ou L'énticelle qui a destitute Ben Ali*, 55.

55 Bouamoud, *Bouâzizi ou L'énticelle qui a destitute Ben Ali*, 60.

56 Butler, *Gender Trouble*, 141.

57 Honwana, *Youth and Revolution in Tunisia*, 11.

58 Aleya-Sghaier, "Tunisian Revolution," 30. The lack of a "clear ideology" has been said about many revolutionary or radical movements, including Occupy Wall Street and even the Cuban revolution. I would distance myself from her claim that the Tunisian uprising was "spontaneous" insofar as, as Scott shows, uprisings play out scenarios that are rehearsed in countless ways by communities while they remain in subservience.

59 After this initial more anarchist mode, the mix of perspectives of "universal" and local views was to come in the fore in Tunisia, which is today held up in the West as a model of the Arab Spring for its transition to a more democratic, moderate form, one that more easily fits into the same networks of capitalist exploitation as Tunisia had occupied previously. This, of course, is not to celebrate the outcome in places like Libya and Syria where the Arab Spring has led to all-out civil war. Rather I wish to point out that there are other options than chaos (Libya and Syria), restoration of dictatorship (Egypt), or the rule of "moderates"—i.e., liberals (Tunisia).

60 In the case of Haiti and the "Wilsonian moment," of course, change was not nearly as quick.

61 See, e.g., Habermas, *Between Facts and Norms*.

62 I should note here that even the question of "becoming" a subject at all (whether good or bad) may keep some of the aperture of interpellation intact

and that misinterpellation may offer ways to make one even "worse" (i.e., more subversive, more resistant) than even a "bad subject."

63 Machiavelli, *Discourses*, 257.

64 Machiavelli, *Discourses*, 258.

65 Machiavelli, *Discourses*, 147.

66 Livy, *Early History of Rome*, 54.

67 Machiavelli, *Discourses*, 147.

68 Machiavelli, *Discourses*, 150–151.

69 Livy, *Early History of Rome*, 97.

70 Machiavelli, *Discourses*, 403.

71 Machiavelli, *Discourses*, 404.

72 Machiavelli, *Discourses*, 157.

73 Machiavelli, *Discourses*, 157.

74 Machiavelli, *Discourses*, 158.

75 Generally, interpellation does not work as it does in the Roman case, where an individual or collective projects authority directly and then goes on to receive it. More often—certainly in the way that Althusser tells it—one set of figures projects (the state) and the other receives (individual members of society), but in either case the larger process of circulation of authority is the same.

76 See Martel, *Textual Conspiracies*.

77 While in the stories Machiavelli offers interpellation seems mainly to benefit the projector, there is, of course, a darker side to the story. Generally the projector of that phantasm is not the same person as the community that suffers from it. Thus, Numa projected and the people of Rome suffered law. The rulers of the French empire projected and the slaves of Haiti lived in the shadow of what came back. Ben Ali projected and Mohamed Bouazizi (maybe) got slapped and then ultimately killed himself. What unites these stories is not the projection itself but what happened next: in these cases, the projection led to not just more suffering but instead a refusal, a reaction that took the determination of subjectivity away from the projecting power and used it as a weapon by which to unmake its projections, along with the political world that it produces.

78 See, e.g., " 'I Felt Like a Five-Year-Old Holding on to Hulk Hogan': Darren Wilson in His Own Words," *Guardian*, November 25, 2014, http://www.theguardian .com/us-news/2014/nov/25/darren-wilson-testimony-ferguson-michael -brown.

79 In this way, Pulcher's rebellion (if that is what we should call it) is not much of a success in practical terms since the army he led did lose its fight and so the "power" of the Roman religion was sustained rather than overturned. Pulcher's example is less one of a way to sure success (or rather to sure failure since the failure of interpellative authority is what is sought) than an indication of where to strike and how, what disobedience to the interpellative mechanism looks like.

1 The English translation of Fanon's chapter in *Black Skin, White Masks*, "L'expérience vécue du noir" (literally the lived experience of the black [person]), is "The fact of blackness." This is not a good translation but it nonetheless suggests, at the experiential level, the kind of undeniable, tangible presence of race for Fanon. Even so, David Macey strongly resists this translation. See Macey, "Fanon, Phenomenology, Race."

2 In this sense, I agree with Lewis Gordon's assessment of Fanon's connection to existentialism. See Gordon, *Fanon and the Crisis of European Man*.

3 Rancière, "Who Is the Subject of the Rights of Man?," 304.

4 Fanon, *Black Skin, White Masks*, 12.

5 Fanon, *Black Skin, White Masks*, 110.

6 Fanon, *Black Skin, White Masks*, 110.

7 Fanon, *Black Skin, White Masks*, 110.

8 Fanon, *Black Skin, White Masks*, 111.

9 Fanon, *Black Skin, White Masks*, 111–112; Fanon, *Peau noire, masques blancs*, 90.

10 Fanon, *Black Skin, White Masks*, 112; Fanon, *Peau noire, masques blancs*, 90. "Y a bon banania" refers to an extremely racist ad for a then-popular breakfast food in France.

11 Fanon, *Black Skin, White Masks*, 111.

12 Fanon, *Black Skin, White Masks*, 112

13 Fanon, *Black Skin, White Masks*, 115; Fanon, *Peau noire, masques blancs*, 92–93.

14 Macey, "Fanon, Phenomenology, Race," 168.

15 Fanon, *Black Skin, White Masks*, 117.

16 Fanon, *Black Skin, White Masks*, 113.

17 Bhabha, "Remembering Fanon," 184.

18 Fanon, *Black Skin, White Masks*, 109.

19 Fanon, *Black Skin, White Masks*, 110.

20 Gordon, *Fanon and the Crisis of European Man*, 35.

21 See Kohn and McBride, *Political Theories of Decolonization*.

22 Fanon, *Toward the African Revolution*, 18.

23 Fanon, *Black Skin, White Masks*, 123.

24 Spivak, *In Other Worlds*, 205.

25 Fanon, *Black Skin, White Masks*, 126.

26 Fanon, *Black Skin, White Masks*, 130.

27 Fanon, *Black Skin, White Masks*, 132.

28 Fanon, *Black Skin, White Masks*, 133.

29 Fanon, *Black Skin, White Masks*, 133–134.

30 Fanon, *Black Skin, White Masks*, 138.

31 Fanon, *Black Skin, White Masks*, 140.

32 Fanon, *Black Skin, White Masks*, 140.

33 Fanon, *Black Skin, White Masks*, 216.

34 Fanon, *Black Skin, White Masks*, 217.

35 Fanon, *Peau noire, masques blancs*, 93.

36 Fanon, *Peau noire, masques blancs*, 176.

37 Fanon, *Black Skin, White Masks*, 217.

38 Fanon, *Black Skin, White Masks*, 217.

39 Fanon, *Black Skin, White Masks*, 218. See also Buck-Morss, *Hegel, Haiti, and Universal History*.

40 Fanon, *Black Skin, White Masks*, 219.

41 Fanon, *Black Skin, White Masks*, 220.

42 However, Susan Buck-Morss argues that Hegel himself had the Haitian slaves in mind when he wrote about the master-slave relationship. See Buck-Morss, *Hegel, Haiti, and Universal History*.

43 Neil Roberts makes this point in *Freedom as Marronage*.

44 Fanon, *Black Skin, White Masks*, 221.

45 Fanon, *Black Skin, White Masks*, 221.

46 Fanon, *Black Skin, White Masks*, 222.

47 Fanon, *Black Skin, White Masks*, 229.

48 Fanon, *Black Skin, White Masks*, 232; Fanon, *Peau noire, masques blancs*, 188.

49 Fanon, *Black Skin, White Masks*, 12.

50 On the other hand, as Sylvain Lazarus argues, it is only when an event has passed from the stage of history that it becomes available for thought, what he calls "saturation." See Lazarus, *Anthropology of the Name*, ix.

51 I am indebted to Keally McBride for this insight.

52 Fanon, *Wretched of the Earth*, 2.

53 Fanon, *Wretched of the Earth*, 2.

54 Fanon, *Les Damnés de la terre*, 40.

55 Fanon, *Wretched of the Earth*, 11.

56 For more on this question, see Macey, *Frantz Fanon: A Biography*; Cherki, *Frantz Fanon: A Portrait*.

57 Fanon, *Wretched of the Earth*, 11

58 Fanon, *Wretched of the Earth*, 11.

59 Fanon, *Wretched of the Earth*, 11.

60 Fanon, *Wretched of the Earth*, 12.

61 Fanon, *Wretched of the Earth*, 12.

62 See Martel, *Textual Conspiracies*, 194–209.

63 Fanon, *Wretched of the Earth*, 21.

64 Fanon, *Wretched of the Earth*, 21.

65 Fanon, *Wretched of the Earth*, 42. He also writes, "The violence of the colonial regime and the counter-violence of the colonized balance each other and respond to each other in an extraordinary reciprocal homogeneity" (46).

66 See Benjamin, "Critique of Violence."

67 Fanon, *Wretched of the Earth*, 50.

68 Fanon, *Wretched of the Earth*, 50.

69 Fanon, *Wretched of the Earth*, 51.

70 We can see some of Fanon's more metaphorical treatment of violence, for example, when he speaks of "atmospheric violence, this violence rippling under the skin" (*Wretched of the Earth*, 31). In considering the context of colonialism where anger and despair have taken over the population in equal measures, violence does not need to be physically present to have its effect. It can exist in the anger itself; it is stored, as it were, in the countless acts of small sabotage and resistance that Scott catalogues in his books. Fanon also tells us that "violence can thus be understood to be the perfect mediation" (44). It is not critical as itself but rather in terms of what mental states and expectations it produces in those who exercise it.

71 Fanon, *Wretched of the Earth*, 51–52.

72 I am grateful to Kojo Koram for this insight.

73 See Arendt, "On Violence." See also Gibson's chapter "Violent Concerns," in *Fanon: The Postcolonial Imagination*.

74 Fanon, *Wretched of the Earth*, 184–185n23.

75 Fanon, *Wretched of the Earth*, 89.

76 Fanon, *Dying Colonialism*, 25.

77 Fanon, *Dying Colonialism*, 25.

78 By contrast to Fanon, Arendt asserts that any turn to violence automatically determines an unhappy ending. By distinguishing between kinds of violence and also by conceptualizing a role for violence that advances rather than undermines agency, Fanon sees violence itself as producing, rather than destroying self-determination, at least under certain circumstances. See Arendt, "On Violence." See also Cocks, *On Commonality, Nationalism and Violence*.

79 See Djebar, *Women of Algiers in Their Apartments*. See also Woodhull, *Transformations of the Maghreb*. The critique is that Fanon adopts the same connection between women and the land as both traditional local practices and French colonial mores dictate. Margaret Kohn and Keally McBride have a different analysis of the role of women and the veil within "Algeria Unveiled," an earlier chapter of *A Dying Colonialism*. Rather than passively receiving the "meaning" of the veil from the French (as a mark of subjection and inferiority), the veil becomes repurposed for revolutionary action. As they put it, "The veiled woman no longer connects to her world through image; instead she uses image—whether of assimilation or traditionalism by donning the veil—to make herself a more effective instrument of revolution. . . . The revolution gives birth to a new woman . . . whose power is in writing her own script and her own future. The veil symbolizes the past, and while the veil is still present, a new relationship to it has emerged. The past becomes a weapon, rather than a fixed identity." Kohn and McBride, *Political Theories of Decolonization*, 75.

80 Fanon, *Dying Colonialism*, 73.

81 Fanon, *Dying Colonialism*, 75.

82 Fanon, *Dying Colonialism*, 76.

83 Fanon, *Dying Colonialism*, 76.

84 Fanon, *Dying Colonialism*, 69.

85 Fanon, *Dying Colonialism*, 84.

86 Fanon, *Dying Colonialism*, 87.

87 Fanon, *Dying Colonialism*, 87.

88 Fanon, *Dying Colonialism*, 87.

89 Richard Joyce and Anne Norton have both convinced me that local is not always good. It is possible to assert challenges on transnational or global levels without reproducing the universal. In a sense it is not the size of the intended assertion about identity and rights that matters (not the universe versus the local) but the way that assertion is framed.

90 Fanon, *Dying Colonialism*, 89.

91 Fanon, *Dying Colonialism*, 90. And, of course, Fanon himself wrote in French.

92 Fanon, *Dying Colonialism*, 96.

93 Benjamin, "Reflections on Radio," 364.

94 In her own thoughts on human relationships forged by and through objects, Arendt argues—quite differently from Benjamin—that, far from producing a chance for radical difference, you get the taint of determinism, a return to the ends/means instrumentalism that is the hallmark of work. As is well known, action and not work in her view is the only form of human endeavor that is not predetermined (even as work certainly has its positive aspects for Arendt insofar as it grounds and locates human actors). I would definitely part company with Arendt on this viewpoint insofar as it seems that, from the perspective of misinterpellation, objects can interfere with the predetermination that is already being produced among and between human subjects. Rather than having some innate quality of their own that somehow transmits its own fixedness to human interactions (as Arendt suggests), the very externality of objects serves as an opportunity (but nothing more than that) to expose and complicate various forms of interpellation that they are associated with.

This helps us to think more about why sometimes misinterpellation itself fails—or more accurately fails to allow for failure—how it can itself be "hijacked" or rendered part of the realm of necessity that is not so much part of nature (as Arendt suggests) but is itself a product of human endeavor (i.e., of interpellation itself). Whereas, as discussed in the previous chapter, interpellation requires some ghostly and transcendent outside to ensure its own circularity, I would argue that misinterpellation, if not requires, then at least greatly benefits from some relationship to the material world; rather than going "up" into the transcendental realms, misinterpellation goes "down" or "into" the physical world for its own forms of authority (or misauthority?). Although material objects can themselves be connected to or even be the purported source of interpellation—as chapter 5 will suggest—ultimately their cooperation with regimes of authority and determinism cannot be guaranteed. The mismatch between claims—both ideological and otherwise—put onto objects and their own status as things tends, as I will argue further, to play its hand toward misinterpellation, toward unmaking, deauthorizing, and decolonizing. The various outcomes we see in misinterpellation may, to a great extent, reflect the varying degrees to which the relationship with the object in question is overdetermined or left to contingency (recognizing that sometimes the "object" in question can even be other people who can be similarly resistant and subversive to such orderings).

95 Djebar says this about Fanon, for example.

96 This might be a fairly uncharitable way to summarize the options posed to him by Sartrean notions of transcendence and the authenticity promised by proponents of négritude.

97 Fitzpatrick, *Modernism and the Grounds of Law*, 47.

98 Kohn and McBride, *Political Theories of Decolonization*, 70–71.

4. "[A Person] Is Something That Shall Be Overcome"

1 This description of this style of reading comes from Bonnie Honig.

2 Ta-Nehisi Coates, the one living and real person in this group, is an exception to this characterization but, as I'll show, he nevertheless epitomizes an approach to police violence that is very much in keeping with misinterpellated subjectivity.

3 See Martel, "Nietzsche's Cruel Messiah."

4 Ultimately, it could be said that the one that Nietzsche is betraying is really only himself; he is giving away his own "birthright" as an author, his control over the meaning and message of his text.

5 Fanon, *Black Skin, White Masks*, 222.

6 Fanon, *Black Skin, White Masks*, 222.

7 Nietzsche, *Genealogy of Morals*, 168.

8 Nietzsche, *Genealogy of Morals*, 168–169.

9 Nietzsche, *Zur Genealogie der Moral*, 780.

10 Nietzsche, *Genealogy of Morals*, 229; Nietzsche, *Zur Genealogie der Moral*, 836.

11 Nietzsche, *Genealogy of Morals*, 229–230.

12 Nietzsche, *Genealogy of Morals*, 149.

13 For more on the question of the noon hour, see Alenka Zupančič, *The Shortest Shadow*.

14 Arthur C. Danto makes a similar argument in "Some Remarks on the Genealogy of Morals," 48.

15 Nickolas Pappas makes a similar argument in *The Nietzsche Disappointment*, 231. According to Pappas, Rüdiger Safranski also acknowledges that Nietzsche's failure to complete stories may have some kind of positive purpose but argues that "in spite of himself, Safranski defers to Nietzsche's wishes even in his fantasy of getting free" (231). See also Safranski, *Nietzsche*.

16 Nietzsche, *Genealogy of Morals*, 157.

17 Nietzsche, *Thus Spoke Zarathustra*, 78.

18 The Hermit tells Zarathustra in the prologue that he should "give [human beings] nothing. . . . Rather take part of their load and help them to bear it— that will be best for them." Nietzsche, *Thus Spoke Zarathustra*, 11.

19 Nietzsche, *Thus Spoke Zarathustra*, 137.

20 In terms of Nietzsche's cruelty, Ivan Soll says, "Because Nietzsche holds the self to be more like a society of many selves rather than a unity, he naturally analyzes the reflexive acts that constitute asceticism—acts such as self-discipline, cruelty to one's self, and self-denial—on the model of interpersonal discipline, cruelty, and denial." Soll, "Nietzsche on Cruelty," 186.

21 As I argued in the previous chapter, Fanon is similar to Nietzsche in the ways that he can help us enhance and expand the opportunities for misinterpellation. I see Fanon and Nietzsche as being quite kindred spirits (as is perhaps suggested by the fact that, as previously noted, Fanon cites Nietzsche in his own work). In a sense, thinking of the two together (or in constellation, to use a Benjaminian term) helps us to develop a richer sense of the kinds of strategies involved in augmenting misinterpellation. Fanon supplies a sense of urgency; to Nietzsche's perspectivism, which essentially says "take it or leave it," Fanon adds an understanding of the hideous politics that come from "taking it." He gives a much more explicitly political sense of the stakes involved in subjectivization and succumbing to authority (and archic) systems of power. Nietzsche, on the other hand, who has relatively more of a privileged position, can thereby afford to see how pernicious it is to risk the phantasms of truth and authenticity that Fanon is more willing to countenance (given the urgency and direness of his situation as well as the situation of the colonial subject more generally). Nietzsche offers Fanon a sense of the costs of the flirtation with the language of truth and ontology (of "using the master's tools to tear down the master's house") that we often see him engaging with. In a way, these two thinkers serve to discipline one another to give a better sense of the possibilities and dangers of any endeavor to enhance the prospects and scope of misinterpellation.

I am grateful to the postgraduate students at the Birkbeck College School of Law for bringing this connection and distinction to my attention.

22 Nietzsche, *Thus Spoke Zarathustra*, 138–139.

23 Nietzsche, *Thus Spoke Zarathustra*, 79.

24 For more on the question of the overman and its paradoxical nature, see Lampert, *Nietzsche's Teaching*. Lampert's argument is that the idea of the overman is meant to be abandoned in favor of eternal recurrence over the course of the book. Here he accepts a basic dissonance to the text that can only be resolved by casting out that part of the text that contradicts the rest (the idea of eternal recurrence, specifically). See also Ansell-Pearson, "Who Is the Ubermensch?" Ansell-Pearson writes that, in order to properly read Nietzsche, we "need to be not *moderner Mensch* [moderns] but *Übermensch*—or at least on the bridge to it" (312). But this assumes that being on the bridge to the overman is the same thing as being the overman (I'd say it is not and by Nietzsche's own argument). He argues further that "the bridge to the overman does not lead to *the* 'way' but to many ways" (315), but I think this still begs the question of

whether Nietzsche's work is meant to lead us to anywhere at all (except for where we start: as a cripple at this bridge).

25 Nietzsche, *Also sprach Zarathustra*, 18.

26 Nietzsche, *Thus Spoke Zarathustra*, 18.

27 Nietzsche, *Thus Spoke Zarathustra*, 14.

28 Nietzsche, *Thus Spoke Zarathustra*, 15; Nietzsche, *Also sprach Zarathustra*, 13.

29 Nietzsche, *Thus Spoke Zarathustra*, 14.

30 Nietzsche, *Thus Spoke Zarathustra*, 14.

31 Nietzsche, *Thus Spoke Zarathustra*, 19.

32 Nietzsche, *Thus Spoke Zarathustra*, 19.

33 Nietzsche, *Thus Spoke Zarathustra*, 20.

34 As Bonnie Honig notes, the gift that Zarathustra gives to the tightrope walker is not the afterlife but burial, the care that he takes with his own hands.

35 Nietzsche, *Thus Spoke Zarathustra*, 12; Nietzsche, *Also sprach Zarahtustra*, 11. This is usually translated into English as "man is something that shall be overcome," but Der Mensch is better translated as "a person." Note that throughout *Thus Spoke Zarathustra*, Nietzsche tends to use the term "Mensch" instead of "Mann" which has more connotations of "man," i.e., male persons. I left the translations alone for the most part (such as the term "overman") but for this one sentence I consistently overrode the English translation.

36 At one point, the jester even threatens Zarathustra himself, telling him "go away from this town, or tomorrow I shall leap over you, one living over one dead." Nietzsche, *Thus Spoke Zarathustra*, 21. Here we see that even the prophet himself can be redeemed, can be overcome.

37 When I presented this paper to the postgraduate students at Birkbeck College in London, I was asked how one could tell if one was a last man or this failed subject. My answer was that the failed subject knows who she is precisely because she has gone through the wringer and suffered from Nietzsche's cruel maneuvers. The last man might think that he is "redeemed" from redemption, but that belief is itself an artifact of his allegiance to phantasm.

38 Nietzsche, *Thus Spoke Zarathustra*, 199. In the original German: "Es gibt vielerlei Weg und Weise der Überwindung: da siehe du zu! Aber nur ein Possenreißer denkt: 'der Mensch kann auch übersprungen werden.' " *Also sprach Zarathustra*, 162. To think such a thing thus makes the reader her- or himself a kind of jester, perhaps in on the joke that Nietzsche is pulling (or "ripping") on us.

39 In my discussions with the students for the Kent Summer School in Paris, one of the students, Kristina Cufar, noted that the overman didn't necessarily have to not exist for the subject to be turned to her own devices. He could also be simply and utterly unavailable, leaving human time and space alone for us mere mortals. In a sense, the overman could work in both senses, first, as failing to appear and, second, as possibly appearing but in a way that is utterly unconnected with human beings and so effectively nonexistent as far as we are concerned.

40 See Nietzsche, *Ecce Homo*.

41 Nietzsche, *Thus Spoke Zarathustra*, 225. This raises important questions about who is doing the leaping here. Is it the overman or the one that the overman "overcomes"?

42 Nietzsche, *Thus Spoke Zarathustra*, 225; Nietzsche *Also sprach Zarathustra*, 185.

43 I think this is what Pappas is accusing Safranski of (see note 15).

44 Tara Mulqueen noted that the overman is often associated with the figure of the child, and I think this is apt for my argument as well. The child represents a new beginning and so, in a sense, does the overman. Because we will never stop our desiring salvation, we will always need to be lured and then disappointed over and over again. When this cycle is complete, we will, like the child, begin anew and reenter into the horizon of the overman, even as we have very recently just left it.

45 Nietzsche, *Thus Spoke Zarathustra*, 195.

46 This too strikes me as a highly anarchist way to think about temporality. The very all-at-onceness of our usual understandings of political solutions smacks too much of eschatology and teleology, that is to say, of archism. To think of history cyclically, of a pattern that we must repeat over and over (with no guarantee of getting it "right," indeed more a guarantee of never doing so) is consistent, I think, with a more anarchist sensibility about time wherein there is no privileged direction but only a sequence of moments that can be read and connected in a variety of ways.

47 Nietzsche, *Ecce Homo*, 68.

48 Nietzsche, *Gay Science*, section 341, 273–274.

49 This is almost exactly what Walter Benjamin counsels when he says of the Sixth Commandment against killing that "neither divine judgment nor the grounds for this judgment can be known in advance. Those who base a condemnation of all violent killing of one person by another on the commandment are therefore mistaken. It exists not as a criterion of judgment, but as a guideline for the actions of persons or communities who have to wrestle with it in solitude and, in exceptional cases, to take on themselves the responsibility of ignoring it." Benjamin, "Critique of Violence," 250.

50 In this way, the claim that the film *Groundhog Day* is "Nietzschean" is, I think, dead wrong. In the film, in which Bill Murray is condemned to repeat the same day over and over (and in which he is conscious of that fact), the plot offers that when Murray "gets it right" (that is, fixes himself, becomes a better person, etc.), he can be released from this repetition. But a Nietzschean movie would have an opposite conclusion. Murray wouldn't be released until he desired to be *himself*, that is, the unpleasant and loutish person that he is at the start of the movie, with no beautiful girlfriend, no sunny disposition, nothing. If he could choose *that*, he would have something far better than a happy ending in Nietzschean terms; he would have experienced himself as he is and not as he should or wishes to be.

51 Some of the complexity of this can be seen in section 276 of *Gay Science* where Nietzsche writes, "I want to learn more and more to see as beautiful what is

necessary in things; then I shall be one of those who make things beautiful. *Amor fati*: let that be my love henceforth! I do not want to wage war against what is ugly. I do not want to accuse; I do not even want to accuse those who accuse. *Looking away* shall be my only negation. And all in all and on the whole: some day I wish to be only a Yes-sayer" (223). Here, we see that Nietzsche is not quite saying yes to everything. He still needs to look away from what he doesn't want. That isn't quite being "only a Yes-sayer."

52 For more on this, see Han-Pile, "Nietzsche and Amor Fati."

53 This is a particularly troubling question I find insofar as love itself—when treated as a political concept—has such a dark and troubling history. In general, as previously noted, I find thinkers who speak of love to have given up on politics. Nietzsche is the one big exception to this. For more on this, see my *Love Is a Sweet Chain*.

54 Quoted in Frost, *Lessons from a Materialist Thinker*, 83.

55 Frost, *Lessons from a Materialist Thinker*, 84.

56 Frost, *Lessons from a Materialist Thinker*, 84.

57 Nietzsche, *Ecce Homo*, 36.

58 Nietzsche, *Ecce Homo*, 36.

59 Nietzsche, *Ecce Homo*, 34.

60 Nietzsche, *Ecce Homo*, 34–35. This is one of the rare places where Nietzsche does approach Hobbes, given the latter's own treatment (and deliberate mistranslation) of *Nosce te ipsum* in the introduction to *Leviathan*. Hobbes, *Leviathan*, 10.

61 Nietzsche, *The Genealogy of Morals*, 178–179. Here again, I am reminded of the value of Samantha Frost's work. In her latest book, *Biocultural Creatures*, Frost shows how the complicated and multiple selves that we are have a basis in biology wherein we are constantly changing and porous subjects who change, not only on the level of society, but also on the level of selves, cells, and even in terms of our DNA. See Frost, *Biocultural Creatures*.

5. *"Come, Come!"*

1 I think "objects" would be a better term because it avoids that sense of being subjected as well as pointing to the material nature of identity. It further appeals because it has the connotation of "objecting" to the modes of identity made possible by interpellation.

2 Aristodemou, *Law, Psychoanalysis, Society*, 6.

3 Coates doesn't really fit any of these definitions. I include him less because I find him to be misinterpellated per se but rather in terms of the way he epitomizes a strategy of refusal that enriches and fleshes out Fanon's own ideas on the subject.

4 Benjamin, "Franz Kafka," 798.

5 See, e.g., Agamben, "Bartleby or On Contingency," in *Potentialities*.

6 Melville, "Bartleby, the Scrivener," 45.

7   Melville, "Bartleby, the Scrivener," 47.

8   Melville, "Bartleby, the Scrivener," 47.

9   Melville, "Bartleby, the Scrivener," 57.

10 Melville, "Bartleby, the Scrivener," 53.

11 Benjamin, "Critique of Violence," 246.

12 I discuss this sort of conspiracy at length (albeit without reference to Bartleby) in *Textual Conspiracies: Walter Benjamin, Idolatry and Political Theory*. In a sense, Bartleby is himself a fetish; like a fetish, like the bust of Cicero too, he can't be thrown away.

13 Agamben sees Benjamin's discussion of the general strike as an example of inoperativity but I see it as instead a deep subversion from within the bounds of operability. Similarly, Bartleby himself evinces many of the strategies of resistance from within the confines of capitalist production. As Bonnie Honig noted to me, he begins by "work to rule," proceeds to a general strike, and eventually resorts to a hunger strike as a way to resist and thwart capitalist forms of subjecthood and productivity. Here, as I'll explain further, Bartleby does not need to be stripped down to "bare life" in order to resist. In fact, the very presumption of a movement down to the pith of his being as a representational figure is called into question by the challenges he poses to the workings of interpellating authority.

14 See Whyte, *Catastrophe and Redemption*.

15 Melville, "Bartleby, the Scrivener," 48.

16 Melville, "Bartleby, the Scrivener," 58.

17 Melville, "Bartleby, the Scrivener," 59.

18 Melville, "Bartleby, the Scrivener," 59. The students in my summer course at the Kent Summer School in Critical Theory noted that, in fact, Nippers and Turkey were in their own way also rebelling against the order that was imposed on them through small acts of sabotage and willed incompetence. (One of them at one point uses a cookie as a seal and they both drink and err in their work on a regular basis.) But there is definitely something much more marked about the way that Bartleby defies and subverts the system than these other characters do.

19 Melville, "Bartleby, the Scrivener," 48.

20 Melville, "Bartleby, the Scrivener," 61.

21 Melville, "Bartleby, the Scrivener," 61.

22 Benjamin, *Origin of German Tragic Drama*, 217–218. As if recognizing this same separation between body and soul in Bartleby, the narrator says, "I might give alms to his body; but his body did not pain him; it was his soul that suffered, and his soul I could not reach." Melville, "Bartleby, the Scrivener," 56. He also speaks of Bartleby's "cadaverous triumph" over him (62). I discuss this radical nature of corpses, and especially unburied ones like Michael Brown in my new book project, *Unburied Bodies: Sovereign Authority and the Subversive Power of the Corpse*.

23 Melville, "Bartleby, the Scrivener," 65.

24 Melville, "Bartleby, the Scrivener," 65.

25 Melville, "Bartleby, the Scrivener," 62.

26 As Bonnie Honig notes, this is akin to granting them a kind of retroactive *amor fati* since it removes the possibility of the false hope that keeps them from loving their own self (and "fate").

27 Melville, "Bartleby, the Scrivener," 73.

28 Melville, "Bartleby, the Scrivener," 73–74.

29 Of course, there is another way to think about this, which is to have more sympathy for those who lost their money and their ring. This certainly doesn't seem like "salvation for them" because they never knew that their letter was coming; they have not been allowed to have their own subjectivity involved or disturbed in the process. This is therefore only a partial and potential salvation, not a direct interference with the phantasms of the affected individuals.

30 Benjamin, "On the Concept of History," 390.

31 Benjamin, "Franz Kafka," 811.

32 Fitzpatrick, *Modernism and the Grounds of Law*, 47.

33 Woolf, *To the Lighthouse*, 4.

34 Woolf, *To the Lighthouse*, 4.

35 Woolf, *To the Lighthouse*, 4.

36 Woolf, *To the Lighthouse*, 6. To be fair, this atmosphere is as much a response to Mrs. Ramsay as to her husband and perhaps foreshadows the way that she too will not provide a satisfying answer to the novel's search for the object.

37 Woolf, *To the Lighthouse*, 4.

38 Woolf, *To the Lighthouse*, 4.

39 Woolf, *To the Lighthouse*, 15.

40 Woolf, *To the Lighthouse*, 15.

41 Woolf, *To the Lighthouse*, 9.

42 Woolf, *To the Lighthouse*, 9.

43 Woolf, *To the Lighthouse*, 10.

44 Woolf, *To the Lighthouse*, 37.

45 Woolf, *To the Lighthouse*, 38.

46 Woolf, *To the Lighthouse*, 14.

47 Woolf, *To the Lighthouse*, 21.

48 Woolf, *To the Lighthouse*, 22.

49 Woolf, *To the Lighthouse*, 22.

50 Woolf, *To the Lighthouse*, 67.

51 Woolf, *To the Lighthouse*, 67–68.

52 Woolf, *To the Lighthouse*, 68.

53 Woolf, *To the Lighthouse*, 68.

54 Woolf, *To the Lighthouse*, 68.

55 Woolf, *To the Lighthouse*, 68.

56 Woolf, *To the Lighthouse*, 69.

57 Woolf, *To the Lighthouse*, 70.

58 Woolf, *To the Lighthouse*, 73.

59 Woolf, To the Lighthouse, 73.

60 Woolf, To the Lighthouse, 72.

61 Here, I am reminded of Lacanian philosophy whereby the *objet petit a* is a flaw that is required in the perception of reality in order to sell it as "real." In Machiavelli's discussion of the Roman religion, we see a similar desire on the parts of the Romans. Their religion has to be light enough for them to manipulate it for their own purposes but solid enough for them to believe that the signs and auguries they have created out of it are meaningful and prophetic.

62 Toril Moi, for one, reads the novel in much the same way insofar as she sees Lily Briscoe as being in some sense the true heroine of the novel (despite the great allure of Mrs. Ramsay). What for Moi is a matter of feminist principles (so that Lily's refusal to bow to misogynist norms harkens to a different form of gender relations) tracks very well with the alternative form of object relations that is also promised in this novel. See Moi, *Sexual/Textual Politics*.

63 Woolf, To the Lighthouse, 11. The reference here to "little Chinese eyes" may show that Woolf herself is not immune to forms of racism and other foibles of interpellation (it doesn't seem to be meant as a compliment). It could also, or simultaneously, reference something else, the line of poetry that initially inspires Mrs. Ramsay's reverie: "The China rose is all abloom and buzzing with the honey bee." But in Lily's case, this reference (if it is indeed accurate) gives us, once again, not magic but its opposite.

64 Woolf, To the Lighthouse, 28.

65 Woolf, To the Lighthouse, 12–13.

66 Woolf, To the Lighthouse, 82.

67 Woolf, To the Lighthouse, 85. That word "presumably" is a mark of her rebellion, perhaps.

68 Woolf, To the Lighthouse, 93.

69 Woolf, To the Lighthouse, 116.

70 Woolf, To the Lighthouse, 99–100.

71 Woolf, To the Lighthouse, 107.

72 Woolf, To the Lighthouse, 108.

73 Woolf, To the Lighthouse, 89.

74 Woolf, To the Lighthouse, 117.

75 Woolf, To the Lighthouse, 116.

76 Benjamin, "Franz Kafka," 811.

77 This is reminiscent too of the moment in *Two Girls, Fat and Thin* as described by Lauren Berlant when Justine walks "with her arms around her middle." If anything, this moment is even more bitter, more failed, or at least more legible as such.

78 Brown, *Politics Out of History*, 4.

79 Woolf, *Orlando*, 201. I am grateful to Başak Ertür for pointing out this wonderful passage and its congruence with my other work.

80 I say this not to belittle Lily Briscoe or Bartleby but rather to point out that there are many ways to experience our anarchic subjectivity and that the Mrs. Ramsays of this world do not have a monopoly on the showier side of things.

6. "Consent to Not Be a Single Being"

1 This is an insight that first attracted me to Benjamin; the idea that when you see the police (at least in the United States) walking around with guns coming out of their holsters, they can literally do whatever they want. And they often do.

2 Benjamin, "Critique of Violence," 243.

3 To be clear, I am not trying to argue that accusation is meaningless or that everyone who has ever been charged with a crime could not have done it. Within the bounds of the legal system, the logic of law prevails. Yet the price we pay for the law's pose of all-knowingness is a system in which the decision is taken away from a community (the community that has suffered under law) and given instead to a system that is based on the usurpation of its authority.

4 Benjamin, "Critique of Violence," 242.

5 To argue that it was would be to deny the very internal multiplicity that I am arguing misinterpellation gives us access to.

6 As Sarah Burgess noted here, being called by the law and being called by the police—for all of Althusser and Rancière's interventions—is not the same thing. One issue with Brown, Garner, and Gray was that they were never given a chance to face the law as opposed to the police. I think this distinction is important to keep in mind. At the same time, Bland's case (where she died while in custody, falsely said to have killed herself) suggests that even when called by the law itself (i.e., hailed in front of a judge and a court), the subject is far from immune from state violence. It is in this sense that Rancière's discussion of the police power of the state works well as a way to understand state violence.

7 Of course, as Ben Ratskoff pointed out in my Kent Summer School in Critical Theory seminar, racial identity and the universal are always present even when subjects of color are not being directly addressed because white people have a race too (despite a marked tendency, in liberal theory but unfortunately even in left discourse at times, to act as if they did not). Silindiwe Sibanda made a similar point when she noted that if race is not specifically mentioned in a text—certainly in a text written by a white person—one can basically assume that the subject in question is considered to be white.

8 Here, as elsewhere, I am using the term "agents" to describe the police merely because that is what they are generally called. I do not think of them as being agents in the philosophical sense of the word because, as I'll argue in this chapter and elsewhere, their decisions are mapped out for them via the operations of interpellation itself.

9   And, of course, there is a class dimension in place here as well; poor whites have a very different relationship to the law than rich ones but even so, it is not the same as black subjects and other people of color have.

10 In this chapter, I focus on the black experience in America although Frank Wilderson III claims that this is true for black people the world over. See Wilderson, *Red, White and Black*.

11 The strategy of refusal can take on many different guises and it is not limited to black subjects. As Audra Simpson tells us in *Mohawk Interruptus*: "The Mohawks of Kahnawà:ke are nationals of a precontact Indigenous polity that simply refuse to stop being themselves. In other words, they insist on being and acting as people who belong to a nation other than the United States or Canada. Their political form predates and survives 'conquest'; it is tangible (albeit strangulated by colonial governmentality) and is tied to sovereign practices. This architecture is not fanciful; it is in place because the Mohawks or Kahnawà:ke share a genealogical kinship relationship with other native peoples of North America and they *know this*. They refuse *to let go of this knowledge*. In fact, they enact this knowledge through marriage practices, political engagements, and the way they live their lives." Simpson, *Mohawk Interruptus*, 2.

12 Kafka, *Amerika*, 185.

13 Kafka, *Amerika*, 186.

14 Kafka, *Amerika*, 187.

15 Kafka, *Amerika*, 187–188.

16 The French continue to use the verb "interpeller" to refer, among other things, to the moment when a police officer stops someone that they are suspicious of.

17 Kafka, *Amerika*, 188.

18 Kafka, *Amerika*, 189.

19 Kafka, *Amerika*, 189.

20 Kafka, *Amerika*, 190.

21 Kafka, *Amerika*, 190.

22 To be fair, Delamarche does also help Karl to escape the police, but it is only so that he can continue to dominate and exploit Karl for his own purposes.

23 Kafka, *Amerika*, 191.

24 Nietzsche, *Genealogy of Morals*, 178–179.

25 As Sarah Burgess points out, the law does this to all of us, but maybe in Karl's case that response is closer to the surface than it normally is because the benefits of the law do not seem as clear to him as it is to many (generally privileged) subjects.

26 Kafka, *Amerika*, 192.

27 Kafka, *Amerika*, 192.

28 Kafka, *Amerika*, 192–193.

29 Kafka, *Amerika*, 194.

30 Besides which, no laws were actually broken.

31 Kafka, *Amerika*, 193.

32 This raises the interesting question of what the "script" of the law actually is for the police. The fact that after shooting unarmed people the police often have recourse to procedural explanations suggests that acting "in the name of the law" doesn't preclude violence. Sometimes it can even incite or cause it. In this way, the violence of the police cannot be said to be the act of poor judgment, individual racism, or what have you but is rather the result of a much more extensive form of state violence.

33 In *Textual Conspiracies*, I make a similar argument based on Machiavelli's reading of the knowledge of the public versus that of the prince. Whereas the public in all of its collective complexity knows everything, the prince only knows what he is told. The prince is thus limited by the quality of his advisors and the limits of their knowledge while the public is only limited by the extent to which it is able to take advantage of its all-knowingness (by being able to talk both individually and collectively).

34 Kafka, *Amerika*, 272.

35 Kafka, *Amerika*, 269.

36 Kafka, *Amerika*, 269.

37 Kafka, *Amerika*, 275.

38 Kafka, *Amerika*, 277.

39 See Thompson, "The Negro Who Disappeared," 195.

40 The reasons for this choice of names appear to come out of Karl's near perfect passivity. We are told that "Negro" was a nickname that he received at a previous job but it is not from any job that we see him as having held (the fractured notion of the text means that any internal chapter where this reference would have been made is either lost to us or was never written). He is thus depicted as offering this name for lack of a better one and also to disguise his true name which, for reasons that are also not really specified, he is reluctant to use.

41 Löwy, *Redemption and Utopia*, 76.

42 I am indebted to Richard Westerman, as well as the larger discussion his comments elicited for this observation. This question reminds me of the recent uproar about Rachel Dolezal, a woman with white parents who nonetheless claimed to be African American (and actually wrote and spoke out on themes related to the black experience in America).

43 In discussing Ellison's critique of the American Communist Party, I do not want to exclude other readings of the party as it actually existed; Jodi Dean for example offers examples of the actual communist party which took the condition of black Americans very seriously. See Dean, *Crowds and Party*. Rather than get drawn into a communist versus anticommunist debate, I'd like to think of the Brotherhood as yet another iteration of a hegemonic interpellating authority, one that runs along the lines of liberalism as I've been describing it in this book so far. This is how Ellison treats "the Brotherhood"—at least in his view—and hence it fits into the larger patterns of what I've been critiquing as well.

44 Ellison, *Invisible Man*, 3.

45 Ellison, *Invisible Man*, 363.

46 In my Kent Summer School in Critical Theory seminar, Silindiwe Sibanda suggested that the marionette Sambo dolls are a kind of foreshadowing of the way that Clifton himself seems to be acting in a marionette play while the narrator sees him killed. She also noted the way that Clifton's rage at his own manipulation by the Brotherhood is reflected in the kind of loathing, and possibly self-loathing, that he expresses in and through the dolls.

47 Ellison, *Invisible Man*, 434.

48 Ellison, *Invisible Man*, 434.

49 Ellison, *Invisible Man*, 439. Silindiwe Sibanda offered this reading, along with the idea that Clifton's beauty was a way for the narrator to fall in love with blackness, during the Kent Summer School in Critical Theory seminar.

50 In saying this, I recognize that "brotherhood" has its own baggage, aligned with the "fraternité" of the French revolution and possibly reinforcing gender and sex hierarchies. Derrida, for one, argues that brotherhood has a bloody history. See Derrida, *The Politics of Friendship*. As I've been arguing and will continue to argue, this form of brotherhood comes from an entirely different position than the French universal. As for its gender and hierarchical exclusions, "siblinghood" might be a better term although it is not one suggested by Ellison himself.

51 Ellison, *Invisible Man*, 436.

52 Ellison, *Invisible Man*, 446.

53 Ellison, *Invisible Man*, 450.

54 Ellison, *Invisible Man*, 453.

55 I would say in this sense that Ellison's evocation of African American culture is not quite the same as the négritude movement that Fanon struggled with. It is not so much "authentic" as interfering or distracting in Ellison's narrative.

56 Nietzsche, *Thus Spoke Zarathustra*, 20.

57 Ellison, *Invisible Man*, 454–455.

58 Ellison, *Invisible Man*, 456.

59 Ellison, *Invisible Man*, 456.

60 Ellison, *Invisible Man*, 458.

61 Ellison, *Invisible Man*, 459. Tellingly, here again the narrator leaves off the "the" that usually precedes Brotherhood.

62 Ellison, *Invisible Man*, 459.

63 Djebar, *Children of the New World*, 120. I discuss this passage at much greater length in *Textual Conspiracies*.

64 Benjamin, *Origin of German Tragic Drama*, 183.

65 Benjamin, *Origin of German Tragic Drama*, 183.

66 Benjamin, *Origin of German Tragic Drama*, 183.

67 Ellison, *Invisible Man*, 455.

68 If "our hope shot down" is less a call than a statement, it nonetheless serves as a form of counterinterpellation. One can dwell on the loss of friends and loved

ones murdered by a legal system that actively desires their deaths—and certainly Ellison's narrator and Coates both do that. But one can also see in the statement that killing hope can lead to some radical and powerful effects. It makes possible what wasn't possible before. Here, one does not count on the venality of the law—its desire to kill black bodies—as a way to kill hope. That particular act of violence must come from within the community itself (hence, it must be purposive). To kill hope (to announce "our hope shot down") is a response, a form of struggle and not simply an act of mourning.

69 Ellison, *Invisible Man*, 16.

70 Indeed, implicitly incorporating his grandfather's advice after the events with Clifton's murder and burial, the narrator later says, "I started yessing [the Brotherhood] the next day and it began beautifully." Ellison, *Invisible Man*, 513.

71 I am grateful to Sarah Burgess for the clarity of her insight on this question.

72 In this case, the officer in question is himself black but that changes nothing for Coates in terms of the workings of institutionalized racism.

73 Coates, *Between the World and Me*, 79.

74 Coates, *Between the World and Me*, 81–82.

75 Coates, *Between the World and Me*, 69–70.

76 Coates, *Between the World and Me*, 70.

77 Djebar, *Children of the New World*, 120.

78 Coates, *Between the World and Me*, 94.

79 Coates, *Between the World and Me*, 94–95.

80 Coates, *Between the World and Me*, 71.

81 Moten and Harney, "General Antagonism," 126.

82 Moten and Harney, "General Antagonism," 129.

83 Moten and Harney, "General Antagonism," 129.

84 Moten and Harney, "General Antagonism," 136.

85 Moten and Harney, "General Antagonism," 154.

86 See Moten, "to consent not to be a single being." That line comes from Glissant, *Poetic Intentions*.

87 Moten, "to consent not to be a single being."

88 See, for example, Irigaray, *To Be Two*. See also Irigaray and Burke, "When Our Lips Speak Together."

89 See Wilderson, "Gramsci's Black Marx," 225. I am grateful to Diego Arrocha for pointing out this essay to me. Wilderson writes, for example, that "the black body in the US is that constant reminder that not only can work not be reformed [the identity Gramsci would opt for as a way to resist liberal capitalist blandishments] but it cannot be transformed to accommodate all subjects: work is a white category. The fact that millions upon millions of black people work misses the point. The point is we were never meant to be workers; in other words, capital/white supremacy's dream did not envision us as being incorporated or incorporative. From the very beginning, we were meant to be accumulated and die." Wilderson, "Gramsci's Black Marx," 238. This quote shows the way that universalism can sneak in on so many levels. It suggests

the dangers of a turn to the universal more generally. Many on the left have argued for a kind of strategic engagement with the universal as a tool to expand rights and power for the subaltern communities that are normally excluded by it. In my view—and I think Wilderson makes this point very clear—the universal has neither a true meaning nor a strategic use. Its assertion or call is just an opportunity to demonstrate its failure to exist. With the misinterpellated subject, and, I would add via Wilderson's intervention, the misinterpellated subject as black body, there is no accommodation to the universal (nor can there be).

90   Or if it does (because one can never tell other anarchists what to do and think), I think its reversion to archism would be very swift, basically instantaneous.

91   Coates, *Between the World and Me*, 151.

92   See Indigenous Action Media, "Accomplices Not Allies." I am grateful to Andrew Dilts for pointing this site out to me. Fred Moten paraphrases the thought of Fred Hampton, saying, "Look: the problematic of coalition is that coalition isn't something that emerges so you can come help me, a maneuver that always gets tracked back to your own interests. The coalition emerges out of your recognition that it's fucked up for you, in the same way that we've already recognized that it's fucked up for us. I don't need your help. I just need you to recognize that this shit is killing you, too, however much more softly, you stupid motherfucker, you know?" Moten and Harney, "General Antagonism," 140–141. He also says, to a question on whether the Italian autonomists should have referenced the black radical movement in their own understanding of strategies and tactics that "the bottom line is I think a whole lot of that kind of work of acknowledging a debt intellectually is really predicated on a notion that somehow the black radical tradition is ennobled when we say that the autonomists picked something up from it. It's as if that makes it more valuable, whereas it doesn't need to be ennobled by its connections to autonomist thought. Rather, what's at stake is the possibility of a general movement that then gets fostered when we recognize these two more or less independent irruptions of a certain kind of radical social action and thinking." Moten and Harney, "General Antagonism," 153.

93   And, anyway, Locke's model is not truly autarkic either because his patriarchal landowners extend their own personal boundaries across the boundaries of other subject people: women, servants, children, and so on.

94   Fanon, *Black Skin, White Masks*, 115.

95   Moten and Harney, "Michael Brown," 84.

96   Moten and Harney, "Michael Brown," 84. This is an allusion to the fact that Darren Wilson in his testimony spoke of Michael Brown as looking like a "demon."

97   I want to reiterate here that I remain generally suspicious of evoking love in political theory but I think that when it comes to Nietzsche's concept of *amor fati*, it becomes possible to think about love in a way that does not replicate

(and actually undoes) the usual workings of love as a political doctrine. For more on this see my forthcoming "What Kind of Love Is *Amor Fati*?"

7. "I Can Believe"

1. In practice, there is no necessary temporal ordering to this circulation of authority; it is generally simultaneous.
2. For more on von Trier's relationship to women and feminism, see Huffer, "Nymph Shoots Back."
3. I tend to shy away from ever using the word "love" as a positive valence in political theory. I wrote an earlier book (*Love Is a Sweet Chain*) about why love generally masks hierarchies and bolsters the very interpellative processes that this book is set in direct opposition to. The love that Nietzsche is talking about could not be more different. It is a kind of antilove, a love that exposes and subverts rather than one that obfuscates and ranks.
4. All quotations from the film are my own transcriptions.
5. This is a question that Bonnie Honig put to me when I presented the paper at a conference that was part of the production of this symposium.
6. Another way to say this is that, although they think they are the consigners, they are, in fact, the consignees.
7. In this way, von Trier's treatment of Bess's God reminds me very much of Franz Rosenzweig's concept of the "ever-new will of God's revelation." This idea offers that God is completely contingent, completely free of determination, and, thus, far from being a source of predestination and law, is a force for change and unpredictability. This was quoted in Batnitzky, *Idolatry and Representation*, 225.
8. Throughout this book, I use the word "local" as a good thing and "universal" as a bad thing. Richard Joyce in a recent work has argued very convincingly that this prejudice may obscure the ways in which international law for one can have very radical implications so that locality need not be as small and as distinct as I (and many other leftists) tend to argue. The international and the global are not the same thing as the universal but, as Joyce argues, their scope allows them to better challenge the universal on its own terms. See Joyce, *Competing Sovereignties*.
9. It is hard to say where this God comes from for Bess. Certainly Bess experiences love and sexuality as a pleasure—as opposed to the rest of her community—and this may constitute the beginning of her own internal split. Or it could be, as already suggested, a form of madness, or a subconscious strategy, or all of the above.
10. See Benjamin, "Meaning of Time in the Moral Universe," 286.
11. Lars Tønder made the great observation that when she speaks as God in this scene, God's deep Scottish accent seems to become more like her own. Perhaps this signals that Bess has become "one" after all, now allowed to go forward as herself and no longer needing the device of God any further.

12 Lori Marso's incisive observations helped me think further about this question.

13 Nietzsche, *Thus Spoke Zarathustra*, 20.

14 It is Jan and not her God who buries her, but the bells in heaven signify God's approval of this final task.

15 And, in a way, von Trier himself enjoys this deprivation. As Lynne Huffer noted to me, von Trier withheld certain key scenes for us, particularly the scene of Bess's murder. This too may be a way to deny us what we secretly desire (the money shot), leaving us bereft in ways that could be both sadistic and—if I were going to be more charitable to von Trier—left to our own devices, much as God does for Bess.

16 Bess's ending is horrible. It may even be tragic, but it is not tragic in the sense in which that term is usually used; it is "fated" but in a way that defies our ordinary usages of such a term. Here, I am thinking of the way that Miriam Leonard defines tragedy in "I Know What Has to Happen."

Conclusion

1 See Hobbes, *Leviathan*, 10. This is Hobbes's undoubtedly deliberate mistranslation of *nosce teipsum*, which means know thyself. Here, as already noted, Hobbes converges with Nietzsche in his evocation of this phrase.

    I discuss this idea at some length in *Subverting the Leviathan: Reading Thomas Hobbes as a Radical Democrat*.

2 See Butler, *Bodies That Matter*, 232. Sometimes the baby's own body resists these binaries and then the real violence and authority of such calls become more legible (even as the gender of the baby becomes less legible).

3 Benjamin, "Critique of Violence," 245.

4 I wrote an essay entitled "Anarchist All the Way Down: Walter Benjamin's Subversion of Authority in Text, Thought and Action," in a special issue of *Parrhesia* (2014). There, I discussed the way that Benjamin is anarchist not only in his politics (which I recognize is a not uncontroversial claim) but also in the way he employs language and the way he engages in political theology.

5 See Rancière, *Disagreement*, 29–30.

6 In Robyn Marasco's great new book, *The Highway of Despair*, the answer to that question is a boisterous yes! I see my arguments and hers as being very much aligned although with very different emphases.

BIBLIOGRAPHY

Agamben, Giorgio. *Potentialities: Collected Essays in Philosophy.* Stanford, CA: Stanford University Press, 1999.

Aleya-Sghaier, Amira. "The Tunisian Revolution: The Revolution of Dignity." In Ricardo René Larémont, *Revolution, Revolt and Reform in North Africa: The Arab Spring and Beyond,* 30–52. New York: Routledge, 2014.

Althusser, Louis. "Ideology and the State." In *Lenin and Philosophy and Other Essays,* 85–126. New York: Monthly Review Press, 2001.

Anderson, Benedict. *Under Three Flags: Anarchism and the Anti-Colonial Imagination.* New York: Verso, 2005.

Ansell-Pearson, Keith. "Who Is the Ubermensch? Time, Truth, and Woman in Nietzsche." *Journal of the History of Ideas* 53, no. 2 (April–June 1992): 309–331.

Arendt, Hannah. "On Violence." In *Crises of the Republic,* 103–184. New York: Harcourt Brace Jovanovich, 1972.

Aristodemou, Maria. *Law, Psychoanalysis, Society: Taking the Unconscious Seriously.* London: Routledge, 2014.

Badiou, Alain. *The Communist Hypothesis.* New York: Verso, 2010.

Badiou, Alain. *Ethics: An Essay on the Understanding of Evil.* New York: Verso, 2001.

Batnitzky, Leora. *Idolatry and Representation: The Philosophy of Franz Rosenzweig Reconsidered.* Princeton, NJ: Princeton University Press, 2000.

Benjamin, Walter. *The Arcades Project.* Translated by Howard Eiland and Kevin McLaughlin. Cambridge, MA: Harvard University Press, 2002.

Benjamin, Walter. "Critique of Violence." In *Walter Benjamin: Selected Writings, Vol. 1, 1913–1926,* edited by Marcus Bullock and Michael W. Jennings, 235–252. Cambridge, MA: Harvard University Press, 2004.

Benjamin, Walter. "Franz Kafka: On the Tenth Anniversary of his Death." In *Walter Benjamin: Selected Writings, Vol. 2, 1927–1934,* edited by Michael W. Jennings, Howard Eiland, and Gary Smith, 794–818. Cambridge, MA: Harvard University Press, 1999.

Benjamin, Walter. "Letter to Gershom Scholem on Franz Kafka." In *Walter Benjamin: Selected Writings, Vol. 3, 1935–1938,* edited by Howard Eiland and Michael W. Jennings, 322–329. Cambridge, MA: Harvard University Press, 2002.

Benjamin, Walter. "The Meaning of Time in the Moral Universe." In *Walter Benjamin: Selected Writings, Vol. 1, 1913–1926*, edited by Marcus Bullock and Michael W. Jennings, 286–287. Cambridge, MA: Harvard University Press, 2004.

Benjamin, Walter. "On the Concept of History." In *Walter Benjamin: Selected Writings, Vol. 4: 1938–1940*, edited by Howard Eiland and Michael W. Jennings, 389–400. Cambridge, MA: Harvard University Press, 2006.

Benjamin, Walter. *Origin of German Tragic Drama*. New York: Verso, 1998.

Benjamin, Walter. "Reflections on Radio." In *Radio Benjamin*, edited by Lecia Rosenthal, 363–364. New York: Verso, 2014.

Benjamin, Walter. "The Work of Art in the Age of Its Technical Reproducibility. (Third Version)." In *Walter Benjamin: Selected Writings, Vol. 4: 1938–1940*, edited by Howard Eiland and Michael W. Jennings, 251–283. Cambridge, MA: Harvard University Press, 2006.

Berlant, Lauren. *Cruel Optimism*. Durham: Duke University Press, 2011.

Bhabha, Homi K. "Remembering Fanon." In *Rethinking Fanon: The Continuing Dialogue*, edited by Nigel C. Gibson, 179–196. New York: Prometheus, 1999.

Bouamoud, Mohamed. *Bouâzizi ou L'énticelle qui a destitué Ben Ali* [Bouâzizi or the spark that deposed Ben Ali]. Tunis, Tunisia: Almaha Editions, 2011.

Brown, Wendy. *Politics Out of History*. Princeton, NJ: Princeton University Press, 2001.

Brown, Wendy. *Undoing the Demos*. Cambridge, MA: MIT Press, 2015.

Buck-Morss, Susan. *Hegel, Haiti and Universal History*. Pittsburgh, PA: University of Pittsburgh Press, 2009.

Butler, Judith. *Bodies That Matter: On the Discursive Limits of Sex*. New York: Routledge, 2011.

Butler, Judith. *Gender Trouble*. New York: Routledge, 1990.

Butler, Judith. *The Psychic Life of Power: Theories in Subjection*. Stanford, CA: Stanford University Press, 1997.

Cherki, Alice. *Frantz Fanon: A Portrait*. Ithaca, NY: Cornell University Press, 2006.

Ciccariello-Maher, George. *We Created Chávez: A People's History of the Venezuelan Revolution*. Durham: Duke University Press, 2013.

Coates, Ta-Nehisi. *Between the World and Me*. New York: Spiegel and Grau, 2015.

Cocks, Joan. "On Commonality, Nationalism and Violence: Hannah Arendt, Rosa Luxemburg, and Frantz Fanon." In *Women in German Yearbook*, Vol. 12, 39–51. Lincoln: University of Nebraska Press, 1996.

Cohen, Margaret. "Benjamin's Phantasmagoria: The *Arcades Project*." In *The Cambridge Companion to Walter Benjamin*, edited by David S. Ferris. New York: Cambridge University Press, 2004.

Culbert, Jennifer. "The Banality of Evil: Cruddy Stuff That Happens on the Bus." Paper presented at the Western Political Science Association, April 2015.

Danto, Arthur. "Some Remarks on the Genealogy of Morals." In *Nietzsche, Genealogy, Morality: Essays on Nietzsche's "On the Genealogy of Morals,"* edited by Richard Shacht, 35–48. Berkeley: University of California Press, 1994.

Dean, Jodi. *The Communist Horizon*. New York: Verso, 2012.

Dean, Jodi. *Crowds and Party*. New York: Verso, 2016.

de Certeau, Michel. *The Practice of Everyday Life*. Berkeley: University of California Press, 1984.

de Gouges, Olympe. "Declaration of the Rights of Woman and Citizen." Pamphlet.

Deleuze, Gilles, Félix Guattari and Robert Brinkley. "What Is a Minor Literature?" *Mississippi Review* 11, no. 3 (Winter/Spring 1983): 13–33.

Derrida, Jacques. *The Politics of Friendship*. New York: Verso, 2006.

Dienst, Richard. *Still Life in Real Time: Theory After Television*. Durham, NC: Duke University Press, 1994.

Djebar, Assia. *Children of the New World: A Novel of the Algerian War*. New York: Feminist Press at the City University of New York, 2005.

Djebar, Assia. *Women of Algiers in Their Apartments*. Charlottesville: University of Virginia Press, 1992.

Dolar, Mladen. "Beyond Interpellation." *Qui Parle* 6, no. 2 (Spring/Summer 1993): 75–96.

Dubois, Laurent. *Avengers of the New World: The Story of the Haitian Revolution*. Cambridge, MA: Harvard University Press, 2005.

Dubois, Laurent, and John D. Garrigus. *Slave Revolution in the Caribbean 1789–1804: A Brief History with Documents*. New York: Bedford/St. Martin's, 2006.

Eagleton, Terry. "Ideology and Its Vicissitudes in Western Marxism." In *Mapping Ideology*, edited by Slavoj Žižek, 179–226. New York: Verso, 2012.

Ellison, Ralph. *Invisible Man*. New York: Vintage, 1995.

Fanon, Frantz. *Black Skin, White Masks*. New York: Grove, 1994.

Fanon, Frantz. *A Dying Colonialism*. New York, Grove, 1965.

Fanon, Frantz. *Les damnés de la terre*. Paris: La Découverte/Poche, 1991.

Fanon, Frantz. *Peau noire, masques blancs*. Paris: Points essais, 1971.

Fanon, Frantz. *Toward the African Revolution*. New York: Grove, 1967.

Fanon, Frantz. *The Wretched of the Earth*. New York: Grove, 2004.

Ferguson, Michaele. *Sharing Democracy*. New York: Oxford University Press, 2012.

Fick, Carolyn E. *The Making of Haiti: The Saint Domingue Revolution from Below*. Knoxville: University of Tennessee Press, 1990.

Fischer, Sibylle. *Modernity Disavowed: Haiti and the Cultures of Slavery in the Age of Revolution*. Durham: Duke University Press, 2004.

Fitzpatrick, Peter. *Modernism and the Grounds of Law*. New York: Cambridge University Press, 2001.

Foucault, Michel. "Truth and Power." In *Power/Knowledge: Selected Interviews and Other Writings, 1972–1977*, 109–133. New York: Pantheon, 1980.

Frank, Thomas. *What's the Matter with Kansas?* New York: Macmillan, 2005.

Frost, Samantha. *Biocultural Creatures: Toward a New Theory of the Human*. Durham: Duke University Press, 2016.

Frost, Samantha. *Lessons from a Materialist Thinker: Hobbesian Reflections on Ethics and Politics*. Stanford, CA: Stanford University Press, 2008.

Gibson, Nigel C. *Fanon: The Postcolonial Imagination*. Cambridge: Polity Press, 2003.

Glissant, Édouard. *Poetic Intentions*. Translated by Nathalie Stephens. Callicoon, NY: Nightboat, 2010.

Gordon, Lewis R. *Fanon and the Crisis of European Man: An Essay on Philosophy and the Human Sciences*. New York: Routledge, 1995.

Gordy, Katherine. *Living Ideology in Cuba: Socialism in Principle and Practice*. Ann Arbor: University of Michigan Press, 2015.

Guha, Ranajit. *Elementary Aspects of Peasant Insurgency in Colonial India*. Durham: Duke University Press, 1999.

Habermas, Jürgen. *Between Facts and Norms*. Cambridge: Polity Press, 1996.

Halberstam, Judith. *The Queer Art of Failure*. Durham: Duke University Press, 2011.

Han-Pile, Béatrice. "Nietzsche and Amor Fati." *European Journal of Philosophy* 19, no. 2 (2009): 224–261.

Hobbes, Thomas. *Leviathan*. Edited by Richard Tuck. New York: Cambridge University Press, 1996.

Honig, Bonnie. *Antigone, Interrupted*. New York: Cambridge University Press, 2013.

Honig, Bonnie. *Emergency Politics*. Princeton, NJ: Princeton University Press, 2011.

Honwana, Alcinda. *Youth and Revolution in Tunisia*. New York: Zed, 2013.

Huffer, Lynne. "The Nymph Shoots Back: Agamben, Nymphomaniac, and the Feel of the Agon." *Theory and Event* 18, no. 2 (2015).

Ileto, Reynaldo Clemeña. *Pasyon and Revolution: Popular Movements in the Philippines, 1840–1910*. Manila: Ateneo de Manila University Press, 1979.

Indigenous Action Media. "Accomplices Not Allies: Abolishing the Ally Industrial Complex." http://www.indigenousaction.org/accomplices-not-allies-abolishing-the-ally-industrial-complex/.

Irigaray, Luce. *To Be Two*. New York: Routledge, 2001.

Irigaray, Luce, and Carolyn Burke. "When Our Lips Speak Together." *Signs* 6, no. 1 (1980): 69–79.

James, C. L. R. *The Black Jacobins: Toussaint L'Ouverture and the San Domingo Revolution*. New York: Vintage, 1989.

Joyce, Richard. *Competing Sovereignties*. New York: Routledge, 2013.

Kafka, Franz. "Abraham." In *Parables and Paradoxes: Bilingual Edition*. New York: Schocken, 1961.

Kafka, Franz. *Amerika*. New York: Schocken, 2008.

Kohn, Margaret, and Keally McBride. *Political Theories of Decolonization: Postcolonialisms and the Problem of Foundations*. New York: Oxford University Press, 2011.

Lampert, Laurence. *Nietzsche's Teaching: An Interpretation of Thus Spoke Zarathustra*. New Haven, CT: Yale University Press, 1986.

Latour, Bruno. *We Have Never Been Modern*. Cambridge, MA: Harvard University Press, 1993.

Lazarus, Sylvain. *Anthropology of the Name*. New York: Seagull, 2015.

Leonard, Miriam. "I Know What Has to Happen: Lars von Trier's Tragic Politics." *Theory and Event* 18, no. 2 (2015).

Livy. *The Early History of Rome*. New York: Penguin Classics, 1984.

Locke, John. "Of the Conduct of the Understanding." In *The Philosophical Works of John Locke*. London: George Bell and Sons, 1908.

L'Ouverture, Toussaint. *Mémoires du Général Toussaint Louverture commentés par Saint-Rémy*. Guitalens-L'Albarède, France: Éditions La Girandole, 2009.

Löwy, Michael. *Redemption and Utopia: Jewish Libertarian Thought in Central Europe: A Study in Elective Affinity*. Stanford, CA: Stanford University Press, 1992.

Macey, David. "Fanon, Phenomenology, Race." *Radical Philosophy* 9 (May/June 1999): 8–14.

Macey, David. *Frantz Fanon: A Biography*. New York: Picador, 2000.

Machiavelli, Niccolò. *The Discourses on the First Ten Books of Livy*. New York: Modern Library, 1950.

Manela, Erez. *The Wilsonian Moment: Self-Determination and the Origins of Anticolonial Nationalism*. New York: Oxford University Press, 2009.

Marasco, Robyn. *The Highway of Despair: Critical Theory After Hegel*. New York: Columbia University Press, 2015.

Martel, James R. "Anarchist All the Way Down: Walter Benjamin's Subversion of Authority in Text, Thought and Action." Special Issue: Continental Philosophy in Australasia. *Parrhesia* 21 (2014): 3–12.

Martel, James R. *Love Is a Sweet Chain: Desire, Autonomy and Friendship in Liberal Political Theory*. New York: Routledge, 2001.

Martel, James R. "Nietzsche's Cruel Messiah." *Qui Parle* 20–22, no. 2 (Spring/Summer 2012): 199–224.

Martel, James R. *The One and Only Law: Walter Benjamin and the Second Commandment*. Ann Arbor: University of Michigan Press, 2014.

Martel, James R. *Subverting the Leviathan: Reading Thomas Hobbes as a Radical Democrat*. New York: Columbia University Press, 2007.

Martel, James R. *Textual Conspiracies: Walter Benjamin, Idolatry and Political Theory*. Ann Arbor: University of Michigan Press, 2011.

Martel, James R. *Unburied Bodies: Sovereign Authority and the Subversive Power of the Corpse*. Amherst, MA: Amherst College Press, forthcoming.

Martel, James R. "What Kind of Love Is Amor Fati?" In *The Radicalism of Romantic Love*, edited by Renata Grossi and David West. Farnham, UK: Ashgate Press, forthcoming.

Marx, Karl. "On the Jewish Question." In *The Marx-Engels Reader*, edited by Robert Tucker, 26–46. New York: W. W. Norton, 1978.

Melville, Herman. "Bartleby, the Scrivener: A Story of Wall-Street." In *Great Short Works of Herman Melville*, 39–74. New York: Perennial Classics, 1969.

Moi, Toril. *Sexual/Textual Politics: Feminist Literary Theory*. New York: Taylor and Francis, 2002.

Mojares, Resil. *Brains of the Nation: Pedro Paterno, T. H. Pardo de Tavera, Isabelo des los Reyes and the Production of Modern Knowledge*. Quezon City: Ateneo de Manila University Press, 2006.

Moten, Fred. "to consent not to be a single being." http://www.poetryfoundation.org/harriet/2010/02/to-consent-not-to-be-a-single-being/.

Moten, Fred, and Stefano Harney. "The General Antagonism: Interview with Ste-vphen Shukaitis." In *The Undercommons: Fugitive Planning and Black Study*, by Fred Moten, 100–159. New York: Autonomedia, 2013.

Moten, Fred, and Stefano Harney. "Michael Brown." *boundary 2* 42, no. 4 (2015): 81–87.

Nietzsche, Friedrich. *Also Sprach Zarathustra: Ein Buch Für Alle und Keinen.* Leipzig, Germany: Goldmann Verlag, 1996.

Nietzsche, Friedrich. *The Birth of Tragedy and The Genealogy of Morals.* New York: Doubleday, 1956.

Nietzsche, Friedrich. *Ecce Homo: How One Becomes What One Is.* New York: Penguin, 1992.

Nietzsche, Friedrich. *The Gay Science.* New York: Vintage, 1974.

Nietzsche, Friedrich. *Thus Spoke Zarathustra: A Book for All and None.* New York: Modern Library, 1995.

Nietzsche, Friedrich. *Zur Genealogie der Moral in Werke in Drei Bänden, Zweiter Band.* Munich, Germany: Carl Hanser Verlag, 1960.

Orwell, George. *Animal Farm.* New York: Signet, 1972.

Pappas, Nickolas. *The Nietzsche Disappointment: Reckoning with Nietzsche's Unkept Promises on Origins and Outcomes.* New York: Rowman and Littlefield, 2005.

Parham, Althéa de Peuch. *My Odyssey: Experience of a Young Refugee from Two Revolutions, by a Creole of Saint-Domingue.* Baton Rouge: Louisiana State University Press, 1959.

Rancière, Jacques. *Disagreement: Politics and Philosophy.* Translated by Julie Rose. Minneapolis: University of Minnesota Press, 2004.

Rancière, Jacques. "On the Theory of Ideology: Althusser's Politics." Translated by Emiliano Battista. In *Althusser's Lesson*, 125–154. London: Continuum, 2011.

Rancière, Jacques. "Who Is the Subject of the Rights of Man?" *South Atlantic Quarterly* 103, nos. 2/3 (2004): 297–310.

Roberts, Neil. *Freedom as Marronage.* Chicago: University of Chicago Press, 2015.

Safranski, Rüdiger. *Nietzsche: A Philosophical Biography.* New York: W. W. Norton, 2002.

Scott, James C. *The Art of Not Being Governed.* New Haven, CT: Yale University Press, 2009.

Scott, James C. *Domination and the Arts of Resistance: Hidden Transcripts.* New Haven, CT: Yale University Press, 1992.

Scott, James C. *Weapons of the Weak: Everyday Forms of Peasant Resistance.* New Haven, CT: Yale University Press, 1985.

Simpson, Audra. *Mohawk Interruptus: Political Life across the Borders of Settler States.* Durham: Duke University Press, 2014.

Soll, Ivan. "Nietzsche on Cruelty, Asceticism, and the Failure of Hedonism." In *Nietzsche, Genealogy, Morality: Essays on Nietzsche's "Genealogy of Morals."* Berkeley: University of California Press, 1994.

Sorel, George. *Reflections on Violence.* New York: Dover, 2004.

Spivak, Gayatri Chakravorty. "Can the Subaltern Speak?" In *Can the Subaltern Speak? Reflections on the History of an Idea*, edited by Rosalind C. Morris, 21–80. New York: Columbia University Press, 2010.

Spivak, Gayatri Chakravorty. *In Other Worlds: Essays in Cultural Politics.* New York: Routledge, 2006.

Taylor, Charles. *Modern Social Imaginaries.* Durham: Duke University Press, 2003.

Thomas, Megan. *Orientalists, Propagandists and Ilustrados: Filipino Scholarship and the End of Spanish Colonialism.* Minneapolis: University of Minnesota Press, 2012.

Thompson, Mark Christian. "The Negro Who Disappeared: Race in Kafka's Amerika." In *Contemplating Violence: Critical Studies in Modern German Culture,* edited by Stefani Engelstein and Carl Niekerk, 183–198. Amsterdam: Rodopi, 2011.

Trouillot, Michel-Rolph. *Silencing the Past: Power and the Production of History.* Boston: Beacon, 1995.

Wall, Illan rua. *Human Rights and Constituent Power: Without Model or Warranty.* New York: Routledge/GlassHouse, 2011.

Whyte, Jessica. *Catastrophe and Redemption: The Political Thought of Giorgio Agamben.* Albany: State University of New York Press, 2013.

Wilderson, Frank B., III. "Gramsci's Black Marx: Whither the Slave in Civil Society?" *Social Identities* 9, no. 2 (2003): 225–240.

Wilderson, Frank B., III. *Red, White and Black: Cinema and the Structure of U.S. Antagonisms.* Durham, NC: Duke University Press, 2010.

Woodhull, Winifred. *Transformations of the Maghreb: Feminism, Decolonization and Literatures.* Minneapolis: University of Minnesota Press, 1993.

Woolf, Virginia. *Orlando.* London: Vintage, 2004.

Woolf, Virginia. *To the Lighthouse.* London: Aziloth, 2010.

Zupančič, Alenka. *The Shortest Shadow: Nietzsche's Philosophy of the Two.* Cambridge, MA: MIT Press, 2003.

Anarchism (continued)

24; "all the way down," 274; anarchist subject, 6, 10; of city, 30; communities and, 160, 225; conspiracy and, 237; fate and, 153; interiority and, 211, 228, 261, 263, 264, 269, 270; Misinterpellation and, 29, 271; Nietzsche and (see Nietzsche, Friedrich); reading and, 11, 26; of soul, 30; of subjectivity, 156, 238; of time, 23, 61, 278n40; "we" and, 30, 271–272

Anderson, Tanisha, 94

Anticolonialism, 9, 59, 71, 73, 74, 76, 79, 82, 84, 95, 109, 115, 133, 272; anticolonial leaders and view of western values, 74; connection to Wilson's Fourteen Points speech, 84; radio and (see Radio)

Ansell-Pearson, Keith, 294n24

Antiheroism, 23–25, 26, 165

Archism, 25, 26, 29, 30, 31, 154, 237, 269, 271, 273; Archist mode of reading, 26; temporality, 154

Arendt, Hannah, 22, 23, 25, 28, 101, 291n78, 292n94; "banality of evil," 22, 25; Little Rock, Arkansas and, 23; On Revolution, 28

Aristotle, 36

Arabs, 71, 79, 85

Arab Spring, (see also Bouazizi) 9, 23, 59, 60, 79–84, 86, 93, 95, 133, 267, 287n59; anarchist response of, 60, 83; beginnings in Tunisia, 80–82

Aristodemou, Maria, 164; Law, Psychoanalysis, Society, 164

Armenians, 71

Asia, 72, 73

Austin, J. L., 22

Authenticity, 61, 115

Authority, 2, 3, 4, 5, 6, 7, 9, 10, 11, 13, 14, 17, 19, 20, 21, 29, 35, 37–48, 50, 51, 52, 53, 54, 56, 58, 59, 60, 61, 62, 68, 70, 76, 77, 79, 82, 84, 85–93, 95, 96, 97, 100, 101–110, 111, 112, 113, 120, 122, 126, 128, 135, 136, 140, 143, 151, 160, 161, 162, 165, 167, 169, 172, 198, 199, 201, 202, 203, 206–212, 218, 226, 233, 237, 239, 243, 248, 249, 254, 259, 260, 268, 274; circuity of, 20, 40, 50, 58, 62, 106; deauthorization, 91; externalization of, 143; failed projection of, 208; disappearance of, 84; liberal power and, 110; projection of, 87; ruination of, 90; source in calling, 92; western, 113

Autonomy, 5, 44, 45, 186, 204

Bhabha, Homi K., 102

Badiou, Alain, 24, 27, 278n47, 284n3; event and, 27

Baltimore, Maryland, 199, 217, 232; west side, 232

Bank of England, 177

"Bartleby the Scrivener," 11, 12, 24, 27, 134. 156, 165–174, 175, 185, 192, 195, 196, 197, 211, 212, 219, 224, 243, 246, 254, 263, 264, 269, 298n13, 298n18, 298n22; agency of, 165, 171, 174; amor fati and, 165; assumption vs. preference, 170; Cicero and (see Cicero); conspiracy and, 168; dead letter office, 173; death of, 167, 172, 173, 224; failure to be a subject, 172; infectious nature of, 174; Messiah and, 174; misinterpellated, 165; "nippers," 170; objectlike nature of, 166; passivity of, 165; theology and, 172–173; "turkey," 169–170; voice of the text, 168

Ben Ali, Zine El Abadine, 80, 81–82, 83, 120; response to demonstrations, 81

Benjamin, Walter, 18, 19, 46, 51, 52, 55, 92, 95, 117–118, 126, 158, 161, 168, 171, 174, 192, 199–201, 212, 225–226, 235, 245, 252, 270, 276n21, 279n49, 282n55, 283n2, 294n21, 296n49, 298n13, 298n22; allegory and, 46, 51, 92, 171, 225; anarchism of everyday life, 161, 270, 273; constellation, 95, 294n21; corpse and, 171; "Critique of Violence," 117, 276n21; Judgment Day (postponement of), 252; Kafka's failure and, 51, 212; law and, 199–200; messianism and, 245; mythic violence, 200; Origin of German Tragic Drama, 171, 225; phantasmagoria and, 18, 51; pure means, 55, 168, 171, 174; radio, radical possibility of, 126; reality

Caesar, Julius, 63

Calls, calling, 1–8, 9, 10, 11, 12, 13, 20, 22, 26, 27, 28, 29, 35, 36–42, 45, 46, 48, 49, 50, 52, 53, 55, 56, 57, 59, 62–64, 71–73, 78, 82, 84–85, 92, 95, 97, 98–101, 106, 107, 111, 114, 115, 123, 125, 127, 135, 136, 139, 140, 143, 148, 149–150, 157, 162, 168, 169, 184, 194–196, 198, 201, 208, 211, 218, 222–223, 233–237, 245, 254, 261, 263, 268–270, 271, 272, 275n1, 279n2, 301n6, 304n68; Abraham and, 1–3, 268; as acknowledgement, 234; alternative forms of, 29; anarchist, 57; calls to order, 233; "come, come!" 12, 27, 194, 196, 233, 235, 268, 269, 271; "consent not to be a single being," 235–237, 245, 254, 269; countercalls, 78, 125, 222, 270; "don't shoot!," 217; by God, 3, 81; "hey, you there!" 8, 11, 20, 26, 36–37, 43, 44–45, 47, 54, 56, 82, 94, 96, 114, 149, 172, 195, 200, 201, 203, 205, 206, 208, 232, 268; "I can believe," 254, 255, 261, 268; "I can't breathe," 217; "I could have you arrested!" 232, 268; "I'll take you there" (Moten), 234; "I would prefer not to," 12, 27, 165, 166, 168, 268, 269; intention of caller, 22; "it's a girl/boy!," 268, 283n64; "men are born free and equal in rights," 62, 236, 268; Moses and, 38 47, 52; network of, 12; "our hope shot down," 222, 226, 227, 304n68; Paul and, 52; "a person is something that shall be overcome," 146, 149, 150, 162, 269, 295n35; radio, 123–126; Soviet Union and, 73; summoning messiah or God, 149; "Tiens, un Nègre!" ("Look, a Negro!"), 8, 10, 98–101, 219, 232, 237, 241, 268; "wait up!," 8, 27, 54–57, 196, 268, 269, 271, 272; "you, you!" 220, 221, 233

Capitalism, 4, 5, 18–19, 165

Caribbean, 15, 68, 70, 72, 235, 236; French Caribbean, 68, 236; memory of Haitian revolution and, 70

Catholic Church, Catholicism, 77; missionaries, 78; ritual, 77

Central America, 72

Césaire, Aimé, 105

China, Chinese, 71, 74, 86

Chinese Cultural Revolution, 27

Charisma, 68, 76

Christ, Jesus, 28, 38, 39, 77, 136, 138, 139, 142, 143, 144, 148, 149, 151, 184, 225–226, 257; Anti-Christ, 139; Gethsemane, 257; Passion plays and, 77–78 (see Ileto; Philippines); Redeemer (Nietzsche), 138; resurrection of, 28; subjectivity of, 38

Christianity, 49, 52, 151, 229

Ciccariello-Maher, George, 279n47, 285n17

Cicero, 166, 167, 172. See also Bartleby; Stoicism

Class, 29

Cleveland, Ohio, 94

Coates, Ta-Nahisi, 11, 26, 100, 133, 134, 162, 163, 164, 203, 217, 229–233, 235, 237, 238, 239, 240, 243, 264, 267, 268, 293n2, 297n3, 303n68, 305n72; Between the World and Me (see Between the World and Me)

Colonial, colonialism, 9, 10, 59, 63, 64, 70, 71, 73, 75, 76, 96–97 102, 104, 105, 106, 107, 110, 111, 112, 113–123, 126, 128, 232, 285n27, 290n65, 291n70, 291n79, 294n21, 302n11; intellectual, 113–121; self-determination and, 71; subjectivity and, 9, 12, 106, 107, 110, 112; unreality of, 101; violence of, 117–121

Communism, 5. See also American Communist Party

Commodity fetishism, 18

Conspiracy, 12, 30, 168, 237, 249

Corbyn, Jeremy, 272

Counterinterpellation, 7, 12, 114, 115

Cuba, 20

Cufar, Kristina, 295, n.39

Culbert, Jennifer, 22–25

Damascus, 52

Dean, Jodi, 28, 29, 43, 44, 278n47, 303n43; interpellation as individuation, 43

De Certeau, Michel, 275n12

Declaration of the Rights of Man and Citizen, 9, 59, 62–65, 68, 69, 72, 284n7; as fetish, 69; Haitian slaves' interpretation of, 65

Karl Rossmann, 11, 24, 134, 201–217, 219, 228, 229, 237, 246; agency of, 210; authority and, 206; chased by police, 209; encounter with the law, 204–210; escape, 209; failure of, 11, 207, 212; possible death of, 216; privilege of, 216; rich uncle and, 204; whiteness of, 202, 216

Korea, Koreans, 71, 74

Kohn, Margaret (*see also* McBride), 72, 103, 128, 286n47, 291n70

Koo, Wellington (Gu Weijun), 71, 92, 109

Kurds, 71

Lacan, Jacques, 29, 56, 252, 257; "Big Other," 257, 258

Lajpat Rai, Lala, 75, 82, 109; views of the United States, 75

Lampert, Laurence, 294n24

Landlords, landlordism. *See* Guha

Latin America, 77

Latinos/as, 199

Latour, Bruno, 276n22

Law, 9, 47, 50–51, 142, 198–204, 210; accusation and, 199–200, 210; attachments to, 50–51; desire of, 200; difference from police, 199; getting it right, 199 (*see also* Interpellation); guilt and, 47, 207, 209, 211; intention of, 63; Karl Rossmann and (*see* Karl Rossman); knowledge, 211; legitimacy of, 198; need for subjects, 202; pose of, 210; recognition and, 142; rule of, 199, 204; vulnerability of, 201, 210

Lazarus, Sylvain, 28, 278n47, 290n50

Leadership, 68

Lebanon, 123

Leclerc, Charles (French General), 66

Lenin, 71, 278n47

Leninism, 28, 29

Leonard, Miriam, 308n16

Liberal capitalism, 4, 17–19, 50

Liberalism, 4, 5, 17, 19; and autonomy, 5; and freedom, 5

Liberal subjectivity, 6, 204

Liberty, 107

Lighthouse (The), 175–186, 188, 189–190, 192; arrival at, 189–190; beauty of, 179; effects of, 181; poetry and, 182

Lily Briscoe, 11, 24, 134, 165, 173, 175, 186–193, 195, 196, 208, 212, 215, 219, 246, 264; agency of, 175, 191–192; appearance of, 187; failure and, 188, 193; invisibility of, 188; Nietzschean subjectivity and, 192; painting and, 187; vision of, 191

Livy, 87, 88; Egeria, 87

Locke, John, 17, 238; "dissolute" land-owner and, 17

Louverture, Toussaint, 9, 59, 63, 65–67, 69, 82, 92, 109; attitudes towards France and, 66; liberal ideology and, 59, 67; *Mémoires*, 66; treatment of ex-slaves and, 67

Love (*see amor fati*), 49, 240–242

Löwy, Michael, 216

Lycurgus, 87

Macey, David, 100

Machiavelli, Niccolò, 9, 61, 85–93, 94, 143, 164, 201, 249, 261, 288n77; Appius Pulcher (*see* Pulcher); approval of deception, 88; conspiratorial reading of, 91; *Discourse on the First Ten Books of Livy*, 86; fortuna, 88, 90; Junius Brutus (*see* Brutus); Medicis and, 88; Numa (*see* Numa); Papirius (*see* Papirius); Pollari and, 89; *The Prince*, 88; prudence and, 90, 91; sacking of Veii, 87, 88, 91; as teller of political stories, 86

McDonald's, 18

Mad Max, 271

Manela, Erez, 71–76, 78, 285n27, 286n33; *The Wilsonian Moment*, 71 (*see* "Wilsonian moment")

Manhattan, 232

Martinique, Martinicans, 9, 96, 121

Marx, Marxism, 48, 217, 228; negation of the negation, 228; "On the Jewish Question," 217

Mary Magdalene, 252

Materialism, 48–49; outside of, 49; and superstructure, 48

McBride, Keally (*see also* Kohn), 72, 103, 128, 286n47, 291n70

Mediterranean, 113

Melville, Herman, 11, 156, 161, 164, 165, 166, 171, 172, 173, 267; "Bartleby the Scrivener" (*see* Bartleby)

Messianism, 10, 27

Middle East, 73

Misinterpellation, 4–7, 8, 10, 12, 13, 15, 16, 17, 23, 26, 27, 28, 29, 31, 35, 36, 38, 40, 41, 45, 46, 48, 50, 51, 52, 55, 56, 58, 59, 60, 61, 63, 65, 70, 73, 74, 75, 78, 82, 84, 91, 93, 94, 97, 100, 105, 109, 111, 112, 115, 116, 119, 120, 123, 124, 127, 128, 134, 140, 141, 148, 150, 155, 160, 164, 168, 239, 244, 263, 264, 267, 271–274; agency and, 112; allegorization of, 92; anarchism and, 29, 271; as antidote to capitalism, 36; authority based on, 91; call of misinterpellation, 150; event and, 28; Fanon and, 9; inoperativity and, 168; male dominance and, 239; maximization of, 244–245; Messiah and, 173; vs. misrecognition, 41; party and, 28; power of, 84; sources of, 28; temporality of, 13; threat of, 20; violence and, 116, 120; visibility of, 23; whiteness and, 239

Misinterpellated reading ("A yet more minor literature"), 11, 26, 27, 134–135, 141, 164–165, 225, 231, 264, 266–268, 270; of flags, 225, 228; of Jesus, 225–226; method of, 26; mundane nature of, 267

Misinterpellated Subject, 2, 5, 10, 40, 105, 157, 262; Abraham as, 2; disruptive power of, 40; par excellence (Fanon), 105; losers, 164; "the one who shows up," 10, 157; payoff of being, 262; self-discovery of, 157

Misrecognition, 40, 41, 44, 45, 47, 52, 58, 70, 79, 88, 93, 95, 97, 111, 117, 134, 195, 202, 229, 240, 277n36, 280n19, 280n23, 281n34, 283n61

Moi, Toril, 300n62

Montag, Warren, 43

Moore, Barrington, 18

Moses, 12, 38–39, 40, 47, 52

Moten, Fred (*see* Stefano Harney), 198, 233–237, 240, 241, 270, 306n92; calls to order, 233; "Michael Brown," 198, 240; other forms of calling, 234

Mr. Ramsay, 175–186, 188, 189, 191, 192, 210; anxieties of, 181; friendship with William Bankes, 180; narrowness of, 177–178; philosophy of, 175; privilege of, 178; widowhood of, 188–189

Mrs. Ramsay, 11, 174, 175–186, 187, 188, 189, 192, 196, 213, 214, 243; beauty of, 179, 182–184; death of, 181, 185, 188; not misinterpellated, 183; personhood and, 183; promise of, 180; seductive nature of, 178, 179

Mulqueen, Tara, 296n44

Murdoch, Rupert, 42

Napoleon, 66; attempt to reimpose Haitian slavery and, 66

Narrator (of "Bartleby"), 166–173, 243

Narrator (of *Invisible Man*), 24, 134, 203, 218–229, 233, 237, 246, 264, 304n68; failure of, 219; invisibility of, 218, 227; refusal of, 219, 240; resistance to heroizing, 223, 228; resistance to teleology (*see also* Teleology), 221, 223, 224, 226; speech of, 222–224, 226

Native Americans, 199

Négritude, 104, 115

Neoliberalism, 19, 275n7

Nietzsche, 6, 10–11, 135–162, 165, 169, 175, 179, 184, 186, 190, 207, 213, 214, 219, 223, 226, 242, 245, 248, 259, 267, 269, 294n21, 296n51, 297n60; abandonment and, 10, 141; *amor fati* (see Amor fati); anarchism and, 159; betrayal by, 136, 159; connection to Fanon, 137, 160; disappointment and, 10, 135, 140, 150, 151; doer and deed, 160, 207; *Ecce Homo*, 138, 149, 153, 157, 158; eternal recurrence, 154, 155; *Gay Science*, 154; *Genealogy of Morals*, 138, 140, 160; "The Greatest Weight," 154; "how one becomes what one is," 148, 158, 190; Jester (*see* Jester); last men, 144; Messianism and (*see* Nietzschean messianism); midday (noon, noontime), 139, 144, 229, 259; "On Old and New Tablets," 147; "On Redemption," 142; "The Other Dancing Song," 148; Overman (Übermensch) (*see* Overman); redeemer and, 138, 148,

Russia, Russian, 66, 74, 84, 272; "czar deliverer," 66; peasantry, 66; revolution, 74, 84

Sacrifice, 3, 26
San Domingo. See Haiti
Sanders, Bernie, 272
Sartre, Jean-Paul, 104–105, 114; *Orphée Noir*, 104
Savonarola, Girolamo, 86
Scotland, Scottish, 244, 246, 252, 263, 307n11
Scott, James C., 13–22, 24, 28, 61, 66, 68, 75, 80, 227, 275n12, 276n18, 276n21, 279n49, 285n16; charisma and (*see* Charisma); critique of Althusser (*see* Althusser); *Domination and the Arts of Resistance*, 13, 66; "taming the Leviathan," 21; vanguard party and, 28; *Weapons of the Weak*, 13, 21, 66
Senghor, Léopold, 104, 105
Sex, sexuality, 29
Shulman, George, 277n37, 277n39
Sicily, 90
Sibanda, Silindiwe, 220, 279n2, 304n46, 304n50
Simpson, Audra, 302n11
Slaves, slavery, 9, 15, 17, 60, 106–107, 231; transatlantic slave trade, 22
Slavic, 207
Smith, Yvette, 94
Soll, Ivan, 294n20
Soul, 158
Spain, 77
Spivak, Gayatri, 104, 283n1; strategic essentialism, 104
Spontaneity, 15, 60, 84
Staples, Mavis, 234; "I'll take you there," 234; Staple Singers, 234
State, 4, 7, 9, 13, 15, 18, 21, 22, 36, 37, 39–42, 44, 47, 48, 58, 66, 67, 82, 92, 117, 199, 203, 217, 232, 235, 241, 260, 280n17, 301n6, 303n32
Staten Island, 94, 199
Skarsgård, Stellan, 246
Stoicism, 167
Solon, 87
Spencer, Herbert, 275, n.8

Subaltern, 9, 59–60, 66–70, 75–79, 110, 113, 116
Subjectivity (*see also* Colonial subject; Liberal subject; Misinterpellated subject), 3, 4, 6, 7, 8, 10, 12, 13, 19, 21, 26, 27, 30, 36, 38, 39, 40, 42, 43, 44, 46–47, 48, 54, 55, 61, 67, 74, 79, 80, 83, 87, 95, 97, 99, 100, 101, 104, 109, 111–113, 119, 120, 125, 128, 134, 135, 137, 140, 143, 151, 153, 157, 158, 160, 161, 163, 164, 169, 171, 172, 175, 177, 178, 180, 181, 183, 184, 190, 192, 193, 194, 195, 202, 204, 209, 213, 214, 219, 227, 228, 233, 235, 236, 240, 241, 243, 245, 253, 261, 263, 271, 274; alternative basis for, 48; anarchic, 44; bad, 46–47, 53; collective, 44; disappointed (Nietzsche), 140, 151; failure of, 24, 26, 61; good, 46–47, 53; to law, 142; liberal (*see* liberalism); objects vs., 163; subversion of, 21
Syria, 123

Tarquins (*see also* Brutus), 88
Taylor, Charles, 284n13
Tea Party, 18
Teleology, 26, 172, 231, 233, 239
Terrorism, 5
Texas, 94, 199
Thatcher, Margaret, 271, 274, 275n8
Theater of Oklahoma (see also *Amerika*), 212–215; disappointment and, 213–215; representation and, 214; reproduction of real world and, 214; size of, 212
Thomas, Megan, 286n39
Tibet, Tibetans, 85; monks and nuns self-immolation, 85–86
Tightrope walker (Nietzsche), 144–152, 171, 223, 257, 258; falls from rope, 145
TINA (there is no alternative), 4, 13, 15, 103, 271, 274, 275n8
To The Lighthouse, 11, 174–194; Andrew Ramsay, 185; Cam Ramsay, 188; Charles Tansley, 178, 179, 182; James Ramsay, 176, 188–189; "The Lighthouse," 187; Lighthouse (*see* Lighthouse); Lily Briscoe (*see* Lily Briscoe); material conspiracy and, 185; Mr. Ramsay (*see* Mr. Ramsay); Mrs. Ramsay,